A COMPREHENSIVE BIBLIOGRAPHY
OF
THE PUBLISHED WORKS OF
CHARLES SANDERS PEIRCE
WITH
A BIBLIOGRAPHY OF SECONDARY STUDIES

SECOND EDITION, REVISED

BIBLIOGRAPHIES OF FAMOUS PHILOSOPHERS

The Philosophy Documentation Center is publishing a series of "Bibliographies of Famous Philosophers," Richard H. Lineback, general editor. Published bibliographies include:

Alfred North Whitehead: A Primary-Secondary Bibliography

Edmund Husserl and His Critics: An International Bibliography (1894-1979)

Jean-Paul Sartre and His Critics: An International Bibliography (1938-1980), Second Edition

Martin Heidegger: Bibliography and Glossary

Hobbes Studies (1879-1979): A Bibliography

George Santayana: A Bibliographical Checklist (1880-1980)

Paul of Venice: A Bibliographical Guide

José Ortega y Gasset: A Bibliography of Secondary Sources

A Bibliography of Vico in English (1884-1984)

Henri Bergson: A Bibliography, Revised Second Edition

A Comprehensive Bibliography of the Published Works of Charles Sanders Peirce with a Bibliography of Secondary Studies

A COMPREHENSIVE BIBLIOGRAPHY OF THE PUBLISHED WORKS OF CHARLES SANDERS PEIRCE WITH A BIBLIOGRAPHY OF SECONDARY STUDIES

SECOND EDITION, REVISED

Edited by

KENNETH LAINE KETNER

With the assistance of

ARTHUR FRANKLIN STEWART
and
CLAUDE V. BRIDGES

Published by

PHILOSOPHY DOCUMENTATION CENTER
BOWLING GREEN STATE UNIVERSITY
BOWLING GREEN, OHIO 43403-0189
U.S.A.

© Copyright 1986 by
Kenneth Laine Ketner
Institute for Studies in Pragmaticism
304K Library
Texas Tech University
Lubbock, Texas 79409

Library of Congress Catalog Card No. 86-061909
ISBN No. 0-912632-84-4

PREFACE TO THE FIRST EDITION

The present work has two purposes. On the one hand it serves as an index and guide to *Charles Sanders Peirce: Complete Published Works, including Selected Secondary Materials,* a microfiche collection published by Johnson Associates in 1977; it is an integral part of that collection in that it shows upon which single fiche (numbered 1 through 149) each given work by Peirce is filmed. On the other hand, and perhaps this is its more important purpose in the long run, it constitutes the first comprehensive bibliography of Peirce's published works since the appearance of the eight volumes of the *Collected Papers,* supplementing and integrating all recent significant advances in Peirce scholarship.

The usefulness of such a bibliography is perhaps better appreciated against the background of a few facts about early Peirce scholarship, about Peirce's life and his manner of working, and about the nature of the materials he produced. It is well known that at his death Peirce left behind a large quantity of manuscript material, the greater part of which is of high and even outstanding quality. By way of comparison, the *Collected Papers* contains decidedly less than half of either the published or the unpublished materials of significance, and due to the plan of organization adopted by the editors of those volumes, complete entities in both categories of material are often broken into fragments. Persons who have depended upon the *Collected Papers* as their source for Peirce's scientific and philosophical work will be pleasantly surprised to find that a more systematic, consistent, and complete Peirce emerges from the materials now being made more generally accessible through this project as well as others.

If the concept of publication is understood, as it is in this bibliography, to include printed items in books and periodicals, public lectures for which written versions may or may not exist, privately printed and circulated brochures and monographs, and papers read before learned societies (with later printed versions or not, with surviving manuscript versions or not) — then a quick survey of Part One of this bibliography will suffice to establish the fact that Peirce published an **ENORMOUS** amount of material during his lifetime. This fact does not coincide with currently prevailing opinion, although it is only fair to say that such an opinion has been, until now, a reasonable one; for a significant part of what Peirce published was anonymous or pseudonymous, or appeared in publications that even today are not available in any single research library. It has also been thought that Peirce published only one book, his *Photometric Researches* (P 00118). But even this can now be shown to be false if one searches no further than the years preceding the date of publication of P 00118. For in that period one finds P 00018 (a privately printed booklet of limited distribution), P 00052 (a paper on logic circulated as a monograph), and P 00102 (an important presentation on geodesy circulated in lithograph form). The first and third of these are admittedly rather brief, but the second is a long piece printed in large-page format. Even lengthier is P 00161, an important report on gravimetry, that was widely circulated as a separate monograph of 144 pages. No doubt other examples could be added to this list if later items were considered.

That Peirce was a severe recluse, both physically and intellectually, has also been a favored allegation among some students of his life and work. This can now be seen to be false, for as late as 1906 Peirce wrote and published articles, often anonymously, in which he reported (for *The Nation*) as an eyewitness those sessions of the National Academy of Sciences that he attended as a member. (Peirce died in 1914, after having been ill with cancer for several years.) Another nonreclusive strain to be discerned from this bibliography is the amount of influence Peirce exercised upon others during his lifetime, and the amount of influence others exercised upon him. For example, it is fashionable to proclaim that Peirce's ability as a philosopher suffered by his lack of a permanent academic chair. Such a chair, it is further said, would have provided him with appropriate critical feedback from students and colleagues, feedback that Peirce would have needed to forestall certain difficulties that are supposed to exist in his works. But by reading through Part One of this bibliography, which includes items about Peirce written by contemporaries during his lifetime or shortly after his death, one realizes that Peirce was constantly, almost until the day he died, responding to and arguing with friends as well as detractors. One will find even more pronounced instances of this in his correspondence or in various parts of his manuscripts, both of which are available on microfilm from Harvard

University. Perhaps some scholars were brought to posit this latter version of the reclusive theory as a way of explaining what they took to be fragmentary or inconsistent work as they read through the *Collected Papers,* not suspecting that this apparent incoherence might better be attributed to the way in which those volumes were edited. And thus we come full circle. The lack of an adequate overview of the "complete" corpus of Peirce's prodigious production in many fields of science and philosophy — to which corpus many more items are sure to be added as time goes by — has had its influence upon the interpretation of the significance of his life and work. Those of us who have worked on this bibliography hope that it will help in the reassessment of his importance as a leading figure in philosophy and science, and that through this, others may come to share our conclusion that Peirce is a master among those who pursue wisdom, a master of such stature that there have been others his equal, but none his better.

The organization of this bibliography should present few difficulties, but perhaps a brief discussion of its mechanics would be helpful. (Details particular to the secondary bibliography are described at the beginning of Part Two.)

Each bibliographic item has been given a number composed of a capital letter prefix, either 'P' (Peirce), 'O' (Others), or 'S' (Secondary), followed by a five-digit number. Items assigned a P number are publications by Peirce himself. Items assigned an O number are works by other authors, written during his life or shortly after his death and concerning Peirce's work in some way. Numbers preceded by O are integrated in Part One, with works by Peirce, and are repeated in a shortened form in Part Two. Items assigned an S number are works by other authors about Peirce which appeared after his death; these together with O numbers make up the secondary bibliography.

The primary bibliography is arranged chronologically, beginning with Peirce's first known publication in *The Harvard Magazine* for 1858, and ending with Jastrow's obituary of Juliette Peirce. Within each year, items are alphabetized according to place of publication. We have devoted considerable effort toward reproducing titles exactly as they appeared in the original publications. When necessary, we have supplied titles, indicated by square brackets. These entries typically have to do with some action or performance by Peirce, such as computations or observations he made in the course of scientific work. We have taken the view that in some sense these actions or performances are, when given in print, publications, even if the description of them is by other authors. Dates are uniformly reckoned on the basis of time of publication, with the year as the basic unit. In a few cases, when two very similar items were published in different ways in different years, we have given additional information to indicate that. A good example of this is "On a New List of Categories," which was presented orally before the American Academy of Arts and Sciences in 1867, and appeared in their *Memoirs* in 1868 (P 00032). Additional information concerning the oral presentation of this item is given just after O 00020. Reviews written by Peirce have the phrase "Review of" preceding the title as it appeared in the printed original. In the case of oral presentations that were not later printed, especially lecture series, we have endeavored to add information about extant manuscripts that might be notes or preparations for such performances. We have made an effort to keep abbreviations to a minimum, preferring short titles and descriptive text to lists of cryptic letter codes. One shortcut we did adopt is the use of 'NF' as a way of indicating that a particular item was Not Filmed: that is, does not appear in the microfiche collection. Short titles refer the reader to bibliographic sources, a list of which is appended to the end of this preface. We decided not to reproduce the contents of these fine resources, but we urge interested readers to consult them, for in many cases they contain annotations that will be of additional value. The present work in no way renders obsolete those earlier studies; instead, it serves to coordinate them so that a fuller picture of Peirce's productions may be obtained. We have been able to add a number of new items as a result of our studies. These can be identified in most instances by a lack of references to previous bibliographies.

There are two Appendixes to the primary bibliography. The first, called Place of Publication Index, organizes all items whose numbers begin with P according to the place where they appeared (book, periodical, report, lecture, and the like). The second, called Titles Index, organizes all such items according to their titles. Having tried several systems of alphabetizing this index, we finally decided to alphabetize Peirce titles letter by letter, except that a title such as "F.E. Abbot" is entered as "Abbot, F.E." Similarly, Peirce's reviews are ordered by author of book being reviewed, or by title if no author is given. Supplied titles, that is, those given in square brackets, are alphabetized by key word. The result of all this is somewhat inexact, but we hope that as a kind of subject index it will be of some help.

It is difficult to draw up a list of acknowledgements, for numerous persons have contributed to the present work. Our project would not have been possible, in this relatively brief span of time, without the important research of previous scholars who have inquired into the extent of Peirce's published productions. Morris Cohen began the task with his early bibliography. Irving C. Smith (the probable author of *List of Articles*), Daniel C. Haskell, and Arthur W. Burks made significant and important strides toward the ideal list. But the most influential Peirce bibliographer has been Max H. Fisch, and in many ways the present work is simply the collation and culmination of the detailed bibliographic researches that he and Ruth B. Fisch began approximately two decades ago. A work such as this typically owes much to professional librarians, and our bibliography is no exception. Ray Janeway, Dean of Library Services at Texas Tech University, has followed our project from its beginning and has made many useful suggestions. Gloria Lyerla and her staff in the Interlibrary Loan office helped us to locate and inspect many scarce items. Ms. Tucker and her staff in the Documents department assisted us in finding our way among Federal Documents, where many of Peirce's publications are located. Mrs. Elle of the Circulation department patiently kept track of the large quantity of items we removed from the Library for inspection and study. During the course of our project, we were aided by several capable student assistants: James Cook, Frances Scott, Peggy Cooper, and Andrea Burbano. Our competent and patient secretary, Sherry Newton, helped us to sort, organize, and prepare the typescript for what seemed like a never-ending flow of materials. Webb Dordick, of Somerville, Massachusetts, came to our rescue by helping us to obtain copies of some Peirce publications in the Harvard University Libraries. Texas Tech University has supported the Institute for Studies in Pragmaticism (under whose auspices the project was undertaken and completed) with funds from Organized Research accounts. Without this support, our project would not have been possible.

BIBLIOGRAPHIC SOURCES

Burchard, E.L. *List and Catalogue of the Publications issued by the U.S. Coast and Geodetic Survey 1816-1902* (Washington: Government Printing Office, 1902). The call number for this document is T 11.2:P 96, as given on p. 1055 in *Checklist of United States Public Documents 1789-1909*.

Cohen, Morris R. "Charles S. Peirce and a Tentative Bibliography of his Published Writings." *The Journal of Philosophy, Psychology, and Scientific Methods,* 13 (1916), 726-737.

[Smith, Irving C.] . "A List of Articles, Mostly Book Reviews, Contributed by Charles S Peirce to 'The Nation' to which is appended Some Additions to the Bibliography of his Published Writings in this Journal, December 21, 1916." *The Journal of Philosophy, Psychology, and Scientific Methods,* 15 (1918), 578-584.

Fisch, Max H., and Haskell, Daniel C. "Some Additions to Morris R. Cohen's Bibliography of Peirce's Published Writings." *Studies in the Philosophy of Charles Sanders Peirce,* edited by Philip P. Wiener and Frederic H. Young (Cambridge: Harvard University Press, 1952).

Burks, Arthur W. "Bibliography of the Works of Charles Sanders Peirce." *Collected Papers of Charles Sanders Peirce,* vol. 8 (Cambridge: Harvard University Press, 1966).

Fisch, Max H. "A First Supplement to Arthur W. Burks's Bibliography of the Works of Charles Sanders Peirce." *Studies in the Philosophy of Charles Sanders Peirce,* edited by Edward C. Moore and Richard S. Robin (Amherst: University of Massachusetts Press, 1964).

Fisch, Max H. "A Second Supplement to Arthur W. Burks's Bibliography of the Works of Charles Sanders Peirce." *Transactions of the Charles S. Peirce Society,* 2 (1966), 51-53.

Fisch, Max H. "Supplements to the Peirce Bibliographies." *Transactions of the Charles S. Peirce Society,* 10 (1974), 94-129.

Charles Sanders Peirce: Contributions to The Nation. Compiled and annotated by Kenneth Laine Ketner and James Edward Cook (Lubbock, Texas Tech University Press, 1977, in three parts). This work contains a complete set of bibliographic notes for Peirce's known works for *The Nation.*

PREFACE TO THE REVISED SECOND EDITION

Sale of the press run of the first edition of this work has provided the occasion to update and revise it in preparation for a new printing.

In conjunction with some revisions in the text of the primary bibliography we have also seized the opportunity to prepare a supplementary set of fiche which will correct some oversights and errors in the first filming. The secondary bibliography of the first edition has been retained here with only a few typographical corrections. We have not attempted to update it; however, there have been recent supplements published elsewhere:

"Bibliography of Charles Peirce, 1976 through 1981," by Christian J.W. Kloesel, in *The Relevance of Charles Peirce*, Ed. Eugene Freeman, The Hegeler Institute, Monist Library of Philosophy: LaSalle, 1983.

"A German Supplement to the Peirce Bibliographies," by Wolfgang M. Ueding, *American Journal of Semiotics*, special issue on Peirce, Ed. K.L. Ketner, 2 (no. 1-2) 1983.

Our revision has been aided considerably by the efforts and cooperation of the following persons, whose assistance and counsel we gratefully acknowledge: Don D. Roberts, William Davenport, E. Dale Cluff, Stewart Dyess, Gloria Lyerla, Ray Janeway, and Barbara Frates.

Max H. Fisch and Charles S. Hardwick were consulting editors for the first edition, and their good advice has influenced this effort.

TABLE OF CONTENTS

Preface to the First Edition. i

Preface to the Revised Second Edition. v

Part One: Bibliography and Index of Published Works. 1

    Appendix One: Places of Publication. 160

    Appendix Two: Titles. 167

Part Two: Bibliography of Secondary Studies. 213

PART ONE:
BIBLIOGRAPHY AND INDEX
OF PUBLISHED WORKS

CHARLES SANDERS PEIRCE
A COMPREHENSIVE BIBLIOGRAPHY

1858

P 00001: Fiche 1
"Think Again!"
    The Harvard Magazine, vol. 4 (April), 100-105. Fisch, *First Supplement.*

1859

P 00002: Fiche 1
"The Thirteenth Annual Meeting of the American Association for the Advancement of Science."
    Boston Daily Evening Traveller (3 August), page 4, column 3. Fisch, *First Supplement.*

P 00003: Fiche 1
"Meeting of the American Association for the Advancement of Science."
    Boston Daily Evening Traveller (4 August), page 4, columns 5-6. Fisch, *First Supplement.*

P 00004: Fiche 1
"Meeting of the American Association for the Advancement of Science."
    Boston Daily Evening Traveller (5 August), page 1, columns 6-7. Fisch, *First Supplement.*

P 00005: Fiche 1
"The Thirteenth Annual Meeting of the American Association for the Advancement of Science."
    Boston Daily Evening Traveller (8 August), page 4, columns 4-5. Fisch, *First Supplement.*

P 00006: Fiche 1
"The Thirteenth Annual Meeting of the American Association for the Advancement of Science."
    Boston Daily Evening Traveller (9 August), page 4, columns 5-6. Fisch, *First Supplement.*

P 00007: Fiche 1
"The Thirteenth Annual Meeting of the American Association for the Advancement of Science."
    Boston Daily Evening Traveller (10 August), page 2, columns 4-5. Fisch, *First Supplement.*

1860

P 00008: Fiche 1
[Azimuth and magnetic observations]
    "Magnetic Observations," in *Report of the Superintendent of the Coast Survey, 1859,* House Ex. Doc. No. 41, 36th Congress, 1st Session, Washington: Thomas H. Ford, p. 36. Burks, *Bibliography.*

1861

P 00009: Fiche 1
[Service as aid]
    "Triangulation of the western side of Isle au Breton sound, La.," in *Report of the Superintendent of the Coast Survey, 1860,* House Ex. Doc. No. 14, 36th Congress, 2d Session, Washington: Government Printing Office, pp. 85-86. Burks, *Bibliography.*

1862

P 00010: Fiche 1
[Computations]
"Report of Professor Benjamin Peirce, LL.D., on an Example for the Determination of Longitudes by Occultations of the Pleiades," in *Report of the Superintendent of the Coast Survey, 1861,* House Ex. Doc. No. 70, 37th Congress, 2d Session, Washington: Government Printing Office, pp. 196-221. Burks, *Bibliography.*

1863

P 00011: Fiche 1
"The Chemical Theory of Interpenetration."
The American Journal of Science and Arts, second series 35, whole series 85 (January 1863), 78-82. The article is dated, "Cambridge, Mass., Dec. 1862." Fisch and Haskell, *Additions to Cohen's Bibliography;* Burks, *Bibliography.*

P 00012: Fiche 1, 2
"The Place of Our Age in the History of Civilization."
Oration delivered at the reunion of the Cambridge High School Association, Thursday evening, 12 November. Extracts printed in *Cambridge Chronicle,* 18 (21 November), no. 47, page 1, columns 1-5. See MS 1638 (Robin, *Catalogue*). Burks, *Bibliography.*

1864

P 00013: Fiche 2
Review of *Lectures on the English Language.* By George P. Marsh. *The Works of William Shakespeare.* By Richard Grant White. *The English of Shakespeare illustrated in a Philological Commentary on his Julius Caesar.* By George L. Craik. *The North American Review,* vol. 98 (April), 342-369.
The page heading of this review is "Shakespearean Pronunciation." Written in collaboration with John Buttrick Noyes. Burks, *Bibliography;* Cohen, *Tentative Bibliography.*

O 00014: Fiche 2
Peirce, Benjamin
[Astronomical Works], in *Report of the Superintendent of the Coast Survey, 1862,* House Ex. Doc. No. 22, 37th Congress, 3d Session, Washington: Government Printing Office, pp. 15-16, 155-156, 157-158.

P 00015: Fiche 2
[Computations]
"Reports of Professor Benjamin Peirce, of Harvard, upon the Occultations of the Pleiades, in 1841 and 1842," *Report of the Superintendent of the Coast Survey, 1863,* House Ex. Doc. No. 11, 38th Congress, 1st Session, Washington: Government Printing Office, pp. 146-154; See also p. 15. Burks, *Bibliography.*

1865

P 00016: (NF)
[Harvard University Lectures of 1865]
Lectures given at Harvard, probably in the University Lecture Series, concerning the logic of science. Eleven lectures of this series survive as MSS 340-350 (see Robin, *Catalogue*). Burks, *Bibliography;* Fisch, *Second Supplement;* Fisch, *Third Supplement.*

1866

P 00017: (NF)
"The Logic of Science; or, Induction and Hypothesis."
>Lectures given for the Lowell Institute at Cambridge, Massachusetts on Wednesday and Saturday evenings, 24 October through 1 December. MSS of this series survive as MSS 351-359 (see Robin, *Catalogue*). Burks, *Bibliography*; Fisch, *First Supplement*.

P 00018: Fiche 2
Memoranda Concerning the Aristotelean Syllogism.
>Privately printed booklet. "Distributed at the Lowell Institute, Nov., 1866, by Charles S. Peirce, of Cambridge, Mass." Fisch and Haskell, *Additions to Cohen's Bibliography*; Burks, *Bibliography*.

P 00019: Fiche 2
[Computations]
>"Report of Professor Benjamin Peirce, of Harvard, on Computations for Longitude from Occultations of the Pleiades," in *Report of the Superintendent of the Coast Survey, 1864*, House Ex. Doc. No. 15, 38th Congress, 2d Session, Washington: Government Printing Office, p. 114; see also p. 11. Burks, *Bibliography*.

1867

"On an Improvement in Boole's Calculus of Logic."
>Paper read on 12 March 1867. See P 00030.

"On the Natural Classification of Arguments."
>Paper read on 9 April 1867. See P 00031.

"On a New List of Categories."
>Paper read on 14 May 1867. See P 00032.

"Upon the Logic of Mathematics."
>Paper read on 10 September 1867. See P 00033.

"Upon Logical Comprehension and Extension."
>Paper read on 13 November 1867. See P 00034.

O 00020: Fiche 2
Wright, Chauncey.
>"Mathematics in Court," *The Nation*, 5(19 September) 238. An answer to a letter by "V.X." who had criticized Benjamin Peirce's testimony in the Sylvia Ann Howland will case. See P 00035.

P 00021: Fiche 2
Review of *The Logic of Chance*. By John Venn.
>*The North American Review*, vol. 105 (July), 317-321. Burks, *Bibliography*; Cohen, *Tentative Bibliography*.

"Deposition of Charles Saunders [sic] Peirce."
>Given on 5 June 1867. See P 00035.

1868

O 00022: (NF)
Winlock, Joseph.
>"Observations of Asteroids Made With the Fifteen Inch Equatorial of the Observatory of Harvard College, Cambridge, U.S.," *Astronomische Nachrichten*, vol. 71, 231-238.

P 00023: (NF)
"Astronomical Explanations."
>*The Atlantic Almanac, 1868.*

1868

P 00024: (NF)
"Calendars."
    The Atlantic Almanac, 1868.

P 00025: F i c h e 2, 3
"Nominalism versus Realism."
    The Journal of Speculative Philosophy, vol. 2, 57-61. The article refers to a previous work in the same journal at 1(1867), 250-256 — those pages are filmed here to facilitate understanding of the issues Peirce and Harris are discussing in P 00025. *List of Articles;* Burks, *Bibliography.*

P 00026: F i c h e 3
"Questions Concerning Certain Faculties Claimed for Man."
    The Journal of Speculative Philosophy, vol. 2, 103-114. Cohen, *Tentative Bibliography;* Burks, *Bibliography.*

P 00027: F i c h e 3
"Some Consequences of Four Incapacities."
    The Journal of Speculative Philosophy, vol. 2, 140-157. Cohen, *Tentative Bibliography;* Burks, *Bibliography;* Fisch, *Third Supplement.* There is a relevant errata list on the back cover of vol. 2, no. 3.

P 00028: F i c h e 3
"What is Meant by 'Determined'."
    The Journal of Speculative Philosophy, vol. 2, 190-191. The article refers to a previous work in the same journal at 1(1867), 116-121 — those pages are filmed here to facilitate understanding of the issues Peirce and Harris are discussing in P 00028. See P 00025. *List of Articles;* Burks, *Bibliography.*

O 00029: F i c h e 3
Harris, William Torrey.
    "Intuition vs. Contemplation," *The Journal of Speculative Philosophy,* vol. 2, 191-192. See P 00025 and P 00028.

P 00030: F i c h e 3
"On an Improvement in Boole's Calculus of Logic."
    Proceedings of the American Academy of Arts and Sciences, vol. 7, 250-261. Read before the Academy on 12 March 1867. Fisch and Haskell, *Additions to Cohen's Bibliography;* Burks, *Bibliography.*

P 00031: F i c h e 3, 4
"On the Natural Classification of Arguments."
    Proceedings of the American Academy of Arts and Sciences, vol. 7, 261-287. Read before the Academy on 9 April 1867. Cohen, *Tentative Bibliography;* Burks, *Bibliography.*

P 00032: F i c h e 4
"On a New List of Categories."
    Proceedings of the American Academy of Arts and Sciences, vol. 7, 287-298. Read before the Academy on 14 May 1867. Cohen, *Tentative Bibliography;* Burks, *Bibliography.*

1868

P 00033: F i c h e 4
"Upon the Logic of Mathematics."
> *Proceedings of the American Academy of Arts and Sciences,* vol. 7, 402-412. Read before the Academy on 10 September 1867. Cohen, *Tentative Bibliography;* Burks, *Bibliography.*

P 00034: F i c h e 4
"Upon Logical Comprehension and Extension."
> *Proceedings of the American Academy of Arts and Sciences,* vol. 7, 416-432. Read before the Academy on 13 November 1867. Cohen, *Tentative Bibliography;* Burks, *Bibliography.*

P 00035: F i c h e 4, 5
"Deposition of Charles Saunders [sic] Peirce."
> *In Supreme Court of the United States, in Equity. Hetty H. Greene & Edward H. Greene, in Equity. vs Thomas Mandell and Others.* Peirce's deposition was given on Wednesday, June 5, 1867, and is printed on pp. 761-765. A deposition by Benjamin Peirce is given on pp. 765-773. Little other bibliographic information on this booklet is available, except that the copy, from which this information is taken, was given to Harvard College Library, and is there catalogued as "Econ 5310.436.7." An article on this case, from the *American Law Review,* vol. 4(1870), 625-663, is filmed in addition here to provide additional background for P 00035.

1869

P 00036: F i c h e 5
[Corrections to an article].
> In "On the spectrum of the Aurora Borealis," *The American Journal of Science and Arts,* second series 48, whole series 98(November), 404-405. Fisch, *First Supplement.*

P 00037: F i c h e 5
"Calendars."
> *The Atlantic Almanac, 1869,* Boston: Ticknor and Fields, pp. 2, 6, 10, 14, 18, 22, 26, 30, 34, 38, 42, and 46. Fisch, *First Supplement.*

P 00038: F i c h e 5
"Chronology, Eclipses, and Tides."
> *The Atlantic Almanac, 1869,* Boston: Ticknor and Fields, pp. 62-64. Fisch, *First Supplement.*

P 00039: (NF)
"British Logicians."
> Lectures given at Harvard University, beginning 14 December 1869 and ending 18 January 1870. Some manuscripts of these lectures have survived: see Robin, *Catalogue,* MSS 584-587; also Fisch describes a surviving set of student's notes. Burks, *Bibliography;* Fisch, *First Supplement.*

P 00040: F i c h e 5
"The Pairing of the Elements."
> *Chemical News, American Supplement.* American reprint vol. 4(June), 339-340. Letter to the editor. See comments by other authors on this same topic at pages 217, 218, 270, 271 in the same year of this journal. Fisch, *First Supplement;* Fisch, *Third Supplement.*

1869

P 00041: Fiche 5
"Grounds of Validity of the Laws of Logic: Further Consequences of Four Incapacities."
The Journal of Speculative Philosophy, vol. 2, 193-208. Burks, *Bibliography*.

O 00042: Fiche Sup. 1
Wasson, David A.
"Being and Nothing—In What Sense They are Identical," *Journal of Speculative Philosophy*, vol. 2, 245-247.

P 00043: Fiche 5, 6
"Professor Porter's 'Human Intellect.'"
The Nation, vol. 8 (18 March) 211-213, pages 23-29.

P 00044: Fiche 6
"Roscoe's Spectrum Analysis."
The Nation, vol. 9 (22 July) 73-74, filmed at P 00043, pages 29-32.

P 00045: Fiche 6
"The English Doctrine Of Ideas."
The Nation, vol. 9 (25 November) 461-462, filmed at P 00043, pages 32-37.

O 00046: Fiche 7
Peirce, Benjamin.
[Astronomical work], "Computing Division," in *Report of the Superintendent of the United States Coast Survey, 1866,* House Ex. Doc. No. 87, 39th Congress, 2d Session, Washington: Government Printing Office, pp. 24-25; see also p. 22 for mention of the "Schooner Peirce," presumably named in honor of Benjamin.

P 00047: Fiche 7
[Observations]
"Latitude observations at Manomet, near Plymouth, Massachusetts," in *Report of the Superintendent of the United States Coast Survey, 1867,* House Ex. Doc. No. 275, 40th Congress, 2d Session, Washington: Government Printing Office, p. 19. Burks, *Bibliography*.

P 00048: Fiche 7
[Observations]
"Magnetic observations at Manomet and at Nantucket, Massachusetts," in *Report of the Superintendent of the United States Coast Survey, 1867,* House Ex. Doc. No. 275, 40th Congress, 2d Session, Washington: Government Printing Office, pp. 19-20, filmed at P 00047. Burks, *Bibliography*.

1870

P 00049: Fiche 7
"Astronomical Information, Etc."
The Atlantic Almanac, 1870, Boston: Fields, Osgood & Co., p. 61. Fisch, *First Supplement*.

P 00050: Fiche 7
"Calendars."
The Atlantic Almanac, 1870, Boston: Fields, Osgood & Co., pp. 2, 6, 10, 14, 18, 22, 26, 30, 34, 38, 42, and 46. Fisch, *First Supplement*.

1870

P 00051: Fiche 7
"The Spectroscope."
>The Atlantic Almanac, 1870, Boston: Fields, Osgood & Co., p. 62.

P 00052: Fiche 7, 8
"Description of a Notation for the Logic of Relatives, Resulting from an Amplification of the Conceptions of Boole's Calculus of Logic."
>Memoirs of the American Academy of Arts and Sciences, new series 9, 317-378. Read before the Academy on 26 January. Reprinted by Welch, Bigelow, and Company: Cambridge, Mass. 1870. Cohen, Tentative Bibliography; Burks, Bibliography; Fisch, Third Supplement.

P 00053: Fiche 8
"Bain's Logic."
>The Nation, vol. 11 (4 August) 77-78, filmed at P 00043, pages 38-40. Probably by Peirce.

P 00054: Fiche 8
Review of The Secret of Swedenborg: being an Elucidation of his Doctrine of the Divine Natural Humanity. By Henry James.
>The North American Review, vol. 110(April), 463-468. Burks, Bibliography.

1871

P 00055: (NF)
"Logic."
>These lectures were announced to be given at Harvard University, but were cancelled because Peirce was out of the country. Burks, Bibliography; Fisch, First Supplement.

P 00056: Fiche 8
Note [on De Morgan].
>The Nation, vol. 12 (20 April) 276, filmed at P 00043, pages 41-42. Probably by Peirce.

P 00057: Fiche Sup. 1
Notes [on Babbage and James Mill Peirce].
>The Nation, vol. 12 (9 November) 307-308.

O 00058: Fiche 8
Wright, Chauncey.
>Note [on Peirce's review of the works of Berkeley in the North American Review]. The Nation, vol. 13 (30 November) 355-356; see also vol. 13 (2 November 1871) 294, filmed at P 00043, pages 43-45.

P 00059: Fiche 8
"Mr. Peirce and The Realists."
>The Nation, vol. 13 (14 December), 386, filmed at P 00043, page 45. Signed letter.

P 00060: Fiche 8
Review of The Works of George Berkeley, D.D., formerly Bishop of Cloyne: including many of his Writings hitherto unpublished. Edited by Alexander Campbell Fraser.
>The North American Review, vol. 113 (October), 449-472. Burks, Bibliography; Cohen, Tentative Bibliography.

1871

P 00061: Fiche 8
"On the Appearance of Encke's Comet as seen at Harvard College Observatory."
>Paper read before the Philosophical Society of Washington, Washington, D.C., 16 December. Cited in *Bulletin of the Philosophical Society of Washington,* vol. 1(1874), 35. Burks, *Bibliography.* Announcement only.

O 00062: Fiche 8
Harley, Robert.
>"On Boole's 'Laws of Thought'," *Report of the Fortieth Meeting of the British Association for the Advancement of Science, held at Liverpool in September 1870,* second sequence of pages, pp. 14-15. See P 00052. Fisch, *Third Supplement.*

1872

P 00063: Fiche 8
[On photometric measurement of the stars]
>Paper read before the American Academy of Arts and Sciences, 12 March. Cited in *Proceedings of the American Academy of Arts and Sciences,* vol. 8(May 1868 to May 1873), Boston and Cambridge: Welch, Bigelow, and Company, 1873, p. 412. Burks, *Bibliography.*

P 00064: Fiche 8
"Astronomical."
>*The Atlantic Almanac, 1872,* Boston: James R. Osgood and Company, p. 4. Fisch, *First Supplement.*

P 00065: Fiche 8
"Calendars."
>*The Atlantic Almanac, 1872,* Boston: James R. Osgood and Company, pp. 2, 6, 10, 14, 18, 22, 26, 30, 34, 38, 42, and 46. Fisch, *First Supplement.*

P 00066: Fiche 8
"Educational Textbooks. II."
>*The Nation,* vol. 14 (11 April) 244-246; see also 14 (4 April 1872) 222. Peirce definitely wrote the review of Wilson's book, and probably also wrote the reviews of the other books mentioned in this review article. Fisch, *First Supplement,* filmed at P 00043, pages 46-51.

P 00067: Fiche 8
"On Stellar Photometry."
>Paper read before the Philosophical Society of Washington, Washington, D.C., 19 October. Cited in *Bulletin of the Philosophical Society of Washington,* vol. 1 (1874), 63. See MSS 1055 and 1059 (Robin, *Catalogue*). Burks, *Bibliography.* Announcement only.

P 00068: Fiche 8
"On the Coincidence of the Geographical Distribution of Rainfall and of Illiteracy, as shown by the Statistical Maps of the Ninth Census Reports."
>Paper read before the Philosophical Society of Washington, Washington, D.C., 21 December. Cited in *Bulletin of the Philosophical Society of Washington,* vol. 1 (1874), 68, abstract given. See MS 1131 (Robin, *Catalogue*). Burks, *Bibliography.* Announcement only.

P 00069: Fiche 8
[Observations]
>"Solar eclipse of August 7, at Shelbyville, Kentucky," in *Report of the Superintendent of the United States Coast Survey, 1869,* House Ex. Doc. No. 206, 41st Congress, 2d Session, Washington: Government Printing Office, pp. 38-39. Burks, *Bibliography.*

1872

P 00070: Fiche 8, 9
[Observations and Research, Solar eclipse of 7 August 1869]
"Reports of Observations of the Eclipse of the Sun on August 7, 1869, made by Parties of the United States Coast Survey, etc.," in *Report of the Superintendent of the United States Coast Survey, 1869,* House Ex. Doc. No. 206, 41st Congress, 2d Session, Washington: Government Printing Office, pp. 116-198. Peirce's participation and work in this cooperative venture is mentioned at pp. 126, 128, 138, 153, and 187. Peirce also wrote two of the sub-reports — one at pp. 126-127 having no title, and another at pp. 181-185 entitled "Report on the Results of the Reduction of the Measures of the Photographs of the Partial Phases of the Eclipse of August 7, 1869, taken at Shelbyville, Kentucky, under the Direction of Professor Winlock." Burks, *Bibliography.*

1873

P 00071: Fiche 9
"Astronomical."
The Atlantic Almanac, 1873, Boston: James R. Osgood and Company, p. 4. Fisch, *First Supplement.*

P 00072: Fiche 9
"Calendars."
The Atlantic Almanac, 1873, Boston: James R. Osgood and Company, pp. 2, 6, 10, 14, 18, 22, 26, 30, 34, 38, 42, and 46. Fisch, *First Supplement.*

P 00073: Fiche 9
"Lazelle's 'One Law in Nature'."
The Nation, vol. 17 (10 July) 28-29, filmed at P 00043, pages 52-54.

O 00074: Fiche 9
Backhouse, T.W.
"Spectrum of Aurora," *Nature,* vol. 7 (17 April), 463.

P 00075: Fiche 9
"On Logical Algebra."
Paper read before the Philosophical Society of Washington, Washington, D.C., 17 May. Cited in *Bulletin of the Philosophical Society of Washington,* vol. 1(1874), 83. Burks, *Bibliography. Bibliography.* Announcement only.

P 00076: Fiche 10
[Observations, Solar Eclipse of 22 December 1870]
"Reports of Observations upon the Total Solar Eclipse of December 22, 1870," in *Report of the Superintendent of the United States Coast Survey, 1870,* House Ex. Doc. No. 112, 41st Congress, 3d Session, Washington: Government Printing Office, pp. 115-177. Peirce wrote a short letter of report which is given at p. 125. Zina Fay Peirce gave a report at pp. 125-127 concerning her participation as a sketcher of the solar corona. Peirce is also mentioned at p. 137. Burks, *Bibliography.*

1873

P 00077: F i c h e 10
"On the Theory of Errors of Observations."
>*Report of the Superintendent of the United States Coast Survey, 1870,* House Ex. Doc. No. 112, 41st Congress, 3d Session, Washington: Government Printing Office, pp. 200-224, with errata sheet. Burchard, *Catalogue;* Cohen, *Tentative Bibliography;* Burks, *Bibliography;* Fisch, *First Supplement.*

P 00078: F i c h e 11
[Observations, Solar Eclipse of 22 December 1870]
>"Report on the Eclipse of the Sun on the 22d of December, 1870. By Benjamin Peirce, LL.D., Superintendent United States Coast Survey," in *Report of the Superintendent of the United States Coast Survey, 1870,* House Ex. Doc. No. 112, 41st Congress, 3d Session, Washington: Government Printing Office, pp. 229-232. Burks, *Bibliography.*

1874

P 00079: F i c h e 11
"Astronomical."
>*The Atlantic Almanac, 1874,* Boston: James R. Osgood and Company, p. 4. Fisch, *First Supplement.*

P 00080: F i c h e 11
"Calendars."
>*The Atlantic Almanac, 1874,* Boston: James R. Osgood and Company, pp. 2, 6, 10, 14, 18, 22, 26, 30, 34, 38, 42, and 46. Fisch, *First Supplement.*

P 00081: (NF)
"Rainfall."
>*The Atlantic Almanac, 1874,* Boston: James R. Osgood and Company, p. 65. Fisch, *First Supplement.*

P 00082: F i c h e 11
"On Quaternions, as Developed from the General Theory of the Logic of Relatives."
>Paper read before the Philosophical Society of Washington, Washington, D.C., 14 March. Cited in *Bulletin of the Philosophical Society of Washington,* vol. 1(1874), 94. See also pp. 39 and 48 for Peirce's appearance on membership list and contributor's list. Burks, *Bibliography. Bibliography.* Announcement only.

P 00083: F i c h e 11
"On various Hypotheses in Reference to Space."
>Paper read before the Philosophical Society of Washington, Washington, D.C., 14 March. Cited in *Bulletin of the Philosophical Society of Washington,* vol. 1(1874), 97. Burks, *Bibliography. Bibliography.* Announcement only.

O 00084: (NF)
Jevons, W. Stanley.
>*The Principles of Science: A Treatise on Logic and Scientific Method.* 2 vols. London: Macmillan and Co. See vol. 1, p. 27.

1874

P 00085: Fiche 11
[Observations, Solar Eclipse of 22 December 1870]
"Solar Eclipse of December 22, 1870," by Benjamin Peirce, in *Report of the Superintendent of the United States Coast Survey, 1871,* House Ex. Doc. No. 121, 42d Congress, 2d Session, Washington: Government Printing Office, pp. 9-14. Charles is mentioned at pp. 10 and 11. Burks, *Bibliography.*

P 00086: Fiche 11
[Observations, Solar Eclipse of 22 December 1870]
"Report of Observation of the Eclipse of the Sun of December 22, 1870, by Dr. C.H.F. Peters, Director of the Litchfield Observatory of Hamilton College," in *Report of the Superintendent of the United States Coast Survey, 1871,* House Ex. Doc. No. 121, 42d Congress, 2d Session, Washington: Government Printing Office, pp. 180-184. Peirce is mentioned at p. 182. Burks, *Bibliography.*

1875

P 00087: Fiche 11
"Photometric Measurements of the Stars."
Paper read before the American Academy of Arts and Sciences, 9 March. Cited in *Proceedings of the American Academy of Arts and Sciences,* new series 2, whole series 10 (May 1874 to May 1875), Boston: Press of John Wilson and Son, 1875, p. 473. Burks, *Bibliography.*

O 00088: Fiche 11
"The Theory of Errors of Observation."
Annual Record of Science and Industry for 1874, edited by Spencer F. Baird, New York: Harper and Brothers, pp. 324-325. Abstract of Peirce's article "On the Theory of Errors of Observation," P 00077. Fisch, *First Supplement.*

P 00089: Fiche 11
"A Plan and an Illustration."
In *The Democratic Party,* by Melusina Fay Peirce, Cambridge: John Wilson and Son, pp. 36-37. Fisch and Haskell, *Additions to Cohen's Bibliography;* Burks, *Bibliography.*

P 00090: Fiche 11
"On the Application of Logical Analysis to Multiple Algebra."
Proceedings of the American Academy of Arts and Sciences, new series 2, whole series 10 (May 1874 to May 1875), 392-394; see also p. 475. Read before the Academy on 11 May. See MS 75 (Robin, *Catalogue*). Cohen, *Tentative Bibliography;* Burks, *Bibliography.*

O 00091: Fiche 11
Peirce, Benjamin
"On the Uses and Transformations of Linear Algebra," *Proceedings of the American Academy of Arts and Sciences,* new series 2, whole series 10 (May 1874 to May 1875), 395-400. Read before the Academy on 11 May.

1875

P 00092: Fiche Sup. 1
[Responsibility for temporary supervision of Coast Survey office]
>"Coast Survey Office," in *Report of the Superintendent of the United States Coast Survey, 1872,* House Ex. Doc. No. 240, 42d Congress, 3d Session, Washington: Government Printing Office, pp. 50-51.

P 00093: Fiche Sup. 1
[Pendulum Research]
>"Pendulum experiments," in *Report of the Superintendent of the United States Coast Survey, 1873,* House Ex. Doc. No. 133, 43d Congress, lst Session, Washington: Government Printing Office, p. 14. Burks, *Bibliography.*

P 00094: Fiche 12
[Administrative Duty]
>"Coast Survey Office," in *Report of the Superintendent of the United States Coast Survey, 1873,* House Ex. Doc. No. 133, 43d Congress, 1st Session, Washington: Government Printing Office, p. 60. Peirce had been in charge of the Survey's office during the temporary absence of Assistant J.E. Hilgard.

P 00095: Fiche 12
"A List of Stars for Observations of Latitude."
>*Report of the Superintendent of the United States Coast Survey, 1873,* House Ex. Doc. No. 133, 43d Congress, 1st Session, Washington: Government Printing Office, pp. 138-174. Burks, *Bibliography;* Fisch, *Third Supplement.*

P 00096: Fiche 12
"Errata in the Heis Catalogue of Stars."
>*Report of the Superintendent of the United States Coast Survey, 1873,* House Ex. Doc. No. 133, 43d Congress, 1st Session, Washington: Government Printing Office, pp. 175-180. Burks, *Bibliography;* Fisch, *Third Supplement.*

P 00097: Fiche 12, 13
[Participation in the meetings of the Permanent Committee of the International Geodetic Association, 1875]
>*Verhandlungen der vom 20. bis 29. September 1876[sic] in Paris vereinigten Permanenten Commission der Europaeischen Gradmessung, 1875,* Berlin: Verlag von Georg Reimer, pp. 13, 16, 19-23, 32, 51, 54, 58-61, 71. Burks, *Bibliography.*

1876

P 00098: Fiche 13
"On a new edition of Ptolemy's catalogue of stars."
>Paper read before the American Academy of Arts and Sciences, 11 October. Cited in *Proceedings of the American Academy of Arts and Sciences,* new series 4, whole series 12 (May 1876 to May 1877), Boston: Press of Wilson and Son, 1877, p. 283. Burks, *Bibliography.*

P 00099: Fiche 13
"Logical Contraposition and Conversion."
>*Mind,* vol. 1(July), 424-425; includes editor's reply on p. 425. Burks, *Bibliography.*

1877

"Note on Grassmann's Calculus of Extension."
    Paper read on 10 October 1877. See P 00125.

P 00100: F i c h e 13
"Note on the Sensation of Color."
    The American Journal of Science and Arts, third series 13, whole series 113 (January to June), 247-251. Burks, *Bibliography.*

O 00101: F i c h e 13
"List of Latitude Stars Employed in the Coast Survey."
    Annual Record of Science and Industry for 1876, edited by Spencer F. Baird, New York: Harper and Brothers, pp. 47-48. Abstract of the star catalogue prepared under Peirce's supervision including the list of errata in the catalogue of Heis. Fisch, *Third Supplement.*

P 00102: F i c h e 13
"De l'influence de la flexibilité du trépied sur l'oscillation du pendule à reversion," par Mr. Peirce du Coast Survey U.S.A. Note Communiquée par Mr. E. Plantamour. Association geodesique internationale.
    This is a lithograph distributed in advance of the Geodesic Conference. Burks, *Bibliography;* Fisch, *First Supplement.*

O 00103: (NF)
Searle, Arthur.
    Historical Account of the Astronomical Observatory of Harvard College, from October, 1855, to October, 1876, Annals of the Astronomical Observatory of Harvard College, vol. 8, 3-65, at 50, 53, 57, 58, 59.

O 00104: F i c h e 13
Peirce, Benjamin.
    "Qualitative Algebra," *Johnson's New Universal Cyclopaedia,* vol. 3, part 2, 1487-1488.

P 00105: F i c h e 13
"Note on the Sensation of Color."
    The London, Edinburgh, and Dublin Philosophical Magazine and Journal of Science, fifth series, 3 (supplement), 543-547. Reprint of P 00100. Fisch and Haskell, *Additions to Cohen's Bibliography;* Burks, *Bibliography.*

O 00106: (NF)
Knobel, E.B.
    "The Chronology of Star Catalogues," *Memoirs of the Royal Astronomical Society,* vol. 43, 1-74, at 61.

P 00107: F i c h e 13, 14
"Illustrations of the Logic of Science. First Paper. — The Fixation of Belief."
    The Popular Science Monthly, vol. 12(November), 1-15. Cohen, *Tentative Bibliography;* Burks, *Bibliography.*

P 00108: F i c h e 14
"Nicholas St. John Green."
    Proceedings of the American Academy of Arts and Sciences, new series 4, whole series 12 (from May, 1876 to May, 1877), Boston: Press of John Wilson and Son, pp. 289-291. Burks, *Bibliography.*

1877

P 00109: Fiche Sup. 1
[Pendulum Observations]
>"Atlantic Coast of Maine, New Hampshire, Massachusetts, and Rhode Island, including Seaport Bays, and Rivers," in *Report of the Superintendent of the United States Coast Survey, 1874*, House Ex. Doc. No. 100, 43d Congress, 2d Session, Washington: Government Printing Office, pp. 17-18. Burks, *Bibliography*.

P 00110: Fiche 14
[References to Peirce's pendulum researches]
>*Verhandlungen der vom 5 bis 10 October 1876 in Brüssel vereinigten Permanenten Commission der Europaeischen Gradmessung,* Berlin: Verlag von Georg Reimer, pp. 2, 3, 12, 16-21, 41-42, 45-49. Burks, *Bibliography*.

[Attendance and remarks, International Geodetic Conference, Stuttgart, 1877]
>Remarks presented September-October 1877. See P 00130.

"De l'influence de la Flexibilité du Trépied sur l'Oscillation du Pendule à Reversion; Note communiquée par Mr. E. Plantamour."
>Paper read September-October 1877. See P 00131.

1878

P 00111: Fiche 14
Review of *Esposizione del Metodo dei Minimi Quadrati.* Per Annibale Ferrero.
>*American Journal of Mathematics,* vol. 1, 59-63. Cohen, *Tentative Bibliography;* Burks, *Bibliography*.

O 00112: (NF)
Anonymous
>[Notice of Charles Sanders Peirce's *Photometric Researches*], *The American Journal of Science and Arts,* 3rd series 16, whole series 116, 329.

O 00113: Fiche 14
"Schwimmende Magnete."
>*Beiblätter zu den Annalen der Physik und Chemie,* vol. 2, p. 661; see also p. 574. Abstracted into German by G. Wiedemann from Peirce's article in *Nature,* vol. 18(1878), 381.

P 00114: Fiche 14
Review of *Popular Astronomy.* By Simon Newcomb.
>*The Nation,* vol. 27 (1 August) 74, filmed at P 00043, page 55.

P 00115: Fiche Sup. 1—2
"On the acceleration of gravity at initial stations."
>Paper read before the National Academy of Sciences, New York City, 5-8 November. Cited in *Report of the National Academy of Sciences for the Year 1883,* Senate Mis. Doc. No. 85, 48th Congress, 1st Session, Washington: Government Printing Office, 1884, Appendix D, p. 49. Burks, *Bibliography*.

1878

O 00116: Fiche 15
Mayer, A.M.
"Floating Magnets," *Nature,* vol. 18 (4 July), 258-260. Conversation with Peirce mentioned at 260.

P 00117: Fiche 15
"Floating Magnets."
Nature, vol. 18(8 August), 381. Fisch, *First Supplement.*

P 00118: Fiche 15, 16, 17
Photometric Researches, Made in the Years 1872-1875.
Annals of the Astronomical Observatory of Harvard College, vol. 9, Leipzig: Wilhelm Engelmann. Cohen, *Tentative Bibliography;* Burks, *Bibliography.*

P 00119: Fiche Sup. 3
"Illustrations of the Logic of Science. Second Paper. — How to make our Ideas Clear."
The Popular Science Monthly, vol. 12 (January), 286-302. Cohen, *Tentative Bibliography;* Burks, *Bibliography.*

P 00120: Fiche Sup. 3
"Illustrations of the Logic of Science. Third Paper. — The Doctrine of Chances."
The Popular Science Monthly, vol. 12(March), 604-615. Cohen, *Tentative Bibliography;* Burks, *Bibliography.*

P 00121: Fiche Sup. 3
"Illustrations of the Logic of Science. Fourth Paper. — The Probability of Induction."
The Popular Science Monthly, vol. 12(April), 705-718. Cohen, *Tentative Bibliography;* Burks, *Bibliography.*

P 00122: Fiche 17
"Illustrations of the Logic of Science. Fifth Paper. — The Order of Nature."
The Popular Science Monthly, vol. 13(June), 203-217. Cohen, *Tentative Bibliography;* Burks, *Bibliography.*

P 00123: Fiche 17, 18
"Illustrations of the Logic of Science. Sixth Paper. — Deduction, Induction, and Hypothesis."
The Popular Science Monthly, vol. 13(August), 470-482. Cohen, *Tentative Bibliography;* Burks, *Bibliography.*

O 00124: (NF)
Anonymous.
[Notice of Peirce's *Photometric Researches*], *The Popular Science Monthly,* vol. 14, 116.

P 00125: Fiche 18
"Note on Grassmann's Calculus of Extension."
Proceedings of the American Academy of Arts and Sciences, new series 5, whole series 13, 115-116; see also 427-428. Read before the Academy on 10 October 1877. Cohen, *Tentative Bibliography;* Burks, *Bibliography.*

1878

P 00126: Fiche 18
"On the Influence of Internal Friction upon the Correction of the Length of the Seconds' Pendulum for the Flexibility of the Support."
    Proceedings of the American Academy of Arts and Sciences, new series 5, whole series 13 (May 1877 to May 1878), pp. 396-401; see also p. 433. Presented by title before the Academy on 13 March. Cohen, *Tentative Bibliography;* Burks, *Bibliography.*

P 00127: Fiche 18
[Pendulum Observations]
    "Pendulum observations," in *Report of the Superintendent of the United States Coast Survey, 1875,* House Ex. Doc. No. 81, 44th Congress, 1st Session, Washington: Government Printing Office, p. 19. Burks, *Bibliography.*

P 00128: Fiche 18
"Description of an Apparatus for Recording the Mean of the Times of a Set of Observations."
    Report of the Superintendent of the United States Coast Survey, 1875, House Ex. Doc. No. 81, 44th Congress, 1st Session, Washington: Government Printing Office, pp. 249-253. *List of Articles;* Burks, *Bibliography;* Burchard, *Catalogue.*

P 00129: Fiche 18
"La Logique de la Science. Première Partie. Comment se fixe la croyance."
    Revue Philosophique de la France et de L'Étranger, vol. 6(December), 553-569. *List of Articles;* Burks, *Bibliography.*

P 00130: Fiche 18
[Attendance and remarks, International Geodetic Conference, Stuttgart, 1877]
    Verhandlungen der vom 27 September bis 2 October 1877 zu Stuttgart abgehaltenen fünften allgemeinen Conferenz der Europäischen Gradmessung, Berlin: Verlag von Georg Reimer, pp. 4, 20, 23, 100-104, 118, and 139. Burks, *Bibliography.*

P 00131: Fiche 18, 19
"De l'influence de la Flexibilite du Trepied sur l'Oscillation du Pendule a Reversion; Note communiquee par Mr. E. Plantamour."
    Verhandlungen der vom 27 September bis 2 October 1877 zu Stuttgart abgehaltenen fünften allgemeinen Conferenz der Europäischen Gradmessung, Berlin: Verlag von Georg Reimer, pp. 171-187. Comments on Peirce's paper by Th. von Oppolzer are at pp. 188-192. Additional comments on Peirce by E. Plantamour are in an appendix entitled "Recherches Experimentales sur le Mouvement Simutane d'un Pendule et de ses Supports," pp. 3-5.

O 00132: (NF)
Sawitsch, M.A.
    "É. Plantamour's Recherches expérimentales sur le mouvement simultané d'un pendule et de ses supports," *Vierteljahrsschrift der Astronomischen Gesellschaft,* 13, 264-274, at 266, 271.

1879

P 00133: Fiche 19
"On the Reference of the Unit of Length to the Wavelengths of Light."
    Paper read before the American Academy of Arts and Sciences, Boston, 11 June. Cited in *Proceedings of the American Academy of Arts and Sciences,* new series 7, whole series 15, 369-370. See MSS 1072-1075 (Robin, *Catalogue*). Burks, *Bibliography.*

1879

P 00134: Fiche Sup. 3
"On the Ghosts in Rutherford's Diffraction-Spectra."
  American Journal of Mathematics, vol. 2, 330-347. Cohen, *Tentative Bibliography;* Burks, *Bibliography.*

P 00135: Fiche Sup. 3
"A Quincuncial Projection of the Sphere."
  American Journal of Mathematics, vol. 2, 394-396, plus map plate. Erratum, *American Journal of Mathematics,* vol. 3(1880), v. Cohen, *Tentative Bibliography;* Burks, *Bibliography,* Fisch, *Second Supplement.*

P 00136: Fiche 19
"Note on the Progress of Experiments for comparing a Wave-length with a Meter."
  The American Journal of Science and Arts, third series 18, whole series 118 (July), 51. See MSS 1072-1075 (Robin, *Catalogue*). Cohen, *Tentative Bibliography;* Burks, *Bibliography.*

P 00137: Fiche 19
"On a method for swinging Pendulums for the determination of Gravity, proposed by M. Faye."
  The American Journal of Science and Arts, third series 18, whole series 118(August), 112-119. Cohen, *Tentative Bibliography;* Burks, *Bibliography.*

O 00138: Fiche 19
Anonymous.
  Annual Record of Science and Industry for 1878, edited by Spencer F. Baird, New York: Harper and Brothers, p. 111. Reference to Peirce's participation in the fifth General Conference of the European International Geodetic Conference.

O 00139: Fiche 19
"Fortschritt von Versuchen, die Wellenlange mit einem Meter zu vergleichen."
  Beiblätter zu den Annalen der Physik und Chemie, vol. 3, p. 711; see also bibliographic references to Peirce at pp. 445, 543, 670, 720, and 765. Abstracted into German by E. Wiedemann from Peirce's article in *The American Journal of Science and Arts,* third series 28(1879), 51.

O 00140: Fiche 19
Faye, Herve.
  "Théorie mathématique des oscillations d'un pendule double, par M. Peirce," *Comtes Rendus, des Seances de L'Academie des Sciences,* vol. 89, 462-463.

O 00141: (NF)
Ranyard, A.C.
  "Observations Made During Total Solar Eclipses," *Memoirs of the Royal Astronomical Society,* vol. 41, 169, 170, 171, 175, 201, 255, 258, 273, 316, 330, 411-414.

O 00142: (NF)
Sawitsch, M.A.
  "Les longueurs du pendule à secondes à Poulkova, à St.-Pétersbourg, et aux différents points de la Russie occidentale, corrigées de l'influence produite par la flexion des supports du pendule construits par M. Repsold," *Memoirs of the Royal Astronomical Society,* vol. 44, 307-315, at 312, 313, 314.

1879

P 00143: Fiche 19
"Questions Concerning certain Faculties, Claimed for Man."
    Read before a meeting of the Metaphysical Club, Johns Hopkins University, on 28 October. Cited in *The Johns Hopkins University Circulars,* vol. 1 (1882), 18. Abstract given. Burks, *Bibliography.*

O 00144: Fiche 19
Hall, G. Stanley.
    "Philosophy in the United States," *Mind,* vol. 4, 89-105, at 101-103, summary of Charles Sanders Peirce's "Illustrations of the Logic of Science."

O 00145: (NF)
Rood, Ogden N.
    Modern Chromatics, With Applications to Art and Industry. New York: D. Appleton & Co., pp. 41, 96, 184-185.

O 00146: Fiche 20
Anonymous.
    [Review of *Photometric Researches* by Charles Sanders Peirce], *Monthly Notices of the Royal Astronomical Society,* vol. 39, 270-273.

O 00147: (NF)
Anonymous.
    "Uranometry," *Monthly Notices of the Royal Astronomical Society,* vol. 40, 245-250, at 245.

P 00148: Fiche 20
"Read's Theory of Logic."
    The Nation, vol. 28 (3 April) 234-235, filmed at P 00043, pages 56-58.

P 00149: Fiche 20
"Rood's Chromatics."
    The Nation, vol. 29 (16 October) 260, filmed at P 00043, pages 58-61. The last two paragraphs are not by Peirce, their author being Russell Sturgis.

P 00150: Fiche 20
Note [on the current number of the *American Journal of Mathematics*].
    The Nation, vol. 29 (25 December) 440, filmed at P 00043, pages 61-62.

P 00151: Fiche 20
"On the projections of the Sphere which preserve the angles."
    Paper read before the National Academy of Sciences, Washington, 15-18 April. Cited in *Report of the National Academy of Sciences for the Year 1883,* Senate Mis. Doc. No. 85, 48th Congress, 1st Session, Washington: Government Printing Office, 1884, Appendix D, p. 50; filmed at P 00115. Burks, *Bibliography.*

P 00152: Fiche 20
"On the errors of pendulum experiments, and on the method of swinging pendulums proposed by Mr. Faye."
    Paper read before the National Academy of Sciences, Washington, 15-18 April. Cited in *Report of the National Academy of Sciences for the Year 1883,* Senate Mis. Doc. No. 85, 48th Congress, 1st Session, Washington: Government Printing Office, 1884, Appendix D, p. 50; filmed at P 00115. Burks, *Bibliography.*

1879

P 00153: F i c h e 20
"Ghosts in the diffraction spectra."
> Paper read before the National Academy of Sciences, Washington, 15-18 April. Cited in *Report of the National Academy of Sciences for the Year 1883,* Senate Mis. Doc. No. 85, 48th Congress, 1st Session, Washington: Government Printing Office, 1884, Appendix D, p. 50; filmed at P 00115. Burks, *Bibliography.*

P 00154: F i c h e 20
"Comparisons of the meter with wave lengths."
> Paper read before the National Academy of Sciences, Washington, 15-18 April. Cited in *Report of the National Academy of Sciences for the Year 1883,* Senate Mis. Doc. No. 85, 48th Congress, 1st Session, Washington: Government Printing Office, 1884, Appendix D, p. 50; filmed at P 00115. See MSS 1072-1075 (Robin, *Catalogue*). Burks, *Bibliography.*

P 00155: F i c h e 20
[Spectroscopic studies]
> "The U.S. National Academy," *Nature,* vol. 20 (29 May), 99-101. Fisch, *First Supplement.*

P 00156: F i c h e 20
"Mutual Attraction of Spectral Lines."
> *Nature,* vol. 21(4 December), 108. Fisch, *First Supplement.*

P 00157: (NF)
"The Relations of Logic to Philosophy."
> Lecture given before the Harvard Philosophical Club, 21 May. Fisch, *First Supplement.*

P 00158: F i c h e 20
[Pendulum Observations]
> "Pendulum-Observations," in *Report of the Superintendent of the United States Coast Survey, 1876,* Senate Ex. Doc. No. 37, 44th Congress, 2d Session, Washington: Government Printing Office, pp. 6-9. Burks, *Bibliography.*

P 00159: F i c h e 20
[Preparation of a Star Catalogue]
> "A Catalogue of Stars for Observations of Latitude," in *Report of the Superintendent of the United States Coast Survey, 1876,* Senate Ex. Doc. No. 37, 44th Congress, 2d Session, Washington: Government Printing Office, pp. 83-129. "The list was selected under the direction of Assistant C.S. Peirce . . ." (p. 83). Burks, *Bibliography.*

P 00160: F i c h e 20
"Note on the Theory of the Economy of Research."
> *Report of the Superintendent of the United States Coast Survey, 1876,* Senate Ex. Doc. No. 37, 44th Congress, 2d Session, Washington: Government Printing Office, pp. 197-201. Cohen, *Tentative Bibliography;* Burchard, *Catalogue;* Burks, *Bibliography;* Fisch, *Third Supplement.*

P 00161: F i c h e 20, 21, 22
"Measurements of Gravity at Initial Stations in America and Europe."
> *Report of the Superintendent of the United States Coast Survey, 1876,* Senate Ex. Doc. No. 37, 44th Congress, 2d Session, Washington: Government Printing Office, pp. 202-337, 410-416. Errata are given in *Report of the Superintendent of the United States Coast Survey, 1883,* p. 476n and in *The American Journal of Science and Arts,* third series 20 (October 1880), 327. Cohen, *Tentative Bibliography;* Burchard, *Catalogue;* Burks, *Bibliography.*

1879

P 00162: Fiche 22
"La Logique de la Science. Deuxieme Partie. Comment rendre nos idees claires."
> *Revue Philosophique de la France et L'Étranger,* vol. 7 (January), 39-57. *List of Articles;* Burks, *Bibliography.*

P 00163: Fiche 22
"Spectroscopic Studies."
> *Science News,* vol. 1(1 May), pp. 196-198. See also pp. 193-198. Abstracts of the two papers Peirce presented at the meeting of the National Academy of Sciences, 15-18 April 1879 ["On Ghosts in Diffraction Spectra" and "Comparison of Wave Lengths with the Metre"]. Reprinted in *Nature,* 20, (29 May 1879), 99-101 with abridgements. Fisch, *First Supplement.*

P 00164: Fiche 22
[Remarks on the four-color problem]
> Given before the Scientific Association, Johns Hopkins University, on 5 November, and 3 December. Cited in *The Johns Hopkins University Circulars,* vol. 1 (1882), 16. Burks, *Bibliography.*

P 00165: Fiche 22
[References to Peirce's pendulum researches]
> *Verhandlungen der vom 4 bis 8 September 1878 in Hamburg Vereinigten Permanenten Commission der Europäischen Gradmessung,* Berlin: Verlag von Georg Reimer, pp. 8-9.

P 00166: Fiche 22
[Report on Peirce's pendulum researches]
> *Verhandlungen der vom 4 bis 8 September 1878 in Hamburg Vereinigten Permanenten Commission der Europäischen Gradmessung,* Berlin: Verlag von Georg Reimer, pp. 116-120. Burks, *Bibliography.*

1880

P 00167: Fiche 22, 23
"On the Algebra of Logic."
> *American Journal of Mathematics,* vol. 3, 15-57. Cohen, *Tentative Bibliography;* Burks, *Bibliography.*

P 00168: Fiche 23
"Results of Pendulum Experiments."
> *American Journal of Science,* third series 20, whole series 120 (October), 327. Reprinted in *The London, Edinburgh, and Dublin Philosophical Magazine and Journal of Science,* fifth series 10 (November 1880), 387; see P 00174. *List of Articles;* Fisch and Haskell, *Additions to Cohen's Bibliography;* Burks, *Bibliography.*

O 00169: Fiche 23
"Ueber eine Methode mit Schwingenden Pendels die Schwere zu bestimmen."
> *Beiblätter zu den Annalen der Physik und Chemie,* vol. 4, p. 240; see also bibliographic references to Peirce at pp. 78, 494, 572, 582, 695, and 846. Abstracted into German by E. Wiedemann from Peirce's article in *The American Journal of Science and Arts,* third series 28(1879), 112-119. In the abstract, the author is given as "J.C. Peirce."

1880

O 00170: F i c h e 23
"Gegenseitige Anziehung von Spectrallinien."
>Beiblätter zu den Annalen der Physik und Chemie, vol. 4, p. 278. Abstracted into German by E. Wiedemann from Peirce's article in Nature, vol. 21(1879), 108.

P 00171: F i c h e 23
"Sur la valeur de la pesanteur à Paris."
>Comptes Rendus des Séances de L'Académie des Sciences, vol. 90(June), 1401-1403. Fisch and Haskell, Additions to Cohen's Bibliography; Burks, Bibliography.

O 00172: F i c h e 23
Faye, Herve.
>"Rapport sur un Mémoire de M. Peirce concernant la constante de la pesanteur à Paris," Comptes Rendus des Seances de L'Academie des Sciences, vol. 90, 1463-1466. Review of "Sur la valeur de la pesanteur a Paris" by Charles Sanders Peirce.

O 00173: (NF)
Clarke, A.R.
>Geodesy. Oxford: Clarendon Press, p. 337.

P 00174: F i c h e 23
"Results of Pendulum Experiments."
>The London, Edinburgh, and Dublin Philosophical Magazine and Journal of Science, fifth series 10 (November), 387. Fisch and Haskell, Additions to Cohen's Bibliography; Burks, Bibliography.

P 00175: (NF)
[Comments on Stringham's paper]
>Given before the Mathematical Seminary, Johns Hopkins University, on 21 January. Cited in The Johns Hopkins University Circulars, vol. 1 (1882), 35. Burks, Bibliography.

P 00176: F i c h e 23
[Remarks on a paper by Marquand]
>Given before the Metaphysical Club, Johns Hopkins University, on 13 January. Cited in The Johns Hopkins University Circulars, vol. 1 (1882), 34. Abstract of Marquand's paper given. Burks, Bibliography.

P 00177: F i c h e 23
"On Kant's 'Critic of the Pure Reason' in the light of Modern Logic."
>Paper read before the Metaphysical Club, Johns Hopkins University, on 9 March. Cited in The Johns Hopkins University Circulars, vol. 1 (1882), 49. Abstract given. Burks, Bibliography.

P 00178: F i c h e 23
"On the ellipticity of the earth as deduced from pendulum experiments."
>Paper read before the National Academy of Sciences, New York City, 16-19 November. Cited in Report of the National Academy of Sciences for the Year 1883, Serate Mis. Doc. No. 85, 48th Congress, 1st Session, Washington: Government Printing Office, 1884, Appendix D, p. 53; filmed at P 00115. Burks, Bibliography.

P 00179: F i c h e 23
"On the Colours of Double Stars."
>Nature, vol. 22(29 July), 291-292. Fisch, First Supplement.

1880

O 00180: (NF)
Peirce, Frederick C.
> *Peirce Genealogy.* Worcester, Mass.: Charles Hamilton.

O 00181: (NF)
Rowland, Henry Augustus.
> "Remarks on Charles Sanders Peirce's Paper on the Ghosts in Rutherford's Grating," *Proceedings of the American Association for the Advancement of Science,* vol. 29, 279.

P 00182: F i c h e 23
[Pendulum Observations]
> "Pendulum experiments," in *Report of the Superintendent of the United States Coast Survey, 1877,* Senate Ex. Doc. No. 12, 45th Congress, 2d Session, Washington: Government Printing Office, pp. 17-18. Burks, *Bibliography.*

P 00183: F i c h e 23
"A Quincuncial Projection of the Sphere."
> *Report of the Superintendent of the United States Coast Survey, 1877,* Senate Ex. Doc. No. 12, 45th Congress, 2d Session, Washington: Government Printing Office, pp. 191-192. Same as *American Journal of Mathematics,* vol. 2(1879), 394-396 plus map plate. Also reprinted in *A Treatise on Projections,* by Thomas Craig, Washington: Government Printing Office, 1882, p. 132. Fisch and Haskell, *Additions to Cohen's Bibliography;* Burchard, *Catalogue;* Burks, *Bibliography.*

P 00184: F i c h e 24
[References to Peirce's pendulum researches]
> *Verhandlungen der vom 16 bis 20 September 1879 in Genf vereinigten Permanenten Commission der Europäischen Gradmessung,* Berlin: Verlag von Georg Reimer, pp. 7-10, 19-29. Burks, *Bibliography.*

O 00185: F i c h e 24
Th. W.
> "Peirce, C.S., Photometric researches. Made in the years 1872-1875," *Vierteljahresschrift der Astron. Gesellschaft,* vol. 15, 193-208.

1881

P 00186: F i c h e 24
"Comparison Between the Yard and Metre by Means of the Reversible Pendulum."
> Paper read before the American Association for the Advancement of Science, Cincinnati, Ohio, August. Cited in *Proceedings of the American Association for the Advancement of Science, Thirtieth Meeting, held at Cincinnati, Ohio, August, 1881,* Salem: 1882, abstract given (presumably by Peirce) on p. 20. Notice of Peirce's election to membership in the Association is given on p. xlix. See MSS 1072-1075 (Robin, *Catalogue*). Fisch, *First Supplement.*

P 00187: F i c h e 24
"On the Logic of Number."
> *American Journal of Mathematics,* vol. 4, 85-95. Cohen, *Tentative Bibliography;* Burks, *Bibliography.*

1881

P 00188: Fiche 24, 25
"Linear Associative Algebra." By Benjamin Peirce. With Notes and Addenda by C.S. Peirce, Son of the Author.
>*American Journal of Mathematics,* vol. 4, 97-229. Cohen, *Tentative Bibliography;* Burks, *Bibliography.*

O 00189: (NF)
Pickering, Edward C.
>"Schreiben des Herrn Professor Edward C. Pickering an den Herausgeber," *Astronomische Nachrichten,* vol. 99, 219-222.

O 00190: Fiche 26
"Resultate von Pendelversuchen."
>*Beiblätter zu den Annalen der Physik und Chemie,* vol. 5, p. 12. Abstracted into German by E. Wiedemann from Peirce's 1880 article in the *American Journal of Science and Arts,* vol. 20, p. 327.

O 00191: Fiche 26
"Ueber Gespenster (ghosts) in den Rutherford'schen Beugungsspectren."
>*Beiblätter zu den Annalen der Physik und Chemie,* vol. 5, pp. 48-50. Abstracted into German by E. Wiedemann from Peirce's 1879 article in the *American Journal of Mathematics,* vol. 2, pp. 330-347. Fisch and Haskell, *Additions to Cohen's Bibliography.*

O 00192: Fiche 26
"Ueber die Weite der Gitterabstande in Rutherford's Gittern."
>*Beiblätter zu den Annalen der Physik und Chemie,* vol. 5, p. 665. Abstracted into German by E. Wiedemann from Peirce's 1881 article in *Nature,* vol. 24, p. 262.

O 00193: Fiche 26
Peirce, Benjamin.
>*Ideality in the Physical Sciences,* Boston: Little, Brown & Co., at 67-68.

P 00194: (NF)
"Proof that there are only Three Linear Associative Algebras in which Division is an Unambiguous Process."
>Paper read before the Mathematical Seminary, Johns Hopkins University, January. Cited in *The Johns Hopkins University Circulars,* vol. 1 (1882), 131. See MS 77 (Robin, *Catalogue*). Burks, *Bibliography.*

P 00195: (NF)
[Comments on Mitchell's paper]
>Given before the Mathematical Seminary, Johns Hopkins University, March. Cited in *The Johns Hopkins University Circulars,* vol. 1 (1882), 128. Burks, *Bibliography.*

P 00196: (NF)
"On Relations between Sensations."
>Read before the Metaphysical Club, Johns Hopkins University, April. Cited in *The Johns Hopkins University Circulars,* vol. 1 (1882), 150. Burks, *Bibliography.*

P 00197: Fiche 26
[Remarks on Gilman's paper]
>Given before the Metaphysical Club, Johns Hopkins University, November. Cited in *The Johns Hopkins University Circulars,* vol. 1 (1882), 177. Burks, *Bibliography.*

1881

P 00198: Fiche 26
Review of *Studies in Deductive Logic.* By W. Stanley Jevons.
    The Nation, vol. 32 (31 March) 227, filmed at P 00043, pages 63-64.

P 00199: Fiche 26
"On the progress of pendulum work."
    Paper read before the National Academy of Sciences, Washington, 19-22 April. Cited in *Report of the National Academy of Sciences for the Year 1883,* Senate Mis. Doc. No. 85, 48th Congress, 1st Session, Washington: Government Printing Office, 1884, Appendix D, p. 53; filmed at P 00115. Burks, *Bibliography.*

P 00200: Fiche 26
"On the logic of number."
    Paper read before the National Academy of Sciences, Philadelphia, 15-17 November. Cited in *Report of the National Academy of Sciences for the Year 1883,* Senate Mis. Doc. No. 85, 48th Congress, 1st Session, Washington: Government Printing Office, 1884, Appendix D, p. 54; filmed at P 00115. See MS 38 (Robin, *Catalogue*). Burks, *Bibliography.*

O 00201: Fiche 26
Jevons, W. Stanley.
    "Recent Mathematico-Logical Memoirs," *Nature,* vol. 23 (24 March), 485-487.

O 00202: Fiche 26
McColl, Hugh.
    "Symbolical Logic," *Nature,* vol. 23 (21 April), 578-579.

O 00203: Fiche 26
McColl, Hugh.
    "Symbolical Logic," *Nature,* vol. 24 (5 May), 5.

P 00204: Fiche 26
"Width of Mr. Rutherford's Rulings."
    Nature, vol. 24 (21 July), 262. Fisch and Haskell, *Additions to Cohen's Bibliography;* Burks, *Bibliography.*

O 00205: Fiche 26
Anonymous.
    "Benjamin Peirce," *Proceedings of the American Academy of Arts and Sciences,* new series 8, whole series 16 (24 May), 443-454. Obituary notice.

O 00206: Fiche 26
McColl, Hugh.
    "A Note on Prof. Peirce's Probability Notation of 1867," *Proceedings of the London Mathematical Society,* vol. 12, 102.

P 00207: Fiche 26
[Pendulum research]
    "Pendulum experiments," in *Report of the Superintendent of the United States Coast and Geodetic Survey, 1878,* Senate Ex. Doc. No. 13, Washington: Government Printing Office, pp. 4, 18. Burks, *Bibliography.*

1881

P 00208: Fiche 26
[Pendulum Research]
"Pendulum observations," in *Report of the Superintendent of the United States Coast and Geodetic Survey, 1879,* Senate Ex. Doc. No. 17, 46th Congress, 2d Session, Washington: Government Printing Office, pp. 27-29. Most of this article consists of quotations from Peirce about work in progress or published in other journals. Burks, *Bibliography.*

O 00209: Fiche 26
Tannery, Paul.
"C.S. Peirce. — On the Algebra of Logic," *Revue Philosophique de la France et de L'Étranger,* vol. 12, 646-650.

P 00210: Fiche 26
"A New Computation of the Compression of the Earth, from Pendulum Experiments."
Paper read before the Scientific Association, Johns Hopkins University, February. Cited in *The Johns Hopkins University Circulars,* vol. 1 (1882), 128. Abstract given. Burks, *Bibliography.*

P 00211: (NF)
"A Fallacy of Induction."
Read before the Scientific Association, Johns Hopkins University, November. Cited in *The Johns Hopkins University Circulars,* vol. 1 (1882), 172. Burks, *Bibliography.*

O 00212: (NF)
Venn, John.
Symbolic Logic. London: Macmillan and Co., 97, 134, 146, 189, 341, 383, 404. (2nd ed., revised and rewritten, 1894, 106, 150, 163, 252, 253, 255, 388, 481, 489).

O 00213: (NF)
Oppolzer, Th. von.
Syzygien-tafeln für den Mond, Leipzig: Engelmann, at 21. On Peirce's quincuncial projection.

O 00214: (NF)
James, William.
"Reflex Action and Theism," *Unitarian Review,* vol. 16, 389-416, at 400.

P 00215: Fiche 26
[Letter to Monsieur Faye]
Verhandlungen der vom 13 bis 16 September 1880 zu München Abgehaltenen Sechsten Allgemeinen Conferenz der Europäischen Gradmessung, Berlin: Verlag von Georg Reimer, pp. 30-32; repeated on pp. 84-86. Burks, *Bibliography.*

P 00216: Fiche 26, 27
[References to Peirce's pendulum researches]
Verhandlungen der vom 13 bis 16 September 1880 zu München Abgehaltenen Sechsten Allgemeinen Conferenz der Europäischen Gradmessung, Berlin: Verlag von Georg Reimer, pp. 43, 96, Appendix II (pp. 1-12), Appendix IIa (pp. 1-8). Burks, *Bibliography.*

1882

O 00217: F i c h e 27
H.A.N.
> *Linear Associative Algebra;* by Benjamin Peirce. *The American Journal of Science and Arts,* third series 23, whole series 123, 336.

P 00218: F i c h e 27
"On Irregularities in the Amplitude of Oscillation of Pendulums."
> *The American Journal of Science,* third series 24, whole series 124 (October), 254-255. Fisch and Haskell, *Additions to Cohen's Bibliography;* Burks, *Bibliography.*

P 00219: F i c h e 27, 28
[Astronomical observations]
> *Micrometric Measurements,* Annals of the Astronomical Observatory of Harvard College, vol. 13, part 1, Cambridge: John Wilson and Son, Peirce's contributions are at pp. iv, 19-61, 63, 66-81, 83, 86, 90, 148, 172, 184-187. Burks, *Bibliography.*

P 00220: F i c h e 28
"Brief Description of the Algebra of Relatives."
> Privately printed brochure, Baltimore: 7 January; with a postscript dated 16 January. Burks, *Bibliography.*

O 00221: F i c h e 28
Michaelis, C.T.
> "C.S. Peirce. On the Algebra of Logic," *Jahrbuch über die Fortschritte der Mathematik,* Jahrgang 1880, vol. 12, part 1, pp. 41-44.

P 00222: F i c h e 28
Abstract of "On the Logic of Number."
> Printed in *The Johns Hopkins University Circulars,* vol. 1 (1882), 184.

O 00223: F i c h e 28
Abstract of *Linear Associative Algebra.* By the late Benjamin Peirce.
> Printed in *The Johns Hopkins University Circulars,* vol. 1 (1882), 214.

P 00224: F i c h e 28
Abstract of "On a Class of Multiple Algebras."
> This paper was read before the Mathematical Society, Johns Hopkins University, 18 October. Printed in *The Johns Hopkins University Circulars,* vol. 2 (1883), 3-4. Burks, *Bibliography.*

P 00225: F i c h e 28
"Introductory Lecture on the Study of Logic."
> An outline of the remarks made by Peirce at the beginning of his course on logic in September, Johns Hopkins University. Given in *The Johns Hopkins University Circulars,* vol. 2 (1883), 11-12. Burks, *Bibliography.*

P 00226: F i c h e 28
"On the Relative Forms of Quaternions."
> Paper read before the Mathematical Seminary, Johns Hopkins University, January. Cited in *The Johns Hopkins University Circulars,* vol. 1 (1882), 179. Abstract given. Burks, *Bibliography.*

1882

O 00227: F i c h e 28
Sylvester, J.J.
> Remarks on C. Peirce's Logic of Relatives, given before the Mathematical Seminary, Johns Hopkins University, April. Cited in *The Johns Hopkins University Circulars,* vol. 1 (1882), 203. Burks, *Bibliography.*

O 00228: (NF)
Pritchard, C.
> "Photometric Determination of the Relative Brightness of the Brighter Stars North of the Equator," *Memoirs of the Royal Astronomical Society,* vol. 47, 353-456, at 364, 375, 376.

P 00229: (NF)
"J.S. Mill's Logic."
> Paper read before the Metaphysical Club, Johns Hopkins University, January. Cited in *The Johns Hopkins University Circulars,* vol. 1 (1882), 178. Burks, *Bibliography.*

P 00230: F i c h e 28
"Remarks on the above paper [by B.I. Gilman]."
> Given before the Metaphysical Club, Johns Hopkins University, April. Cited in *The Johns Hopkins University Circulars,* vol. 1 (1882), 240. Abstract given. Burks, *Bibliography.*

O 00231: F i c h e 28
Gilman, B.I.
> "On Propositions called Spurious," paper given before the Metaphysical Club, Johns Hopkins University, May. Cited in *The Johns Hopkins University Circulars,* vol. 1 (1882), 241. Abstract given.

P 00232: F i c h e 28
[Opening remarks for the Metaphysical Club]
> Given before that club, Johns Hopkins University, on 14 November. Cited in *The Johns Hopkins University Circulars,* vol. 2 (1883), 38. Note attendance by J. Dewey. Burks, *Bibliography.*

P 00233: F i c h e 28
"On a fallacy of induction."
> Paper read before the National Academy of Sciences, Washington, 18-21 April. Cited in *Report of the National Academy of Sciences for the Year 1883,* Senate Mis. Doc. No. 85, 48th Congress, 1st Session, Washington: Government Printing Office, 1884, Appendix D, p. 54; filmed at P 00113. Burks, *Bibliography.*

P 00234: F i c h e 28
"On the determination of the figure of the earth by the variations of gravity."
> Paper read before the National Academy of Sciences, New York City, 14-17 November. Cited in *Report of the National Academy of Sciences for the Year 1883,* Senate Mis. Doc. No. 85, 48th Congress, 1st Session, Washington: Government Printing Office, 1884, Appendix D, p. 55; filmed at P 00115. Burks, *Bibliography.*

P 00235: F i c h e 28
"On the logic of relatives."
> Paper read before the National Academy of Sciences, New York City, 14-17 November. Cited in *Report of the National Academy of Sciences for the Year 1883,* Senate Mis. Doc. No. 85, 48th Congress, 1st Session, Washington: Government Printing Office, 1884, Appendix D, p. 55; filmed at P 00115.

1882

P 00236: F i c h e 28
"On Ptolemy's catalogue of stars."
    Paper read before the National Academy of Sciences, New York City, 14-17 November. Cited in *Report of the National Academy of Sciences for the Year 1883,* Senate Mis. Doc. No. 85, 48th Congress, 1st Session, Washington: Government Printing Office, 1884, Appendix D, p. 55; filmed at P 00115. Burks, *Bibliography*.

P 00237: F i c h e 28
[Pendulum research, metrology, diffraction spectra]
    "Pendulum observations," in *Report of the Superintendent of the United States Coast and Geodetic Survey, 1880,* Senate Ex. Doc. No. 12, 46th Congress, 3d Session, Washington: Government Printing Office, pp. 19-20. Burks, *Bibliography*.

P 00238: F i c h e 28
"Quincuncial Projection of the Sphere."
    In *A Treatise on Projections,* by Thomas Craig, Treasury Department, Document No. 61, Coast and Geodetic Survey, Washington: Government Printing Office, pp. 132, 247. This is extracted from Peirce's report on this topic in the Coast Survey Report for 1877. Burks, *Bibliography*.

1883

O 00239: (NF)
Orff, Carl von.
    "Bestimmung der Länge des einfachen Secundenpendels auf der Sternwarte zu Bogenhausen," *Abhandlungen der Akademie der Wissenschaften,* Munchen (Mathematisch-Physikalischen Classe), vol. 14, 163-294, at 164, 268, 272, 274, 276, 277, 278.

O 00240: F i c h e S u p. 4
Peirce, Benjamin Osgood, Jr.
    "On the Sensitiveness of the Eye to Slight Differences of Color," *The American Journal of Science*, third series 26, whole series 126 (October), 299-302.

P 00241: F i c h e 28
"C.S. Peirce.—Irregularidades en las oscilaciones del péndulo."
    Crónica Cientifica (Barcelona), vol. 6 (25 October), 447-449. Fisch, *First Supplement*.

P 00242: F i c h e 28
"Preface to Contributions to Logic by Members of the Johns Hopkins University. C.S. Peirce, Editor. (Little, Brown & Co., Boston, 1882)."
    Printed in *The Johns Hopkins University Circulars,* vol. 2 (1883), 34. Burks, *Bibliography*.

O 00243: F i c h e 28
Sylvester, J.J.
    "Erratum," *The Johns Hopkins University Circulars,* vol. 2, 46. Burks, *Bibliography*.

O 00244: (NF)
Sylvester, J.J.
    "A Note from Professor Sylvester," *The Johns Hopkins University Circulars,* vol. 2, 86 Burks, *Bibliography*.

1883

P 00245: Fiche 28
"A Communication from Mr. Peirce."
    The Johns Hopkins University Circulars, vol. 2, 86-88. See the related note by Sylvester printed immediately above Peirce's "Communication." Burks, *Bibliography.*

O 00246: (NF)
Angot, Alfred.
    Review of "On Irregularities in the Amplitude of Oscillation of Pendulums" by Charles Sanders Peirce. *Journal de Physique,* second series 12, 145-146.

P 00247: (NF)
"Reply to Professor Morris on 'Life'."
    Remarks before the Metaphysical Club, Johns Hopkins University, 13 November. Cited in *The Johns Hopkins University Circulars,* vol. 3 (1884), 46. Burks, *Bibliography.*

O 00248: Fiche 29
Venn, J.
    Review of *Studies in Logic.* By Members of the Johns Hopkins University. *Mind,* vol. 8, 594-603.

P 00249: Fiche 29
Note [on Peirce's comparison of U.S. yard no. 57 with British yard no. 1].
    Nature, vol. 29 (29 November), 110-111.

O 00250: (NF)
Anonymous.
    Notice of *Studies in Logic,* edited by Peirce. *Popular Science Monthly,* vol. 24, 131.

O 00251: (NF)
Müller, Gustav.
    "Photometrische Untersuchungen," *Publicationen des Astrophysikalischen Observatoriums zu Potsdam,* No. 12, 3: 227-293, at 236, 243, 244, 245, 293.

P 00252: Fiche 29
[Pendulum research, metrology]
    "Pendulum observations," in *Report of the Superintendent of the United States Coast and Geodetic Survey, 1881,* Washington: Government Printing Office, p. 26. Burks, *Bibliography.*

P 00253: Fiche 29, 30
"On the Flexure of Pendulum Supports."
    Report of the Superintendent of the United States Coast and Geodetic Survey, 1881, Washington: Government Printing Office, pp. 359-441. Burchard, *Catalogue;* Cohen, *Tentative Bibliography;* Burks, *Bibliography;* Fisch, *First Supplement.*

P 00254: Fiche 30
"On the Deduction of the Ellipticity of the Earth from Pendulum Experiments."
    Report of the Superintendent of the United States Coast and Geodetic Survey, 1881, Washington: Government Printing Office, pp. 442-456. Burchard, *Catalogue;* Cohen, *Tentative Bibliography;* Burks, *Bibliography;* Fisch, *First Supplement.*

1883

P 00255: Fiche 30
"On a Method of Observing the Coincidence of Vibration of Two Pendulums."
> *Report of the Superintendent of the United States Coast and Geodetic Survey, 1881,* Washington: Government Printing Office, pp. 457-460. Burchard, *Catalogue;* Fisch and Haskell, *Additions to Cohen's Bibliography;* Burks, *Bibliography;* Fisch, *First Supplement.*

P 00256: Fiche 30
"On the Value of Gravity at Paris."
> *Report of the Superintendent of the United States Coast and Geodetic Survey, 1881,* Washington: Government Printing Office, pp. 461-463. Burchard, *Catalogue;* Fisch and Haskell, *Additions to Cohen's Bibliography;* Burks, *Bibliography;* Fisch, *First Supplement.*

P 00257: Fiche 30
[Pendulum research]
> "Figure of the Earth," in *Report of the Superintendent of the United States Coast and Geodetic Survey, 1882,* Senate Ex. Doc. No. 77, 47th Congress, 2d Session, Washington: Government Printing Office, p. 4. Burks, *Bibliography.*

P 00258: Fiche 30
[Measurement of absolute gravity]
> "Measurement of the Force of Gravity," in *Report of the Superintendent of the United States Coast and Geodetic Survey, 1882,* Senate Ex. Doc. No. 77, 47th Congress, 2d Session, Washington: Government Printing Office, p. 19. Burks, *Bibliography.*

P 00259: Fiche 30
[Measurement of absolute gravity, economy of research]
> "Force of gravity," in *Report of the Superintendent of the United States Coast and Geodetic Survey, 1882,* Senate Ex. Doc. No. 77, 47th Congress, 2d Session, Washington: Government Printing Office, pp. 32-33. Burks, *Bibliography.*

P 00260: Fiche 30
[Gravity research]
> "Report of a Conference on Gravity Determinations, held at Washington, D.C., in May, 1882,." in *Report of the Superintendent of the United States Coast and Geodetic Survey, 1882,* Senate Ex. Doc. No. 77, 47th Congress, 2d Session, Washington: Government Printing Office, pp. 503-516. Peirce is mentioned a few times in the report, and his recorded remarks are given at several points.

P 00261: Fiche 30
"Six Reasons for the Prosecution of Pendulum Experiments."
> *Report of the Superintendent of the United States Coast and Geodetic Survey, 1882,* Senate Ex. Doc. No. 77, 47th Congress, 2d Session, Washington: Government Printing Office, pp. 506-508; filmed at P 00260. Burks, *Bibliography.*

P 00262: Fiche 30
"Opinions Concerning the Conduct of Gravitation Work."
> *Report of the Superintendent of the United States Coast and Geodetic Survey, 1882,* Senate Ex. Doc. No. 77, 47th Congress, 2d Session, Washington: Government Printing Office, pp. 512-516; filmed at P 00260. Burks, *Bibliography.*

1883

P 00263: F i c h e 30
"Experimental Researches on the Force of Gravity."
> *Report of the Superintendent of the United States Coast and Geodetic Survey, 1882,* Senate Ex. Doc. No. 77, 47th Congress, 2d Session, Washington: Government Printing Office, p. 557. "Owing to the already bulky proportions of this volume, Appendix No. 23 [this title] has been transferred to, and will appear in, the Annual Report of the Superintendent for the year 1883." Probably the article in the Report for 1883 that is the successor of this unprinted piece is "Determinations of Gravity at Allegheny, Ebensburgh, and York, Pa., in 1879 and 1880." Burks, *Bibliography.*

P 00264: F i c h e 30
[Eulogy]
> "Tribute to the Memory of Carlile P. Patterson, Superintendent of the Coast and Geodetic Survey from 1874 to 1881," in *Report of the Superintendent of the United States Coast and Geodetic Survey, 1882,* Senate Ex. Doc. No. 77, 47th Congress, 2d Session, Washington: Government Printing Office, pp. 559-563; Peirce's comments are at p. 563. Fisch, *Third Supplement.*

O 00265: F i c h e 30
Anonymous.
> "Studies in Logic," *Science,* vol. 1 (8 June), 514-516.

P 00266: F i c h e 30
"A New Rule for Division in Arithmetic."
> *Science,* vol. 2 (21 December), 788-789. Fisch and Haskell, *Additions to Cohen's Bibliography;* Burks, *Bibliography.*

O 00267: (NF)
Farrer, T.H.
> Report of the Board of Trade on their Proceedings and Business under the Weights and Measures Act, 1878. Great Britain, House of Commons. *Sessional Papers,* vol. 27, 853-878, at 854.

P 00268: F i c h e 31, 32, 33
Studies in Logic, By Members of the Johns Hopkins University. Edited by C.S. Peirce, Boston: Little, Brown, and Company.
> The following parts of the book are by Peirce: "Preface," iii-vi;"A Theory of Probable Inference," 126-181; "Note A (On a Limited Universe of Marks)," 182-186; "Note B (The Logic of Relatives)," 187-203. Cohen, *Tentative Bibliography;* Burks, *Bibliography.*

1884

O 00269: F i c h e 33
Rowland, Henry Augustus.
> Remarks in accepting the Rumford Medal. *American Academy of Arts and Sciences,* vol. 19, 477-483, at 483.

1884

P 00270: Fiche Sup. 4
"On Weights and Measures."
    A discussion of pendulum experiments and weights and measures given before the American Metrological Society meeting at Columbia College in New York City, 30 December. Cited (with summary account of the discussion) in *Proceedings of the American Metrological Society, from May, 1884, to December, 1885,* New York: Published by the Society, 1885, pp. 46-48, 83. Burks, *Bibliography;* Fisch, *First Supplement.*

P 00271: Fiche Sup. 4
[Astronomical Observations]
    Observations with the Meridian Photometer During the Years 1879-1882, Annals of the Astronomical Observatory of Harvard College, vol. 14, part 1: 98, 102-284, 330, 337-340, 361, 374-376, 432, 436, 442, 444, 456, 460, 464, 468, 472, 489, 490, 500, 502, 504.

O 00272: Fiche 36
Michaelis, C.T.
    "C.S. Peirce. Remarks," *Jahrbuch über die Fortschritte der Mathematik,* Jahrgang 1882, vol. 14, part 1, pp. 28-29.

P 00273: (NF)
"On the Mode of Representing Negative Quantity in the Logic of Relatives."
    Paper read before the Mathematical Society, Johns Hopkins University, 16 January. Cited in *The Johns Hopkins University Circulars,* vol. 3 (1884), 70. Burks, *Bibliography.*

P 00274: (NF)
"Design and Chance."
    Paper read before the Metaphysical Club, Johns Hopkins University, on 17 January. Cited in *The Johns Hopkins University Circulars,* vol. 3 (1884), 70. See MS 875 (Robin, *Catalogue).* Burks, *Bibliography.*

P 00275: (NF)
"The Logic of Religion."
    Paper read before the Metaphysical Club, Johns Hopkins University, on 13 May. Cited in *The Johns Hopkins University Circulars,* vol. 3 (1884), 138. Burks, *Bibliography.*

P 00276: (NF)
"On 'The Magnet': a fourteenth century manuscript of Petrus Peregrinus."
    Paper read before the Metaphysical Club, Johns Hopkins University, on 18 November. Cited in *The Johns Hopkins University Circulars,* vol. 4 (1885), 28. Burks, *Bibliography.*

O 00277: Fiche 37
Hall, G. Stanley and Hartwell, E.M.
    "Bilateral Asymmetry of Function, " *Mind,* vol. 9, 93-109, at 107-108.

O 00278: Fiche 37
Mitchell, O.H. and Venn, J.
    [Comments on *Studies in Logic*], *Mind,* vol. 9, 321-322. Also includes a comment by C. Ladd-Franklin at 322.

1884

P 00279: Fiche 37
"The Reciprocity Treaty With Spain."
> *The Nation,* vol. 39 (18 December) 521, filmed at P 00043, pages 65-66. Signed letter, with editor's reply.

O 00280: Fiche 37
Anonymous.
> Note [on Peirce's article concerning the Old Stone Mill at Newport], *The Nation,* vol. 39 (18 December), 522.

P 00281: Fiche Sup. 4
"On Gravitation Survey."
> Paper read before the National Academy of Sciences, Newport, 14-17 October. Cited in *Report of the National Academy of Sciences for the Year 1884,* Senate Mis. Doc. No. 68, 48th Congress, 2d Session, Washington: Government Printing Office, 1885, p. 12. Burks, *Bibliography.*

P 00282: Fiche 37
"On Minimum Differences of Sensibility." [co-authored with Joseph Jastrow]
> Paper read before the National Academy of Sciences, Newport, 14-17 October. Cited in *Report of the National Academy of Sciences for the Year 1884,* Senate Mis. Doc. No. 68, 48th Congress, 2d Session, Washington: Government Printing Office, 1885, p. 12; filmed at P 00281. Burks, *Bibliography.*

P 00283: Fiche 37
"On the Algebra of Logic."
> Paper read before the National Academy of Sciences, Newport, 14-17 October. Cited in *Report of the National Academy of Sciences for the Year 1884,* Senate Mis. Doc. No. 68, 48th Congress, 2d Session, Washington: Government Printing Office, 1885, p. 13; filmed at P 00281. Burks, *Bibliography.*

O 00284: Fiche 37
Cayley, Arthur.
> "On Double Algebra," *Proceedings of the London Mathematical Society,* vol. 15 (3 April) 185-197, at 186-187, 194-197.

O 00285: (NF)
Schroder, Ernst.
> "Exposition of a Logical Principle, as disclosed by the Algebra of Logic, but overlooked by the Ancient Logicians," *Report of the Fifty-Third Meeting of the British Association for the Advancement of Science.* London: John Murray, p. 412.

P 00286: Fiche 37
[Pendulum research]
> "Determinations of the force of gravity at Montreal, Canada, Albany, N.Y., and Hoboken, N.J.," in *Report of the Superintendent of the United States Coast and Geodetic Survey, 1883,* Senate Ex. Doc. No. 29, 48th Congress, 1st Session, Washington: Government Printing Office, p. 27. Burks, *Bibliography.*

1884

P 00287: Fiche 37
[Pendulum research]
"Determinations of gravity by pendulum experiments at Baltimore and Washington," in *Report of the Superintendent of the United States Coast and Geodetic Survey, 1883,* Senate Ex. Doc. No. 29, 48th Congress, 1st Session, Washington: Government Printing Office, pp. 36-37; see also pp. 96-97. Burks, *Bibliography.*

P 00288: Fiche 37
[Pendulum research, determination of longitude]
"Occupation of the station at Savannah, Ga., for the determination of the longitude of Saint Augustine, Fla., by exchange of telegraphic signals," in *Report of the Superintendent of the United States Coast and Geodetic Survey, 1883,* Senate Ex. Doc. No. 29, 48th Congress, 1st Session, Washington: Government Printing Office, pp. 41-42. Burks, *Bibliography.*

P 00289: Fiche Sup. 4
[Determination of longitude]
"Determination of the longitude of the Transit of Venus station at Saint Augustine, Fla., by exchange of telegraph signals with Savannah," *Report of the Superintendent of the United States Coast and Geodetic Survey, 1883,* Senate Ex. Doc. No. 29, 48th Congress, 1st Session, Washington: Government Printing Office, p. 42. Burks, *Bibliography.*

P 00290: Fiche Sup. 4
"Determinations of Gravity at Allegheny, Ebensburgh, and York, Pa., in 1879 and 1880."
Report of the Superintendent of the United States Coast and Geodetic Survey, 1883, Senate Ex. Doc. No. 29, 48th Congress, 1st Session, Washington: Government Printing Office, pp. 473-487. Burchard, *Catalogue;* Cohen, *Tentative Bibliography;* Burks, *Bibliography.*

O 00291: Fiche Sup. 4
Minot, C.S.
"The October Meeting of the National Academy of Sciences," *Science,* vol. 4 (24 October), 396-400.

P 00292: Fiche Sup. 5
"The Numerical Measure of the Success of Predictions."
Science, vol. 4 (14 November), 453-454. *List of Articles;* Burks, *Bibliography;* Fisch, *Third Supplement.*

P 00293: Fiche Sup. 5
"The 'Old Stone Mill' at Newport."
Science, vol. 4 (5 December), 512-514. *List of Articles;* Burks, *Bibilography.*

O 00294: Fiche Sup. 5–6
[References to Peirce's pendulum researches]
Verhandlungen der vom 15 bis zum 24 Oktober 1883 in Rom Abgehaltenen Siebenten Allgemeinen Conferenz der Europäischen Gradmessung, Berlin: Verlag von Georg Reimer, Appendix VIb (pp. 41, 44-45, 50-52, 59-60), pages repeated. Burks, *Bibliography.*

O 00295: (NF)
Oppolzer, Theodor von.
"Ueber die Bestimmung der Schwere mit Hilfe verschiedener Apparate," *Zeitschrift für Instrumentenkunde,* vol. 4, 303-316, 379-387, at 305, 308, 313, 314, 315, 383, 384.

1885

P 00296: Fiche Sup. 6
"On the Algebra of Logic: A Contribution to the Philosophy of Notation."
    American Journal of Mathematics, vol. 7 (January), 180-202. Burks, *Bibliography;* Fisch, *Second Supplement.*

P 00297: Fiche 39
"Gravimetric Surveys."
    Lecture given before the Association of Engineers, Cornell University, Friday, 4 December. Cited in *The Cornell Daily Sun,* Ithaca, New York (Thursday, 3 December), page 1. Fisch, *Third Supplement.* Filmed at P 00302.

O 00298: (NF)
Farquhar, Henry.
    "Empirical Formulae for the Diminution of Amplitude of a Freely-Oscillating Pendulum," *Bulletin of the Philosophical Society of Washington,* vol. 7, 89-92, at 90.

O 00299: (NF)
Doolittle, M.H.
    "The Verification of Predictions," *Bulletin of the Philosophical Society of Washington,* vol. 7, 122-127, at 124-125, 127.

P 00300: Fiche 39
"The Coast Survey Investigation."
    The Evening Post, New York City, vol. 84 (Friday, 10 August), page 3, column 3. Burks, *Bibliography.*

O 00301: Fiche 39
Schlegel.
    "C.S. Peirce. On the relative forms of quaternions," *Jahrbuch über die Fortschritte der Mathematik,* Jahrgang 1882, vol. 14, part 2, pp. 594-595.

P 00302: Fiche 39
"Connected Pendulums."
    Lecture given before the Mathematical Seminary, Cornell University, Tuesday, 1 December. Cited in *The Cornell Daily Sun,* Ithaca, New York, Monday, 30 November and Thursday, 3 December. Fisch, *Third Supplement.*

P 00303: Fiche 39
"On Small Differences of Sensation." [Co-authored with Joseph Jastrow]
    Memoirs of the National Academy of Sciences, 1884, Washington: Government Printing Office, 73-83. Read before the Academy on 17 October 1884 under the title, "On Minimum Differences of Sensibility." Cohen, *Tentative Bibliography;* Burks, *Bibliography.* For paper read, see P 00282.

O 00304: (NF)
Schubert, Johannes.
    Review of "The Numerical Measure of the Success of Predictions," by Charles Sanders Peirce, *Meteorologische Zeitschrift,* vol. 2, 39-40.

O 00305: (NF)
James, William.
    "On the Function of Cognition," *Mind,* vol. 10, 27-44, at 43.

1885

P 00306: Fiche 39
"The Spanish Treaty Once More."
    The Nation, vol. 40 (1 January) 12, filmed at P 00043, page 67. Signed letter.

P 00307: Fiche 39
Review of *The Common Sense of the Exact Sciences.* By the late William Kingdon Clifford.
    The Nation, vol. 41 (3 September) 203, filmed at P 00043, pages 68-69. Probably by Peirce.

P 00308: Fiche 39
Review of *The Religion of Philosophy; or, The Unification of Knowledge.* By Raymond S. Perrin.
    The Nation, vol. 41 (19 November) 431, filmed at P 00043, pages 69-70.

O 00309: Fiche 39
Anonymous.
    Notice of *United States Coast and Geodetic Survey. Determination of Gravity at Stations in Pennsylvania, 1879-1880. Appendix No. 19, Report for 1883. Nature.* vol. 32 (15 October), 572-573.

P 00310: Fiche 39
[Pendulum research, metrology]
    "Determinations of Gravity and Comparisons of Standards," in *Report of the Superintendent of the United States Coast and Geodetic Survey, 1884,* House Ex. Doc. No. 43, 48th Congress, 2d Session, Washington: Government Printing Office, pp. 6-7; see also a reference to these pages (which identifies this as an account of Peirce's work) at pp. 80-81. Compare a similar brief reference at p. 2; pp. 80-81 filmed at P 00312.

P 00311: Fiche 39
[Pendulum research, metrology]
    "Determinations of gravity by pendulum experiments, and comparisons of standards in Europe and in the United States," in *Report of the Superintendent of the United States Coast and Geodetic Survey, 1884,* House Ex. Doc. No. 43, 48th Congress, 2d Session, Washington: Government Printing Office, p. 40. Burks, *Bibliography.*

P 00312: Fiche 39
[Metrology, pendulum research]
    "Comparisons of standards of weight and measure, and investigations relating to determinations of gravity," in *Report of the Superintendent of the United States Coast and Geodetic Survey, 1884,* House Ex. Doc. No. 43, 48th Congress, 2d Session, Washington: Government Printing Office, pp. 80-81. Burks, *Bibliography.*

P 00313: Fiche 39
[Metrology, pendulum research]
    "Distributions of the parties of the Coast and Geodetic Survey upon the Atlantic, Gulf of Mexico, and Pacific coasts and the interior of the United States during the fiscal year 1883-'84," in *Report of the Superintendent of the United States Coast and Geodetic Survey, 1884,* House Ex. Doc. No. 43, 48th Congress, 2d Session, Washington: Government Printing Office, pp. 87-93; Peirce is mentioned at p. 89 and p. 93. Burks, *Bibliography.*

1885

P 00314: F i c h e 39, 40
[Pendulum research]
"Determinations of Gravity with the Kater Pendulums at Auckland, New Zealand; Sydney, New South Wales; Singapore, British India; Tokio, Japan; San Francisco, Cal.; and Washington, D.C.," by Edwin Smith, Assistant, in *Report of the Superintendent of the United States Coast and Geodetic Survey, 1884,* House Ex. Doc. No. 43, 48th Congress, 2d Session, Washington: Government Printing Office, pp. 439-473; Peirce is mentioned at p. 439, p. 442, and p. 443; a letter and a quotation from Peirce are printed at pp. 442-443. Burks, *Bibliography.*

P 00315: F i c h e 40
"On the Use of the Noddy for Measuring the Amplitude of Swaying in a Pendulum Support."
Report of the Superintendent of the United States Coast and Geodetic Survey, 1884, House Ex. Doc. No. 43, 48th Congress, 2d Session, Washington: Government Printing Office, pp. 475-482. Burchard, *Catalogue;* Burks, *Bibliography.*

P 00316: F i c h e 40
"Note on the Effect of the Flexure of a Pendulum upon its Period of Oscillation."
Report of the Superintendent of the United States Coast and Geodetic Survey, 1884, House Ex. Doc. No. 43, 48th Congress, 2d Session, Washington: Government Printing Office, pp. 483-485. Burchard, *Catalogue;* Cohen, *Tentative Bibiliography;* Burks, *Bibliography.*

P 00317: F i c h e 40
Note [on Peirce and the investigation of the Coast Survey].
Science, vol. 6 (21 August), 158. The letter is dated "Ann Arbor, Mich., Aug. 10." Burks, *Bibliography.*

[Testimony on the office of weights and measures, and on the gravimetric survey, Coast Survey]
Testimony given 24 January 1885. See P 00339.

O 00318: F i c h e 40
Anonymous.
"Exhorbitant Expenditures," *The Washington Post* (Saturday, 25 July), page 1, column 7.

O 00319: F i c h e 40
Anonymous.
"How the Money was Spent," *The Washington Post* (Sunday, 26 July), page 2, column 1.

O 00320: F i c h e 40
Anonymous.
"The Coast Survey Scandal," *The Washington Post* (Monday, 3 August), page 1, column 7.

O 00321: F i c h e 40
Anonymous.
"The Coast Survey Inquiry," *The Washington Post* (Thursday, 6 August), page 1, column 7.

O 00322: F i c h e 40
Anonymous.
"Intoxicated — Demoralized," *The Washington Post* (Friday, 7 August), page 1, columns 6-7.

1885

O 00323: F i c h e 40
Anonymous.
    "The Geological Survey Next," *The Washington Post* (Wednesday, 12 August), page 1, column 7.

1886

P 00324: F i c h e 40
[Pendulum research at Cornell]
    Cited in *Cornell Daily Sun,* Ithaca, New York, vol. 6 (5 February), page 1, columns 1-2. Fisch, *Third Supplement.*

O 00325: (NF)
Anonymous.
    Notice of *On Small Differences of Sensation.* By C.S. Peirce and J. Jastrow. *Mind,* vol. 11 (January), 128.

P 00326: F i c h e 6
"Dr. F.E. Abbot's Philosophy."
    The Nation, vol. 42 (11 February) 135-136, filmed at P 00043, pages 71-74.

P 00327: F i c h e 40, 41
"Review of Paper on Color Contrast."
    Paper read before the National Academy of Sciences, Washington, 20-23 April. Cited in *Report of the National Academy of Sciences for the Year 1886,* Senate Mis. Doc. No. 30, Part 1, 49th Congress, 2d Session, Washington: Government Printing Office, 1887, p. 6. Burks, *Bibliography.*

O 00328: F i c h e 41
Marquand, Allen.
    "A New Logical Machine," *Proceedings of the American Academy of Arts and Sciences,* new series 13, whole series 21, 303-307. Paper read before the Academy on 11 November 1885.

O 00329: (NF)
Gibbs, J. Willard.
    "Multiple Algebra," *Proceedings of the American Association for the Advancement of Science,* vol. 35, 37-66, at 42,54.

O 00330: F i c h e 41
Anonymous.
    "Executive Proceedings," *Proceedings of the American Association for the Advancement of Science, Thirty-fourth Meeting Held at Ann Arbor, Mich., August, 1885,* Salem: Published by the Permanent Secretary, pp. 545-546, minutes for the executive meeting of Friday Morning, August 28, 1885.

P 00331: F i c h e 41
[Pendulum research, metrology]
    "Gravity determinations and experimental researches at Washington, D.C., and in Virginia," in *Report of the Superintendent of the United States Coast and Geodetic Survey, 1885,* Washington: Government Printing Office, pp. 37-38. Burks, *Bibliography.*

1886

P 00332: Fiche Sup. 6—8
[Pendulum research]
>"Determination of gravity at Key West," in *Report of the Superintendent of the United States Coast and Geodetic Survey, 1885,* Washington: Government Printing Office, p. 46. Burks, *Bibliography.*

P 00333: Fiche 41
[Pendulum research, metrology]
>"Distributions of the parties of the Coast and Geodetic Survey upon the Atlantic, Gulf of Mexico, and Pacific coasts, and in the interior of the United States during the fiscal year ending with June, 1885," in *Report of the Superintendent of the United States Coast and Geodetic Survey, 1885,* Washington: Government Printing Office, pp. 81-86; Peirce is mentioned at p. 83 and p. 84; compare p. 99. Burks, *Bibliography.*

P 00334: Fiche 41
"Note on a Device for Abbreviating Time Reductions."
>*Report of the Superintendent of the United States Coast and Geodetic Survey, 1885,* Washington: Government Printing Office, pp. 503-508. Burchard, *Catalogue;* Fisch and Haskell, *Additions to Cohen's Bibliography;* Burks, *Bibliography.*

P 00335: Fiche 41
"On the Influence of a Noddy on the Period of a Pendulum."
>*Report of the Superintendent of the United States Coast and Geodetic Survey, 1885,* Washington: Government Printing Office, pp. 509-510. Burchard, *Catalogue;* Cohen, *Tentative Bibliography;* Burks, *Bibliography.*

P 00336: Fiche 41
"On the Effect of Unequal Temperature upon a Reversible Pendulum."
>*Report of the Superintendent of the United States Coast and Geodetic Survey, 1885,* Washington: Government Printing Office, pp. 511-512. Burchard, *Catalogue;* Cohen, *Tentative Bibliography;* Burks, *Bibliography.*

O 00337: Fiche 41
Anonymous.
>Note [on investigation of Coast Survey], *Science,* vol. 7 (9 April), 325-326.

O 00338: Fiche 41
Anonymous.
>"The Present Condition of the Coast Survey," *Science,* vol. 8 (22 October), 359-360.

P 00339: Fiche 41
[Testimony on the office of weights and measures, and on the gravimetric survey, Coast Survey].
>*Testimony before the Joint Commission* [etc.], Senate Mis. Doc. No. 82, 49th Congress, 1st Session, Washington: Government Printing Office, pp. 370-378; see also pp. 839, 852. Peirce's testimony was presented on 24 January 1885. Fisch and Haskell, *Additions to Cohen's Bibliography;* Burks, *Bibliography.*

O 00340: Fiche 41, 42
Greely, Adolphus W.
>*Three Years of Arctic Service,* New York: Charles Scribner's Sons, vol. 1, pp. 67-68, 124-133, 135-136, 178-180.

1886

O 00341: F i c h e 42
Anonymous.
"The Coast Survey Scandal," *The Washington Post* (Sunday, 17 October), page 2, column 2.

O 00342: F i c h e 42
Anonymous.
"Mr. Thorn Heard From," *The Washington Post* (Monday, 18 October), page 2, column 6.

1887

O 00343: F i c h e 42
Jastrow, Joseph.
"The Psycho-Physic Law and Star Magnitudes," *American Journal of Psychology,* vol. 1 (November), 112-127, at 116, 118, 121n, 125-126.

P 00344: F i c h e 42
"Logical Machines."
The American Journal of Psychology, vol. 1 (November), 165-170. *List of Articles;* Burks, *Bibliography.*

O 00345: F i c h e 42
Bell, Louis.
"On the Absolute Wave-Length of Light," *The American Journal of Science*, third series 33, whole series 133, 167-182, at 175, 181, 182.

O 00346: F i c h e 42
Rowland, Henry A.
"On the Relative Wave-Length of the Lines of the Solar Spectrum," *The American Journal of Science*, third weries 33, whole series 133, 182-190, at 183, 184.

P 00347: (NF)
[Contribution on Science and Immortality]
The Christian Register, Boston, vol. 66 (7 April), page 214, columns 2-4. Final version filmed at P 00348. *List of Articles;* Burks, *Bibliography.*

P 00348: F i c h e 42, 43
[Contribution to the *Christian Register* symposium on Science and Immortality]
In *Science and Immortality; the Christian Register Symposium, Revised and Enlarged,* Edited and Reviewed by Samuel J. Barrows, Boston: Geo. H. Ellis, pp. 69-76; comments on Peirce's contribution are at pp. 109-111; a brief biographical statement on Peirce is at p. 135. *List of Articles;* Burks, *Bibliography.*

O 00349: (NF)
Rowland, Henry Augustus.
"On the Relative Wavelengths of the Lines of the Solar Spectrum," *The London, Edinburgh, and Dublin Philosophical Magazine and Journal of Science,* fifth series, vol. 23, 257-265, at 258, 259, 263, 265.

O 00350: (NF)
Bell, Louis.
"On the Absolute Wave-length of Light," *The London, Edinburgh, and Dublin Philosophical Magazine and Journal of Science,* fifth series, vol. 23, 265-282, at 266, 273, 280, 281, 282.

1887

O 00351: F i c h e 43
Michelson, Albert A. and Morley, Edward W.
> "On a Method of making the Wave-length of Sodium Light the actual and practical Standard of Length," *The London, Edinburgh, and Dublin Philosophical Magazine and Journal of Science,* fifth series, vol. 24, 463-466, at 463.

P 00352: F i c h e 43
"Criticism on 'Phantasms of the Living.' An Examination of an Argument of Messrs. Gurney, Myers, and Podmore."
> *Proceedings of the American Society for Phychical Research,* old series vol. 1 (December), 150-157. *List of Articles,* Burks, *Bibliography.*

O 00353: F i c h e 43, 44
Gurney, Edmund.
> "Remarks on Professor Peirce's Paper," *Proceedings of the American Society for Psychical Research,* old series vol. 1 (December), 157-179.

P 00354: F i c h e 44
"Mr. Peirce's Rejoinder."
> *Proceedings of the American Society for Psychical Research,* old series vol. 1 (December), 180-215. *List of Articles;* Burks, *Bibliography.*

O 00355: F i c h e 44
Kempe, A.B.
> "Note to a Memoir on the Theory of Mathematical Form," *Proceedings of the Royal Society of London,* vol. 42, 193-196.

P 00356: F i c h e 44
[Pendulum research]
> "Determinations of gravity and pendulum experiments," in *Report of the Superintendent of the United States Coast and Geodetic Survey, 1886,* House Ex. Doc. No. 40, 49th Congress, 2d Session, Washington: Government Printing Office, p. 41; see also p. 12. Burks, *Bibliography.*

P 00357: F i c h e 44
[Pendulum research]
> "Gravity research. — Pendulum oscillations at Washington," in *Report of the Superintendent of the United States Coast and Geodetic Survey, 1886,* House Ex. Doc. No. 40, 49th Congress, 2d Session, Washington: Government Printing Office, p. 49. Burks, *Bibliography.*

P 00358: F i c h e 44
[Pendulum research]
> "Determinations of gravity at Ann Arbor, Mich., and at Madison, Wis.," in *Report of the Superintendent of the United States Coast and Geodetic Survey, 1886,* House Ex. Doc. No. 40, 49th Congress, 2d Session, Washington: Government Printing Office, pp. 85-86. Burks, *Bibliography.*

P 00359: F i c h e 44
[Pendulum research]
> "Distribution of the Parties of the Coast and Geodetic Survey upon the Atlantic, Gulf of Mexico, and Pacific Coasts, and in the Interior of the United States during the Fiscal Year ending June 30, 1886," in *Report of the Superintendent of the United States Coast and Geodetic Survey, 1886,* House Ex. Doc. No. 40, 49th Congress, 2d Session, Washington: Government Printing Office, pp. 97-103, see pp. 99, 100, 103. Burks, *Bibliography.*

1887

P 00360: F i c h e 44
[Records of pendulum research]
    "Archives and Library, Coast and Geodetic Survey Office. Report for the Fiscal Year ending June 30, 1886," in *Report of the Superintendent of the United States Coast and Geodetic Survey, 1886,* House Ex. Doc. No. 40, 49th Congress, 2d Session, Washington: Government Printing Office, pp. 134-137, see pp. 135, 137. Burks, *Bibliography.*

O 00361: (NF)
Rogers, William A.
    "Report of Professor William A. Rogers," in *Standards of Length and Their Practical Application,* Hartford, Conn.: The Pratt and Whitney Co., at pp. 2, 39, 40.

1888

O 00362: F i c h e 44, 45
Jastrow, Joseph.
    "A Critique of Psycho-Physic Methods," *American Journal of Psychology,* vol. 1 (February), 271-309, at 280, 285n., 288, 304.

O 00363: F i c h e 45
Bell, Louis.
    "The Absolute Wave-length of Light," *The American Journal of Science,* third series 35, whole series 135, 265-282 plus 347-367.

O 00364: F i c h e 45
Trowbridge, John.
    "Wave-lengths of standard lines," *The American Journal of Science,* third series 35, whole series 135, 337-338.

O 00365: (NF)
Kurlbaum, Ferdinand.
    "Bestimmung der Wellenlänge Fraunhofer'sche Linien," *Annalen der Physik und Chemie,* vol. 269, 159-193 plus 381-412, at 167, 412.

O 00366: (NF)
Defforges, Charles.
    "Sur L'Intensite Absolue de la Pesanteur," *Journal de Physique,* second series 7, 239-250 plus 347-364 plus 455-478, at 355, 357, 359, 362, 463-464.

O 00367: F i c h e 45
Lockyer, J. Norman.
    "Notes on the Spectrum of the Aurora," *Nature,* vol. 37 (9 February), 358-359, at 359.

P 00368: F i c h e 45, 46
Proceedings of the Assay Commission of 1888; Also, Laws of the United States Relating to the Annual Assay, and Rules for the Organization and Government of the Board of Assay Commissioners.
    Treasury Department, Document no. 1089. Director of the Mint. Burks, *Bibliography.*

1888

P 00369: F i c h e 46
"Pendulum Observations."
> In *Report on the Proceedings of the United States Expedition to Lady Franklin Bay, Grinnell Land,* by Adolphus W. Greely, House Misc. Doc. 393, Part 2, 49th Congress, 1st Session, Washington: Government Printing Office, pp. 701-714; see also comments by Greely at p. 715 plus comments and tables by Henry Farquhar at pp. 716-729. Includes Index, pp. 735-736. Burks, *Bibliography.*

P 00370: F i c h e 46
[References to Peirce's pendulum researches]
> *Verhandlungen der vom 21 bis zum 29 October 1887 auf der Sternwarte zu Nizza abgehalten Conferenz der Permanenten Commission der Internationalen Erdmessung,* Berlin: Verlag von Georg Reimer; Neuchatel: Imprimé par Attinger Frères, pp. 3-7. 15-16, Appendix IIa (pp. 1-7, 15-16, and Table IV), Appendix IIf (pp. 1-3, 15-17, and Table IV). Burks, *Bibliography.*

O 00371: (NF)
Kempf, Paul.
> Review of "On the Absolute Wave-length of Light," by Kurlbaum and Bell, *Vierteljahrsschrift der Astronomischen Gesellschaft,* vol. 23, 262-286, at 285.

1889

P 00372: F i c h e 46
[Astronomical observations]
> *Meteorological Observations made during the years 1840 to 1888 inclusive,* Annals of the Astronomical Observatory of Harvard College, vol. 19, part 1: 50, 66-70, 79, 81.

P 00373: Fiche 47-88, Sup. 8-9
[Definitions]
> In *The Century Dictionary and Cyclopedia,* Editor-in-Chief, William D. Whitney, 10 volumes, New York: The Century Company. Peirce was responsible for definitions in the fields of Logic, Metaphysics, Mathematics, Mechanics, Astronomy, Weights and Measures, Color Terms, and many common words of philosophical import (see the list of collaborators plus the editor's general introduction in volume one). Identification of Peirce's definitions (or his partial role in definitions) is possible due to his marked copy of the 1889 edition in Houghton Library, Harvard University. We have duplicated those markings in the 1900 edition of the Dictionary we are using for filming. The following list of definitions does not distinguish between partial or total authorship. That can be determined to some extent by checking the actual definition as filmed which will show Peirce's markings. These take the form of vertical lines at the left of the relevant definition. Duplication of Peirce's annotations of definitions is with the permission of the Department of Philosophy, Harvard University, which we gratefully acknowledge. Peirce made extensive handwritten notes in his copy of the *Century;* those are not reproduced here. For further study of those notes, see MS 1597, Robin, *Catalogue.* To use this listing, find the word desired in the alphabetical sequence below, then locate the fiche through the number provided. Burks, *Bibliography.*

47: A, p. 1.
a², p. 1.
aam, p. 3.
A.B., p. 3.
abacist, p. 3.
aback, p. 3.
abacus, p. 3.
abandon, p. 4.
abandoned, p. 4.
abandonment, p. 4.
abase, p. 5.
abasement, p. 5.
abash, p. 5.
abashment, p. 5.
abate, p. 5.
abatement, p. 5.
abbas, p. 6.
abbreviate, p. 7.
abbreviation, p. 7.
Abderite, p. 7.
abdicate, p. 8.
abdication, p. 8.
abdicative, p. 8.
abdomen, p. 8.
abdominous, p. 8.
abduct, p. 9
abduction, p. 9.
abecedarium, p. 9.
abed, p. 9.
abele, p. 9.
Abelian², p. 9.
aberrancy, p. 9.
aberration, p. 10.
abet, p. 10.
abetter, abettor, p. 10.
abeyance, p. 10.
abhor, p. 10.
abhorrence, p. 11.
abhorrent, p. 11.
abhorrently, p. 11.
abhorrer, p. 11.
abide¹, p. 11.
ability, p. 11.
ab initio, p. 12.
abject, p. 12.
abjectness, p. 12.

abjuration, p. 12.
abjure, p. 12.
ablative, p. 13.
ablaze, p. 13.
able¹, p. 13.
able-bodied, p. 13.
abloom, p. 14.
ablution, p. 14.
abnegation, p. 14.
abnormal, p. 14.
abode, p. 14.
abolish, p. 15.
abolition, p. 15.
abolitionism, p. 15.
abolitionist, p. 15.
abominable, p. 15.
abominableness, p. 15.
abominably, p. 15.
abominate, p. 15.
abomination, p. 15.
aboriginal, p. 15.
aborigines, p. 16.
abortion, p. 16.
abortionist, p. 16.
abortive, p. 16.
abortively, p. 16.
abortment, p. 16.
abound, p. 16.
abounding, p. 16.
about, p. 16.
To be about, p. 17.
above, p. 17.
aboveboard, p. 17.
above-ground, p. 17.
abovo, p. 17.
abracadabra, p. 17.
abrade, p. 17.
abrasion, p. 18.
Abraxas, p. 18.
abreast, p. 18.
abridge, p. 18.
abridger, p. 18.
abridgment, p. 19.
To set abroach, p. 19.
abroad, p. 19.
abrogate, p. 19.

abrogation, p. 19.
abrood, p. 19.
abrupt, p. 19.
abruptly, p. 19.
abruptness, p. 19.
abscess, p. 19.
abscissa, p. 20.
abscissio infiniti, p. 20.
abscission, p. 20.
abscond, p. 20.
absence, p. 20.
absence of mind, p. 20.
absent, p. 20.
absentee, p. 20.
absenteeism, p. 20.
absenter, p. 20.
absent-minded, p. 20.
absent-mindedness, p. 20.
absinthe, p. 20.
absinthine, p. 21.
absolute, p. 21.
absolutely, p. 21.
absolution, p. 22.
absolutism, p. 22.
absolutist, p. 22.
absolve, p. 22.
absonant, p. 22.
absorb, p. 22.
absorption, p. 22.
abstain, p. 23.
abstainer, p. 23.
abstemious, p. 23.
abstemiousness, p. 23.
abstention, p. 23.
abstergent, p. 23.
abstersion, p. 23.
abstersive, p. 23.
abstinence, p. 23.
abstinent, p. 24.
abstract, p. 24.
Abstract of title, p. 24.
abstractedness, p. 24.
abstraction, p. 24.
abstractive, p. 25.
Abstractive cognition, p. 25
abstractly, p. 25.

A Comprehensive Bibliography

abstractness, p. 25.
abstrahent, p. 25.
abstruse, p. 25.
abstrusely, p. 25.
abstruseness, p. 25.
absurd, p. 25.
absurdity, p. 25.
abundance, p. 26.
abundant, p. 26.
abundant definition, p. 26.
abuse, p. 26.
abuse, p. 26.
abut, p. 26.
abutment, p. 27.
abuttal, p. 27.
abuy, p. 27.
abuzz, abuz, p. 27.
abyss, p. 27.
A.C., p. 27.
academic, p. 28.
academical, p. 28.
academician, p. 28.
Academics, p. 28.
academy, p. 28.
acatalepsy, p. 31.
acataleptic, p. 31.
accede, p. 31.
acceleration, p. 31.
accent, p. 32.
accentual, p. 32.
accoutre, accouter, p. 39.
accredit, p. 40.
accure, p. 40.
accumbent, p. 40.
accumulate, p. 41.
accumulation, p. 41
accumulation of degrees, p. 41.
accumulative, p. 41.
accuracy, p. 41.
accurate, p. 41.
accurately, p. 41.
accursed, accurst, p. 41.
accusation, p. 41.
accuse, p. 42.
accuser, p. 42.
Accustom, p. 42.
accustomed, p. 42.
ace, p. 42.
Aceldama, p. 42.
acerbity, p. 43.
acetose, p. 45.

acetous, p. 45.
ache[1], ake, p. 45.
ache[1], ake, p. 45.
achievable, p. 46.
achieve, p. 46.
achievement, p. 46.
achiever, p. 46.
acid, p. 47.
acidity, p. 48.
acidulate, p. 48.
acidulous, p. 48.
acknowledgement, p. 49.
acme, p. 49.
acnodal, p. 49.
acnode, p. 49.
acold, p. 50.
acolyte, p. 50.
acorn, p. 51.
accentuate, p. 32.
accentuation, p. 32.
accept, p. 32.
acceptable, p. 33.
acceptance, p. 33.
acceptation, p. 33.
acceptilation, p. 33.
acception, p. 33.
accessible, p. 33.
accession, p. 33.
accessory, p. 34.
accidence, p. 34.
accident, p. 34.
accidental, p. 34.
accidentally, p. 35.
accidented, p. 35.
accidentiary, p. 35.
acclaim, p. 35.
acclamation, p. 35.
acclimate, p. 35.
acclimation, p. 36.
acclimatization, p. 36.
acclimatize, p. 36.
acclivity, p. 36.
accloy, p. 36.
acclade, p. 36.
accommodate, p. 36.
Accommodate distribution, p. 36.
accommodation, p. 36-37.
accompaniment, p. 37.
accompanist, p. 37.
accomplice, p. 37.
accomplish, p. 37.
accord, p. 38.

accord, p. 38.
accordance, p. 38.
accordant, p. 38.
according, p. 38.
accoucheur, p. 38.
account, p. 39.
accountability, p. 39.
accountable, p. 39.
accountance, p. 39.
accountant, p. 39.
account-book, p. 39.
accouplement, p. 39.
acorn-cup, p. 51.
acorn-shell, p. 51.
acosmism, p. 51.
acousmatic, p. 51.
acoustic, p. 51.
acoustics, p. 51.
acquaint, p. 52.
acquaintance, p. 52.
acquainted, p. 52.
acquiesce, p. 52.
acquiescence, p. 52.
acquiescent, p. 52.
acquiescently, p. 52.
acquire, p. 52.
acquired logic, p. 52.
acquirement, p. 52.
acquisition, p. 53.
Acquisitive, p. 53.
acquisitive faculty, p. 53.
acquit, p. 53.
acquittal, p. 53.
acquittance, p. 53.
acre, p. 53.
acrid, p. 54.
acridity, p. 54.
acrimonious, p. 54.
acrimony, p. 54.
acroamatic, p. 55.
acroamatical, p. 55.
acroamatics, p. 55.
acroatic, p. 55.
acroatics, p. 55.
acronychal, p. 56.
acronychally, p. 56.
across, p. 57.
acrostic, p. 57.
act, p. 57-58
act, p. 58.
acting, p. 59.

action, p. 60-61.
actionable, p. 61.
active, p. 61-62.
actively, p. 62.
activity, p. 62.
actor, p. 62.
actress, p. 62.
actual, p. 62.
actualism, p. 62.
actuality, p. 62.
actualization, p. 62-63.
actually, p. 63.
actuary, p. 63.
actuate, p. 63.
acumen, p. 63.
acuminate, p. 63.
acutangular, p. 64.
acute, p. 64.
acute-angled, p. 64.
acute-angular, p. 64.
acutely, p. 64.
acuteness, p. 64.
adage, p. 65.
adagia, p. 65.
Adam's ale, Adam's wine, p. 65.
Adams apple, p. 65.
adamant, p. 65
adamantine, p. 65.
Adamic, p. 65.
adapt, p. 66.
adaptable, p. 66
Adaptability, p. 66.
Adaptation, p. 66.
adaptive, p. 66.
adaptively, p. 66.
adaptiveness, p. 66.
adarme, p. 66.
add, p. 67.
adder[1], p. 67.
adder[2], p. 67
addict, p. 68.
addictedness, p. 68.
adding-machine, p. 68.
additament, p. 68.
addition, p. 68.
additional, p. 68.
additionally, p. 68.
additive, p. 68.
addle, p. 68.
address, p. 68-69.
address, p. 69.
adduce, p. 69

adept, p. 71.
adequacy, p. 71.
adequateness, p. 71.
adequation, p. 71.
adequative, p. 71.
ad eundem, p. 71.
adfected or affected equation, p. 71.
adhere, p. 71.
adherence, p. 72.
adherence, p. 72.
adherency, p. 72.
adherent, p. 72.
adhesion, p. 72.
adhesive, p. 72.
adhesive knowledge, p. 72.
Argumentum ad hominem, p. 72.
Adiabatic curve or line, p. 72.
adiaphorism, p. 72.
adiaphorous, p. 73.
adieu, p. 73.
adieu, p. 73.
ad indefinitum, p. 73.
adipocere, p. 73.
adipose, p. 73.
adit, p. 73.
adjacene, p. 73.
adjacency, p. 73.
adjacent, p. 73.
adjectitious, p. 74.
adjectival, p. 74.
adjective, p. 74.
adjunct, p. 74-75.
adjunction, p. 75.
adjuvant, p. 76.
admeasure, p. 76.
admeasurement, p. 76.
admit, p. 78.
48: adscititious, p. 83.
advenient, p. 86.
adventitious, p. 86.
adversative, p. 87.
aegrotans, p. 92.
aegrotant, p. 92.
aegrotat, p. 92.
Reading aegrotat, p. 92.
aeolotropic, p. 93.
aelotropy, p. 93.
aetiological, etiological, p. 96.
aetiologically, etiologically, p. 96.
aetiologist, etiologist, p. 96.
aetiology, etiology, p. 96.
affection, p. 98.

affective quality, p. 98.
affinity, p. 99-100.
affirmation, p. 100.
affirmative, p. 100.
affirmatory, p. 100.
a fortiori, p. 103.
acrogens, p. 108.
agency, p. 109.
agent, p. 109.
catalytic agent, p. 110.
aggregate, p. 111.
aggregation, p. 111.
agnoiology, p. 114.
agnostic, p. 114.
agnosticism, p. 114.
agrimensor, p. 118.
alamodality, p. 127.
albedo, p. 130.
Albertist, p. 130.
Algebar, p. 138.
algebraic, p. 138.
algebraical, p. 138.
algebraically, p. 138.
algebraist, p. 138.
algebrist, p. 138.
algebrist, p. 138.
algorist, p. 139.
algoristic, p. 139.
algorithm, p. 139.
algorithimic, p. 139.
alichel, p. 139.
alictisal, p. 139.
alidade, p. 139.
aliety, p. 140.
aline, p. 142.
Alineation, p. 142.
aliquant, p. 142.
aliquot, p. 142.
all[2], p. 143.
alligation, p. 148.
almamater, p. 153.
almanac, p. 153.
almena, p. 153.
almucantar, almucanter, p.
almucantar-staff, p. 155.
almud, almude, p. 155.
almury, p. 155.
almuten, p. 155.
alnage, p. 155.
alnager, p. 155.
alagership, p. 155.
alogical, p. 155.

alogism, p. 155.
alogy, p. 155.
Alphonsine, p. 157.
alquier, p. 158.
alternant, p. 160.
alternate, p. 160.
alternate, p. 160.
alternative, p. 161.
altitude, p. 160.
altruism, p. 161.
altruist, p. 161.
altruistic, p. 161.
altruistically, p. 161.
ambigen, ambigene, p. 168.
ambigenal, p. 168.
amicable, p. 175.
ampere, p. 181-182.
amphibology, p. 183.
amphibolous, p. 183.
amphiboly, p. 183.
amphichiral, p. 183.
amphora, p. 186.
ampliation, p. 187.
ampliative, p. 187.
amplification, p. 187.
amplificative, p. 187.
amplificatory, p. 187.
amplitude, p. 187.
analemma, p. 194.
anallagmatic, p. 194.
analogal, p. 194.
analogical, p. 194.
analogically, p. 194.
analogism, p. 194.
analogan, p. 195.
analogous, p. 195.
analogue, p. 195.
analogy, p. 195.
analysis, p. 195.
analytic, analytical, p. 195.
analytics, p. 196.
anamneis, p. 196.
anareta, p. 197.
anaretic, p. 197.
anaretical, p. 197.
Anaxagorean, p. 200.
anchor-ring, p. 202.
Andromeda, p. 206.
angle, p. 212.
angular, p. 216.
anharmonic, p. 216.

anima, p. 217.
anamastic, p. 219.
animism, p. 220.
animodar, p. 220.
anomaly, p. 228.
antartic, p. 233.
Antares, p. 233.
antecedence, p. 233.
antecedent, p. 233.
antecedental, p. 233.
antenumber, p. 235.
antepredicament, p. 236.
anthelion, p. 236.
anticipation, p. 243.
anticlastic, p. 243.
antinomy, p. 247.
Antiochian, p. 247.
antiparallel, p. 247.
antiperistasis, p. 248.
antipode, p. 248.
antipodes, p. 249.
antipoint, p. 249.
antiscian, p. 250.
apagoge, p. 254.
apagogic, p. 254.
aparithmeis, p. 255.
a parte ante, p. 255.
a parte post, p. 255.
apathist, p. 255.
apathistical, p. 255.
aoathy, p. 255.
aphereton, p. 257.
apex, p. 257.
aphelion, p. 257.
apheta, p. 258.
aphetical, p. 258.
49: aplanatic, p. 260.
apocopate, apocopated, p. 261-262.
apodictic, apodeictic, p. 262.
apodictically, apodeictically, p. 263.
apodixis, apodeixis, p. 263.
apogaeum, apogeum, apogaeon, apogeon, p. 263.
apogeal, p. 263.
apogean, p. 263.
apogee, p. 263.
apolaustic, p. 263.
Apollonian, p. 264.
apomecometer, p. 264.
apomecometry, p. 264.
apophantic, p. 264.

aporeme, p. 265.
aporetic, p. 265.
aporia, p. 265.
aposaturn, p. 265.
a posteriori, p. 266.
aposterioristic, p. 266.
Apothecaries weight, p. 267.
apothem, apotheme, p. 267.
apotome, p. 268.
apparent, p. 269.
apparition, p. 269.
apparitional, p. 269.
apparitor, p. 269.
appearance, p. 270.
appellation, p. 271.
apperceive, p. 272.
apperceiving, p. 272.
apperception, p. 272.
active apperception, p. 272.
apperceptive, p. 272.
Apperceptive union, p. 272.
appetite, p. 273.
appetition, p. 273.
appetizing, p. 273.
apple-green, p. 274.
applicable, p. 274.
applicate number, p. 274.
apply, p. 275.
appreciate, p. 276.
appredicate, p. 277.
apprehend, p. 277.
apprehension, p. 277.
simple apprehension, p. 277.
apprehensive, p. 277-278.
approbativeness, p. 279.
appropriative, p. 279.
approximate, p. 280.
Approximate value or formular, p. 280.
approximation, p. 280.
a priori, p. 281.
apriorist, p. 281.
aprioristic, p. 281.
apriority, p. 281.
apse, p. 281.
Apsidal chapel, p. 282.
apsis, p. 282.
apsychical, p. 282.
aptitude, p. 283.
Aptitudinal relaxation, p. 283.
aquarium, p. 284.

Aquarius, p. 284.
Aquila, p. 284-285.
Ara¹, p. 285.
Ara², p. 285.
Arabic figures or characters, p. 286.
arbitrary, p. 289.
Arbitrary constant, p. 289.
arbutus, p. 291.
arc-cosine, p. 292.
arch, p. 292.
archaeus, p. 292.
archaelogy, p. 295.
archesthetism, p. 295-296.
archetypal, p. 296.
archetype, p. 296.
Archimedean, p. 297.
architectonic, p. 297.
Architectonic idea, p. 297.
architypographer, p. 298.
archology, p. 298.
arcograph, p. 299.
arc-tangent, p. 299.
Arcturus, p. 300.
ardeb, p. 301.
are², p. 301.
Argo, p. 305.
arguable, p. 306.
argue, p. 306.
argument, p. 306.
argumentable, p. 306.
argumental, p. 307.
argumentation, p. 307.
argumentative, p. 307.
argumentum, p. 307.
Aries, p. 308.
Aristotelian, p. 310.
Aristotelianism, p. 310.
Aristotelic, p. 310.
arithmetic, p. 310.
arithmetical complement, p. 310.
arithmetically, p. 310.
arithmetician, p. 310.
arithmetico-geometrical, p. 310.
arithmometer, p. 310.
arithmo-planimeter, p. 310.
armillary sphere, p. 313.
arpent, p. 317.
arroba, p. 320
arshin, arshine, p. 322.
art², p. 323.
Bachelor of Arts, p. 323.

artaba, p. 323.
article, p. 326.
articulate, p. 326-327.
Artificial argument, p. 327.
Artium Baccalaureus, p. 328.
Artium Magister, p. 328.
artsman, p. 329.
arura, p. 329.
asar, p. 331.
ascend, p. 332.
ascendant, ascendent, p. 332.
ascending, p. 332.
ascension, p. 333.
Ascensional difference, p. 333.
ascent, p. 333.
ascertain, p. 333.
aseity, p. 335.
asellus, p. 335.
ash-color, p. 336.
ash-colored, p. 336.
aspect, p. 339.
ass¹, p. 343.
assent, p. 345.
assert, p. 345-346.
assertoric, assertorical, p. 346.
assertory proposition, p. 346.
assignable, p. 347.
assimilation, p. 348.
assistant form, p. 349.
associable, p. 349.
associate, p. 349.
Articles of association or incorporation, p. 350.
associational, p. 350.
associationalism, p. 350.
associationism, p. 350.
associationist, p. 350.
associative, p. 350.
associativeness, p. 350.
assume, p. 351.
assumption, p. 351.
assurance, p. 351-352.
asterism, p. 354.
asteroid, p. 354.
asteroidal, p. 354.
astral, p. 356.
astrolabe, p. 357.
astrologer, p. 357.
astrologian, p. 357.
astrologic, p. 357.
astrological, p. 357.
astrologically, p. 357.

astrologize, p. 357.
astrologue, p. 357.
astrology, p. 357.
astrometeorology, p. 357.
astrometer, p. 357.
astrometry, p. 357.
astronomer, p. 357.
astronomian, p. 358.
astronomic, p. 358.
astronomical, p. 358.
astronomically, p. 358.
astronomicon, p. 358.
astronomics, p. 358.
astronomize, p. 358.
astronomy, p. 358.
astrophotography, p. 358.
astrophotometer, p. 358.
astrophotometrical, p. 358.
astrophysical, p. 358.
astroscope, p. 358.
astroscopy, p. 358.
asymmetric, p. 359.
asymmetrical, p. 359.
asymmetrous, p. 359.
asymmetry, p. 359.
asymptote, p. 359.
asystaton, p. 359-360.
asyzygetic, p. 360.
atazir, p. 361.
atheism, p. 362.
atom, p. 365-366.
atomic, p. 366.
atomism, p. 366.
atomist, p. 366.
atomistic, p. 366.
atomistical, p. 366.
atomistically, p. 366.
attention, p. 372.
attentive, p. 372.
attitude, p. 374.
attract, p. 374.
attraction, p. 374-375.
attribute, p. 375.
attributive, p. 375.
audition, p. 378.
Argumented interval, p. 379.
augrim, p. 379.
augrim-stones, p. 379.
auncel, p. 381.
aune, p. 381.
Auriga, p. 383.

author, p. 386.
Argument from authority, p. 387.
automatism, p. 389.
automatist, p. 389.
automaton, p. 389.
autonomy, p. 390.
autopisty, p. 390.
autumn, p. 391.
autumnal, p. 391.
auxiliary, p. 391.
aver, p. 394.
average², p. 394.
Averroism, Averrhoism, p. 395.
Averroist, Averrhoist, p. 395.
Averroistic, p. 395.
aversion, p. 395.
avoirdupois, p. 397.
awareness, p. 399.
axial, p. 401.
axiom, p. 402.
axiomatic, p. 402.
axiomatical, p. 402.
axiomatically, p. 402.
axis¹, p. 402-403.
axisymmetric, p. 403.
axonometry, p. 404.
azimuth, p. 405.
azimuthal, p. 405.
azimuthally, p. 405.
azumbre, p. 406.
B, p. 407.
baccalaurean, p. 409.
bachelor, p. 410.
Baconian, p. 415-416.
bahar, p. 420.
balance, p. 424-425.
bale³, p. 428.
bamalip, p. 435.
bamalipton, p. 435.
bambara, p. 435.
bamboo, p. 435.
baralipton, p. 447.
barbara, p. 447.
barbari, p. 447.
barleycorn, p. 454.
barn-gallon, p. 455.
baraco¹, p. 455-456.
barra², p. 457.
barrel, p. 458.
barycentric, p. 461.
barytrope, p. 462.

base², p. 463.
base-line, p. 463-464.
basic, p. 465.
basket, p. 468.
batch¹, p. 472.
bath², p. 474.
batman², p. 475.
battel⁴, p. 476.
battel⁴, p. 476.
batteler, p. 476.
bazaar-maund, p. 483.
beadle, p. 486.
beakment, p. 487.
beam-compass, p. 487.
beat¹, p. 493.
beauty, p. 495.
because, p. 496.
becoming, p. 498.
bedel, bedell, p. 499.
bedmaker, p. 500.
beer-measure, p. 503.
Beg¹, p. 505-506.
being, p. 510.
beknottedness, p. 511.
belacedness, p. 511.
Bellatrix, p. 515.
bell-shaped, p. 517.
Benthamic, p. 527.
Benthamism, p. 527.
Benthamite, p. 527.
Bereleian, p. 529.
Berkeleianism, p. 529.
berkovets, p. 529.
berkowitz, p. 529.
51: Bernoullian, p. 530.
berri, p. 530.
bes, p. 531.
besa, p. 531.
Besselian, p. 533.
bestial, p. 534.
bevel-angle, p. 539.
bever³, p. 539.
Bezoutian, p. 541.
bezoutiant, p. 541.
bezoutoid, p. 541.
bialar, p. 542.
biblic, p. 543.
bicircular, p. 545.
bicircloid, p. 545.
biennial, p. 547.
bind, p. 548.

bifilar, p. 548.
biflecnode, p. 548.
bifolium, p. 548.
bilateral, p. 551.
bilinear, p. 552.
billion, p. 554.
bimedial, p. 555.
binariant, p. 556.
binode, p. 557.
binomial, p. 557.
binormal, p. 558.
biometry, p. 559.
biordinal, p. 559.
bipartient, p. 559.
bipartite, p. 559.
biplane, p. 560.
bipunctual, p. 560.
biquadratic, p. 560.
biquaternion, p. 560.
biquintile, p. 560.
bisaccia, p. 563.
bisector, p. 563.
bisectrix, p. 563.
bismerpund, p. 565.
bissext, p. 565.
bissextile, p. 565-566.
bissextus, p. 566.
bitangent, p. 567.
biterminal, p. 567.
bitter¹, p. 568.
boccale, p. 607.
body, p. 609.
boisseau, p. 612.
boll², p. 614.
bolometer, p. 614.
Boolian, p. 626.
Bootes, p. 628.
bordered, p. 630.
bore², p. 631.
braccio, p. 650.
brachistochrome, p. 652.
branch, p. 659.
breadth, p. 668.
broad, p. 688.
broken, p. 692.
bullfinch¹, p. 716.
bundle, p. 716.
burden¹, burthen¹, p. 724.
bursar, p. 730.
bursary, p. 730.
bushel¹, p. 731.
butt, p. 736.

butter-weight, p. 738.
by-fellow, p. 742.
cab, kab, p. 744.
cable's-length, p. 748.
cadent, p. 753.
cafisso, p. 755.
cahiz, p. 755.
calculate, p. 761.
calculating-machine, p. 761.
calculation, p. 761.
calculus, p. 762.
calendar, p. 762.
calends, kalends, p. 763.
calory, p. 771.
camestres, p. 778
campo, p. 781.
can, p. 783.
cana, p. 783.
canada, p. 783.
52: cancer, p. 786.
candy, kandy, p. 789.
caneh, kaneh, p. 789.
Canicula, p. 790.
canicular, p. 790.
canne, p. 792.
canon, p. 794.
canonic, p. 794.
canonical, p. 795.
canonizant, p. 795.
Canopus, p. 795.
cantar, p. 797.
cantara, p. 797.
capacity, p. 802.
Capella, p. 802.
capillary, p. 804.
Capricorn, p. 808.
carat, karat, p. 814.
cardinal, p. 820.
cardiod, p. 821.
carga, p. 823.
Carlylism, p. 826.
carnok, p. 828.
carotel, caroteel, p. 829.
carriage, p. 832.
carro, p. 834.
carry, p. 834.
Cartesian, p. 836.
case, p. 841.
Cassegrainian, p. 844.
Cassinian, p. 845.
cassinoid, p. 845.
Cassiope, p. 845.

cast, p. 847-848.
Castor and Pollux, p. 851.
casualism, p. 852.
casualist, p. 852.
casuality, p. 852.
casualness, p. 852.
catacaustic, p. 853.
catadioptric, catadioptrical, p. 854.
catalecticant, p. 854.
catasterism, p. 857.
categorem, p. 860.
categorematic, p. 860.
categorematical, p. 860.
catagorematically, p. 860.
categorical, p. 860.
categorically, p. 860.
categorically, p. 860.
categoricalness, p. 860.
categorist, p. 860.
categorization, p. 860.
categorize, p. 860.
category, p. 860.
catena, p. 860.
cartenarian, p. 860.
catenary, p. 860.
catty, p. 866.
causal, p. 868.
causality, p. 868.
causally, p. 868.
causation, p. 868.
causationism, p. 868.
causationist, p. 868.
causative, p. 868.
causativity, p. 868.
causator, p. 868.
cause, p. 868.
Cayleyan, p. 874.
celantes, p. 876.
celarent, p. 877.
cent, p. 883.
cental, p. 884.
Centaurus, p. 884.
centenaar, p. 884.
center^1, centre^1, p. 884.
centesimal, p. 886.
centigram, p. 886.
centiliter, p. 886.
centimeter, p. 886.
centner, p. 886.
central, p. 886.
centrobaric, p. 888.
centroid, p. 888.

centrosurface, p. 889.
centuple, p. 889.
century^1, p. 889.
Cepheus, p. 892.
ceratine^2, p. 894.
certain, p. 900.
certainty, p. 901.
cesare, p. 903.
cetus, p. 906.
chain, p. 909-910.
chain-syllogism, p. 910.
chaldron^1, p. 912.
chamberdakin, chamberdekin, p. 915.
chameleon, p. 916.
chance, p. 918.
chancellor, p. 919.
change, p. 920.
Change of the moon, p. 920.
chaos, p. 923.
chapel-clerk, p. 924.
53: char^7, p. 926.
character, p. 927.
characteristic, p. 927-928.
charge, p. 929.
chart, p. 933.
chebbo, p. 940.
check, p. 940.
cheki, p. 944.
cheme, p. 946.
chest^1, p. 950.
chetverik, p. 951.
chetvert, p. 951.
chetvertak, p. 951.
chetvertka, p. 951.
chih, p. 957.
chiliad, p. 958.
chiliaedron, chiliahedron, p. 958.
chiliagon, p. 958.
chlak, p. 970.
choenix, p. 973.
chomer, p. 976.
chopin, choppin, p. 979.
chop-logic, p. 979.
chord, p. 980.
chordel, p. 980.
chorography^1, p. 982.
chous, p. 983.
chow^5, p. 983.
chroma, p. 986.

chronograph, p. 989.
chronology, p. 989.
chronometer, p. 989.
chronoscope, p. 989.
chuck⁴, p. 992.
chum¹, p. 993.
chunam, p. 993.
chupah, p. 994.
cipher, p. 1005.
Circinus, p. 1006.
circle, p. 1006-1007.
circle-reading, p. 1007.
circle-squarer, p. 1007.
circuit, p. 1007-1008.
circulant, p. 1008.
circular, p. 1008-1009.
circulate, p. 1009.
circulation, p. 1009.
circulator, p. 1009.
circulus, p. 1009.
circumarea, p. 1010.
circumcenter, p. 1010.
circumcentral, p. 1010.
circumcone, p. 1010.
circumconic, p. 1010.
circumcubic, p. 1010.
circumference, p. 1011.
circumferentor, p. 1011.
circumjovial, p. 1011.
circummeridian, p. 1012.
circumpapallelogram, p. 1012.
circumpentagon, p. 1012.
circumpolar, p. 1012.
circumpolygon, p. 1012.
circumradius, p. 1012.
circumscribe, p. 1012.
circumsolar, p. 1013.
circumstance, p. 1013.
circumstantial, p. 1014.
circumtorsion, p. 1014.
cissoid, p. 1016.
citrine, p. 1019.
clamp¹, p. 1025.
clang, p. 1026.
class, p. 1029.
class-day, p. 1030.
classification, p. 1030.
clear, p. 1037.
clearness, p. 1038.
climax, p. 1046.
clock, p. 1051.

close, p. 1054-1054.
close-plane, p. 1055.
close-point, p. 1055.
cloth-measure, p. 1057.
cloth-yard, p. 1057.
clove⁵, p. 1060.
cnicnode, p. 1065.
cnictrope, p. 1065.
coadjacence, p. 1066.
coadjacent, p. 1066.
coal-sack, p. 1069.
cobado, p. 1072.
cobezoutiant, p. 1073.
cobezoutoid, p. 1073.
cochlear², p. 1075.
cochleoid, p. 1076.
cocktail, p. 1081.
coefficient, p. 1084.
coenesthesis, coenaesthesis, p. 1086.
54: cogency, p. 1089-1090.
cogent, p. 1090.
cogitability, p. 1090.
cogitable, p. 1090.
cogitate, p. 1090.
cogitation, p. 1090.
cogito ergo sum, p. 1090.
cognate, p. 1090.
cognition, p. 1090-1091.
cognitive, p. 1091.
cognitum, p. 1091.
cognizability, p. 1091.
cognizable, p. 1091.
cognize, p. 1091.
cognoscence, p. 1091.
cognoscible, p. 1092.
cognoscitive, p. 1092.
cogrediency, p. 1092.
cogredient, p. 1092.
cohere, p. 1092.
coherence, coherency, p. 1092.
coherent, p. 1092.
cohesion, p. 1092.
cohobate, p. 1093.
coincide, p. 1094.
coincidence, p. 1094.
coincident, p. 1094.
coinhere, p. 1094.
colatitude, p. 1096.
collect, p. 1101.
collection, p. 1101.
collective, p. 1102.

college, p. 1102.
collegian, p. 1102.
colligation, p. 1104.
collimation, p. 1104.
collimator, p. 1104.
collinear, p. 1104.
collineation, p. 1104.
color, colour, p. 1109.
color-box, p. 1111.
color-chart, p. 1111.
color-circle, p. 1111.
color-combination, p. 1111.
color-comparator, p. 1111.
color-cone, p. 1111.
color-contrast, p. 1111.
color-cylinder, p. 1111.
color-diagram, p. 1111.
color-equation, p. 1111.
color-sensation, p. 1112.
color-triangle, p. 1112.
colure, p. 1116.
coma², p. 1116.
combinant, p. 1118.
combination, p. 1118.
combinatorial, p. 1118.
combinatory, p. 1118.
combust, p. 1119.
combustion, p. 1119.
comet, p. 1122.
cometarium, p. 1122.
cometary, p. 1122.
comet-finder, p. 1122.
cometic, p. 1122.
cometographer, p. 1122.
cometography, p. 1122.
cometology, p. 1122.
comet-seeker, p. 1122.
commence, p. 1126.
commencement, p. 1126.
commencer, p. 1126.
commensurability, p. 1127.
commensurable, p. 1127.
common, p. 1133.
commorant, p. 1135.
commutative, p. 1138.
comparator, p. 1141.
compass, p. 1142.
compensation, p. 1144.
complement, p. 1147.
complementary, p. 1147.
complete, p. 1148.

completive, p. 1148.
complex, p. 1148.
complex, p. 1148.
component, p. 1151.
composite, p. 1152.
composition, p. 1152.
compossibility, p. 1153.
compossible, p. 1153.
compound¹, p. 1154.
comprehend, p. 1154.
comprehension, p. 1155.
compression, p. 1155.
compulsion, p. 1157.
computation, p. 1158.
compute, p. 1158.
computer, p. 1158.
Comtian, p. 1158.
Comtism, p. 1158.
Comtist, p. 1158.
conation, p. 1159.
conative, p. 1159.
conaxial, p. 1159.
concave, p. 1159.
concavo-concave, p. 1159.
concavo-convex, p. 1159.
conceit, p. 1160.
conceivability, p. 1161.
conceive, p. 1161.
concentration, p. 1162.
concentric, p. 1162.
concept, p. 1162.
conception, p. 1162.
conceptualism, p. 1163.
conceptualist, p. 1163.
conchoid, p. 1165.
conclude, p. 1167.
conclusion, p. 1167.
conclusive, p. 1167-1168.
conclusively, p. 1168.
conclusiveness, p. 1168.
concomitance, concomitancy, p. 1168.
concomitant, p. 1168.
concrete, p. 1170.
concretion, p. 1170.
concurrent, p. 1171-1172.
concyclic, p. 1172.
condition, p. 1174-1175.
conditional, p. 1175.
conditioned, p. 1175.
conditio sine qua non, p. 1175.

conduction, p. 1177.
cone, p. 1178-1179.
configuration, p. 1184.
confocal, p. 1186.
conform, pp. 1186-1187.
confuse, p. 1188.
confused, p. 1188.
confutation, p. 1189.
cong, p. 1189.
conge¹, p. 1189.
conge², p. 1189.
congius, p. 1191.
congruence, p. 1194.
congruency, p. 1194.
congruent, p. 1194.
congruity, p. 1194.
congruous, p. 1194.
conic, p. 1194.
conical, p. 1194.
conjectural, p. 1195.
conjecture, p. 1195.
conjugate, p. 1196-1197.
conjunction, p. 1197.
conjunctive, p. 1197.
connate, p. 1198.
connex, p. 1199.
connotate, p. 1200.
connotation, p. 1200.
connotative, p. 1200.
connote, p. 1200.
connotive, p. 1200.
conocuneous, p. 1201.
conoid¹, p. 1201.
conoidal, p. 1201.
conormal, p. 1201.
conscience, p. 1202-1203.
concious, p. 1203.
conciousness, p. 1203-1204.
consecution, p. 1204.
consecutive, p. 1204-1205.
consequence, p. 1205-1206.
55: consequent, p. 1206.
consequential, p. 1206.
conservative, p. 1206-1207.
consideration, p. 1208.
consignificant, p. 1209.
consignificate, p. 1209.
consignification, p. 1209.
consistence, consistency, p. 1209.
consistent, p. 1209.
constant, p. 1214.

constellation, pp. 1214-1215.
constituent, p. 1215.
constituted, p. 1215.
constitutive, p. 1216-1217.
constraint, p. 1217.
construction, pp. 1217-1218
contact, p. 1221.
contain, p. 1221-1222.
contemplate, p. 1223.
contemplation, p. 1223.
contemplative, p. 1223.
content², p. 1225.
contentious, p. 1225.
context, p. 1226.
contiguity, p. 1227.
contingency, contingence, p. 1228.
contingent, p. 1228.
continual, p. 1228.
continuant, p. 1228.
continuation, p. 1228.
continue, p. 1229.
continued, p. 1229.
continuity, p. 1229.
continuous, p. 1229-1230.
continuun, p. 1230.
conto, p. 1230.
contour, p. 1230.
contour-line, p. 1230.
contra-arithmetical, p. 1230
contract, p. 1231.
contradiction, p. 1233.
contradictory, p. 1233.
contradistinctive, p. 1233.
contradistinguish, p. 1233.
contrafocal, p. 1233.
contrageometric, p. 1233.
contragredience, p. 1233.
contragredient, p. 1233-1234
contraharmonical, p. 1234.
contrapose, p. 1234.
contraposita, p. 1234.
contraposition, p. 1234.
contraprovectant, p. 1234.
contraprovector, p. 1234.
contrariety, p. 1234.
contrary, p. 1235.
contravarient, p. 1235.
control, p. 1237.
convergence, convergency, p. 1242.

convergent, p. 1242.
converging, p. 1242.
converse², p. 1243.
conversion, p. 1243.
convertend, p. 1244.
convertibility, p. 1244.
convertible, p. 1244.
convex, p. 1244.
conviction, p. 1245.
convince, p. 1246.
convocation, p. 1246.
coom², p. 1250.
coop, p. 1250.
coordinate, p. 1251.
Copernican, p. 1253.
coppo, p. 1256.
copula, p. 1257.
copulation, p. 1257.
cor¹, p. 1258.
cor⁴, p. 1258.
cord¹, p. 1262.
coreciprocal, p. 1265.
co-relation, p. 1265.
co-relative, p. 1265.
co-relatively, p. 1265.
co-residual, p. 1266.
corf, p. 1266.
corollary, p. 1273.
corona, p. 1273.
corporal¹, p. 1275.
corporeal, p. 1276.
corpse-candle, p. 1276.
corpuscle, p. 1277.
corpuscular, p. 1277.
corpuscularian, p. 1277.
correct, p. 1278.
correction, p. 1278.
correctness, p. 1279.
correlate, p. 1279.
correlation, p. 1279.
correlative, p. 1279.
correspond, p. 1279.
correspondence, p. 1280.
correspondential, p. 1280.

Corvus, p. 1285.
cosecant, p. 1287.
cosine, p. 1287.
cosmic, cosmical, p. 1288.

cosmism, p. 1288.
cosmogony, p. 1288.

cosmography, p. 1288.
cosmolabe, p. 1288.
cosmology, p. 1288-1289.
cosmometry, p. 1289.
cosmos¹, p. 1289.
cosmotheism, p. 1289.
cosmothetic, p. 1289.
coss², p. 1289.
coss³, p. 1289.
cossic, cossical, p. 1289.
cotangent, p. 1292.
cotidal, p. 1293.
cotriple, p. 1293.
cotyle, p. 1296.
coude, p. 1298.
count¹, p. 1300.
count¹, p. 1300.
counter-clockwise, p. 1303.
counter-earth, p. 1303.
counter-paradox, p. 1305.
counterpedal, p. 1305.
couple, p. 1309.
coupure, p. 1310.
course¹, p. 1311-1312.
covado, p. 1316.
covariant, p. 1316.
co-versed, p. 1318.
covid, p. 1319.
cow-mass, p. 1321.
cowry, p. 1321.
coxcombity, p. 1322.
crab¹, p. 1323.
crackling, p. 1326.
cram, p. 1328.
cram, p. 1328.
crambo, p. 1328.
cramp-iron, p. 1329.
crater, p. 1335.
56: cream-colored, p. 1338.
create, p. 1339.
creation, p. 1339.
creationism, p. 1339.
creative, p. 1339.
creatural, p. 1339.
credence, p. 1340.
credencive, p. 1340.
credibility, p. 1340.
credulity, p. 1341.
Cretan, p. 1347.
crib¹, p. 1348.
cribrum, p. 1349.

criterion, p. 1354.
crith, p. 1354.
critic, p. 1354-1355.
critical, p. 1355.
criticism, p. 1355.
critique, p. 1355.
crocodile, p. 1357.
crocodilite, p. 1357.
croft, p. 1357-1358.
crohol, p. 1358.
croislet, p. 1358.
cross¹, p. 1361-1362.
cross-curve, p. 1363.
cross-hair, p. 1364.
cross-section, p. 1365.
cross-staff, p. 1365.
crotchet, p. 1366.
crown, p. 1369-1370.
crozier, crosier, p. 1372.
crucial, p. 1372.
crude, p. 1373.
crunodal, p. 1375.
crunode, p. 1375.
crux, p. 1378.
cryptic, p. 1379.
crystalline, p. 1382.
cuadra, p. 1384.
cuartilla, p. 1384.
cuartillo, p. 1384.
cuarto, p. 1384.
cubangle, p. 1385.
cubation², p. 1385.
cube, p. 1385.
cubic, p. 1385.
cubical, p. 1385.
cubicone, p. 1385.
cubicontravariant, p. 1385.
cubicovariant, p. 1385.
cubicriticoid, p. 1385.
cuerda, p. 1389.
culeus, p. 1391.
culminate, p. 1392.
culmination, p. 1392.
culture, p. 1393.
cumulant, p. 1395.
cumulative, p. 1395-1396.
cunning¹, p. 1397.
curl, p. 1403-1404.
curvature, p. 1409-1410.
curve, p. 1410.
curvilinead, p. 1410.

curvilinear, p. 1410.
curvital, p. 1411.
cusp, p. 1411-1412.
custos, p. 1414.
cut-chundoo, p. 1416.
cutra, p. 1417.
cycle[1], p. 1421-1422.
cyclic, p. 1422.
cyclide, p. 1422.
cyclifying, p. 1422.
cyclode, p. 1422.
cycloid, p. 1423.
cycloimber, p. 1423.
cyclometer, p. 1423.
cyclometric, p. 1423.
cyclometry, p. 1423.
cyclotomic, p. 1425.
Cygnus, p. 1425-1426.
cylinder, p. 1426.
cylindroid, p. 1427.
cynic, p. 1429.
cynicism, p. 1429.
Cyrenaic, p. 1433.
D, p. 1437.
daalder, p. 1437.
dabitis, p. 1438.
dactyl, dactyle, p. 1439.
dandiprat, dandyprat, p. 1451.
darapti, p. 1454.
darli, p. 1455.
darriba, p. 1458.
date-line, p. 1461.
datisi, p. 1462.
datum, p. 1462.
daubery, p. 1463.
day[1], p. 1465-1466.
day-house, p. 1466.
day-work, p. 1467.
dean[2], p. 1472-1473.
deanthropomorphism, p. 1473.
deanthropomorphization, p. 1473.
deanthropomorphize, p. 1473.
debility, p. 1477.
decad, decade, p. 1479.
decadianome, p. 1479.
decagon, p. 1479.
decagonal, p. 1479.
decagram, decagramme, p. 1479.

decahedron, p. 1479.
decaliter, decalitre, p. 1479.
decameter, decametre, p. 1479.
decanate, p. 1479.
57: decastere, p. 1480.
decency, p. 1482.
deci-, p. 1483.
deciare, p. 1483.
decigram, decigramme, p. 1484.
decil, decile, p. 1484.
deciliter, decilitre, p. 1484.
decillion, p. 1484.
decillionth, p. 1484.
decimal, p. 1484.
decimeter, p. 1484.
decimo, p. 1484.
declination, p. 1488.
declinational, p. 1488.
decliner, p. 1488.
decrement, p. 1492.
decretist, p. 1492.
decuman, p. 1493.
decumbiture, p. 1493.
decuple, p. 1493.
dedo, p. 1494.
deduce, p. 1495.
deducement, p. 1495.
deducibility, p. 1495.
deducible, p. 1495.
deduct, p. 1495.
deductio, p. 1495.
deduction, p. 1495.
deductive, p. 1495.
defective, p. 1500.
deferent, p. 1502.
deficient, p. 1503.
define, p. 1503.
definite, p. 1504.
definition, p. 1504.
definitional, p. 1504.
definitive, p. 1504.
definitum, p. 1504.
deflection, p. 1505.
deform[1], p. 1505.
deformation, p. 1506.
degorder, p. 1508.
degrade, p. 1509.
degree, p. 1509-1510.
deism, p. 1511.

deist, p. 1511.
deistic, p. 1511.
dejection, p. 1512.
dekass, p. 1512.
Delian, p. 1515.
delicacy, p. 1515.
Delphinus, p. 1520.
demideify, p. 1525.
demigod, p. 1525.
demiurge, p. 1526.
Democritical, p. 1527.
Democriteau, p. 1527.
demonstrability, p. 1528.
demonstrable, p. 1528.
demonstrableness, p. 1528.
demonstrably, p. 1528.
demonstrate, p. 1528-1529.
demonstration, p. 1529.
demonstrative, p. 1529.
demonstrator, p. 1529.
denarius, p. 1530-1531.
denaro, p. 1531.
denary, p. 1531.
denial, p. 1533.
denomination, p. 1534.
denominator, p. 1534.
denotate, p. 1534.
denotation, p. 1534-1535.
denotative, p. 1535.
denotatively, p. 1535.
denote, p. 1535.
density, p. 1535-1536.
denumerant, p. 1538.
deny, p. 1538.
deontology, p. 1539.
departure, p. 1541.
depend, p. 1541.
dependence, p. 1542.
dependent, p. 1542.
depression, p. 1548.
depth, p. 1548.
derham, p. 1551.
derivant, p. 1551.
derivation, p. 1551-1552.
derivative, p. 1552.
descension, p. 1556.
descensional, p. 1556.
descent, p. 1556-1557.

A Comprehensive Bibliography

describe, p. 1557.
describent, p. 1557.
describer, p. 1557.
description, p. 1557.
descriptive, p. 1557.
design, p. 1560.
dessiatine, dessyatine, p. 1567.
destiny, p. 1568.
detached, p. 1570.
determinance, p. 1571.
determinant, p. 1571-1572.
determinantal, p. 1572.
determinate, p. 1572.
determination, p. 1572.
determinative, p. 1572-1573.
determine, p. 1573.
determiner, p. 1573.
determinism, p. 1573.
detriment, p. 1575.
detur, p. 1575.
deuce[2], p. 1576.
develop, p. 1577.
developable, p. 1577-1578.
development, p. 1578.
deviation, p. 1578.
devil, p. 1579.
dha, p. 1586.
dhadium, p. 1586.
dhan, p. 1586.
dharri, p. 1586.
diacaustic, p. 1587.
diachylon, diachylum, p. 1587.
diagonal, p. 1588-1589.
diagram, p. 1589.
diagrammatic, p. 1589.
diagrammatically, p. 1589.
dial, p. 1589-1590.
dialect, p. 1590.
dialectic, p. 1590.
dialectical, p. 1590.
dialectrician, p. 1590.
dialing, dialling, p. 1590-1591.
diallelon, p. 1591.
diallelous, p. 1591.
diallelus, p. 1591.
dialogic, dialogical, p. 1591.
dialogism, p. 1591.
diameter, p. 1592.
diametral, p. 1592.
diametrical, p. 1592.
diamond, p. 1592.

dianodal, p. 1593.
dianoetic, p. 1593.
dianoialogy, p. 1593.
dianome, p. 1593.
diaulos, p. 1598.
dichotomy, p. 1600.
dicker[1], p. 1601.
dictum, p. 1603.
difference, p. 1608.
difference, p. 1609.
difference-engine, p. 1609.
difference-equation, p. 1609.
different, p. 1609.
differentia, p. 1609.
differential, p. 1609.
differentiant, p. 1609.
differentiate, p. 1609.
differentiation, p. 1609-1610.
differentio-differential, p. 1610.
diffraction, p. 1611.
diffractive, p. 1611.
diffuse, p. 1611.
diffusibility, p. 1611.
diffusible, p. 1611.
diffusion, p. 1612.
digit, p. 1614.
dignity, p. 1615-1616.
58: dihedral, p. 1616.
dilation, p. 1618.
dilemma, p. 1618.
dilemmatic, p. 1618.
dimaris, dimatis, p. 1620.
dime, p. 1620.
dimension, p. 1621.
dimensional, p. 1621.
dimensionality, p. 1621.
dimensity, p. 1621.
dimidation, p. 1621.
diminute, p. 1622.
dinar, p. 1624.
dinero, p. 1624.
dinner, p. 1624.
diorism, p. 1628.
dip, p. 1629.
dip, p. 1629.
dipolar, p. 1634.
dipper, p. 1634.
direct, p. 1636.
directing, p. 1637.
direction, p. 1637.
directly, p. 1637.

directrix, p. 1638.
dirigent, p. 1638.
dirigo-motor, p. 1638.
disablement, p. 1639.
disamis, p. 1641.
disbelief, p. 1644.
discern, p. 1645.
discernment, p. 1645.
discerpibility, p. 1645.
discerpible, p. 1645.
discharge, p. 1646.
discommon, p. 1650.
discontinuity, p. 1652.
discontinuous, p. 1652.
discourse, p. 1654.
discover, p. 1654.
discovery, p. 1655.
discreet, p. 1655.
discrete, p. 1656.
discretion, p. 1656.
discretive, p. 1656.
discriminant, p. 1656.
discriminantal, p. 1656.
discriminate, p. 1656.
discursive, p. 1657.
discursus, p. 1657.
dish, p. 1664.
disjunct, p. 1668.
disjunction, p. 1688.
disjunctive, p. 1668.
disk, disc, p. 1668.
disparate, p. 1673.
disposition, p. 1679.
disproof, p. 1680.
disputation, p. 1681.
disquiparancy, disquiparance, p. 1682.
dissentaneous, p. 1685.
dissimilar, p. 1687.
dissimilation, p. 1687.
dissimilitude, p. 1687.
dissipative, p. 1687-1688.
dissipativity, p. 1688.
distance, p. 1690.
distinct, p. 1693.
distinction, p. 1693.
distinguish, p. 1694.
distortion, p. 1695.
distraction, p. 1696.
distribution, p. 1697.
distributive, p. 1698.

distributively, p. 1698.
distributiveness, p. 1698.
disyntheme, p. 1700.
dittany, p. 1701.
ditty, p. 1701.
diurnal, p. 1702.
diverge, p. 1703.
divergent, p. 1703.
diverse, p. 1703.
diversity, p. 1704.
divide, p. 1705.
divided, p. 1705.
dividend, p. 1705-1706.
dividing-engine, p. 1706.
dividual, p. 1706.
divisibility, p. 1707.
divisible, p. 1707.
division, p. 1707-1708.
divisive, p. 1708.
divisor, p. 1708-1709.
dobbeldaler, p. 1712.
dobla, p. 1712.
dobra, p. 1712.
doctor, p. 1714.
doctorate, p. 1715.
dodecahedron, p. 1716.
dodecatemorion, p. 1717.
dodecatemory, p. 1717.
dog-days, p. 1719.
dog-hole, p. 1720.
dogma, p. 1720.
dogmatic, p. 1720.
dogmatism, p. 1721.
dogmatist, p. 1721.
dollar, p. 1724-1725.
domain, p. 1726.
dominant, p. 1728.
dominical, p. 1729.
doppia, p. 1734.
doppietta, p. 1734.
Dorado, p. 1735.
double, p. 1741-1742.
double-bodied, p. 1743.
double-first, p. 1743.
doubloon, p. 1744.
doubt[1], p. 1745.
59: drachma, p. 1753.
Draco, p. 1753.
dracontic, p. 1753.
dragon, p. 1756.
dram, p. 1758.

droop, p. 1777.
drumslade, p. 1783.
Drusian, p. 1784.
dry, p. 1784.
dualism, p. 1786.
dualist, p. 1786.
dualistic, p. 1786.
duality, p. 1786.
dubiety, p. 1787.
dubious, p. 1787.
dubiousness, p. 1787.
dubitation, p. 1787.
ducat, p. 1788.
duck, p. 1788-1789.
dulcify, p. 1794.
dunce, p. 1797.
Dunce-man, Duns-man, p. 1797.
duodecimal, p. 1799.
duplicate, p. 1800.
duplication, p. 1800.
duration, p. 1800.
dryad, p. 1807.
dyadic, p. 1807.
dygogram, p. 1808.
dynam, p. 1808.
dynamic, p. 1808.
dynamics, p. 1809.
dynamism, p. 1809.
dynamist, p. 1809.
dynamistic, p. 1809.
dysis, p. 1811.
dyslogistic, p. 1811.
eagle, p. 1814.
eaglestone, p. 1815.
earth, p. 1819.
earwitness, p. 1821.
Easter, p. 1823.
eccentric, p. 1828.
eclectic, p. 1835.
eclecticism, p. 1835.
eclimeter, p. 1835.
eclipse, p. 1835.
ecliptic, p. 1835.
eddy, p. 1841.
educate, p. 1845.
education, p. 1845.
educe, p. 1845.
educt, p. 1845.
effect, p. 1847.
effection, p. 1848.
effictive, p. 1848.

effectual, p. 1848.
effectuous, p. 1848.
effeminant, p. 1848.
efficiency, p. 1849.
efficient, p. 1849.
effluent, p. 1850.
efflux, p. 1850.
effluxion, p. 1850.
effort, p. 1850.
egg-nog, p. 1853.
ego, p. 1854.
ego-altruistic, p. 1854.
egoism, p. 1854.
egoist, p. 1854.
egoistic, egoistical, p. 1854.
egoity, p. 1854.
egotism, p. 1854.
egress, p. 1855.
egrimony[1], p. 1855.
Egyptian, p. 1855.
eighteen, p. 1856-1857.
eighteenth, p. 1857.
eighth, p. 1857.
eightieth, p. 1857.
eighty, p. 1857.
eikosarion, p. 1857.
eimer, p. 1857.
eject, p. 1858.
elaborative, p. 1859.
elastic, p. 1862.
elasticity, p. 1862.
elate, p. 1862.
elater[2], p. 1863.
elaterist, p. 1863.
elderberry, p. 1865.
election, p. 1866.
Electic, p. 1865.
Eleaticism, p. 1865.
elect, p. 1865.
Electra, p. 1867.
electrochronographic, p. 1869.
electrum, p. 1871.
element, p. 1873.
elench, p. 1874.
elenchic, elenchical, p. 1874.
elevation, p. 1876.
eleven, p. 1877.
eleventh, p. 1877.
elf-shot, p. 1877.
Eliac, p. 1877.
elicitation, p. 1878.

eligible, p. 1878.
eliminant, p. 1878.
eliminate, p. 1878.
elimination, p. 1878.
elixation, p. 1879.
elixir, p. 1879.
Elixir of vitriol, p. 1879.
ell[1], p. 1879-1880.
ellipse, p. 1880.
ellipsis, p. 1880.
ellipsograph, p. 1880.
ellipsoid, p. 1880.
elliptic, elliptical, p. 1880.
ellipticity, p. 1880.
elliptois, p. 1880.
elliptoid, p. 1880.
ellwand, elwand, p. 1881.
emanation, p. 1885.
emanative, p. 1885.
emerge, p. 1897.
emergent year, p. 1897.
emersion, p. 1898.
empirema, p. 1903.
empiric, p. 1903.
empirical, p. 1903.
empiricism, p. 1903.
empiricist, p. 1903.
empty, p. 1905.
empyrean, p. 1906.
encounter, p. 1915.
end, p. 1917-1918.
60: energy, p. 1926-1927.
engine, p. 1930-1931.
engyscope, p. 1935.
enlightenment, p. 1937-1938.
ennead, p. 1938.
ens, p. 1942.
ensemble, p. 1942.
entelechy, p. 1946.
enthusiasm, p. 1950.
enthymematical, p. 1950.
enthymeme, p. 1950.
entire, p. 1951.
entitative, p. 1951.
entitatively, p. 1951.
entity, p. 1951.
enumerable, p. 1956.
enumerate, p. 1956.
enumeration, p. 1956.
enumerator, p. 1956.
enunciation, p. 1957.

enunciative, p. 1957.
envelop, envelope, p. 1957.
envy[1], p. 1958.
eon, aeon, p. 1959.
epact, p. 1960.
epagote, p. 1960.
epagomenal, p. 1960.
epanthem, p. 1961.
ephah, epha, p. 1962.
ephemeris, p. 1962-1963.
epichirema, p. 1965.
Epictetian, p. 1966.
epicure, p. 1966.
Epicurean, p. 1966-1967.
epicycle, p. 1967.
epicycloid, p. 1967.
epithymetical, p. 1977.
epitomator, p. 1977.
epitome, p. 1977-1978.
epitrochoid, p. 1978.
epoch, p. 1979.
equal, p. 1980.
equality, p. 1980.
equant, p. 1981.
equation, p. 1981-1982.
equator, p. 1983.
equatorial, p. 1983.
equiangular, p. 1983.
equianharmonic, p. 1983.
equianharmonically, p. 1983.
equiconvex, p. 1983.
equicrescent, p. 1983.
equicrural, p. 1983.
equicrure, p. 1983.
equidistant, p. 1983.
equilateral, p. 1984.
equilibrant, p. 1984.
equilibrate, p. 1984.
equilibration, p. 1984.
equilibrism, p. 1984.
equilibrium, p. 1984.
equimomental, p. 1984.
equimultiple, p. 1984.
equinoctial, p. 1984-1985.
equinox, p. 1985.
equiparance, equiparancy, p. 1985.
equiparant, p. 1985.
equipollence, equipollency, p. 1986.
equipollent, p. 1986.
equiponderant, p. 1986.
equipotential, p. 1986.

equisegmental, p. 1986.
equivalence, p. 1987.
equivalent, p. 1987.
equivocal, p. 1988.
equivocate, p. 1988.
equivocation, p. 1988.
equivoke, equivoque, p. 1988.
Equuleus, p. 1988.
era, p. 1989.
erect, p. 1991.
Eretrian, p. 1992.
erg, p. 1992.
ergo, p. 1993.
ergometer, p. 1993.
ergotism, p. 1993.
Eridanus, p. 1993.
eristic, p. 1995.
erotematic, p. 1996.
error, p. 1997-1998.
escribe, p. 2003.
escuage, p. 2004.
escudo, p. 2004.
esoteric, p. 2005.
esotery, p. 2005.
essence, p. 2007-2008.
Essenes, p. 2008.
essential, p. 2008.
essentiality, p. 2008.
essentially, p. 2008.
establishment, p. 2009.
estadal, p. 2009.
estimation, p. 2012.
Etamin, p. 2014.
et cetera, etcetera, p. 2014.
eteopolymorphism, p. 2014.
eternity, p. 2015.
ethical, p. 2017.
ethics, p. 2017.
etiquette, p. 2019.
Euclidean, p. 2022.
Eulerian, p. 2025.
euthymia, p. 2033.
euthytatic, p. 2033.
evaluate, p. 2034.
evaluation, p. 2034.
evanesce, p. 2034.
evanscible, p. 2035.
evaporation, p. 2036.
evectant, p. 2037.
evection, p. 2037.
evectional, p. 2037.

evector, p. 2037.
even¹, p. 2037-2038.
evening, p. 2038.
everlasting, p. 2040.
every, p. 2041.
evidence, p. 2042.
evolute, p. 2044.
evolution, p. 2044.
evolvent, p. 2045.
exact, p. 2046.
exactly, p. 2047.
examination, p. 2048.
examination paper, p. 2048.
examine, p. 2049.
examiner, p. 2049.
example, p. 2049.
exception, p. 2053.
exceptious, p. 2053.
exceptive, p. 2053-2054.
excircle, p. 2055.
61: exclusion, p. 2057.
exclusive, p. 2057.
excursion, p. 2060.
exegesis, p. 2063.
exegetic, p. 2063.
exemplar, p. 2063.
exercise, p. 2064-2065.
exhaustion, p. 2067.
exhaustive, p. 2067.
exhibition, p. 2067-2068.
exhibitioner, p. 2068.
exigent, p. 2069.
existence, p. 2070.
existential, p. 2070.
existible, p. 2070.
exoterical, p. 2074.
exotery, p. 2074.
exotic, p. 2074.
expanse, p. 2074.
expansion, p. 2074-2075.
expectation, p. 2076.
expectatorium, p. 2076.
expense, p. 2078.
experience, p. 2079.
experiential, p. 2079.
experiment, p. 2079.
experimental, p. 2079.
explain, p. 2081.
explanation, p. 2081-2082.
explement, p. 2082.
explicand, p. 2082.

explication, p. 2082.
explicative, p. 2082.
explicit¹, p. 2082.
explosion, p. 2084.
exponent, p. 2084.
exponential, p. 2084.
exponible, p. 2084.
exposition, p. 2085.
expository, p. 2085.
express, p. 2086.
expression, p. 2086-2087.
expurgation, p. 2088.
extended, p. 2091.
extension, p. 2091.
extensity, p. 2092.
extensive, p. 2092.
extent, p. 2092.
exterior, p. 2093.
exterminate, p. 2093.
extermination, p. 2093.
external, p. 2093-2094.
extraconstellary, p. 2096.
extract, p. 2096.
extraction, p. 2097.
extralogical, p. 2097.
extralogically, p. 2097.
extramundane space, p. 2097.
extraneous factor, p. 2098.
extraordinary, p. 2098.
extrapolation, p. 2098.
extreme, p. 2099-2100.
extrinsic, p. 2100.
fabricate, p. 2108.
face¹, p. 2109-2110.
facient, p. 2111.
fact, p. 2112-2113.
factor, p. 2113-2114.
factor, p. 2114.
factorial, p. 2114.
factory-maund, p. 2114.
facula, p. 2114.
facultative, p. 2114.
faculty, p. 2114-2115.
fadge¹, p. 2116.
fag¹, p. 2116.
fagot, faggot, p. 2116.
fair-book, p. 2120.
fairing, p. 2120.
faisceau, p. 2121.
faith, p. 2121-2122.
faitor, faitour, p. 2123.

falcated, p. 2124.
fall¹, p. 2127-2128.
fall², p. 2128.
fallacet, p. 2128.
fallacious, p. 2128.
fallacy, p. 2128.
fallax, p. 2128.
fallible, p. 2129.
falling-from, p. 2129.
falling-star, p. 2129.
fan, p. 2134-2135.
fancy, p. 2136.
fapesmo, p. 2139.
fardingdeal, p. 2141.
farthing, p. 2145-2146.
fashionably, p. 2148.
fatalism, p. 2152.
fatality, p. 2152.
fate, p. 2153.
father, p. 2153-2154.
fathom, p. 2154-2155.
fathom, p. 2155.
feeling, p. 2171.
feeze, feaze¹, p. 2172.
felapton, p. 2172.
felicity, p. 2173.
fellow, p. 2174-2175.
fellowship, p. 2175.
ferio, p. 2183.
ferison, p. 2183.
fermatian, p. 2183.
Acetic ferment, p. 2184.
festino, p. 2189.
fiddling, p. 2201.
fiddling, p. 2201.
figment, p. 2208.
figural, p. 2208.
figurate number, p. 2208.
figuration, p. 2208.
figure, p. 2209.
62: figured, p. 2210.
finesse, p. 2223.
finger, p. 2223.
fingerbreadth, p. 2224.
finger-counting, p. 2224.
finite, p. 2225-2226.
fire, p. 2227.
firesmo, p. 2231.
firkin, p. 2232.
firlot, p. 2232.
first¹, p. 2233-2234.

fishy, p. 2238.
fist¹, p. 2240.
fit¹, p. 2241.
five-square, p. 2243.
fixed, p. 2244.
flashy¹, p. 2255-2256.
flat¹, p. 2256-2257.
flatus, p. 2259.
flaw¹, p. 2260.
flecnodal, p. 2262.
flecnode, p. 2262.
fleflecnodal, p. 2265.
fleflecnode, p. 2265.
flexure, p. 2268.
flocculent, p. 2275.
flock-bed, p. 2276.
Florentine, p. 2279.
flotation, p. 2280-2281.
fluent, p. 2286.
fluid, p. 2286-2287.
flunk, p. 2288.
flunk, p. 2288.
fluorescence, p. 2288.
flux, p. 2292.
fluxion, p. 2292.
fluxional, p. 2292.
fluxionist, p. 2292.
focal, p. 2297.
focaloid, p. 2297.
focus, p. 2297.
foin¹, p. 2300.
folium, p. 2303.
foot, p. 2309-2310.
foot-breadth, p. 2311.
foot-pound, p. 2312.
footpoundal, p. 2312.
force¹, p. 2318-2319.
force-function, p. 2320.
forejudgement, p. 2325.
foreknowledge, p. 2325.
foresight, p. 2327.
form, p. 2335-2336.
formal, p. 2336-2337.
formalism, p. 2337.
formalist, p. 2337.
formality, p. 2337.
formally, p. 2337.
formula, p. 2338.
Fornax, p. 2340.
forpet, p. 2341.
forthcomingness, p. 2343.

fortitude, p. 2344.
fortuitous, p. 2344-2345.
fortune, p. 2345.
fother¹, p. 2349.
fotmal, p. 2349.
foundation, p. 2351.
fraction, p. 2357.
free, p. 2366-2367.
freedom, p. 2368.
freeness, p. 2370.
free-thinker, p. 2370.
free-thinking, p. 2370.
freewill, p. 2370.
freezing-point, p. 2371.
fremd, p. 2371.
frequency, p. 2373.
freshman, p. 2374.
fresison, p. 2375.
63: friarly, p. 2377.
friction, p. 2377.
frigid, p. 2381.
frisesomorum, p. 2383.
front, p. 2388.
F.R.S., p. 2393.
fruitful, p. 2395.
frustration, p. 2396.
fuga contrarii, p. 2399.
fulminate, p. 2404.
funambulo, p. 2407.
function, p. 2407-2408.
functional, p. 2408.
fundamental, p. 2409.
funicular, p. 2411.
funiculus, p. 2411.
furlong, p. 2414.
furmenty, furmety, furmity,
 p. 2414-2415.
G, p. 2423.
galactic, p. 2431.
Galilean², p. 2436.
gallon, p. 2441-2442.
gamic, p. 2448.
gas, p. 2460-2461.
gauche, p. 2470.
Gaussian, p. 2471.
gematria, p. 2479.
Gemini, p. 2479.
genderlike, p. 2481.
general, p. 2482.
generale, p. 2482.
generality, p. 2483.

generalizable, p. 2483.
generalization, p. 2483.
generalize, p. 2483.
generant, p. 2483.
generate, p. 2483.
generative, p. 2484.
generator, p. 2484.
generatrix, p. 2484.
generic, p. 2484.
generification, p. 2484.
genethliac, p. 2485.
genethlialogy, p. 2485.
genethliatic, p. 2485.
genetic, p. 2485.
genus, p. 2492.
geocentric, p. 2492.
geocyclic, p. 2493.
geodesic, p. 2493.
geodesist, p. 2493.
geodesy, p. 2493.
geometer, p. 2494.
Geometra, p. 2494.
geometriant, p. 2494.
geometric, geometrical,
 p. 2494.
geometrically, p. 2495.
geometrician, p. 2495.
geometry, p. 2495.
Geoguim Sidus, p. 2496.
ghost, p. 2506.
gill⁴, p. 2513.
globe, p. 2539-2540.
glomerel, p. 2542.
glomery, p. 2542.
gnomon, p. 2555.
gnomonic, p. 2555.
gnomonics, p. 2555.
grace, p. 2587.
grade¹, p. 2589.
graduate, p. 2590.
grain¹, p. 2592.
gram², gramme, p. 2594.
gram-centimeter, p. 2594.
graph, p. 2600.
graphic, graphical, p. 2601.
graphometric, graphometrical,
 p. 2601.
graphometrics, p. 2601.
graphonym, p. 2601.
grating², p. 2606.
gravimeter, p. 2608.

gravitation, p. 2609.
gravitational, p. 2609.
gravitative, p. 2609.
gravity, p. 2609.
gray, grey, p. 2609-2610.
green¹, p. 2616-2617.
grind, p. 2625.
group¹, p. 2637-2638.
Gude², p. 2647.
Gudermannian, p. 2647.
64: gymnasiast, p. 2664.
gymnasium, p. 2664.
gyration, p. 2668.
gyrational, p. 2668.
gyratory, p. 2668.
gyroscope, p. 2669.
gyroscopic, p. 2669.
gyrostat, p. 2669.
habit, p. 2673.
habitual, p. 2673-2674.
hæcceity, p. 2677.
hairbreadth, p. 2683.
hair-splitting, p. 2683.
half, p. 2686.
half-and-half, p. 2686.
half-blood, p. 2686.
half-fou, p. 2687.
half-tangent, p. 2689.
half-thought, p. 2689.
half-yard, p. 2689.
hallucination, p. 2692.
Hamiltonian, p. 2696.
Hamiltonism, p. 2696.
hammock¹, p. 2698.
hanap, p. 2699.
hand, p. 2699-2700.
handbreadth, p. 2702.
handful, p. 2703.
happiness, p. 2713.
harmonic, p. 2722-2724.
harmonically, p. 2723.
harmonicism, p. 2723.
harmonics, p. 2723.
harmonious, p. 2724.
harmony, p. 2724-2725.
harrysoph, p. 2729.
Hartleian, p. 2730.
harvest-moon, p. 2731.
hay-band, p. 2744.
hayz, p. 2745.
hazard, p. 2745.

haze, p. 2746.
hazer, p. 2747.
hazing, p. 2747.
heap, p. 2754.
heap, p. 2754.
heart, p. 2755-2756.
heart-shaped, p. 2759.
Hecatombæon, p. 2766.
hectare, p. 2767.
hectogram, hectogramme, p. 2767.
hectoliter, hectolitre, p. 2767.
hectometer, p. 2767.
hectostere, p. 2767.
hedonics, p. 2769.
hedonism, p. 2769.
hedonist, p. 2769.
hedonistic, p. 2769.
Hegelianism, p. 2772.
Hegelianize, p. 2772.
height, hight¹, p. 2773.
heinously, p. 2773.
hejira, p. 2774.
heliacal, p. 2774.
helicograph, p. 2775.
helicoid, p. 2775.
helicosophy, p. 2776.
heliocentric, p. 2776.
heliocomete, p. 2776.
heliometer, p. 2776.
helioscope, p. 2777.
heliotrope, p. 2777.
heliotroper, p. 2777.
helispheric, helispherical, p. 2778.
helix, p. 2778.
hemerologium, p. 2787.
hemicycle, p. 2787.
hemicylindrical, p. 2787.
hemihedral, p. 2788.
hemina, p. 2788.
hemisphere, p. 2789.
hemispheroid, p. 2790.
hence, p. 2792.
hencemeant, p. 2793.
hendecagon, p. 2793.
hendecagonal, p. 2793.
hendecahedron, p. 2793.
heptace, p. 2796.
heptad, p. 2796.
heptagon, p. 2796.
heptagonal, p. 2796.
heptahedral, p. 2796.

heptahedron, p. 2796.
Heraclitean, p. 2797.
herculean, p. 2800.
hermaphrodeity, p, p. 2805.
Hermetic, p. 2805.
herpolhode, p. 2809.
herring-pond, p. 2810.
herring-vessel, p. 2810.
Herschel, p. 2810.
Herschelian, p. 2810.
Hesse's equation, p. 2812.
Hessian², p. 2812.
heterogeneal, p. 2814.
heterogeneity, p. 2814.
heterogeneous, p. 2814.
heteronomy, p. 2816.
heteronymous, p. 2816.
heteropolar, p. 2816.
heteroscian, p. 2817.
heterostatic, p. 2817.
heterozetesis, p. 2818.
hexace, p. 2819.
hexad, p. 2819.
hexadic, p. 2819.
hexagon, p. 2819.
hexagonal, p. 2819.
hexagram, p. 2819.
hexahedral, p. 2819.
hexahedron, p. 2819.
hiemal, p. 2824.
high, p. 2827-2828.
hin, p. 2833.
historical, p. 2842.
hitchcock, p. 2844.
65: Hobbesian, p. 2847.
Hobbism, p. 2847.
hod¹, p. 2849.
hogshead, p. 2852-2853.
hogsheadweight, p. 2853.
holochrone, p. 2859.
holometer, p. 2860.
holomorphy, p. 2860.
homaloidal, p. 2860.
homeoid, homoeoid, p. 2864.
homeoidal, p. 2864.
homer³, p. 2865.
homodromous, p. 2867.
homoeomery, p. 2867.
homogeneity, p. 2868.
homogeneous, p. 2868.
homogeneum, p. 2868.

homogeny, p. 2868.
homographic, p. 2868.
homography, p. 2868.
homological, p. 2868.
homologous, p. 2868.
homolographic, p. 2868.
homology, p. 2869.
homonym, p. 2869.
homonymous, p. 2869.
horizon, p. 2883-2884.
horizon-glass, p. 2884.
horizontal, p. 2884.
horograph, p. 2887.
horography, p. 2887.
horologirm, p. 2887.
horometry, p. 2888.
horopter, p. 2888.
horopteric, p. 2888.
horoscope, p. 2888.
horoscopy, p. 2888.
horse-power, p. 2892.
hostel, p. 2897.
hour, p. 2900.
hour-circle, p. 2900.
house[1], p. 2901.
huddle, p. 2909.
hue[1], p. 2909-2910.
huge, p. 2911.
hull[1], p. 2912.
hum[1], p. 2913.
human, p. 2913.
humane, p. 2913.
humanist, p. 2913.
Humian, p. 2916.
humorist, p. 2918.
hundred, p. 2919.
Huygenian, p. 2929.
Hyades, p. 2929.
hydra, p. 2931.
hydrodynamic, p. 2935.
hydrographer, p. 2936.
hydrography, p. 2936.
hydrokinetic, p. 2937.
hydrokinetical, p. 2937.
hydrokinetics, p. 2937.
hydromantic, p. 2937.
hydromechanics, p. 2937.
hydromel, p. 2937.
hydrostatic, p. 2940.
hydrostatics, p. 2940.
Hydrus, p. 2941.

hyleg, p. 2943.
hylism, p. 2943.
hylogenesis, p. 2943.
hylogeny, p. 2943.
hyloidealism, p. 2943.
hylopathic, p. 2943.
hylopathism, p. 2943.
hylopathist, p. 2943.
hylozoical, p. 2943.
hylozoism, p. 2943.
hylozoist, p. 2943.
hylozoistic, p. 2943.
hylozoistically, p. 2943.
hyperabelian, p. 2947.
hyperbola, p. 2947-2948.
hyperbolic, p. 2948.
hyperbolograph, p. 2948.
hyperboloid, p. 2948.
hypercomplex, p. 2948.
hyperconic, p. 2948.
hypercycle, p. 2949.
hyperdeterminant, p. 2949.
hyperdistributive, p. 2949.
hyperelliptic, p. 2949.
hyperfuchsian, p. 2949.
hypergeometric, p. 2949.
hyperjacobian, p. 2949.
hyperspace, p. 2951.
hyperspherical, p. 2951.
hypertridimensional, p. 2951.
hypocycloid, p. 2954.
hypostasis, p. 2954.
hypostatic, p. 2957.
hypostatization, p. 2958.
hyposyllogistic, p. 2958.
hypotenusal, hypothenusal, p. 2958.
hypotenuse, hypothenuse, p. 2958.
hypothesis, p. 2959.
hypothetic, p. 2959.
hypothetical, p. 2959.
hypothetico-disjunctive, p. 2959.
hypotrochoid, p. 2960.
hypotyposis, p. 2960.
hysteron-proteron, p. 2962.
I, p. 2963.
I[2], p. 2963.
icon, p. 2970-2971.
iconantidyptic, p. 2971.
icosahedron, p. 2972.
icosian, p. 2972.
icosidodecahedron, p. 2972.

idea, p. 2973.
ideal, p. 2973-2974.
idealism, p. 2974.
idealist, p. 2974.
ideality, p. 2974.
ideal-realism, p. 2974.
ideate, p. 2974.
ideation, p. 2974.
ideational, p. 2974.
idemfaciand, p. 2974.
idemfacient, p. 2974.
idemfactor, p. 2974.
idempotent, p. 2975.
identical, p. 2975.
identically, p. 2975.
identism, p. 2975.
identity, p. 2975.
ideology, p. 2975.
idol, p. 2978.
idolon, idolum, p. 2979.
Idomenean, p. 2979.
ignorance, p. 2981-2982.
ignoration, p. 2982.
illapse, p. 2985.
illation, p. 2985.
illative, p. 2985-2986.
illumination, p. 2989.
illuminative, p. 2989.
illusion, p. 2990.
image, p. 2991.
imaginary, p. 2992.
imagination, p. 2992.
imaginative, p. 2992.
imagine, p. 2992-2993.
imbrue, p. 2994.
immanence, p. 2995.
immanent, p. 2995-2996.
immaterial, p. 2996.
immaterialism, p. 2996.
immaterialist, p. 2996.
immateriality, p. 2996.
immaterialize, p. 2996.
immaterially, p. 2996.
immaterialness, p. 2996.
immateriate, p. 2996.
immeability, p. 2996.
immeasurable, p. 2996.
immeasurability, p. 2996.
immeasurably, p. 2996.
immediacy, p. 2996-2997.
immediate, p. 2997.

immerge, p. 2997.
immersion, p. 2998.
66: immutation, p. 3000-3001.
imp, p. 3001.
impact, p. 3001.
impar, p. 3002.
imparity, p. 3002.
impedite, p. 3005.
impenetrability, p. 3005.
imperate, p. 3006.
imperative, p. 3006.
imperceptible, p. 3006.
imperfect, p. 3007.
impetus, p. 3010.
implex, p. 3011.
implicit, p. 3012.
imply, p. 3012.
imponderable, p. 3013.
import, p. 3013.
important, p. 3014.
impose, p. 3015.
impossible, p. 3015.
impotence, p. 3016.
impression, p. 3018.
imprint, p. 3019.
improperly, p. 3020.
improportion, p. 3020.
impulse, p. 3023.
impulsor, p. 3023.
impure, p. 3023.
impute, p. 3024.
in^1, p. 3024-3025.
in^1, p. 3025.
inane, p. 3027.
inartificial, p. 3029.
inbeing, p. 3030.
incast, p. 3032.
inception, p. 3034.
inceptive, p. 3034.
inch^1, p. 3035.
inch-pound, p. 3035.
incidence, p. 3035-3036.
incident, p. 3036.
incidental, p. 3036.
incipient, p. 3036.
in-circle, p. 3036.
incircle, p. 3036.
inclination, p. 3037-3038.
incliner, p. 3038.
inclusion, p. 3038.
incogitability, p. 3039.

incogitable, p. 3039.
incognizible, p. 3039.
incognoscible, p. 3039.
incommensurability, p. 3040.
incommensurable, p. 3040.
incomplete, p. 3041.
incomplexly, p. 3041.
incomposite, p. 3042.
incompossibility, p. 3042.
incompossible, p. 3042.
incomprehensibility, p. 3042.
incomprehensible, p. 3042.
incomprehensibleness, p. 3042.
incomprehensibly, p. 3042.
incomprehension, p. 3042.
incomprehensive, p. 3042.
inconceivability, p. 3042.
inconceivable, p. 3042.
inconceivableness, p. 3042.
inconceivably, p. 3042.
inconceptible, p. 3042.
inconcludent, p. 3043.
inconcluding, p. 3043.
inconclusion, p. 3043.
inconclusive, p. 3043.
inconclusively, p. 3043.
inconclusiveness, p. 3043.
inconcrete, p. 3043.
inconditional, p. 3043.
inconditionate, p. 3043.
incongrue, p. 3043.
incongruent, p. 3043.
incongruity, p. 3043.
incongruous, p. 3043.
in-conic, p. 3043.
inconscient, p. 3043.
inconcious, p. 3043.
inconsecutive, p. 3044.
inconsecutiveness, p. 3044.
inconsequence, p. 3044.
inconsequent, p. 3044.
inconsequential, p. 3044.
inconsequentiality, p. 3044.
inconsequentially, p. 3044.
inconsequently, p. 3044.
inconsequentness, p. 3044.
inconsistency, p. 3044.
incontestable, p. 3045.
incopresentability, p. 3046.
incopresentable, p. 3046.
incorporal, p. 3046.

incorporealism, p. 3047.
increase, p. 3048.
increment, p. 3048.
in-cubic, p. 3049.
indagatory, p. 3051.
indeficiency, p. 3053.
indeficient, p. 3053.
indefinite, p. 3053.
indefinitude, p. 3053.
indemonstrability, p. 3054.
indemonstrable, p. 3054.
independent, p. 3055.
indeterminate, p. 3056.
indeterminateness, p. 3056.
indetermination, p. 3056.
indeterminism, p. 3056.
indeterminist, p. 3056.
index, p. 3056-3057.
index-correction, p. 3057.
index-error, p. 3057.
index-glass, p. 3057.
index-law, p. 3057.
indicate, p. 3058.
indication, p. 3058.
indicatrix, p. 3059.
indiction, p. 3059.
indifference, p. 3059-3060.
indifferentism, p. 3060.
indigo, p. 3061.
indirect, p. 3062.
indiscernible, p. 3062.
indisputable, p. 3063.
indistinct, p. 3064.
indistinctness, p. 3064.
individual, p. 3064.
individualism, p. 3064-3065.
individuality, p. 3065.
individualization, p. 3065.
individuand, p. 3065.
individuant, p. 3065.
individuate, p. 3065.
individuate, p. 3065.
individuation, p. 3065.
indivisibility, p. 3065.
indivisible, p. 3065.
indubitable, p. 3067.
induction, p. 3068.
inductive, p. 3069.
inelastic, p. 3072.
inequal, p. 3073.
inequality, p. 3073.

inertia, p. 3074.
in esse, p. 3074.
ineunt, p. 3075.
inexistence[1], p. 3075.
inexistence[2], p. 3075.
inexistency, p. 3075.
inexistent[1], p. 3075.
inextensible, p. 3077.
infer, p. 3080.
inference, p. 3080-3081.
inferential, p. 3081.
inferior, p. 3081.
inferiority, p. 3081.
infinitant, p. 3083.
infinitary, p. 3083.
infinitate, p. 3083.
infinitation, p. 3083.
infinite, p. 3083-3084.
infiniteness, p. 3084.
infinitesimal, p. 3084.
infinitesimally, p. 3084.
infinition, p. 3084.
infinituple, p. 3084.
infinity, p. 3084.
infirmity, p. 3085.
inflection, inflexion, p. 3086.
inflectional, inflexional, p. 3086.
influence, p. 3087.
influx, p. 3087-3088.
influxionism, p. 3088.
influxionist, p. 3088.
informant, p. 3088.
information, p. 3088.
informed[1], p. 3089.
informed[2], p. 3089.
infortune, p. 3890.
infra-red, p. 3090.
ingrain, p. 3095.
ingress, p. 3096.
inhere, p. 3097.
inherence, p. 3097.
inherent, p. 3097.
inhesion, p. 3098.
in-hexagon, p. 3098.
inn[1], p. 3105.
innate, p. 3105.
innervation[2], p. 3106.
innumerability, p. 3108.
innumerable, p. 3108.
inobservable, p. 3108.
inordinate, p. 3109.

in-parabola, p. 3110.
in-polygon, p. 3110.
in potentia, p. 3110.
inscribe, p. 3114.
inscriptible, p. 3114.
insensate, p. 3116.
inseparable, p. 3116.
insight, p. 3118.
67: inspiration, p. 3121.
in-square, p. 3121.
instance, p. 3122.
instant, p. 3122.
instantaneous, p. 3122.
instinct, p. 3123-3124.
institute, p. 3124.
instrument, p. 3125-3126.
integer, p. 3130.
integrability, p. 3130.
integrable, p. 3130.
integral, p. 3130-3131.
integrant, p. 3131.
integrate, p. 3131.
integrate, p. 3131.
integration, p. 3131.
integrator, p. 3131.
integrity, p. 3131.
intellect, p. 3131-3132.
intellectible, p. 3132.
intellection, p. 3132.
intellective, p. 3132.
intellectual, p. 3132.
intellectualism, p. 3132.
intellectualist, p. 3132.
intellectualistic, p. 3132.
intellectuality, p. 3132.
intellectualization, p. 3132.
intellectualize, p. 3132.
intelligence, p. 3132.
intelligible, p. 3133.
intend, p. 3134.
intension, p. 3135.
intensity, p. 3135.
intensive, p. 3135.
intensively, p. 3135.
intention, p. 3136.
intentional, p. 3136.
intercalary, p. 3137.
intercalate, p. 3137.
intercalation, p. 3137-3138.
intercept, p. 3138.
intercepted, p. 3138.

interfacial, p. 3142.
interface, p. 3142.
interior, p. 3144.
intermediary, p. 3147.
intermediate, p. 3147.
internal, p. 3149.
interpenetration, p. 3151.
interplanetary, p. 3151.
interpolate, p. 3151-3152.
interpolation, p. 3152.
interpretation, p. 3153.
interrogatedness, p. 3153.
interscendent, p. 3154.
intersect, p. 3154.
intersection, p. 3154.
intestine, p. 3158.
intramercurial, p. 3162.
intransitive, p. 3162.
intrant, p. 3162.
intraphilosophic, p. 3162.
in-triangle, p. 3163.
intrinsic, p. 3164.
introspection, p. 3165.
introspectionist, p. 3165.
introspective, p. 3165.
intuit, p. 3166.
intuition, p. 3166-3167.
intuitional, p. 3167.
intuitionalism, p. 3167.
intuitionalist, p. 3167.
intuitionism, p. 3167.
intuitionist, p. 3167.
intuitive, p. 3167.
intuitively, p. 3167.
intuitivism, p. 3167.
intuitivist, p. 3167.
invalidity, p. 3169.
invariable, p. 3169.
invariance, p. 3169.
invariant, p. 3169.
invariantive, p. 3169.
invariod, p. 3169.
inverse, p. 3171.
inversely, p. 3171.
inversion, p. 3171.
invisible, p. 3174.
involuntary, p. 3176.
involutant, p. 3176.
involute, p. 3176.
involution, p. 3176.
involutorial, p. 3176.

involve, p. 3176.
inward, p. 3177.
inwardness, p. 3177.
Ionic, p. 3178.
irrational, p. 3185.
irreconcilable, p. 3186.
irrepressible, p. 3189.
irresolbable, p. 3189.
irriguous, p. 3189.
irrotational, p. 3191.
isagoge, p. 3192.
isentropic, p. 3193.
isochronal, p. 3195.
isogoniostat, p. 3197.
isomeria, p. 3197.
isometric, p. 3197.
isomorphism, p. 3197.
isoperimetrical, p. 3198.
isoperimetry, p. 3198.
isosceles, p. 3198.
isotropic, p. 3198.
isotropy, p. 3199.
iteration, p. 3203.
iterative, p. 3203.
itinerary, p. 3204.
izar, p. 3206.
J, p. 3207.
jack, p. 3208.
Jacobian^2, p. 3212.
Jacob's-staff, p. 3213.
jocoserious, p. 3236.
joculary, p. 3236.
jordan, p. 3241.
jostle, p. 3242.
Jovial, p. 3243.
judge, p. 3247.
judgment, judgement, p. 3247.
jugum, p. 3250.
Julian, p. 3250.
junior, p. 3253.
Jupiter, p. 3255.
jutty, p. 3260.
K, p. 3261.
Kantian, p. 3265.
Kantianism, p. 3265.
keg, p. 3272.
68: Keplerian, p. 3275.
kilderkin, p. 3284.
kilo, p. 3286.
kilodyne, p. 3286.
kilogram, kilogramme, p. 3286.

kilogrammeter, kilogrammetre, p. 3286.
kiloliter, kilolitre, p. 3286.
kilometer, kilometre, p. 3286.
kilostere, p. 3286.
kilowatt, p. 3286.
kin^3, p. 3287.
kind^2, p. 3287.
kinematics, p. 3289.
kinetics, p. 3289.
knot^1, p. 3305-3306.
knotfulness, p. 3306.
knottiness, p. 3307.
know^1, p. 3307.
knowledge, p. 3308.
L, p. 3315.
label^1, p. 3315-3316.
lacunary, p. 3326.
Lagrangian, p. 3332.
lambdaic, p. 3334.
Lampadias, p. 3338.
lamp-fly, p. 3339.
lampion, p. 3339.
land-measure, p. 3344.
land-measurer, p. 3344.
land-measuring, p. 3344.
lap^3, p. 3351.
laparocolotomy, p. 3351.
laparo-enterotomy, p. 3351.
laparohysterectomy, p. 3351.
laparonephrectomy, p. 3351.
laparonephrotomy, p. 3351.
laparostict, p. 3351.
laparotomic, p. 3351.
laparotomist, p. 3351.
laparotomize, p. 3351.
laparotomy, p. 3351.
lap-bander, p. 3351.
lap-dovetail, p. 3351.
lapel, p. 3351.
lapelhout, p. 3351.
lapelled, p. 3351.
lapful, p. 3351.
Laphria, p. 3351.
Laphygma, p. 3351.
lapidarist, p. 3352.
lapidary, p. 3352.
lapidate, p. 3352.
lapidation, p. 3352.
lapideon, p. 3352.
lapidescent, p. 3352.

lapidific, p. 3352.
lapidifical, p. 3352.
lapidification, p. 3352.
lapidify, p. 3352.
lapidose, p. 3352.
lapillus, p. 3352.
lapis, p. 3352.
Lapith, p. 3352.
Laplacian, p. 3353.
Laportea, p. 3353.
Lapp, p. 3353.
lapper-milk, p. 3353.
lappet-end, p. 3353.
lappet-frame, p. 3353.
lappet-head, p. 3353.
lappet-moth, p. 3353.
lappet-weaving, p. 3353.
lapping^1, p. 3353.
lapping-engine, p. 3353.
lapping-machine, p. 3353.
Lappish, p. 3353.
Lapponian, p. 3353.
lappy, p. 3353.
lapsable, p. 3353.
Lapsana, Lampsana, p. 3353.
Lapsaneae, Lampsaneae, p. 33
lapse, p. 3353-3354.
lap-stone, p. 3354.
lapstreak, p. 3354.
lapstreaked, p. 3354.
lapstreaker, p. 3354.
lapsus, p. 3354.
lapwing, p. 3354.
laquear, p. 3354.
Lar^1, p. 3354.
lararium, p. 3354.
larboard, p. 3354.
larbowlines, p. 3354.
larcener, p. 3354.
larcenist, p. 3354.
larch, p. 3355.
larch-bark, p. 3355.
larchen, p. 3355.
lard, p. 3355.
lard, p. 3355.
lardacein, p. 3355.
lardaceous, p. 3355.
lard-boiler, p. 3355.
lard-cooler, p. 3355.
larder^1, p. 3355.
larder^2, lardure, p. 3355.

larderellite, p. 3355.
larderer, p. 3355.
larder-house, p. 3355.
lardery, p. 3355.
lardiner, p. 3355.
larding-needle, p. 3355.
lard-oil, p. 3355.
lard-press, p. 3355.
lard-renderer, p. 3355.
lardry, p. 3355.
lardstone, p. 3355.
lardy, p. 3355.
Larentia, p. 3355.
Larentidæ, Larentiidæ, p. 3355.
lareover, p. 3356.
largamente, p. 3356.
large, p. 3356.
large, p. 3356.
last^1, p. 3360-3361.
last^3, p. 3361.
last^5, p. 3361.
latch-string, p. 3363.
latent, p. 3363-3364.
lateral, p. 3364.
Latiner, p. 3368.
latitude, p. 3368-3369.
latrant, p. 3369.
latus, p. 3370.
laughter, p. 3371.
lavender^2, p. 3374.
law, p. 3375-3377.
law-worthy, p. 3379.
lay^1, p. 3381.
lazzarone, p. 3383.
league^2, p. 3388.
leave^1, p. 3393.
ledger-book, p. 3397.
legality, p. 3400.
Legendrian, p. 3401.
legitimate, p. 3403.
Leibnitzian, p. 3404.
lemma, p. 3405.
lemniscate, p. 3405-3406.
lemniscatic, p. 3406.
lemon, p. 3406.
lemon-yellow, p. 3406.
length, p. 3407-3408.
Leo, p. 3410.
Leonides, p. 3410.
Lepus, p. 3416.
level^1, p. 3425.

leveling, levelling, p. 3426.
leveling-instrument, p. 3426.
leveling-screw, p. 3426.
leveling-staff, p. 3426.
lever^1, p. 3427.
levitation, p. 3428.
levity, p. 3428.
lherzolite, p. 3430.
liar, p. 3430.
libella, p. 3431.
libertarian, p. 3433.
liberty, p. 3433.
libra, p. 3434.
libration, p. 3434-3435.
licentiate^2, p. 3435.
light^1, p. 3445-3446.
likelihood, p. 3452-3453.
likeness, p. 3453.
lilac, p. 3453.
limacon, p. 3455.
limb^2, p. 3455
69: limbo, p. 3456.
limit, p. 3458.
limit, p. 3458.
limitary, p. 3458.
limitation, p. 3458-3459.
limited, p. 3459.
limit-point, p. 3459.
line^1, p. 3462-3463.
linear, p. 3464.
line-coordinate, p. 3465.
line-equation, p. 3465.
line-integral, p. 3465.
lineolinear, p. 3465.
lineopolar, p. 3465.
link^1, p. 3467-3468.
linkage, p. 3468.
link-motion, p. 3468.
linkwork, p. 3468.
lipogram, p. 3472.
lippy^2, lippie, p. 3473.
liquid, p. 3474.
listred, p. 3478.
liter^2, litre^1, p. 3479.
literal, p. 3479.
litigious, p. 3483.
liver-color, p. 3488.
livid, p. 3489.
lizard, p. 3489-3490.
load^2, p. 3490-3491.
local, p. 3495-3496.

locale, p. 3496.
localization, p. 3496.
Lockian, p. 3498.
log^4, p. 3503.
log, p. 3503.
logarithm, p. 3503-3504.
logarithmic, p. 3504.
logic, p. 3504-3505.
logical, p. 3505.
logicality, p. 3505.
logicalization, p. 3505.
logicalize, p. 3505.
logically, p. 3505.
logicalness, p. 3505.
logic-chopping, p. 3505.
logician, p. 3505.
logicianer, p. 3505.
logicize, p. 3505.
logics, p. 3505.
logist, p. 3505.
logistic, p. 3505.
logistics, p. 3505.
logocyclic, p. 3505.
logometer^1, p. 3506.
Logos, p. 3506.
long^1, p. 3509-3510.
longitude, p. 3512.
longitudinal, p. 3512.
loxocosm, p. 3532.
loxodrome, p. 3532.
loxodromic, p. 3532.
lozenge, p. 3532.
lucida, p. 3534.
Lucifer, p. 3534.
luck^1, p. 3535.
lucky^1, p. 3535-3536.
ludicrously, p. 3537.
Ludolphian, Ludolfian, p. 3537.
lug^1, p. 3537.
lug^3, p. 3538.
lug-perch, p. 3538.
luke^1, p. 3538.
luminary, p. 3540.
luminosity, p. 3540.
lunar, p. 3541.
lunarian, p. 3541.
lunarist, p. 3541.
lunariun, p. 3542.
lune^1, p. 3542.
lunisolar, p. 3543.
lunistice, p. 3543.

lunistitial, p. 3543.
lunitidal, p. 3543.
lunula, p. 3544.
lunule, p. 3544.
Lupus[1], p. 3544.
lurid, p. 3545.
luteous[1], p. 3548.
lyceum, p. 3551.
lynx, p. 3554.
Lyra, p. 3555.
lyraid, p. 3556.
M, p. 3557.
Macaroni, p. 3558.
machina, p. 3560.
machine, p. 3560.
macrocosm, p. 3563.
macrocosmic, p. 3563.
macroscian, p. 3565.
macula, p. 3566.
madam-town, p. 3567.
Magellanic, p. 3571.
magic, p. 3571-3572.
magister, p. 3572.
magisterial, p. 3572.
magistery, p. 3572-3573.
magistral, p. 3573.
magistrality, p. 3573.
magistrally, p. 3573.
magnanimity, p. 3573.
magnification, p. 3576.
magnificence, p. 3576.
magnitude, p. 3577.
maidenhead, p. 3580.
maieutic, p. 3581.
maigre day, p. 3581.
maim, p. 3582.
main[1], p. 3582.
main[2], p. 3582.
major, p. 3585.
majoration, p. 3585.
makebate, p. 3588.
malachite-green, p. 3589.
malconceived, p. 3591.
malefic, p. 3592-3593.
malevolent, p. 3593.
malgrado, p. 3593.
manifold, p. 3611-3612.
manifoldness, p. 3612.
70: mansion, p. 3616.
mantissa, p. 3618.
map[1], p. 3622.

map-measurer, p. 3623.
mappemounde, p. 3623.
mappery, p. 3623.
mappist, p. 3623.
mark[1], p. 3631-3632.
mark[2], p. 3633.
Marlowism, p. 3635.
maroon[1], p. 3636.
marriage, p. 3637.
Mars, p. 3638.
Martinish, p. 3643.
Martinist, p. 3643.
mass[2], p. 3648.
Massalia, p. 3649.
mass-area, p. 3649.
mass-center, p. 3649.
mass-vector, p. 3650.
master[1], p. 3650-3651.
matachin, matachine,
  p. 3654-3655.
match-terms, p. 3656.
material, p. 3657.
materialism, p. 3658.
materialist, p. 3658.
materialistic, p. 3658.
materiality, p. 3658.
materiarian, p. 3658.
materiate, p. 3658.
materiantion, p. 3658.
materiature, p. 3658.
mathematic, p. 3659.
mathematical, p. 3659.
mathematically, p. 3659.
mathematician, p. 3659.
mathematicize, p. 3659.
mathematicize, p. 3659.
mathematics, p. 3659.
mathesis, p. 3659.
matricula, p. 3660.
matriculant, p. 3660.
matriculant, p. 3660.
matriculate, p. 3660.
matriculate, p. 3660.
matriculate, p. 3660.
matriculation, p. 3660.
matriculator, p. 3660.
matrix, p. 3661.
matter, p. 3661.
matterless, p. 3663.
maund, p. 3665.
maxim, p. 3667.

maximal, p. 3667.
maximal, p. 3667.
maximally, p. 3667.
maximum, p. 3667.
mean[1], p. 3673.
mean[3], p. 3674.
meander, p. 3674.
meander, p. 3675.
meaning, p. 3675.
measureable, p. 3676.
measurableness, p. 3676.
measure, p. 3676.
measure, p. 3677.
measurement, p. 3677.
measurer, p. 3677.
measuring-chain, p. 3677.
mechanic, p. 3678-3679.
mechanical, p. 3679.
mechanician, p. 3679.
mechanics, p. 3679.
mechanism, p. 3679.
mechanist, p. 3680.
mediacy, p. 3681.
mediacy, p. 3681.
mediate, p. 3682.
mediate, p, 3682.
mediately, p. 3682.
mediateness, p. 3682.
mediation, p. 3682.
meditation, p. 3686.
medium, p. 3686-3687.
megacosm, p. 3690.
megadyne, p. 3690.
magaerg, p. 3690.
megafarad, p. 3690.
Megarian, p. 3691.
Megaric, p. 3691.
meliorism, p. 3697.
member, p. 3703.
memoria technica, p. 3705.
mempry, p. 3705.
menstrual, p. 3709.
mensuration, p. 3710.
mensurative, p. 3710.
mental[1], p. 3710.
mental[2], p. 3710.
mental[3], p. 3710.
mentery, p. 3710.
mercurialist, p. 3714.
Mercury, p. 3714.
mere, p. 3715.

meridian, p. 3717.
meridian-circle, p. 3717.
meridian-mark, p. 3717.
meridional, p. 3717.
meridionality, p. 3717.
meridionally, p. 3717.
meromorphic, p. 3719.
mesolabe, p. 3724.
metabatic, p. 3729.
metacenter, metacentre, p. 3729.
metagnostic, p. 3730.
metagnostics, p. 3730.
metamathematics, p. 3732.
metaphysical, p. 3734.
metaphysically, p. 3734.
metaphysician, p. 3734.
metaphysics, p. 3734.
metapsychosis, p. 3735.
metaptosis, p. 3735.
metatatic, p. 3736.
metempiric, p. 3737.
metempirical, p. 3737.
metempiricism, p. 3737.
metempiricist, p. 3737.
metempsychosis, p. 3737.
metemptosis, p. 3737.
meter^3, metre^2, p. 3739.
metesthetic, p. 3739.
metesthetism, p. 3739.
metewand, p. 3739.
method, p. 3740.
Methodist, p. 3741.
methodization, p. 3741.
methodology, p. 3741.
metrete, p. 3742.
Metonic, p. 3742.
metric^1, p. 3742.
metric^3, p. 3742.
metrics^1, p. 3743.
metrology, p. 3743.
micro-, p. 3747.
microcosm, p. 3747.
microgram, p. 3750.
microhm, p. 3750.
micrometer, p. 3750.
micrometer-screw, p. 3750.
micromillimeter, micromillimetre, p. 3751.
micron, p. 3751.
middle, p. 3754-3755.
mile, p. 3760.
milk-punch, p. 3763.

Milky Way, p. 3763.
71: milli-, p. 3766.
milliampere, p. 3766.
milliard, p. 3766.
milliare^1, p. 3766.
milliare^2, p. 3766.
milligram, milligramme, p. 3766.
milliliter, millilitre, p. 3766.
millimeter, millimetre, p. 3766.
million^1, p. 3766.
millionth, p. 3767.
millistere, p. 3767.
mina^1, p. 3770.
mind^1, p. 3771.
minim, p. 3775.
minimum, p. 3775.
minor, p. 3778.
minuend, p. 3780.
minus, p. 3780.
minute^2, p. 3780-3781.
miskal, p. 3792.
mittimus, p. 3806.
mixed^1, p. 3806.
mnemonic, p. 3807.
mnemonical, p. 3807.
mnemonician, p. 3807.
mnemonics, p. 3807.
mnemonist, p. 3807.
mnemotechnic, p. 3807.
mnemotechnics, p. 3807.
mnemotechny, p. 3807.
modal, p. 3811.
modality, p. 3811.
modality, p. 3811.
mode^1, p. 3811-3812.
moderation, p. 3813.
moderator, p. 3813-3814.
modicum, p. 3815.
modification, p. 2815.
modius, p. 3815.
modular, p. 3816.
module, p. 3816.
modulus, p. 3816-3817.
modus, p. 3817.
Molinist^2, p. 3823.
moment, p. 3826-3827.
momental, p. 3827.
momentum, p. 3827.
monad, p. 3827.
monadelphic, p. 3828.
monadic, p. 3828.
monadism, p. 3829.

monadology, p. 3829.
monism, p. 3834.
monist, p. 3834.
monistic, p. 3834.
monoaxal, p. 3836.
monoceros, p. 3837.
monochromatic, p. 3837.
monodromic, p. 3839.
monogeneous, p. 3839.
monogenous, p. 3839.
monomachy, p. 3840.
Monomial, p. 3841.
monotonous, p. 3845.
Mons Maenalus, p. 3846.
Mons Mensae, p. 3846.
month, p. 3848.
mood^2, p. 3850.
moon-culminating, p. 3851.
moon-calmination, p. 3851.
moral, p. 3855.
morality, p. 3856.
moralization, p. 3856.
motion, p. 3872-3873.
motive, p. 3873-3874.
motivity, p. 3874.
motor, p. 3874.
multeity, p. 3892.
multidimensional, p. 3893.
multifarious, p. 3893.
multiform, p. 3893.
multiformity, p. 3893.
multigenerate, p. 3893.
multilateral, p. 3893.
multinomial, p. 3893.
multiple, p. 3894.
multiplex, p. 3894.
multiplicand, p. 3894.
multiplication, p. 3894.
multiplicity, p. 3894.
multiply, p. 3894-3895.
multitude, p. 3895.
mumchance, p. 3896.
mundane, p. 3898.
mural, p. 3900.
Musca, p. 3903.
mutability, p. 3913.
mutchkin, p. 3913.
mutual, p. 3916.
myriagram, myriagramme, p. 3921.
myrialiter, myrialitre, p. 3921.

myriameter, myriametre, p. 3921.
myriare, p. 3921.
N, p. 3927.
nadir, p. 3927.
nail, p. 3928-3929.
naked, p. 3930.
nap², p. 3932.
nation, p. 3939.
native, p. 3940.
nativism, p. 3940.
nativist, p. 3940.
nativistic, p. 3940.
nativity, p. 3940.
natural, p. 3941-3942.
nature, p. 3943-3944.
n-dimensional, p. 3948.
neap¹, p. 3948.
nebula, p. 3950.
nebular, p. 3950.
nebulous, p. 3950.
necessarian, p. 3951.
necessarianism, p. 3951.
necessary, p. 3951.
necessitarian, p. 3951.
necessity, p. 3951-3952.
necromancy, p. 3953.
necromantic, p. 3954.
need, p. 3955.
negation, p. 3958.
negationist, p. 3958.
negative, p. 3958.
negativeness, p. 3958.
negativism, p. 3958.
negativity, p. 3958.
72: negus¹, p. 3961.
neoid, p. 3965.
neo-Kantian, p. 3965.
Neopythagorean, p. 3966.
nephroid, p. 3968.
Neptune, p. 3969.
net¹, p. 3974.
Newtonian, p. 3983.
nihilism, p. 3994.
nihilist, p. 3994.
nilfaciend, p. 3994.
nilfacient, p. 3994.
nilfactor, p. 3994.
nilpotent, p. 3995.
nineteen, p. 3996.

noddy², p. 4006.
node, p. 4006.
node-and-flecnode, p. 4006.
node-and-spinode, p. 4006.
node-couple, p. 4006.
node-cusp, p. 4006.
node-plane, p. 4006.
node-triplet, p. 4006.
nodical, p. 4006.
noematic, p. 4007.
noemayical, p. 4007.
noematically, p. 4007.
noemics, p. 4007.
noetic, p. 4007.
nolition, p. 4008.
nolleity, p. 4008.
nome³, p. 4009.
nominal, p. 4009.
nominalism, p. 4009.
nomology, p. 4010.
nonagesimal, p. 4011.
nonagon, p. 4011.
non-ego, p. 4012.
non-egoistical, p. 4012-4013.
nonentity, p. 4013.
non-essential, p. 4013.
non-existence, p. 4013.
non-existent, p. 4013.
nonfeasance, p. 4013.
non-folium, p. 4013.
nonillion, p. 4013.
nonius, p. 4013.
nonsubstantialism, p. 4015.
nonsubstantialist, p. 4015.
norma, p. 4017.
normal, p. 4017.
normalcy, p. 4017.
normative, p. 4017.
north, p. 4018.
northeast, p. 4018.
northern, p. 4018.
northwest, p. 4019.
notation, p. 4022.
nothing, p. 4025-4026.
notion, p. 4026.
notional, p. 4026.
not-self, p. 4029.
noumenal, p. 4029.
noumenon, p. 4029.

nous, p. 4030.
nuance, p. 4033.
nubecula, p. 4034.
number, p. 4038.
number, p. 4038.
numerable, p. 4039.
numeral, p. 4039.
numerant, p. 4039.
numerary, p. 4039.
numerate, p. 4039.
numeration, p. 4039.
numerative, p. 4039.
numerator, p. 4039.
numerical, p. 4039.
nutation, p. 4044.
nychthemeron, p. 4046.
O, p. 4049.
object, p. 4056.
objectification, p. 4056.
objectify, p. 4056.
objective, p. 4057.
objectivism, p. 4057.
objectivity, p. 4057.
objectivize, p. 4057.
objectize, p. 4057.
object-object, p. 4057.
objectual, p. 4058.
obligation, p. 4059.
obligatum, p. 4059.
oblique, p. 4059-4060.
obliquity, p. 4060.
Oblong, p. 4061.
obscure, p. 4061-4062.
observation, p. 4064.
observational, p. 4064.
observatory, p. 4065.
observer, p. 4065.
obverse, p. 4069-4070.
obversion, p. 4070.
Occamism, p. 4070.
Occamist, p. 4070.
occasion, p. 4070-4071.
occasional, p. 4071.
occasionalism, p. 4071.
occasive, p. 4071.
occident, p. 4071.
occult, p. 4073.
occultation, p. 4073.
occultism, p. 4073.

occultist, p. 4073.
octad, p. 4077.
octadic, p. 4077.
octagon, p. 4077.
octahedral, p. 4077.
octahedron, p. 4077.
Octans Hadleianus, p. 4077.
octant, p. 4077.
octolateral, p. 4079.
odd, p. 4081.
omnipercipience, p. 4106.
omnipercipient, p. 4106.
one, p. 4111.
ontological, p. 4115.
ontologically, p. 4115.
ontology, p. 4115.
operation, p. 4121.
operator, p. 4122.
Ophiuchus, p. 4125.
opinion, p. 4127.
opponency, p. 4130.
opponent, p. 4130.
opposite, p. 4131.
opposition, p. 4131.
optimism, p. 4133.
optimist, p. 4133.
orange, p. 4136.
orb[1], p. 4138-4139.
orbit, p. 4139.
73: order, p. 4142-4144.
order-class, p. 4145.
ordinal, p. 4145.
ordinate, p. 4147.
orectic, p. 4148.
organic, p. 4150.
organon, p. 4151.
origin, p. 4154.
original, p. 4155.
oriolus, p. 4156.
Orion, p. 4156.
orrery, p. 4160.
orthogon, p. 4162.
orthogonal, p. 4162.
orthogonally, p. 4162.
orthographic, p. 4162.
orthographically, p. 4162.
orthomorphic, p. 4162.
ortive, p. 4164.
oscillation, p. 4165.

oscnode, p. 4166.
osculant, p. 4166.
oscular, p. 4166.
osculate, p. 4166.
osculatrix, p. 4166.
ostensive, p. 4169.
ounce[1], p. 4177.
outness, p. 4186.
oval[1], p. 4192.
P, p. 4221.
pace, p. 4221.
pale, p. 4240.
palm, p. 4246.
panel, p. 4258.
pangeometry, p. 4259.
pangrammatist, p. 4259.
pantology, p. 4264.
panometric, p. 4264.
pantometry, p. 4264.
parabola[2], p. 4272.
parabolic[2], p. 4272.
paraboliform, p. 4272.
paraboloid, p. 4272.
paraboloidal, p. 4272.
paracentric, p. 4272.
paradox, p. 4274-4275.
paradoxer, p. 4275.
paradoxical, p. 4275.
parallatic, p. 4277.
parallax, p. 4277.
parallel, p. 4277.
parallelogram, p. 4278.
parallelogrammatic, p. 4278.
paralogism, p. 4279.
paralogy, p. 4279.
parameter, p. 4280.
parasang, p. 4283.
part, p. 4302-4303.
partial, p. 4304-4305.
partibility, p. 4305.
partible, p. 4305.
particate, p. 4305.
particular, p. 4306.
partition, p. 4308.
parva logicalia, p. 4310.
passion, p. 4318.
passive, p. 4319.
patient, p. 4328.
Pavo, p. 4336.

peach-blossom, p. 4341.
pedal, p. 4351-4352.
pedimeter, p. 4355.
pedimetric, p. 4355.
pedimetry, p. 4355.
Pegasus, p. 4359.
pelecoid, p. 4361.
pencil, p. 4369.
pendulum, p. 4371.
penetrability, p. 4372.
peninvariant, p. 4374.
penny, p. 4376.
pennyweight, p. 4377.
pensioner, p. 4378.
penta-, p. 4378.
pentace, p. 4378.
pentad, p. 4378-4379.
pentagon, p. 4379.
pentagram, p. 4379.
pentahedral, p. 4379.
pentagrammatic, p. 4379.
pentahedrical, p. 4379.
pentahedron, p. 4379.
pentalemma, p. 4379.
pentalpha, p. 4379.
pentagle, p. 4379.
pentangular, p. 4379.
penumbra, p. 4381.
peonia, p. 4382.
74: percase, p. 4386.
perceivable, p. 4386.
perceive, p. 4386.
percentage, p. 4386.
percentile, p. 4386.
percept, p. 4386.
perceptibility, p. 4386.
perceptible, p. 4386.
perceptibleness, p. 4386.
perceptibly, p. 4386.
perception, p. 4386-4387.
perceptional, p. 4387.
perceptive, p. 4387.
perceptiveness, p. 4387.
perceptivity, p. 4387.
perceptivity, p. 4387.
perceptual, p. 4387.
pearch, p. 4387.
percipency, p. 4388.
percipiency, p. 4388.

percipient, p. 4388.
perdurability, p. 4390.
perdurable, p. 4390.
peremptory, p. 4391.
perfect, p. 4391-4392.
perfection, p. 4392.
periastral, p. 4395.
periastron, p. 4395.
perigean, p. 4398.
perigee, p. 4398.
perigon, p. 4398.
perigonal, p. 4398.
perihelion, perihelium, p. 4398.
perihelioned, p. 4398.
perijove, p. 4398.
perimeter, p. 4399.
perimetric, p. 4399.
peroid, p. 4400.
peripatetic, p. 4401.
peripatetical, p. 4401.
Peripateticism, p. 4401.
periphery, p. 4401.
periphratic, p. 4401.
periphraxy, p. 4402.
perisaturnium, p. 4402.
Periscii, p. 4402.
perk^2, p. 4406.
permanent, p. 4407.
permutant, p. 4408.
permutation, p. 4408.
perpendicular, p. 4410.
Peroetuant, p. 4410.
perrotatory, p. 4412.
perse, p. 4412.
Persepoliation, p. 4412-4413.
person, p. 4414.
personal, p. 4415.
personality, p. 4415.
perspective, p. 4416-4417.
persymmetric, p. 4419.
persymmetrical, p. 4419.
pertinent, p. 4419.
perturbation, p. 4420.
perturbation, p. 4420.
perturbative, p. 4420.
perverse, p. 4421.
pervision, p. 4421.
pessimission, p. 4422.
pessimist, p. 4422.
pessimistic, p. 4422.

pessimistical, p. 4422.
petitio principii, p. 4426.
pfaffian, p. 4431.
Pfaff's equation, p. 4431.
Pfaff's problem, p. 4431.
phenomenal, p. 4441.
phenomenalism, p. 4441.
phenomenalist, p. 4441.
phenomenality, p. 4441.
phenomenalize, p. 4441.
phenomenally, p. 4441.
phenomenism, p. 4441.
phenomenist, p. 4441.
phenomenize, p. 4441.
phenomenological, p. 4441.
phenomenology, p. 4441.
Phenomenon, p. 4441.
philosoph, p. 4445.
philosophaster, p. 4445.
philosophate, p. 4445.
philosophation, p. 4445.
philosophdom, p. 4445.
philosophema, p. 4445.
philosopheme, p. 4445.
philosopher, p. 4445.
philosophic, p. 4445.
philosophical, p. 4446.
philosophically, p. 4446.
philosophicalness, p. 4446.
philosophise, philosophiser, p. 4446.
philosophism, p. 4446.
philosophistic, p. 4446.
philosophistical, p. 4446.
philosophize, p. 4446.
philosophy, p. 4446.
Phobos, p. 4448.
phoronomics, p. 4452.
phoronomy, p. 4452.
photogrammetry, p. 4454.
phototachometer, p. 4456.
phototachometrical, p. 4456.
phototachometry, p. 4456.
phototheodolite, p. 4456.
physic, p. 4464.
physicomathematics, p. 4465.
physicomental, p. 4465.
physicophilosophy, p. 4465.
physics, p. 4465.
physiophilosophy, p. 4466.
pi^2, p. 4469.

pik, p. 4483.
pill-box, p. 4489.
pinch-plane, p. 4495.
pink^2, p. 4499.
pint, p. 4502.
pipe^1, p. 4504.
Pippian, p. 4507.
Pisces, p. 4510.
Piscis Austrinus, p. 4510.
Piscis Volans, p. 4510.
place, p. 4520.
plain^1, p. 4525.
plane^1, p. 4527-4528.
planet, p. 4528.
plane-table, p. 4528-4529.
plane-table, p. 4529.
plane-tabler, p. 4529.
plane-tabling, p. 4529.
planetarium, p. 4529.
planetary, p. 4529.
planetic, p. 4529.
planetical, p. 4529.
planeting, p. 4529.
planetist, p. 4529.
planetoid, p. 4529.
planimeter, p. 4529-4530.
planimetric, p. 4530.
planimetry, p. 4530.
planisphere, p. 4530.
planispheric, p. 4530.
plano-concave, p. 4530.
plano-conical, p. 4530.
plano-convex, p. 4530.
planographist, p. 4530.
plano-horizontal, p. 4530.
planometry, p. 4531.
plastic, p. 4535.
platic, p. 4539.
Platonic^1, p. 4540.
Platonism, p. 4540.
Platonist, p. 4541.
Platonist, p. 4541.
Platonistic, p. 4541.
Platonizer, p. 4541.
pleasure, p. 4549.
Pleiad, p. 4551.
plenist, p. 4552.
plenum, p. 4553.
75: plexus, p. 4557-4558.
plot^1, p. 4561.

plum¹, p. 4565.
plump¹, p. 4568.
plus, p. 4571.
pneumatology, p. 4574.
pococurante, p. 4577.
pococurantism, p. 4577.
point¹, p. 4582-4584.
polar, p. 4589.
polarity, p. 4590.
pole², p. 4590.
poll³, p. 4597.
polygon, p. 4603.
polygonal, p. 4603.
polygynoecial, p. 4604.
polygynous, p. 4604.
polyhedral, p. 4604.
polyhedric, p. 4604.
polyhedrical, p. 4604.
polyhedrometric, p. 4604.
polyhedron, p. 4604.
polylemma, p. 4604.
polynome, p. 4606.
polynomial, p. 4606.
pons, p. 4616.
porism, p. 4626.
porismatic, p. 4626.
poristic, p. 4626.
poser, p. 4635.
posit, p. 4635.
position, p. 4635.
positive, p. 4635-4636.
positivism, p. 4636.
Positivist, p. 4636.
positivistic, p. 4636.
posology, p. 4636.
posse, p. 4636.
possibility, p. 4638.
possible, p. 4638.
postulate, p. 4645-4646.
postulate, p. 4646.
potential, p. 4650.
potentiality, p. 4650-4651.
potentialize, p. 4651.
potentially, p. 4651.
pound¹, p. 4657-4658.
poundal, p. 4658.
power¹, p. 4662-4663.
practice, p. 4665.
pragmatic, p. 4667.
pram¹, p. 4669.

precession, p. 4676.
precessional, p. 4676.
precise, p. 4678-4679.
precision, p. 4679.
precisive, p. 4679.
precritical, p. 4681.
predesignate, p. 4682.
predesignate, p. 4682.
predesignation, p. 4682.
predesignatory, p. 4682.
predetermination, p. 4682.
predicable, p. 4682-4683.
predicament, p. 4683.
predicamental, p. 4683.
predicate, p. 4683.
predicate, p. 4683.
predication, p. 4683.
predicative, p. 4683.
predicatory, p. 4683.
pregnant, p. 4688.
preindesignate, p. 4689.
preinstruct, p. 4689.
preintimation, p. 4689.
prejacent, p. 4689.
prescind, p. 4700-4701.
prescindent, p. 4701.
prescission, p. 4701.
presentable, p. 4703.
presentation, p. 4703.
presentation², p. 4704.
presentationism, p. 4704.
presentationist, p. 4704.
presentative, p. 4704.
presential, p. 4704.
presentially, p. 4704.
presentialness, p. 4704.
presentiate, p. 4704.
presentient, p. 4704.
presentific, p. 4704.
presentificly, p. 4704.
presentiment, p. 4704.
presentimental, p. 4704.
presention, p. 4704.
presentive, p. 4704.
presentiveness, p. 4704.
pressly, p. 4708.
pressural, p. 4709.
pressure, p. 4709.
presupposition, p. 4711.
preteach, p. 4711.

preternatural, p. 4711.
prevaricator, p. 4711.
primary, p. 4723-4724.
prime, p. 4724-4725.
primigenious, p. 4726.
primitive, p. 4726.
primitivity, p. 4727.
primordial, p. 4727.
primovant, p. 4727.
Primuleæ, p. 4728.
primulin, p. 4728.
primum frigidum, p. 4728.
primum mobile, p. 4728.
principal, p. 4729-4730.
principium, p. 4730.
principle, p. 4730-4731.
prism, p. 4735.
prismatic, p. 4735-4736.
privation, p. 4738.
privative, p. 4738.
76: probability, p. 4741.
Probable, p. 4741.
problem, p. 4742-4743.
problematic, p. 4743.
procatarctic, p. 4744.
procatarctical, p. 4744.
Procyon, p. 4751.
product, p. 4753.
proegumenal, p. 4753.
proemptosis, p. 4754.
professor, p. 4755-4756.
profound, p. 4757.
progress, p. 4760.
progression, p. 4760.
prohibition, p. 4761.
project, p. 4761.
projection, p. 4762-4763.
projective, p. 4763.
projectivity, p. 4763.
projector, p. 4763-4764.
prolate, p. 4764.
prolegomenon, p. 4764.
prolepsis, p. 4764.
proleptic, p. 4764.
promiscuity, p. 4767.
proof, p. 4772-4773.
proper, p. 4776.
property, p. 4777.
proportion, p. 4780.
proportional, p. 4781.

proposition, p. 4781-4782.
propositional, p. 4782.
propositionally, p. 4782.
propositum, p. 4782.
proproctor, p. 4783.
prosthaphæresis, p. 4790.
protension, p. 4794.
protensity, p. 4794.
protensive, p. 4794.
prototype, p. 4800.
prove, p. 4802.
provectant, p. 4803.
provector, p. 4803.
proxy, p. 4808.
pseudodox, p. 4815.
pseudospherical, p. 4818.
psychal, p. 4821.
psycheometry, p. 4821.
psychic, p. 4821.
psychical, p. 4821.
psychically, p. 4821.
psychics, p. 4821.
psychism, p. 4821.
psychist, p. 4821.
psychoblast, p 4821.
psychodectic, p. 4821.
psychodometer, p. 4821.
psychodynamic, p. 4821.
psychodynamics, p. 4821.
psycho-ethical, p. 4821.
psychogenesis, p. 4821.
psychogenetical, p. 4821.
psychogenetically, p. 4821.
psychogeny, p. 4821.
psychogonic, p. 4821.
psychogonical, p. 4821.
psychogony, p. 4821.
psychographic, p. 4821.
psychography, p. 4821.
psychological, p. 4822.
psychology, p. 4822.
psychomachy, p. 4822.
psychomancy, p. 4822.
psychomantic, p. 4822.
psychometric, p. 4822.
psychometrical, p. 4822.
psychometrize, p. 4822.
psychomotor, p. 4822.
psychoneurology, p. 4822.
psychoneurosis, p. 4822.

psychonomy, p. 4822.
psychonosology, p. 4822.
psychopannychism, p. 4822.
psychopannychist, p. 4822.
psychoparesis, p. 4822.
psychopath, p. 4822.
psychopathic, p. 4822.
psychopathist, p. 4822.
psychophysic, p. 4822.
psychophysical, p. 4822.
psychophysicist, p. 4822.
psychophysics, p. 4822.
psychophysiological, p. 4822.
psychophysiology, p. 4822.
psychoplasm, p. 4822.
psychoplasmic, p. 4822.
psychopomp, p. 4822.
psychoscope, p. 4822.
psychosensorial, p. 4823.
psychosensory, p. 4823.
psychosis, p. 4823.
psychosomatic, p. 4823.
psychosophy, p. 4823.
psychostasia, p. 4823.
psychostasy, p. 4823.
psychostatic, p. 4823.
psychostatical, p. 4823.
psychostatically, p. 4823.
psychostatics, p. 4823.
psychotheism, p. 4823.
psychotherapeutic, p. 4823.
psychotherapeutics, p. 4823.
psychotherapy, p. 4823.
Ptolemaic, p. 4828.
Ptolemaist, p. 4828.
pulley, p. 4838.
pulsion, p. 4842.
puncheon[2], p. 4846.
punctate, p. 4846.
punctated, p. 4846.
pure, p. 4853.
purple, p. 4857.
pyramid, p. 4872-4873.
pyramidoid, p. 4873.
Pyrrhonic, p. 4878.
Pythagorean, p. 4878.
pyxis, p. 4880.
Q.E.D., p. 4881.
Q.E.F., p. 4881.
Q.E.I., p. 4881.

quadrable, p. 4882.
quadrangle, p. 4882.
quadrans, p. 4882-4883.
quadrant, p. 4883.
quadrantal, p. 4883.
quadrantal, p. 4883.
quadrat, p. 4883.
quadrate, p. 4883.
quadratic, p. 4883-4884.
quadratically, p. 4884.
quadratocubic, p. 4884.
quadrator, p. 4884.
quadratrix, p. 4884.
quadrature, p. 4884.
quadrible, p. 4884.
quadric, p. 4884.
quadricone, p. 4885.
quadricuspidal, p. 4885.
quadriderivative, p. 4885.
quadrilateral, p. 4885.
quadrilateralness, p. 4885.
quadrillion, p. 4886.
quadrinomial, p. 4886.
quadrinominal, p. 4886.
quadrinvariant, p. 4886.
quadripartite, p. 4886.
quadriplanar, p. 4886.
quadriplicated, p. 4886.
quadriquadric, p. 4886.
quadrisection, p. 4886.
quadritactic, p. 4887.
quadrivial, p. 4887.
quadrivium, p. 4887.
quadro-quadro-quartic, p. 488
quadruplane, p. 4887.
quadruple, p. 4887.
quadruplicate, p. 4887.
quadruplicate, p. 4887.
quadruplication, p. 4887.
quadruplicity, p. 4887.
quadruply, p. 4888.
quæsitum, p. 4888.
quale[4], p. 4890.
qualifiable, p. 4890.
qualification, p. 4890.
qualificative, p. 4890.
qualify, p. 4890.
qualitative, p. 4891.
quality, p. 4891-4892.
quantative, p. 4892.

quantic, p. 4892.
quantical, p. 4892.
quantification, p. 4892.
quantitative, p. 4892.
quantitativeness, p. 4892.
quantitive, p 4892.
quantity, p. 4892-4893.
quantuplicity, p. 4893.
quart^1, p. 4896.
quartan, p. 4896.
quarter^1, p. 4896.
quarter-aspect, p. 4897.
quarter-cask, p. 4897.
quaternary, p. 4901.
quaternion, p. 4901.
quaternion, p. 4901.
quaternionist, p. 4901.
quaternity, p. 4901.
question, p. 4907-4908.
questionist, p. 4908.
quidditative, p. 4911.
quiddity, p. 4911.
quinary, p. 4914.
quincuncial, p. 4914.
quincunx, p. 4914.
quindecagon, p. 4914.
quinquangular, p. 4915.
quinquepartite, p. 4915.
quinquesect, p. 4915.
quinquesection, p. 4915.
quintal, p. 4916.
quintessence, p. 4916.
quintessential, p. 4916.
quintic, p. 4916.
quintile, p. 4917.
quintillion, p. 4917.
quintuple, p. 4917.
quintuple, p. 4917.
quippian, p. 4917.
quodlibet, p. 4921.
quodlibetal, p. 4921.
quodlibetarian, p. 4921.
quodlibetic, p. 4921.
quodlibetical, p. 4921.
quodlibetically, p. 4921.
quote, p. 4922.
quotient, p. 4922.
quotiety, p. 4922.
R, p. 4923.

77: radial, p. 4931.
radian, p. 4931.
radiant, p. 4932.
radiation, p. 4932-4933.
radical, p. 4933.
radicand, p. 4933.
radiometer, p. 4934.
radirs, p. 4935.
radix, p. 4935.
Ramism, p. 4950.
Ramist, p. 4950.
random, p. 4954.
rank^2, p. 4956-4957.
rank-axis, p. 4957.
rank-curve, p. 4957.
rank-plane, p. 4958.
rank-point, p. 4958.
rank-radiant, p. 4958.
rank-surface, p. 4958.
rare^1, p. 4963.
rarefaction, p. 4964.
ratio, p. 4970-4971.
ratiocinant, p. 4971.
ratiocinate, p. 4971.
ratiocinate, p. 4971.
ratiocination, p. 4971.
ratiocinative, p. 4971.
rationability, p. 4971.
rationable, p. 4971.
rational, p. 4971-4972.
rationale, p. 4972.
rationalism, p. 4972.
rationalist, p. 4972.
rationalistic, p. 4972.
rationalistical, p. 4972.
rationalistically, p. 4972.
rationality, p. 4972.
rationalization, p. 4972.
rationalize, p. 4972.
rationalizer, p. 4972.
ratiuncule, p. 4972.
ray^1, p. 4978.
razor, p. 4979.
react, p. 4981.
reaction, p. 4981.
reaction-time, p. 4981.
reader, p. 4983.
ready-reckoner, p. 4984.
real^1, p. 4985.

realism, p. 4986.
realist, p. 4986.
realistic, p. 4986.
realistically, p. 4986.
reality^1, p. 4986.
realization, p. 4986.
ream^3, p. 4987.
reaper, p. 4988.
reason^1, p. 4990.
reason^1, p. 4990-4991.
reasonable, p. 4991.
reasoned, p. 4991.
reasoner, p. 4991.
reception, p. 4998.
receptive, p. 4998.
receptiveness, p. 4998.
receptivity, p. 4998.
reciprocal, p. 5000.
reciprocality, p. 5000.
reciprocally, p. 5000.
reciprocant, p. 5000.
reciprocantive, p. 5000.
reciprocate, p. 5000.
reciprocation, p. 5001.
reciprocity, p. 5001.
recitation, p. 5001.
reckmaster, p. 5002.
reckon, p. 5002.
reckoning, p. 5002-5003.
reckoning-penny, p. 5003.
reclamation, p. 5003.
reclination, p. 5003.
recline, p. 5003.
recognition^1, p. 5004.
recognize^1, p. 5004.
recollectedness, p. 5005.
recollection, p. 5005.
recollective, p. 5005.
rectangle, p. 5012.
rectangular, p. 5012.
rectangularity, p. 5012.
rectification, p. 5012-5013.
rectify, p. 5013.
recurring, p. 5015.
red^1, p. 5016.
redintegration, p. 5021.
reduce, p. 5024.
reductio ad absurdum, p. 5025.
reduction, p. 5025.

reduction-compasses, p. 5025.
reduction-formula, p. 5025.
reductive, p. 5025.
refigure, p. 5033.
reflect, p. 5034.
reflecting, p. 5034-5035.
reflectionist, p. 5035.
reflective, p. 5035.
reflectoire, p. 5035.
reflex, p. 5036.
reflexibility, p. 5036.
regent, p. 5045.
region, p. 5046-5047.
registrar, p. 5048.
registrary, p. 5048.
regress, p. 5049.
regression, p. 5049.
regula, p. 5050.
regular, p. 5050.
regulative, p. 5051.
regulus, p. 5051.
reification, p. 5052.
reify, p. 5052.
relate, p. 5057.
related, p. 5057.
relation, p. 5057-5058.
relational, p. 5058.
relationist, p. 5058.
relative, p. 5058-5059.
relativeness, p. 5059.
relativity, p. 5059.
relatum, p. 5059.
relief-perspective, p. 5062.
remember, p. 5068.
remembrance, p. 5068.
reminiscence, p. 5069.
reminiscent, p. 5069.
reminiscential, p. 5069.
remote, p. 5072.
remotely, p. 5072.
remoteness, p. 5072.
remotive, p. 5072.
rendezvous, p. 5076.
renown, p. 5078.
renowner, p. 5078.
repeat, p. 5082.
repetend, p. 5083.
replication, p. 5085.
represent, p. 5088.

representability, p. 5088.
representable, p. 5088.
representamen, p. 5088.
representation, p. 5088.
representational, p. 5089.
representationism, p. 5089.
representationist, p. 5089.
representative, p. 5089.
reproduction, p. 5091-5092.
reproductive, p. 5092.
reproductiveness, p. 5092.
reproductivity, p. 5092.
reptation, p. 5093.
repugnance, p. 5094.
repullulate, p. 5095.
repulsion, p. 5095.
78: resentment, p. 5100.
residual, p. 5102-5103.
residuate, p. 5103.
residuation, p. 5103.
residue, p. 5103.
resilience, p. 5103.
resistance, p. 5104.
resolution, p. 5105.
resolutive, p. 5106.
resolve, p. 5106.
resolvend, p. 5107.
resolvent, p. 5107.
respective, p. 5109.
respond, p. 5111.
respondent, p. 5111.
responsibility, p. 5112.
restraint, p. 5116.
restrict, p. 5116.
restrict, p. 5117.
restriction, p. 5117.
restrictive, p. 5117.
restringend, p. 5117.
restringent, p. 5117.
result, p. 5117.
resultant, p. 5117.
resultate, p. 5117.
resuscitation, p. 5119.
resuscitative, p. 5119.
retard, p. 5120.
retention, p. 5121.
retentive, p. 5121.
reticle, p. 5122.
reticule, p. 5122.

reticulum, p. 5122.
revelation, p. 5133.
revenant, p. 5133.
reverie, revery, p. 5136.
reversible, p. 5137.
revie, p. 5139.
revolution, p. 5142.
rhamphoid, p. 5147.
rheostatics, p. 5149.
rhinæthesia, p. 5151.
rhinæsthesis, p. 5151.
rhinæsthetics, p. 5151.
rhizic, p. 5154.
rhombicosidodecahedron, p. 5158.
rhomboid, p. 5158.
rhomboides, p. 5158.
rhomb-solid, p. 5158.
rhombus, p. 5158.
rhumb, rumb, p. 5159.
rhumb-line, p. 5159.
right, p. 5177.
right-handed, p. 5180.
rigid, p. 5180-5181.
rigidity, p. 5181.
ring-dial, p. 5186.
ring-vortex, p. 5188.
rise[1], p. 5192.
rising, p. 5193.
riverish, p. 5197.
road, p. 5199.
road-measurer, p. 5199.
roan[1], p. 5200.
Robervallian, p. 5202.
Robur Caroli, p. 5204.
rod[1], p. 5209.
rodman, p. 5210.
role, p. 5213.
roll, p. 5213.
rolling, p. 5215.
rolling, p. 5215.
Roman, p. 5216-5217.
rood, p. 5220.
root, p. 5224-5225.
roral, p. 5227.
rose, p. 5229-5230.
roseaker, p. 5230.
rose-pink, p. 5232.
rose-red, p. 5232.

A Comprehensive Bibliography

rosette, p. 5232.
Rosminianism, p. 5233.
rotary, p. 5236.
rotate, p. 5236.
rotation, p. 5236-5237.
rotational, p. 5237.
rotation-area, p. 5237.
rotative, p. 5237.
rotatory, p. 5237.
rotl, p. 5238.
rotor, p. 5238.
rottolo, p. 5239.
roulette, p. 5242.
round, p. 5242-5243.
rove[5], p. 5249.
row[2], p. 5249.
row[3], p. 5249.
royal, p. 5251.
ruby, p. 5256.
ruck[3], p. 5256.
ruddy, p. 5258.
rudiment, p. 5259.
Rudolphine, p. 5259.
rufescence, p. 5260.
rufescent, p. 5260.
rufous, p. 5262.
rulable, p. 5264.
rule[1], p. 5264-5265.
rule[1], p. 5265.
rule-driller, p. 5265.
ruler, p. 5265-5266.
rumfustian, p. 5267.
ruminate, p. 5267.
rumination, p. 5267.
rumper, p. 5268.
run[1], p. 5271-5272.
rundlet, runlet[2], p. 5273.
rupture, p. 5276.
russet, p. 5278.
rust-colored, p. 5280.
rusticate, p. 5280.
rustication, p. 5280.
S, p. 5285.
sack[1], p. 5291.
sagacious, p. 5302.
sagacity, p. 5302.
sage[1], p. 5302.
sage-green, p. 5303.
sagene[2], p. 5303.

sagitta, p. 5303.
Sagittarius, p. 5304.
sagittary, p. 5304.
Sagmarius, p. 5304.
sallow[2], p. 5313.
salmon-color, p. 5315.
salmon-pink, p. 5315.
same, p. 5323-5324.
sameness, p. 5324.
sample, p. 5325.
sanction, p. 5327.
sansculottide, p. 5336.
sapharensian, p. 5338.
sapience, p. 5338.
sapient, p. 5338.
sapphire, p. 5339-5340.
sapphirine[1], p. 5340.
sappy, p. 5340.
saros, p. 5345.
79: sarplar, sarpler, p. 5345.
sasse, p. 5347.
satelite, p. 5348.
satisfaction, p. 5350.
satisfy, p. 5350.
Saturn, p. 5351-5352.
Saturnian[1], p. 5352.
Saturnicentric, p. 5352.
Saturnine, p. 5352.
saucy, p. 5353-5354.
saum, p. 5354.
save[1], p. 5357-5358.
scale[2], p. 5369.
scale[3], p. 5369.
scalene, p. 5370.
scalenon, p. 5370.
scalenum, p. 5370.
scalet, p. 5381.
scenographer, p. 5385.
scenographic, p. 5385.
scenographically, p. 5385.
scenography, p. 5385.
Sceptrum Brandenburgicum, p. 5386.
Sceptrum et Manus Justiciae, p. 5386.
schediasm, p. 5387.
schema, p. 5387.
schematic, p. 5387.
schematism, p. 5387.

scheme, p. 5387-5388.
schemist, p. 5388.
schene, p. 5388.
scholar, p. 5392.
scholarch, p. 5392.
scholarship, p. 5392.
scholastic, p. 5392.
scholasticism, p. 5392-5393.
scholium, p. 5393.
school[1], p. 5393-5394.
school-name, p. 5394.
schuit, p. 5395.
schwartzian, p. 5395.
schwelle, p. 5395.
sciagraph, p. 5396.
sciagraphic, p. 5396.
sciagraphical, p. 5396.
sciagraphically, p. 5396.
sciagraphy, p. 5396.
sciametry, p. 5396.
sciatheric, p. 5396.
scibile, p. 5396.
science, p. 5396-5397.
sciential, p. 5397.
scientific, p. 5397.
scientifically, p. 5397.
scientist, p. 5397.
scientistic, p. 5397.
scintillant, p. 5398.
scintillation, p. 5398.
sciography, p. 5398.
scioptic, p. 5398-5399.
sciotheism, p. 5399.
score[1], p. 5408.
Scorpio, p. 5410.
Scotism, p. 5412.
Scotist, p. 5412-5413.
Scotistic, p. 5413.
scrape[1], p. 5417.
screw[1], p. 5420.
scripturient, p. 5425.
scrolar, p. 5426.
scroll, p. 5426.
scruple, p. 5428.
80: Scutum Sobiescianum,

sea-green, p. 5440.
sea-level, p. 5443.
seam[2], p. 5444.

seat, p. 5449.
seat of the soul, p. 5449.
secant, p. 5451.
secern, p. 5451.
second¹, p. 5452-5453.
second², p. 5453.
secondary, p. 5453-5454.
second-hand¹, p. 5454.
second-hand², p. 5454.
second-mark, p. 5454.
seconds-pendulum, p. 5454.
secretiveness, p. 5456.
sect¹, p. 5456.
sectant, p. 5457.
section, p. 5457.
sector, p. 5458.
sectorial, p. 5458.
secundo-primary, p. 5459.
secundum, p. 5459.
see¹, p. 5463.
seer⁴, p. 5467.
see-saw, p. 5467.
segment, p. 5468.
segregate, p. 5469.
seleniscope, p. 5474.
selenitic, p. 5474.
selenocentric, p. 5474.
selenograph, p. 5474.
selenographer, p. 5474.
selenographic, p. 5474.
selenographical, p. 5474.
selenographist, p. 5474.
selenography, p. 5474.
selenological, p. 5474.
selenologist, p. 5474.
selenology, p. 5474.
self, p. 5474-5475.
self-abasement, p. 5475.
self-activity, p. 5475.
self-adjusting, p. 5475.
self-asserting, p. 5475.
self-assertion, p. 5475.
self-assertiveness, p. 5475.
self-command, p. 5475.
self-complacency, p. 5476.
self-complacent, p. 5476.
self-conceit, p. 5476.
self-confidence, p. 5476.
self-confident, p. 5476.
self-conjugate, p. 5476.
self-conscious, p. 5476.
self-consciousness, p. 5476.
self-consistency, p. 5476.
self-consistent, p. 5476.

self-contradiction, p. 5476.
self-correspondence, p. 5476.
self-corresponding, p. 5476.
self-creation, p. 5476.
self-denial, p. 5476.
self-dependence, p. 5477.
self-determination, p. 5477.
self-determined, p. 5477.
self-determining, p. 5477.
self-end, p. 5477.
self-enjoyment, p. 5477.
self-esteem, p. 5477.
self-estimation, p. 5477.
self-evidence, p. 5477.
self-evident, p. 5477.
self-evidently, p. 5477.
self-existence, p. 5477.
self-existent, p. 5477.
self-focusing, p. 5477.
self-help, p. 5477.
self-importance, p. 5477.
self-indulgence, p. 5478.
self-interest, p. 5478.
selfish, p. 5478.
self-knowing, p. 5478.
self-knowledge, p. 5478.
self-love, p. 5478.
self-motion, p. 5478.
self-moved, p. 5478.
self-murder, p. 5478.
selfness, p. 5478.
self-opinion, p. 5478.
self-opinionated, p. 5478.
self-perception, p. 5478.
self-realization, p. 5479.
self-respect, p. 5479.
self-sacrifice, p. 5479.
self-scorn, p. 5479.
self-substantial, p. 5480.
self-sufficiency, p. 5480.
self-sufficient, p. 5480.
selfthinking, p. 5480.
self-will, p. 5480.
sematology, p. 5481.
semester, p. 5482.
semicircle, p. 5483.
semiconjugate, p. 5483.
semiconscious, p. 5483.
semiconvergent, p. 5483.
semicritical, p. 5483.
semicubical, p. 5483.

semidefinite, p. 5483.
semiduiurna, p. 5484.
semi-infinite, p. 5484.
semilogical, p. 5484.
seminar, p. 5485.
seminary, p. 5485.
seminvariant, p. 5485.
seminvariantive, p. 5485.
semiological, semeiological, p. 5485.
semi-ordinate, p. 5486.
semiotic, semeiotic, p. 5486.
semiotics, semeiotics, p. 548
semi-parabola, p. 5486.
semiquintile, p. 5486.
semireflex, p. 5486.
semi-regular, p. 5487.
semisextile, p. 5487.
semisolid, p. 5487.
semisquare, p. 5487.
semisubstitution, p. 5487.
semi-tangent, p. 5487.
semitychonic, p. 5487.
sempiternal, p. 5488.
senary, p. 5489.
sensation, p. 5492.
sensational, p. 5492.
sensationalism, p. 5492.
sensationalist, p. 5492.
sense¹, p. 5492-5493.
sense-element, p. 5493.
sense-impression, p. 5493.
senseless, p. 5493.
sense-perception, p. 5493.
sensibility, p. 5494.
sensible, p. 5494.
sensifacient, p. 5494.
sensific, p. 5494.
sensificatory, p. 5494.
sensigenous, p. 5494.
sensigerous, p. 5494.
sensile, p. 5494.
sension, p. 5494.
sensism, p. 5494.
sensitive, p. 5494-5495.
sentiveness, p. 5495.
sensitivity, p. 5495.
sensitory, p. 5495.
sensomotor, p. 5495.
sensor, p. 5495.
sensorial, p. 5495.

sensorimotor, p. 5495.
sensorium, p. 5495.
sensorivolitional, p. 5495.
sensory, p. 5495.
sensual, p. 5495.
sensualism, p. 5495.
sensualist, p. 5495-5496.
sensualistic, p. 5496.
sensuism, p. 5496.
sensuist, p. 5496.
sensuous, p. 5496.
sensuosity, p. 5496.
sentence, p. 5496.
sententiarian, p. 5496.
sententiary, p. 5496.
sentience, p. 5497.
sentient, p. 5497.
sentiment, p. 5497.
sentimental, p. 5497.
sentimentalism, p. 5497.
sentimentalist, p. 5497.
sentimentally, p. 5497.
separability, p. 5498.
separable, p. 5498.
separableness, p. 5498.
separate, p. 5498.
septangle, p. 5500.
septangular, p. 5500.
septenary, p. 5501.
Septentrio, p. 5501.
septentrion, p. 5501.
septilateral, p. 5501.
septillion, p. 5502.
septuagesimal, p. 5502.
sequacious, p. 5503.
sequacity, p. 5503.
sequence, p. 5503.
series, p. 5509.
servitor, p. 5519.
sesqui-, p. 5520.
sesquialteral, p. 5520.
sesquialterate, p. 5520.
sesquiduple, p. 5520.
sesquiduplicate, p. 5520.
sesquinonal,p 5520.
sesquioctaval, p. 5520.
sesquiplicate, p. 5520.
sesquiquadrate, p. 5520.
sesquiquartal, p. 5520.

sesquiquintal, p. 5520.
sesquiquintile, p. 5520.
sesquiseptimal, p. 5520.
sesquisextal, p. 5520.
set, p. 5524.
set, p. 5526.
setting, p. 5528.
seven, p. 5530-5531.
seven-fold, p. 5531.
seven-point, p. 5531.
seventeen, p. 5531.
seventeenth, p. 5531.
seventh, p. 5531.
seventieth, p. 5532.
seventy, p. 5532.
sexadecimal, p. 5535.
sexagecuple, p. 5535.
sexagenal, p. 5535.
sexagenarian, p. 5535.
sexagenary, p. 5535.
sexagene, p. 5535-5536.
sexagesimal, p. 5536.
sexagesimally, p. 5536.
sexagesm, p. 5536.
sexangle, p. 5536.
sexangled, p. 5536.
sexangular, p. 5536.
sexangularly, p. 5536.
sexcentenary, p. 5536.
sextactic, p. 5536.
sextans, p. 5536.
sextant, p. 5536-5537.
sextantal, p. 5537.
sextarius, p. 5537.
sextary[1], p. 5537.
sexter, p. 5537.
sextern, p. 5537.
Sextian, p. 5537.
sextic, p. 5537.
sextile, p. 5537.
sextillion, p. 5537.
sextine, p. 5537.
sextinvariant, p. 5537.
sextipartite, p. 5537.
sextiply, p. 5537.
shame, p. 5547.
shear[1], p. 5557.
shearer, p. 5557.
sheet[1], p. 5562-5563.

ship-pound, p. 5577.
shirt, p. 5578.
shrink, p. 5600.
shrub[2], p. 5602.
sibiconjugate, p. 5609.
side[1], p. 5612-5613.
sideral, p. 5615.
sidereal, p. 5615-5616.
siderostatic, p. 5616.
siderotechry, p. 5616.
sieve, p. 5619.
sigma, p. 5622.
sign, p. 5622-5623.
signaletic, p. 5624.
signature, p. 5625.
significance, p. 5625.
significancy, p. 5625.
significant, p. 5626.
significate, p. 5626.
signification, p. 5626.
significative, p. 5626.
significatively, p. 5626.
significator, p. 5626.
significatory, p. 5626.
signifier, p. 5626.
signify, p. 5626.
signless, p. 5626.
sign-symbol, p. 5626.
siling-dish, p. 5629.
siliqua, p. 5629.
81: sillometer, p. 5631.
similar, p. 5636.
similitude, p. 5636.
simple, p. 5638-5639.
simpliciter, p. 5640.
simplicity, p. 5640.
simulacrum, p. 5640.
simultaneity, p. 5641.
simultaneous, p. 5641.
sin, p. 5642.
sine, p. 5643.
sine-integral, p. 5643.
sinew, p. 5643-5644.
singeingly, p. 5645.
single, p. 5645-5646.
singular, p. 5647-5648.
singularity, p. 5648.
sinical, p. 5648.
sinister, p. 5648.

sinusoid, p. 5652.
sinusoidal, p. 5652.
sinusoidally, p. 5652.
Sirus, p. 5656.
sixer, p. 5662.
sixpoint, p. 5662.
sizar, p. 5663.
size^1, p. 5663.
skeptic, sceptic, p. 5668.
skeptical, sceptical, p. 5668.
skepticism, scepticism, p. 5668.
skew, p. 5669.
skin, p. 5672.
skip-kennel, p. 5674.
sky-blue, p. 5679.
slantendicular, p. 5684.
slidder, p. 5694.
slide, p. 5694.
slipping-peice, p. 5699.
smash, p. 5712.
smolder, smoulder, p. 5719-5720.
smug^1, p. 5722.
snob, p. 5732.
snub-cube, p. 5737.
snub-dodecahedron, p. 5737.
snudging, p. 5737.
snug, p. 5738.
sociability, p. 5743.
sociality, p. 5744.
socialism, p. 5744.
sociality, p. 5744.
society, p. 5744-5745.
sociogeny, p. 5745.
sociography, p. 5745.
sociology, p. 5745.
socionomy, p. 5745.
Socratic, p. 5746.
Socratical, p. 5746.
Socratically, p. 5746.
Socraticism, p. 5746.
Socratism, p. 5746.
Socratist, p. 5746.
Socratize, p. 5746.
Soe, p. 5747.
solar, p. 5752.
solid, p. 5758-5759.
solidity, p. 5760.
solipsism, p. 5761.
solitaire, p. 5761.
Solomon's-seal, p. 5762.

solsticion, p. 5262-5263.
solstitial, p. 5763.
soluble, p. 5763.
solvability, p. 5764.
solve, p. 5764.
Somatic, p. 5764.
somatism, p. 5764.
somatist, p. 5764.
somatology, p. 5764.
some, p. 5765.
sonation, p. 5768.
soph, p. 5772.
sophist, p. 5772.
sophister, p. 5772-5773.
sophisticism, p. 5773.
sophomore, p. 5773.
sophomoric, p. 5773.
sophrosyne, p. 5774.
sophorate, p. 5774.
Sorbonne, p. 5775.
Sothiac, p. 5780.
Sothic, p. 5780.
soul^1, p. 5781.
soul-blindness, p. 5782.
soul-deaf, p. 5782.
soul-deafness, p. 5782.
sour, p. 5785.
source, p. 5785.
soy, p. 5790.
space, p. 5790.
span, p. 5793.
spatil, p. 5801.
spatiality, p. 5801.
special, p. 5805.
species, p. 5806.
specifically, p. 5807.
specification, p. 5807.
speillum, p. 5808.
specious, p. 5508.
speculate, p. 5812.
speculation, p. 5812.
speculatist, p. 5812.
speculative, p. 5812.
Spencerianism, p. 5816.
spheral, p. 5825.
sphere, p. 5825.
82/83: spherical, p. 5825-5826.
sphericity, p. 5826.
spherics, p. 5826.
spheroconic, p. 5826.

spheroid, p. 5826.
spicular, p. 5829.
spin, p. 5834.
spindle, p. 5835.
spinode, p. 5837.
spinode-curve, p. 5837.
spinode-torse, p. 5837.
Spinozism, p. 5837.
Spinozist, p. 5837.
spinister, p. 5837.
spiral, p. 5838-5839.
spire, p. 5840.
spiric, p. 5840.
spirit, p. 5840-5841.
spiritual, p. 5842.
spiritual, p. 5842.
spiritualism, p. 5842.
spiritualist, p. 5842.
spiritualist, p. 5842.
spirituality, p. 5842.
spiritually, p. 5842.
spiritual-mindedness, p. 584
spontaneity, p. 5854.
spontaneous, p. 5854.
spread, p. 5861.
square, p. 5875-5876.
stability, p. 5884.
stacca, p. 5884.
stack, p. 5885.
stadia, p. 5886.
stadiometer, p. 5886.
stadium, p. 5886.
staff, p. 5886.
Stagrite, p. 5889.
standard^2, p. 5900.
star, p. 5904-5905.
star-catalogue, p. 5906.
star-cluster, p. 5906.
star-drift, p. 5906.
star-map, p. 5908.
state, p. 5911-5912.
static, p. 5913.
statical, p. 5913.
statics, p. 5913.
station, p. 5913.
stationary, p. 5913.
statistical, p. 5914.
statistics, p. 5914.
steelyard^2, p. 5924.
steganography, p. 5927.

Steinerian, p. 5927.
stellar, p. 5928.
stentorophonic, p. 5931.
step, p. 5932.
stere², p. 5934.
stereogram, p. 5934.
stereographic, p. 5934-5935.
stereographical, p. 5935.
stereographically, p. 5935.
stereography, p. 5935.
stereometer, p. 5935.
stereometric, p. 5935.
stereometry, p. 5935.
stickle³, p. 5943.
stickler, p. 5944.
stone, p. 5961.
stook, p. 5965.
straight¹, p. 5975.
strain¹, p. 5977.
strain-normal, p. 5977.
strain-type, p. 5977.
Stratonical, p. 5982.
straw-color, p. 5983.
stream, p. 5984.
stress¹, p. 5988.
striction, p. 5990.
stride, p. 5990.
strike, p. 5991-5992.
strob, p. 5996.
strobic, p. 5996.
stroke¹, p. 5997.
Sturmian, p. 6010.
stut¹, p. 6010.
style¹, p. 6011-6012.
style-curve, p. 6012.
suasion, p. 6014.
subalternant, p. 6015.
subalternate, p. 6015.
subalternation, p. 6015.
subconscious, p. 6017.
subconsciousness, p. 6017.
subcontrariety, p. 6017.
subcontrary, p. 6017.
subdecimal, p. 6017.
subdeterminant, p. 6017.
subdivide, p. 6018.
subdivision, p. 6018.
subdivisive, p. 6018.
subduce, p. 6018.
subduction, p. 6018.
subduple, p. 6018.

subduplicate, p. 6018.
subequal, p. 6018.
subfactorial, p. 6019.
subgroup, p. 6019.
subimaginal, p. 6020.
subingression, p. 6020.
subinvariant, p. 6020.
subjacent, p. 6020.
subject, p. 6020-6021.
subjective, p. 6021.
subjectively, p. 6021.
subjectiveness, p. 6021.
subjectivism, p. 6021.
subjectivist, p. 6021.
subjectivity, p. 6021.
subjectless, p. 6022.
subject-matter, p. 6022.
subject-notion, p. 6022.
subject-object, p. 6022.
subjicible, p. 6022.
sublate, p. 6022.
sublation, p. 6022.
sublative, p. 6022.
sublime, p. 6023.
subliminal, p. 6023.
submultiple, p. 6025.
subnormal, p. 6025.
subpolar, p. 6027.
subrational, p. 6027.
subrhomboidal, p. 6027.
83: subsidiary, p. 6029.
subsist, p. 6029-6030.
subsistence, p. 6030.
subsistent, p. 6030.
substance, p. 6030-6031.
substantialism, p. 6031.
substantialist, p. 6031.
substantiality, p. 6031.
substitute, p. 6032.
subsume, p. 6033.
subsumption, p. 6033.
subsurface, p. 6033.
subtangent, p. 6033.
subtent, p. 6033.
subtense, p. 6033.
subtract, p. 6035.
subtraction, p. 6035.
subtractive, p. 6035.
subtrahend, p. 6035.
subtriple, p. 6035.
subtriplicate, p. 6035.

succedent, p. 6037.
succession, p. 6037.
suggestedness, p. 6047.
suggestibility, p. 6047.
suggestible, p. 6047.
suggestio falsi, p. 6047.
suggestion, p. 6047-6048.
suggestionism, p. 6048.
suggestionist, p. 6048.
suggestive, p. 6048.
suggestively, p. 6048.
suggestiveness, p. 6048.
sulphur, p. 6052.
sum¹, p. 6054.
sum-calculus, p. 6054.
summation, p. 6054.
summational, p. 6054.
summative, p. 6055.
summit, p. 6056.
summula, p. 6056.
summulist, p. 6056.
summum bonum, p. 6056.
sumption, p. 6057.
sun-dial, p. 6060.
superbipartient, p. 6063.
superbiquintal, p. 6063.
supercelestial, p. 6064.
supercurve, p. 6064.
superdeterminate, p. 6064.
superessential, p. 6065.
superfice, p. 6065.
superficial, p. 6065.
superficiary, p. 6065.
superficies, p. 6065.
superimaginary, p. 6066.
superindue, p. 6066.
superior, p. 6067.
super-line, p. 6067.
superlinear, p. 6067.
superlunar, p. 6067.
supernatural, p. 6068.
supernormal, p. 6068.
superordination, p. 6068.
superorganic, p. 6068.
superosculate, p. 6068.
superparticular, p. 6068.
superparticularity, p. 6068.
superpartient, p. 6068.
superphosphate, p. 6068.
superphysical, p. 6068.
superposable, p. 6069.

superposition, p. 6069.
superquadriquintal, p. 6069.
superquadripartient, p. 6069.
supersensible, p. 6069.
supersensory, p. 6069.
supersensual, p. 6069.
supersensuous, p. 6069.
superstruct, p. 6070.
supersubstantial, p. 6070.
supersurface, p. 6070.
supertelluric, p. 6070.
supertripartient, p. 6070.
supertriquartal, p. 6070.
supplement, p. 6072.
supplemental, p. 6072.
supplementary, p. 6072.
supplete, p. 6073.
suppletive, p. 6073.
suppletory, p. 6073.
supplial, p. 6073.
suppliance^1, p. 6073.
suppliance^2, p. 6073.
suppliant^1, p. 6073.
supplicantly, p. 6073.
supplicat, p. 6073.
supplicate, p. 6073.
supplicatingly, p. 6073.
supplication, p. 6073.
supplicator, p. 6073.
supplier, p. 6073.
supply, p. 6073.
supply, p. 6073.
suppose, p. 6075.
supposition, p. 6075.
suppositionless, p. 6075.
suppositive, p. 6076.
suppositum, p. 6076.
suppress, p. 6076.
supputate, p. 6076.
supputuation, p. 6076.
suppute, p. 6076.
supra-entity, p. 6077.
supramundane, p. 6077.
supreme, p. 6079.
surd, p. 6080.
surdesolid, p. 6080.
surface, p. 6081-6082.
survey, p. 6088.
survey, p. 6088.
surveying, p. 6089.
susceptibility, p. 6089.

susceptive, p. 6090.
suttle^3, p. 6094.
sweep, p. 6105.
sweet, p. 6107.
Swiss, p. 6116.
syllogism, p. 6123-6124.
syllogistic, p. 6124.
syllogistical, p. 6124.
syllogistically, p. 6124.
syllogization, p. 6124.
syllogize, p. 6124.
syllogizer, p. 6124.
symbol^1, p. 6125.
symbolic, p. 6125.
symbolical, p. 6125.
symmetral, p. 6126.
symmetral, p. 6126.
symmetric, p. 6126.
symmetrical, p. 6126.
symmetroid, p. 6126.
symmetry, p. 6126-6127.
sympiesometer, p. 6129.
sympolar, p. 6130.
symptosis, p. 6130.
synacral, p. 6130.
synaugeia, p. 6132.
syncategorematic, p. 6132.
syncategorematically, p. 6132.
synchronous, p. 6133.
synclastic, p. 6133.
syncopate, p. 6133.
synechiology, p. 6135.
synetic, p. 6135.
synod, p. 6136.
syntatic, p. 6139.
synteresis, p. 6139.
syntheme, p. 6139.
synthesis, p. 6139.
synthetic, p. 6139.
syntractrix, p. 6140.
syntypic, p. 6140.
syntypicism, p. 6140.
syntypous, p. 6140.
syrrhizoristic, p. 6141.
system, p. 6142-6143.
syzygant, p. 6144.
syzygetic, p. 6144.
syzygial, p. 6144.
syzygy, p. 6144.
tabula, p. 6151.
tabular, p. 6151.

tac-locus, p. 6155.
tacnode, p. 6155.
tacnode-cusp, p. 6155.
tact, p. 6155.
Tag^1, p. 6157-6158.
talent^1, p. 6168.
tang^2, p. 6178.
tangency, p. 6178.
tangent, p. 6178-6179.
tangental, p. 6179.
tangential, p. 6179.
tangentiality, p. 6179.
tantipartite, p. 6182.
tantity, p. 6182.
tarantulated, p. 6188.
tare^4, p. 6189.
84: tasimetric, p. 6194.
taurus, p. 6199.
tautobayrd, p. 6200.
tautochrone, p. 6200.
tautochronism, p. 6200.
tautochronous, p. 6200.
tawny, p. 6201.
teal^3, p. 6206.
telekinesis, p. 6215.
telekinetic, p. 6215.
telemeter, p. 6215.
teleologic, p. 6215.
teleological, p. 6215.
teleologically, p. 6215.
teleologism, p. 6215.
teleologist, p. 6215.
teleology, p. 6215.
teleophobia, p. 6215.
Telescopium, p. 6218.
telestic, p. 6218.
temporary, p. 6226.
ten, p. 6227.
tender, p. 6229.
tension, p. 6233-6234.
tensional, p. 6234.
tensor, p. 6234.
term, p. 6240-6242.
terminal, p. 6242.
terminism, p. 6243.
terminist, p. 6243.
terminus, p. 6243.
terræ filius, p. 6245.
tertian, p. 6248-6249.
tertium quid, p. 6249.
tessarace, p. 6249.

tessarescædecahedron, p. 6249.
tetragon, p. 6256.
tetragonal, p. 6256.
tetragonism, p. 6256.
tetragram, p. 6256.
tetrahedral, p. 6256.
tetrahedroid, p. 6256.
tetrahedron, p. 6256-6257.
tetrahexahedral, p. 6257.
tetrahexahedron, p. 6257.
tetralemma, p. 6257.
tetrastigm, p. 6258.
tetratop, p. 6259.
Thalia, p. 6263.
thalweg, p. 6263.
thaumatography, p. 6267.
thaumaturge, p. 6267.
thaumatirgic, p. 6267.
theatrical, p. 6269.
Theban, p. 6270.
thema, p. 6271.
thematic, p. 6271.
theme, p. 6271-6272.
theocrasy, p. 6272.
theodicy, p. 6273.
theodolite, p. 6273.
theorem, p. 6275-6277.
theorematic, p. 6277.
theorematical, p. 6277.
theorematist, p. 6277.
theoremic, p. 6277.
theoretic, p. 6277.
theoretical, p. 6277.
theoretically, p. 6277.
theoretician, p. 6277.
theoretics, p. 6277.
theoric[1], p. 6277.
theorist, p. 6278.
theorization, p. 6278.
theorize, p. 6278.
theorizer, p. 6278.
theorizing, p. 6278.
theorizing, p. 6278.
theory, p. 6278.
theosophist, p. 6278.
theosophy, p. 6278.
thermodynamics, p. 6282.
thesis, p. 6285.
theta, p. 6286.
think[1], p. 6292-6293.
third[1], p. 6294.

thirdendeal, p. 6294.
thirteenth, p. 6295.
thirtieth, p. 6295.
thirteen, p. 6295.
Thomism, p. 6298.
thought[1], p. 6303.
thought-reader, p. 6304.
thought-transfer, p. 6304.
thousandth, p. 6304.
thrave, threave, p. 6305.
three, p. 6307-6308.
three-dimensional, p. 6308.
threefold, p. 6308.
threshold, p. 6309-6310.
thrust[1], p. 6318.
tical, p. 6327.
tidal, p. 6329-6330.
tide[1], p. 6330.
tide-gage, p. 6330.
tide-predictor, p. 6331.
tierce, p. 6332.
time[1], p. 6340-6341.
tint[1], p. 6348.
Titan[1], p. 6354-6355.
tithonometer, p. 6356.
tocsin, p. 6364.
tod[1], p. 6364.
tohu bohu, p. 6367.
toise, p. 6368.
tom[1], p. 6371.
85: ton[1], p. 6373.
topic, p. 6386.
topical, p. 6386.
topography, p. 6387.
topology, p. 6387.
toroidal, p. 6391.
torpify, p. 6392.
torsal[2], p. 6394.
torse[1], p. 6394.
torsion, p. 6394.
torsional, p. 6394.
total, p. 6398.
totient, p. 6399.
totitive, p. 6400.
trace[1], p. 6410.
traction, p. 6415.
tractrix, p. 6415.
traduction, p. 6418.
trajectory, p. 6423.
trammel, p. 6424.
transcendent, p. 6426-6427.

transcendental, p. 6427.
transcendentalism, p. 6427.
transcendentalist, p. 6427.
transcendentality, p. 6427.
transcendentalize, p. 6427.
transcendentally, p. 6427.
transform, p. 6429.
transformation, p. 6430.
transit, p. 6432.
transit-circle, p. 6432.
transit-instrument, p. 6432.
transitive, p. 6433.
transitivity, p. 6433.
translation, p. 6433.
transmutant, p. 6435.
transmutation, p. 6435.
transponibility, p. 6437.
transposition, p. 6438-6439.
transrotatory, p. 6439.
transvectant, p. 6440.
transvection, p. 6440.
transversal, p. 6440.
transverse, p. 6440.
trapezoid, p. 6442.
trencherman, p. 6459.
tret, p. 6461.
triadic, p. 6462.
triad, p. 6462.
triakisicosahedral, p. 6462.
triakisicosahedron, p. 6462.
triakisoctahedral, p. 6462.
triakisoctahedron, p. 6462.
triakistetrahedral, p. 6462.
triakistetrahedron, p. 6462.
trialism, p. 6463.
triangle, p. 6463-6464.
triangular, p. 6464.
Triangulum, p. 6464.
trichotomic, p. 6470.
trichotomous, p. 6470.
trichotomously, p. 6470.
trichotomy, p. 6470.
tricircular, p. 6470.
tricuspida, p. 6472.
trident, p. 6473.
tridimensional, p. 6474.
trigon[1], p. 6477.
trigon[2], p. 6477.
trigonal, p. 6477.
trigonic, p. 6477.
trigonoid, p. 6478.

trigonometer, p. 6478.
trigonometrical, p. 6478.
trigonometrically, p. 6478.
trigonometry, p. 6478.
trihedral, p. 6478.
trilemma, p. 6478.
trillion, p. 6479.
trillionth, p. 6479.
trinary, p. 6481.
trinodal, p. 6483.
trinode, p. 6483.
trinomial, p. 6483-6484.
triorthogonal, p. 6485.
trip^4, p. 6485.
tripartite, p. 6485.
triple, p. 6486.
triplet, p. 6487.
triplicate, p. 6487.
triplicity, p. 6487.
tripos, p. 6488.
triquetric, p. 6489.
trisection, p. 6489.
trisectory, p. 6489.
trivial, p. 6493.
trivium, p. 6494.
trizomal, p. 6494.
trochoid, p. 6495.
trochoidal, p. 6495.
trone^1, p. 6498.
trope, p. 6499.
tropic, p. 6500.
trouble, p. 6502.
troy weight, p. 6504.
true, p. 6506.
trusion, p. 6511.
truss, p. 6511.
trustworthiness, p. 6513.
truth, p. 6514.
tub, p. 6517.
tube, p. 6517.
tubus, p. 6521.
Tucana, p. 6522.
tuck^1, p. 6522.
tuck^1, p. 6522.
86: tuft^1, p. 6524.
tuft-hunter, p. 6524.
tuism, p. 6525.
tun^1, p. 6528.
Turdus Solitarius, p. 6534.
turgid, p. 6535.
tutor, p. 6547.

tutorial, p. 6547.
twin^1, p. 6552-6553.
twinkling, p. 6554.
twist, p. 6555-6556.
twist-velocity, p. 6557.
twitch^1, p. 6557.
twofold, p. 6558.
two-way, p. 6558.
typocosmy, p. 6564.
ubication, p. 6567.
ubiety, p. 6567.
ubiquity, p. 6567.
ullage, p. 6569.
ulna, p. 6570.
ultimate, p. 6570.
ultrabernoullian, p. 6571.
ultranominalistic, p. 6571.
ultra-violet, p. 6571.
ultra-zodiacal, p. 6571.
ultromotivity, p. 6571.
umberer, p. 6572.
umbilic, p. 6573.
umbilicar, p. 6573.
umbilicus, p. 6573.
umbra^1, p. 6573.
umbral, p. 6574.
unaffectedness, p. 6579.
unattainable, p. 6580.
unboundedness, p. 6584.
unconditional, p. 6589.
unconditionality, p. 6589.
unconditionally, p. 6589.
unconditionalness, p. 6589.
unconditioned, p. 6589-6590.
unconscious, p. 6590.
unconsciously, p. 6590.
unconsciousness, p. 6590.
understand, p. 6599.
understandable, p. 6599.
understander, p. 6599.
understanding, p. 6599.
understanding, p. 6599.
understandingly, p. 6599.
undetermined, p. 6601.
uneven, p. 6606.
unformed, p. 6608.
ungula, p. 6612.
unicorn, p. 6615.
unicursal, p. 6615.
unidimensional, p. 6616.
unification, p. 6616.

uniform, p. 6616.
unimodular, p. 6617.
unipartite, p. 6619-6620.
uniplanar, p. 6620.
unit, p. 6620-6621.
unitarian, p. 6621.
Unitarianism, p. 6621.
unitary, p. 6621.
unitate, p. 6621.
unitate, p. 6621.
unitation, p. 6621.
unitism, p. 6622.
unity, p. 6622.
universal, p. 6623.
universe, p. 6623.
university, p. 6623-6624.
universology, p. 6624.
univocal, p. 6624.
univocation, p. 6624.
unknowable, p. 6625.
unknown, p. 6625.
unlike, p. 6626.
unlimited, p. 6626-6627.
unlimitedly, p. 6627.
unlimitedness, p. 6627.
unnaturalness, p. 6631.
unode, p. 6632.
unsensible, p. 6644.
unsolid, p. 6646.
Uraniun, p. 6665.
uranology, p. 6665.
uranometry, p. 6665.
Uranus, p. 6665-6666.
Ursa, p. 6672.
utilitarian, p. 6678.
utilitarianism, p. 6678.
vacation, p. 6681.
vacuist, p. 6683.
vacuum, p. 6683.
vague, p. 6685.
valedictorian, p. 6687.
valedictory, p. 6687.
valid, p. 6689.
value, p. 6691.
vanish, p. 6695.
variability, p. 6698-6699.
variable, p. 6699.
variation, p. 6699-6700.
87: vary, p. 6703.
vector, p. 6708.
Vega^2, p. 6709.

vehicle, p. 6710.
vehicular, p. 6710.
velleity, p. 6713.
Venus, p. 6724.
veracity, p. 6725.
verbalist, p. 6725.
verbicide¹, p. 6726.
vergee, p. 6728.
verger¹, p. 6728.
verisimility, p. 6729.
vernier, p. 6732.
versed, p. 6734.
version, p. 6734.
vertex, p. 6736.
vertical, p. 6736.
verticity, p. 6737.
vespertine, p. 6739.
via¹, p. 6744.
vibration, p. 6745.
vice-chancellor, p. 6747.
vicinal, p. 6748.
vinculum, p. 6757.
Vindemiatrix, p. 6757.
violet¹, p. 6761.
virgin, p. 6764.
Virgo, p. 6765.
virial, p. 6765.
virtual, p. 6766.
virtuality, p. 6766.
virtually, p. 6766.
virtue, p. 6766-6767.
virtuoso, p. 6767.
vis³, p. 6768.
visitation, p. 6771.
visitatorial, p. 6771.
visual, p. 6772.
visualization, p. 6772.
visualize, p. 6772.
vital, p. 6772-6773.
viz, p. 6778.
Volans, p. 6782.
volition, p. 6784.
volitional, p. 6784.
volitionally, p. 6784.
volitionary, p. 6784.
volitive, p. 6784.
volume, p. 6785-6786.
voluntary, p. 6786.
volutation, p. 6788.
vortex, p. 6789-6790.
vortex-filament, p. 6790.

vortex-motion, p. 6790.
Vulcan, p. 6793.
Vulpecula cum Ansere, p. 6794-6795.
W, p. 6797.
warp, p. 6826-6827.
wash, p. 6830.
watch, p. 6835.
water-language, p. 6843.
water-line, p. 6844.
water-measure, p. 6844.
water-poise, p. 6845.
Watling street, p. 6849.
wave¹, p. 6851.
wave-surface, p. 6852.
wedge¹, p. 6866-6867.
week¹, p. 6868.
weigh¹, p. 6870-6871.
weigh¹, p. 6871.
weight¹, p. 6871-6872.
well-being, p. 6875.
west, p. 6880.
westing, p. 6881.
wey¹, p. 6883.
whatness, p. 6887.
white¹, p. 6908-6909.
wide, p. 6920.
Sup. 8: wilding, p. 6925.
will¹, p. 6927.
wine-measure, p. 6939.
wingedly, p. 6941.
wire¹, p. 6945.
wisdom, p. 6947.
wit¹, p. 6950.
witch¹, p. 6951.
withdraw, p. 6953.
witheringly, p. 6954.
witness, p. 6956.
Wolfian¹, p. 6960.
work, p. 6975-6976.
worm, p. 6980.
worse, p. 6982.
wrangler, p. 6986.
wranglership, p. 6986.
wrappage, p. 6986.
wrongous, p. 6995.
X, p. 6997.
Xenocratean, p. 7000.
Xenophanean, p. 7000.
Y, p. 7006.
yard¹, p. 7009.

year, p. 7012.
year (cont'd.), p. 7013.
Sup. 9: yellow, p. 7015.
zenity, p. 7032.
zenith-collimater, p. 7032.
zenith-distance, p. 7032.
zenith-sector, p. 7032.
zenith-telescope, p. 7032.
Zenonian, p. 7032.
zero, p. 7033.
zeta¹, p. 7033.
zetetic, p. 7033.
zodiac, p. 7037.
zodiacal, p. 7037.
zone, p. 7038.

1889

O 00374: (NF)
Wolf, C.
> *Collection de Mémoirs relatifs à la Physique,* Paris: La Société Francaise de Physique, vol 4, pp. 183-214.

O 00375: F i c h e 88
Newcomb, S.
> "The Century Dictionary," *The Nation,* vol. 48 (13 June) 488, filmed at P 00043 page 75. Letter.

P 00376: F i c h e 88
"The Century Dictionary."
> *The Nation,* vol. 48 (20 June) 504-505, filmed at P 00043 pages 75-78. Signed letter.

O 00377: F i c h e 88
Newcomb, S.
> "The Century Dictionary," *The Nation,* vol. 48 (27 June) 524, filmed at P 00043, pages 77-78. Letter.

P 00378: F i c h e 88
Review of *Deductive Logic.* By St. George Stock.
> *The Nation,* vol. 49 (15 August) 136-137, filmed at P 00043, pages 78-80. Probably by Peirce.

P 00379: F i c h e 88, 89
"On Sensations of Color."
> Paper read before the National Academy of Sciences, Washington, 16-19 April. Cited in *Report of the National Academy of Sciences for the Year 1889,* Senate Mis. Doc. No. 47, 51st Congress, 2d Session, Washington: Government Printing Office, 1891, p. 6. Notice of research grants to Peirce are given at p. 38. Burks, *Bibliography.*

P 00380: F i c h e 89
"On Determinations of Gravity."
> Paper read before the National Academy of Sciences, Washington, 16-19 April. Cited in *Report of the National Academy of Sciences for the Year 1889,* Senate Mis. Doc. No. 47, 51st Congress, 2d Session, Washington: Government Printing Office, 1891, p. 6; filmed at P 00379. Burks, *Bibliography.*

O 00381: F i c h e 89
Gurney, Edmund
> "Remarks on Mr. Peirce's Rejoinder" [with a "Postscript to Mr. Gurney's Reply to Professor Peirce," by Frederic W.H. Myers], *Proceedings of the American Society for Psychical Research,* old series 4 (March), 286-301.

O 00382: (NF)
Lockyer, J. Norman.
> "Appendix to the Bakerian Lecture, Session 1887-1888," *Proceedings of the Royal Society of London,* vol. 45, 157-262, at 232.

O 00383: (NF)
Huggins, William.
> "On the Wave-length of the Principal Line in the Spectrum of the Aurora," *Proceedings of the Royal Society of London,* vol. 45, 430-436, at 433.

1889

P 00384: Fiche 89
[Pendulum research]
> *Report of the Superintendent of the United States Coast and Geodetic Survey, 1887,* House Ex. Doc. No. 17, 50th Congress, 1st Session, Washington: Government Printing Office, references to Peirce's research at p. 116-117, 88. Burks, *Bibliography.*

P 00385: Fiche 89, 90, 91, 92
Report on Gravity at the Smithsonian, Ann Arbor, Madison, and Cornell.
> This typescript report was not published, although it was received by the Superintendent of the United States Coast and Geodetic Survey on 22 November 1889. It is copied in this edition to make it available to students of Peirce's work; it has not been reproduced in books or microformat prior to this edition. A full account of the history and significance of this typescript is given in Victor F. Lenzen, "An Unpublished Scientific Monograph by C.S. Peirce," *Transactions of the Charles S. Peirce Society,* vol. 5 (1969), 5-24. This typescript is MS 1096a in Robin's *Catalogue.*

1890

O 00386: (NF)
Taber, Henry.
> "On the Theory of Matrices," *American Journal of Mathematics,* vol. 12, 337-396, at 388, 340 n., 346 n., 349 n., 352-354, 386 n.

O 00387: (NF)
Nagy, Albino.
> "Fondamenti del calcolo logico," *Giornale di matematiche,* vol. 28, 1-35, at 2, 6, 27-28, 29-30.

O 00388: Fiche 92
Stearns, J.W.
> "Philosophy in American Colleges and Universities: University of Wisconsin," *The Monist,* vol. 1 (October), 148-156, at 155. Mention that Peirce's logic is taught in an advanced course instructed by Jastrow.

P 00389: Fiche 92
Review of *The Science of Metrology; or Natural Weights and Measures. A Challenge to the Metric System.* By E. Noel.
> *The Nation,* vol. 50 (27 February) 184, filmed at P 00043, pages 81-82.

P 00390: Fiche 92
Review of *Epitome of the Synthetic Philosophy.* By F. Howard Collins.
> *The Nation,* vol. 50 (27 March) 265, filmed at P 00043, page 82.

P 00391: Fiche 92
"Ribot's Psychology of Attention."
> *The Nation,* vol. 50 (19 June) 492-493, filmed at P 00043, pages 83-86.

P 00392: Fiche 92
Review of *Pure Logic, and Other Minor Works.* By W. Stanley Jevons.
> *The Nation,* vol. 51 (3 July) 16, filmed at P 00043, pages 86-88.

P 00393: Fiche 92
Review of *Fundamental Problems: The Method of Philosophy as a Systematic Arrangement of Knowledge.* By Paul Carus.
> *The Nation,* vol. 51 (7 August) 118-119, filmed at P 00043, pages 88-89.

1890

P 00394: Fiche 92
Review of *The Theory of Determinants in the Historical Order of its Development. Part I.* By Thomas Muir.
    The Nation, vol. 51 (28 August) 177, filmed at P 00043, page 90.

P 00395: Fiche 92
Review of *Elements of Logic as a Science of Propositions.* By E.E. Constance Jones.
    The Nation, vol. 51 (18 September) 234, filmed at P 00043, pages 91-93. Probably by Peirce.

P 00396: Fiche 92
Review of *Locke.* By Alexander Campbell Fraser.
    The Nation, vol. 51 (25 September) 254-255, filmed at P 00043, pages 93-96.

P 00397: Fiche 92
Note [on the first number of the *Monist*].
    The Nation, vol. 51 (23 October) 326, filmed at P 00043, pages 96-97. Probably by Peirce.

P 00398: Fiche 92
Review of *Our Dictionaries, and Other English-Language Topics.* By R.O. Williams.
    The Nation, vol. 51 (30 October) 349, filmed at P 00043, pages 97-98.

O 00399: Fiche 92
A.B.C.
    "The 'Pons Asinorum'," *New York Daily Tribune* (Friday, 8 Dec., 1800), page 10, column 2.

O 00400: Fiche 92
W.L.S.
    "The 'Pons Asinorum'," *New York Daily Tribune* (Tuesday, 19 Dec., 1890), page 16, columns 5-6.

O 00401: Fiche 92
Anonymous.
    "Herbert Spencer Attacked [editorial]," *The New York Times,* vol. 39 (Sunday, 23 March), page 4, column 4.

P 00402: Fiche 92
"Herbert Spencer's Philosophy. Is it Unscientific and Unsound? — Its Pretensions Attacked and a Demonstration Called For."
    The New York Times, vol. 39 (Sunday, 23 March), page 4, columns 6-7. Signed "Outsider."
    Fisch, *First Supplement.*

O 00403: Fiche 92
Anonymous.
    "Herbert Spencer Defended [editorial]," *The New York Times,* vol. 39 (Sunday, 30 March), page 4, column 4.

O 00404: Fiche 92
Anonymous.
    "Spencer Ably Defended [editorial]," *The New York Times,* vol. 39 (Sunday, 30 March), page 13, column 1.

O 00405: Fiche 92
KAPPA
    "Flaws in 'Outsider's' Reasoning," *The New York Times,* vol. 39 (Sunday, 30 March), page 13, columns 1-2.

1890

O 00406: F i c h e 93
R.G.E.
"A Call for Specifications," *The New York Times,* vol. 39 (Sunday, 30 March), page 13, columns 2-4.

O 00407: F i c h e 93
Messenger, H.J., Jr.
"Two Points Fairly Met," *The New York Times,* vol. 39 (Sunday, 30 March), page 13, column 4.

O 00408: F i c h e 93
Anonymous.
"Where are the Foes of Spencer? [editorial]" *The New York Times,* vol. 39 (Sunday, 6 April), page 4, columns 3-4.

O 00409: F i c h e 93
Anonymous.
"Spencer's Philosophy [editorial]," *The New York Times,* vol. 39 (Sunday, 6 April), page 13, column 1.

O 00410: F i c h e 93
Osborn, Henry Fairfield.
"The Spencerian Biology," *The New York Times,* vol. 39 (Sunday, 6 April), page 13, columns 1-2.

O 00411: F i c h e 93
Dawson, Edgar R.
"Asking Too Much," *The New York Times,* vol. 39 (Sunday, 6 April), page 13, columns 2-3.

O 00412: F i c h e 93
Opperg, Carl.
"Experience and Intuition," *The New York Times,* vol. 39 (Sunday, 6 April), page 13, columns 3-4.

O 00413: F i c h e 93
W.H.B.
"A Philosophical Critic," *The New York Times,* vol. 39 (Sunday, 6 April), page 13, column 4.

O 00414: F i c h e 93
Anonymous.
"The Critics of Spencer [editorial]," *The New York Times,* vol. 39 (Sunday, 13 April), page 4, column 4.

O 00415: F i c h e 93
Anonymous.
"A Fair Field and No Favor [editorial]." *The New York Times,* vol. 39 (Sunday, 13 April), page 13, column 1.

P 00416: F i c h e 93
"'Outsider' Wants More Light. He Cometh After his Critics and Searcheth Them — Spencer's Standing in Science — His Theory of Evolution — 'Outsider' is an Inquirer, Not an Assailant."
The New York Times, vol. 39 (Sunday, 13 April), page 13, columns 1-2. Signed "Outsider."
Fisch, *First Supplement.*

1890

O 00417: Fiche 93
W.S.N.
"Mathematical Weakness of Spencer's Philosophy," *The New York Times,* vol. 39 (Sunday, 13 April), page 13, columns 2-3.

O 00418: Fiche 93
H.L.P.
"Specialists and Generalizers," *The New York Times,* vol. 39 (Sunday, 13 April), page 13, column 3.

O 00419: Fiche 93
S.D.R.
"Where Spencer Fails," *The New York Times,* vol. 39 (Sunday, 13 April), page 13, columns 3-4.

O 00420: Fiche 93
Dawson, Edgar R.
"The Spencer Discussion as to Reversed Velocities," *The New York Times,* vol. 39 (Sunday, 20 April), page 13, column 1.

O 00421: Fiche 93
R.G.E.
"Force and Life," *The New York Times,* vol. 39 (Sunday, 20 April), page 13, columns 1-2.

O 00422: Fiche 93
W.E.S.
"Space and Form," *The New York Times,* vol. 39 (Sunday, 20 April), page 13, columns 2-3.

O 00423: Fiche 93
West, George E.
"Evolution and Gravitation," *The New York Times,* vol. 39 (Sunday, 20 April), page 13, column 3.

O 00424: Fiche 93
W.H.B.
"The Evolution of Scientific Religion," *The New York Times,* vol. 39 (Sunday, 20 April), page 13, column 3.

O 00425: Fiche 93
Anonymous.
"Light for 'Outsider' [editorial]," *The New York Times,* vol. 39 (Sunday, 27 April), page 4, column 5.

O 00426: Fiche 93
Anonymous.
"Facts about Spencer [editorial]," *The New York Times,* vol. 39 (Sunday, 27 April), page 13, column 1.

O 00427: Fiche 93
Youmans, W.J.
"Mr. Spencer's Rank as a Philosopher," *The New York Times,* vol. 39 (Sunday, 27 April), page 13, columns 1-3.

1890

O 00428: Fiche 93
Janes, Lewis G.
> "The Grandeur of Spencer's System," *The New York Times,* vol. 39 (Sunday, 27 April), page 13, columns 3-4.

O 00429: Fiche 93
Iles, George.
> "Seventy Years Old To-day," *The New York Times,* vol. 39 (Sunday, 27 April), page 13, columns 4-6.

O 00430: Fiche 94
Hegeler, Edward C.
> "Religion and Science," *The Open Court,* vol. 4, 2473-2474.

O 00431: Fiche 94
Carus, Paul.
> "The Unity of Truth," *The Open Court,* vol. 4, 2501-2502.

O 00432: Fiche 94
Carus, Paul.
> "The Superscientific and Pure Reason," *The Open Court,* vol. 4, 2509-2511.

P 00433: Fiche 94
[Pendulum and metrological research]
> *Report of the Superintendent of the United States Coast and Geodetic Survey, 1889,* House Ex. Doc. No. 55, 51st Congress, 1st Session, Washington: Government Printing Office, references to Peirce's research at p. 100, 112, 151, 179-188. Burks, *Bibliography.*

O 00434: (NF)
Clerke, A.M.
> *The System of the Stars.* London: Longmans, Green, & Co., at p. 361.

O 00435: Fiche 94, 95, 96
Schröder, Ernst.
> *Vorlesungen über die Algebra der Logik* (Exakte Logik), vol. 1, Leipzig: B.G. Teubner, pp. I-IX, 1-125, 133, 140, 141, 191, 193, 194, 211, 243, 253, 257, 274-276, 285, 290, 291, 297, 301, 302, 314, 350, 354, 363-365, 376, 378, 379, 418, 419, 423, 457, 496, 525, 532, 553, 559, 560, 573, 588, 589, 591, 717.

1891

O 00436: Fiche 96
Reyes y Prósper, Ventura.
> "Cristina Ladd Franklin: Matemática Americana y su Influencia en la lógica Simbólica," *El Progreso Matemático,* vol. 1 (20 December), 297-300.

O 00437: (NF)
Husserl, E.G.
> Review of Schröder's *Vorlesungen über die Algebra der Logik,* vol. 1, *Gottingische gelehrte Anzeigen,* vol. 1, 243-278.

O 00438: (NF)
Scheffers, Georg.
> "Zuruckfúhring Complexer Zahlensysteme auf typische Formen," *Mathematische Annalen,* vol. 39, 293-390 at 388-389.

1891

P 00439: F i c h e 96
"The Architecture of Theories."
    The Monist, vol. 1 (January), 161-176. Cohen, *Tentative Bibliography;* Burks, *Bibliography.*

O 00440: F i c h e 96
Carus, Paul.
    "The Criterion of Truth." *The Monist,* vol. 1 (January), 229-244, at 241-244.

P 00441: F i c h e 6
Note [on Shea's history of Duns Scotus].
    The Nation, vol. 52 (12 February) 139, filmed at P 00043, page 99.

P 00442: F i c h e 6
Note [on Cajori's *The Teaching and History of Mathematics in the United States*].
    The Nation, vol. 52 (19 February) 160, filmed at P 00043, pages 100-101. Probably by Peirce.

O 00443: F i c h e 6
X. "A Caricature."
    The Nation, 52 (26 February) 178, filmed at P 00043, page 101. Letter.

O 00444: F i c h e 6
F.H.L. [F.H. Loud].
    "The Teaching of Mathematics," *The Nation,* vol. 52 (12 March) 217-218, filmed at P 00043, pages 101-103. Letter.

O 00445: F i c h e 6
Cajori, Florian.
    "The Teaching of Mathematics," *The Nation,* vol. 52 (12 March) 217-218, filmed at P 00043, pages 101-103. Letter.

P 00446: F i c h e 6
"The Teaching of Mathematics."
    The Nation, vol. 52 (12 March) 217-218, filmed at P 00043, pages 101-103. Reply to letters. Probably by Peirce.

P 00447: F i c h e 6
"James's Psychology. — I."
    The Nation, vol. 53 (2 July) 15, filmed at P 00043, pages 104-106.

P 00448: F i c h e 6
"James's Psychology. — II."
    The Nation, vol. 53 (9 July) 32-33, filmed at P 00043, pages 107-110.

P 00449: F i c h e 6
Review of *Vorlesungen uber die Algebra der Logik.* By Dr. Ernst Schröder.
    The Nation, vol. 53 (13 August) 129, filmed at P 00043, pages 110-111. Probably by Peirce.

P 00450: F i c h e 6
Review of *Essays, Scientific, Political, and Speculative.* By Herbert Spencer.
    The Nation, vol. 53 (8 October) 283, filmed at P 00043, pages 112-113.

P 00451: F i c h e 6
Review of *Geodesy.* By J. Howard Gore.
    The Nation, vol. 53 (15 October) 302, filmed at P 00043, page 114.

1891

O 00452: F i c h e 6
Hoskins, L.M.
> The Law of "Vis Viva." *The Nation,* 53 (22 October) 313-314, filmed at P 00043, pages 114-115. Letter.

P 00453: F i c h e 6
"The Law of 'Vis Viva'."
> *The Nation,* vol. 53 (22 October) 313-314, filmed at P 00043, pages 114-115, Reply to letter.

P 00454: F i c h e 6
"Abbot Against Royce."
> *The Nation,* vol. 53 (12 November) 372, filmed at P 00043, pages 115-117. Signed letter.

P 00455: F i c h e 6
Note [a reply to Hoskins in regard to a dispute about the law of *vis viva*].
> *The Nation,* vol. 53 (12 November) 375, filmed at P 00043, page 117.

O 00456: F i c h e 6
James, William.
> "Abbot Against Royce." *The Nation,* vol. 53 (19 November) 389-390, filmed at P 00043, pages 118-120. Letter.

O 00457: F i c h e 6
Warner, Joseph B.
> "The Suppression of Dr. Abbot's Reply," *The Nation,* 53 (26 November) 408, filmed at P 00043, pages 120-122. Letter.

P 00458: F i c h e 6
Review of *Pictorial Astronomy for General Readers.* By George F. Chambers.
> *The Nation,* vol. 53 (26 November) 415, filmed at P 00043, pages 123-124.

O 00459: F i c h e 6
Abbot, Francis E.
> "Mr. Warner's 'Evidence in Full' completed," *The Nation,* 53 (3 December) 426, filmed at P 00043, pages 124-127. Letter.

P 00460: F i c h e 6
Review of *An Introduction to Spherical and Practical Astronomy.* By Dascom Greene
> *The Nation,* vol. 53 (17 December) 474, filmed at P 00043, pages 127-128.

P 00461: F i c h e 97
"Astronomical Methods of Determining the Curvature of Space."
> Paper read before the National Academy of Sciences, New York City, 10-12 April. Cited in *Report of the National Academy of Sciences for the Year 1891,* Senate Mis. Doc. No. 170, 52d Congress, 1st Session, Washington: Government Printing Office, 1892, p. 16. MS 1028 (Robin, *Catalogue*) may be relevant to this paper. Burks, *Bibliography.*

P 00462: F i c h e 97
[Discussion of a paper by O.N. Rood]
> O.N. Rood's paper, "On a Color System," was read before the National Academy of Sciences, New York City, 10-12 April, and was "discussed by Mr. Peirce." Cited in *Report of the National Academy of Sciences for the Year 1891,* Senate Mis. Doc. No. 170, 52d Congress, 1st Session, Washington: Government Printing Office, p. 16; see P 00461.

1891

O 00463: F i c h e 97
W.
> "Not 'Pons,' But 'Pontes Asinorum,' Perhaps," *New York Daily Tribune,* (Friday, 2 January), page 5, column 5.

P 00464: F i c h e 97
"The 'Pons Asinorum' Again. Mr. Peirce sets forth the History of the Phrase from the Times of Duns Scotus's Followers."
> *New York Daily Tribune,* (Tuesday, 6 January), page 14, column 5. This is a response to several earlier articles which were critical of Peirce's account of this phrase in the *Century Dictionary.* Those earlier articles are in the same newspaper at: Friday 19 December 1890, page 10, column 2; Tuesday 23 December 1890, page 16, columns 5-6; Friday 2 January 1891 page 5, column 5. Fisch, *First Supplement.*

P 00465: F i c h e Sup. 9
[Reference to gravity research].
> *Report of the Superintendent of the U.S. Coast and Geodetic Survey, 1890,* House Ex. Doc. No. 80, 51st Congress, 2d Session, Washington: Government Printing Office, p. 104. Burks, *Bibliography.*

O 00466: (NF)
Preston, E.D.
> "Determinations of Gravity and the Magnetic Elements in Connection with the U.S. Scientific Expedition to the West Coast of Africa, 1889-1890," *Report of the Superintendent of the United States Coast and Geodetic Survey, 1890,* House Ex. Doc. No. 80, 51st Congress, 2d Session, Washington: Government Printing Office, pp. 625-684, at 626, 632, 652, 683.

O 00467: (NF)
Husserl, E.G.
> "Der Folgerungscalcul und die Inhaltslogik," *Vierteljahrsschrift für wissenschaftliche Philosophie,* vol. 15, 168-189 and 351-356.

O 00468: F i c h e 97, 98
Schröder, Ernst.
> *Vorlesungen über die Algebra der Logik (Exakte Logik),* vol. 2, Leipzig: B.G. Teubner, pp. i-xxiv, 8, 24, 27, 29, 33, 69, 73. 89, 182, 197, 198, 199, 210, 258, 262, 263, 266, 270, 272, 273, 276, 291, 295, 297-302, 316, 320, 326, 327, 334, 346, 354, 402-404, 405, 438, 445, 447-450, 455, 460, 463, 464, 476, 482-488, 516, 597, 603, 606.

1892

O 00469: F i c h e 98
Reyes y Prosper, Ventura.
> "Charles Santiago Peirce y Oscar Honward [sic.] Mitchell," *El Progreso Matemático, vol. 2,* 170-173.

P 00470: (NF)
"Synechism."
> Paper read before the Graduate Philosophical Society of Harvard University, Cambridge, 21 May. Notes for this lecture survive as MS 955 (Robin, *Catalogue*). Fisch, *First Supplement* and *Third Supplement.*

P 00471: (NF)
"The History of Science."
> Lectures given for the Lowell Institute at Cambridge, Massachusetts on Monday and Thursday evenings, 28 November 1892 through 5 January 1893. Notes for this series survive as MSS 1274-1283 (Robin, *Catalogue*). Burks, *Bibliography;* Fisch, *First Supplement.*

1892

O 00472: F i c h e S u p. 9—10
Johnson, William Ernest.
    "The Logical Calculus," *Mind,* new series 1, 3-30, 235-250, 340-357, at 16, 29, 235, 237, 240, 241, 247, 249, 250.

O 00473: F i c h e 99
Franklin, Christine Ladd.
    Review of *Vorlesungen über die Algebra der Logik (Exakte Logik),* vol. 1, by Ernst Schröder, *Mind,* new series 1, 126-132.

P 00474: F i c h e 99
"The Doctrine of Necessity Examined."
    The Monist, vol. 2 (April), 321-337. Cohen, *Tentative Bibliography;* Burks, *Bibliography.*

O 00475: F i c h e 99
Carus, Paul.
    "Mr. Charles S. Peirce on Necessity." *The Monist,* vol. 2 (April), 442.

O 00476: F i c h e 99
Carus, Paul.
    "What does Anschauung Mean?" *The Monist,* vol. 2 (July), 527-532, at 528-529.

P 00477: F i c h e 99
"The Law of Mind."
    The Monist, vol. 2 (July), 533-559. Cohen, *Tentative Bibliography;* Burks, *Bibliography.*

O 00478: F i c h e 100
Carus, Paul.
    "Mr. Charles S. Peirce's Onslaught on the Doctrine of Necessity," *The Monist,* vol. 2 (July), 560-582.

O 00479: F i c h e 100
"Kappa rho sigma [pseudonym]."
    Review of *Vorlesungen über die Algebra der Logik (Exakte Logik),* erster band. By Ernst Schröder. *The Monist,* vol. 2 (July), 618-623.

P 00480: F i c h e 100
"Man's Glassy Essence."
    The Monist, vol. 3 (October), 1-22. Cohen, *Tentative Bibliography;* Burks, *Bibliography.*

O 00481: F i c h e 100
Carus, Paul.
    "The Idea of Necessity, Its Basis and Its Scope," *The Monist,* vol. 3 (October), 68-96.

P 00482: F i c h e 101
"The Comtist Calendar."
    The Nation, vol. 54 (21 January) 54-55.

O 00483: F i c h e 101
Stille, Werner A.
    "Science in America," *The Nation,* vol. 54 (11 February) 110. Letter.

P 00484: F i c h e 101
"Science in America."
    The Nation, vol. 54 (11 February) 110, see O 00483. Peirce's editorial reply.

1892

P 00485: Fiche 101
"The Non-Euclidean Geometry."
The Nation, vol. 54 (11 February) 116.

O 00486: Fiche 101
Bocher, Maxime.
"Geometry Not Mathematics," *The Nation,* vol. 54 (18 February) 131. Letter.

P 00487: Fiche 101
Review of *The Man of Genius.* By Cesare Lombroso.
The Nation, vol. 54 (25 February) 151-153.

O 00488: Fiche 101
Smith, William Benjamin.
"Science in America," *The Nation,* vol. 54 (3 March) 169. Letter.

P 00489: Fiche 101
"Science in America."
The Nation, vol. 54 (3 March) 169, see O 00488. Reply to a letter. Probably by Peirce.

O 00490: Fiche 101
J. McL. S.
"Is Induction an Inference?" *The Nation,* vol. 54 (10 March) 190-191.

P 00491: Fiche 101
"Is Induction an Inference?"
The Nation, vol. 54 (10 March) 190-191, see O 00451. Reply to a letter.

O 00492: Fiche 101
Stille, Werner A.
"Experimental Psychology," *The Nation,* vol. 54 (17 March) 211-212. Letter commenting on Peirce's review of Lombroso.

P 00493: Fiche 101
Note [on Halsted's translation of Bolyai's Non-Euclidean Geometry].
The Nation, vol. 54 (17 March) 212.

P 00494: Fiche 101
Note [on the abridged edition of James' *Principles of Psychology*].
The Nation, vol. 54 (17 March) 214.

P 00495: Fiche 101
Review of *A Treatise on the Geometry of the Circle, and some Extensions to Conic Sections by the method of Reciprocation.* By William J. McClelland.
The Nation, vol. 54 (24 March) 237.

P 00496: Fiche 101
Note [on Netto's *Theory of Substitutions*].
The Nation, vol. 54 (12 May) 358.

P 00497: Fiche 101
Note [on Edwards' *Elementary Treatise on the Differential Calculus*].
The Nation, vol. 54 (12 May) 358, see P 00496.

1892

P 00498: F i c h e 101
Review of *Mathematical Recreations, and Problems of Past and Present Times.* By W.W. Rouse Ball.
    The Nation, vol. 54 (12 May) 366.

P 00499: F i c h e 101
Review of *Moral Teachings of Science.* By Arabella B. Buckley.
    The Nation, vol. 54 (2 June) 417.

P 00500: F i c h e 101
Review of *The Origin of Metallic Currency and Weight Standards.* By William Ridgeway.
    The Nation, vol. 54 (23 June) 472-473.

P 00501: F i c h e 101.
Review of *The Grammar of Science.* By Karl Pearson.
    The Nation, vol. 55 (7 July) 15.

P 00502: F i c h e 101
Review of *The Province of Expression: A search for principles underlying adquate methods of developing Dramatic and Oratoric Delivery.* By S.S. Curry.
    The Nation, vol. 55 (14 July) 35.

P 00503: F i c h e 101
Review of *Dynamics of Rotation: An Elementary Introduction to Rigid Dynamics.* By A.M. Worthington.
    The Nation, vol. 55 (11 August) 114-115.

P 00504: F i c h e 101
Review of *The Philosophy of Spinoza.* By George Stuart Fullerton.
    The Nation, vol. 55 (25 August) 152.

P 00505: F i c h e 101
Review of *Dreams of the Dead.* By Edward Stanton.
    The Nation, vol. 55 (8 September) 190-191.

P 00506: F i c h e 101
"The Boston Public Library."
    The Nation, vol. 55 (6 October) 260. Signed letter.

P 00507: F i c h e 101
Review of *Distinction and the Criticism of Belief.* By Alfred Sidgwick.
    The Nation, vol. 55 (27 October) 324-325.

P 00508: F i c h e 101
Review of *Logarithmic and Other Mathematical Tables.* By William J. Hussey.
    The Nation, vol. 55 (10 November) 359-360.

P 00509: F i c h e 101
[announcement, correspondence lessons in the Art of Reasoning]
    The Open Court, vol. 6 (1 September), 3374.

P 00510: F i c h e 101
"Pythagorics."
    The Open Court, vol. 6 (8 September), 3375-3377. Cohen, *Tentative Bibliography;* Burks, *Bibliography.*

1892

P 00511: F i c h e 102
"The Critic of Arguments. I. Exact Thinking."
> *The Open Court,* vol. 6 (22 September), 3391-3394. Cohen, *Tentative Bibliography;* Burks, *Bibliography.*

P 00512: F i c h e 102
"Dmesis."
> *The Open Court,* vol. 6 (29 September), 3399-3402. Cohen, *Tentative Bibliography;* Burks, *Bibliography;* Fisch, *First Supplement.*

P 00513: F i c h e 102
"The critic of Arguments. II. The Reader is Introduced to Relatives."
> *The Open Court,* vol. 6 (13 October), 3415-3418. Burks, *Bibliography.*

P 00514: F i c h e 102
[Pendulum research]
> *Report of the Superintendent of the United States Coast and Geodetic Survey, 1891, Part I,* House Ex. Doc. No. 43, 52nd Congress, 1st Session, Washington: Government Printing Office, references to Peirce's research at p. 67-68,97. Burks, *Bibliography.*

O 00515: F i c h e 102
Mendenhall, Thomas Corwin.
> [Note on Peirce's resignation from the Coast Survey], *Science,* vol. 19 (8 January), 17-18.

O 00516: F i c h e 102
Anonymous.
> [Note on Peirce's *Open Court* articles], *Science,* vol. 20 (23 September), 173.

O 00517: F i c h e 102
Anonymous.
> "Charles Sanders Peirce," *Sun and Shade,* vol. 4 (August), photogravure numbered XC, with short biographical sketch.

1893

O 00518: F i c h e 102
Strobel, Fr.
> [Bibliographic references to Peirce's work] "Namenregister zum 1-15 Bande (1877-1891)," von Fr. Strobel, *Beiblätter zu den Annalen der Physik und Chemie.* Peirce's name is given at p. 132 with references to mentions of his work in the *Beiblätter.* Additional bibliographic references to Peirce's articles are to be found in the following volumes of the *Beiblätter:* 6(1882), 830; 7(1883), 80.

P 00519: F i c h e 102
"Napoleon Intime."
> Part one of a review of *Napoleon Intime,* by Arthur Levy, *The Independent,* vol. 45 (21 December), 1725-1726. *List of Articles;* Burks, *Bibliography.*

P 00520: F i c h e 102
"Napoleon Intime. Second Article."
> Part two of a review of *Napoleon Intime,* by Arthur Levy, *The Independent,* vol. 45 (28 December), p. 1760. *List of Articles;* Burks, *Bibliography.*

P 00521: F i c h e 102
"Evolutionary Love."
> *The Monist,* vol. 3 (January), 176-200. Cohen, *Tentative Bibliography;* Burks, *Bibliography.*

1893

O 00522: F i c h e 102
Russell, Francis C.
    "Logic as Relation-Lore," *The Monist,* vol. 3 (January), 272-285, at p. 275.

O 00523: F i c h e 103
Dewey, John.
    "The Superstition of Necessity," *The Monist,* vol. 3 (April), 362-379.

O 00524: F i c h e 103
McCrie, G.M.
    "The Issues of 'Synechism'," *The Monist,* vol. 3 (April), 380-401.

P 00525: F i c h e 103
"Reply to the Necessitarians."
    The Monist, vol. 3 (July), 526-570. Cohen, *Tentative Bibliography;* Burks, *Bibliography.*

O 00526: F i c h e 104
Carus, Paul.
    "The Founder of Tychism, His Methods, Philosophy and Criticisms: In Reply to Mr. Charles Sanders Peirce," *The Monist,* vol. 3 (July), 571-622. On p. 571 there is part of a letter from Peirce concerning his "Reply to the Necessitarians..."

O 00527: F i c h e 104
Kappa kappa [pseudonym].
    Review of *The Science of Mechanics.* By Dr. Ernst Mach, *The Monist,* vol. 4 (October), 152-153, at p. 153.

P 00528: F i c h e 104
Review of *A Treatise on the Mathematical Theory of Elasticity.* By A.E. H. Love.
    The Nation, vol. 56 (2 February) 90.

P 00529: F i c h e 104
Note [on volume xix, part 2, *Annals of the Harvard College Observatory*].
    The Nation, vol. 57 (27 July) 65.

P 00530: F i c h e 104
Review of *The Meaning and Method of Life: A Search for Religion in Biology.* By George M. Gould.
    The Nation, vol. 57 (3 August) 88-89.

P 00531: F i c h e 104
"Hale's New England Boyhood."
    The Nation, vol. 57 (17 August), 123-124.

P 00532: F i c h e 104
Review of *An Elementary Treatise on Pure Geometry.* By John Wellesley Russell. *An Elementary Treatise on Modern Pure Geometry.* By R. Lachlan.
    Geometry in the Grammar School. By Paul H. Hanns. *The Nation,* vol. 57 (24 August) 143.

P 00533: F i c h e 104
Review of *Pioneers of Science.* By Oliver Lodge.
    The Nation, vol. 57 (7 September) 178-179.

O 00534: F i c h e 104
Kral, J.J.
    "Was Copernicus a German?" *The Nation,* vol. 57 (5 October) 248. Letter.

1893

P 00535: F i c h e 104
"Was Copernicus a German?"
>The Nation, vol. 57 (5 October) 248. Reply to a letter; see O 00534.

P 00536: F i c h e 104
"Mach's Science of Mechanics."
>The Nation, vol. 57 (5 October) 251-252.

P 00537: F i c h e 105
Review of *Negative Beneficence and Positive Beneficence. Being Parts V. and VI. of the Principles of Ethics.* By Herbert Spencer.
>The Nation, vol. 57 (19 October) 293-294.

P 00538: F i c h e 105
Review of *Personal Recollections of Werner von Siemens.* Translated by W.C. Coupland.
>The Nation, vol. 57 (26 October) 313-314.

P 00539: F i c h e 105
Note [on Beckford's *Vathek*].
>The Nation, vol. 57 (9 November) 350.

P 00540: F i c h e 105
"Conundrum."
>The Nation, vol. 57 (16 November) 370. Signed letter.

P 00541: F i c h e 105
"Ritchie's Darwin and Hegel."
>The Nation, vol. 57 (23 November) 393-394.

P 00542: F i c h e 105
"Leland's Memoirs."
>The Nation, vol. 57 (30 November) 414-415.

O 00543: F i c h e 105
F.E.M.,
>Note [on Peirce's review of Leland's *Memoirs*], The Nation, vol. 57 (7 December) 431.

P 00544: F i c h e 105
Review of *L'Ennemi des Lois.* Par Maurice Barrès.
>The Nation, vol. 57 (7 December) 436-437.

P 00545: F i c h e 105
"The Marriage of Religion and Science."
>The Open Court, vol. 7 (16 February), 3559-3560. *List of Articles;* Burks, *Bibliography.*

O 00546: F i c h e 105
Carus, Paul
>"Religion Inseparable from Science," The Open Court, vol. 7 (16 February), 3560.

P 00547: F i c h e 105
"Cogito Ergo Sum."
>The Open Court, vol. 7 (15 June), 3702. Compare p. 3670. Burks, *Bibliography.*

P 00548: F i c h e 105
"What is Christian Faith?"
>The Open Court, vol. 7 (27 July), 3743-3745. Cohen, *Tentative Bibliography;* Burks, *Bibliography.*

A Comprehensive Bibliography

1893

O 00549: F i c h e 105
Carus, Paul.
> "Note [on Peirce's article, "What is Christian Faith?"]," *The Open Court,* vol. 7 (27 July), 3750.

P 00550: F i c h e 105
[Statement of the mechanical units in use in the United States and Great Britain].
> In *The Science of Mechanics,* by Ernst Mach, translated from the second German edition by Thomas J. McCormack, Chicago: The Open Court Publishing Co., 1893, p. 280-286. "The thanks of the translator are due to Mr. C.S. Peirce, well known for his studies both of analytical mechanics and the history and logic of physics, for numerous suggestions and notes. Mr. Peirce has read all the proofs and has rewritten [Paragraph] 8 in the chapter on Units and Measures, where the original was inapplicable to this country and slightly out of date." Fisch, *First Supplement;* see Burks, *Bibliography,* G-1902-4.

P 00551: F i c h e 105
"Prospectus. The Treatise of Petrus Peregrinus on the Lodestone: Latin Text, English Version, and Notes. With an Introductory History of Experimental Science in the Middle Ages. By C.S. Peirce. Printed in two colors on hand-made paper. Bound in full Persian Morocco, hand-tooled. 140 pages."
> Privately printed prospectus for an edition of Peregrinus. P. 16. An announcement of this prospectus appeared in *The Nation,* vol. 58 (11 January 1894) 30, which suggests that it had already been printed in 1893. Burks, *Bibliography.*

P 00552: F i c h e 106
"The Principles of Philosophy: Or, Logic, Physics and Psychics, Considered as a Unity, In the Light of the Nineteenth Century."
> Privately printed brochure announcing Peirce's proposed work in twelve volumes, planned for sale through subscription. Burks, *Bibliography.*

1894

P 00553: F i c h e 106
"Rough notes on geometry. Constitution of real space."
> Paper read before the American Mathematical Society, 24 November. Cited in *Bulletin of the American Mathematical Society,* vol. 1 (December), 77. Burks, *Bibliography.*

O 00554: (NF)
> *Hearings before the Committee on Naval Affairs, U.S. House of Representatives . . . on the Bill H.R. 6338, to Abolish the Bureau in the Treasury Department Known as the Coast and Geodetic Survey . . . ,* Washington: Government Printing Office. This publication contains the Thorn Commission report (1885) on the Coast Survey (relevant portions are already filmed at O 00322). This document is rare; however, a copy available in the Library of Congress was examined.

O 00555: (NF)
Korselt, A.
> "Bemerkung zur Algebra der Logik," *Mathematische Annalen,* vol. 44, 156-157.

O 00556: F i c h e 106
Russell, Francis C.
> "Logic as Relation-Lore: Rejoinder to M. Mouret by Mr. Russell," *The Monist,* vol. 4 (April) 448-463.

P 00557: F i c h e 106
Review of *Utility of Quaternions in Physics.* By A.C. McAulay.
> *The Nation,* vol. 58 (4 January) 19.

1894

P 00558: F i c h e 106
Note [on Peirce's *Principles of Philosophy* and his edition of *On the Lodestone*].
    The Nation, vol. 58 (11 January) 30. Probably by Peirce.

P 00559: F i c h e 106
Note [on Langley's "The Internal Work of the Wind"].
    The Nation, vol. 58 (11 January) 31. Probably by Peirce.

P 00560: F i c h e 106
"Huxley's Essays."
    The Nation, vol. 58 (11 January) 34-35.

P 00561: F i c h e 106
"Scott's Familiar Letters."
    The Nation, vol. 58 (8 February) 105-107.

P 00562: F i c h e 106
"Early Magnetical Science. — I."
    The Nation, vol. 58 (15 February) 124-125.

P 00563: F i c h e 106
Note [on Langley's *Internal Work of the Wind*].
    The Nation, vol. 58 (22 February) 139. Probably by Peirce.

P 00564: F i c h e 106
"Early Magnetical Science. — II."
    The Nation, vol. 58 (22 February) 141-142.

P 00565: F i c h e 106
"Funk's Standard Dictionary."
    The Nation, vol. 58 (8 March) 180-181.

P 00566: F i c h e S u p. 10
"Mathematical Functions."
    The Nation, vol. 58 (15 March) 197-199.

P 00567: F i c h e 106
"Lockyer's Dawn of Astronomy."
    The Nation, vol. 58 (29 March) 234-236.

P 00568: F i c h e S u p. 10
Reviews of *The Monism of Man.* By David Allyn Gorton. *Genetic Philosophy.* By David Jayne Hill.
    The Nation, vol. 58 (12 April) 278.

P 00569: F i c h e 106
Review of *An Elementary Treatise on Fourier's Series and Spherical and Ellipsoidal Harmonics.* By William Elwood Byerly. *Lectures on Mathematics, delivered in August and September, 1893, at Evanston, Ill.* By Felix Klein.
    The Nation, vol. 58 (19 April) 299.

P 00570: F i c h e 106
"Cajori's History of Mathematics."
    The Nation, vol. 58 (26 April) 316-317.

P 00571: F i c h e 106
Review of *Total Eclipses of the Sun.* By Mabel Loomis Todd.
    The Nation, vol. 58 (3 May) 335.

1894

P 00572: F i c h e S u p. 10
Review of *New Light from the Great Pyramid*. By Albert Ross Parsons.
> *The Nation,* vol. 58 (31 May) 415-416.

P 00573: F i c h e 106
Review of *Johnson's Universal Cyclopaedia: A New and Enlarged Edition.* Charles Kendall Adams, Editor-in-chief.
> *The Nation,* vol. 59 (5 July) 17.

P 00574: F i c h e 106
Review of *Basal Concepts in Philosophy.* By Alexander T. Ormond.
> *The Nation,* vol. 59 (12 July) 34-35. Probably by Peirce.

P 00575: F i c h e 106
Review of *The Animal as a Machine and a Prime Mover, and the Laws of Energetics.* By R.H. Thurston.
> *The Nation,* vol. 59 (19 July) 52-53.

P 00576: F i c h e 106
"Alchemy and Chemistry."
> *The Nation,* vol. 59 (23 August) 144-145.

P 00577: F i c h e 106
"Helmholtz."
> *The Nation,* vol. 59 (13 September) 191-193.

P 00578: F i c h e 107
"Four Histories of Philosophy. — I."
> *The Nation,* vol. 59 (27 September) 237-238.

P 00579: F i c h e 107
"Four Histories of Philosophy. — II."
> *The Nation,* vol. 59 (4 October) 251-252.

P 00580: F i c h e 107
Review of *Essays in Historical Chemistry.* By T.E. Thorpe.
> *The Nation,* vol. 59 (25 October) 312-313. Probably by Peirce.

O 00581: F i c h e 107
Anonymous.
> Note [on the *Proceedings of the Psychical Research Society*], *The Nation,* vol. 59 (8 November) 343. Peirce refers to this note in his letter at 59 (22 November 1894) 381.

P 00582: F i c h e 107
"Spinoza's Ethic."
> *The Nation,* vol. 59 (8 November) 344-345.

P 00583: F i c h e 107
"Hallucinations."
> *The Nation,* vol. 59 (22 November) 381. Signed letter.

P 00584: F i c h e 107
Note [on Wundt's *Vorlesungen über Menschen und Thierseele* (English translation)].
> *The Nation,* vol. 59 (22 November) 383. Probably by Peirce.

1894

O 00585: F i c h e 107
Anonymous.
> Note [on Peirce's review of Spinoza's *Ethic* in *The Nation* at vol. 59 (8 November 1894) 344-345], *The Nation,* 59 (29 November) 409.

P 00586: F i c h e 107
Review of *Modern Scientific Whist.* By C.D.P. Hamilton.
> *The Nation,* vol. 59 (6 December) 430-431.

P 00587: F i c h e 107
"Descartes and His Works."
> *The Nation,* vol. 59 (27 December) 476-477.

O 00588: (NF)
Greenhill, A.G.
> Review of *Science of Mechanics* by Ernst Mach. *Nature,* vol. 51, 49-52, at 51-52.

P 00589: F i c h e 107
[Exhibition of the arithmetic of Rollandus]
> Presented at the meeting of the New York Mathematical Society on 7 April. Cited in *Bulletin of the New York Mathematical Society,* vol. 3 (May 1894), 199-200. Burks, *Bibliography;* Fisch, *First Supplement.*

P 00590: F i c h e 107
"Mathematics Their Theme."
> *The New York Times* (8 April), page 8, column 1. This article is a report on the 7 April 1894 meeting of the New York Mathematical Society at which Peirce exhibited an arithmetic by Rolandus (dated 1424). A translation (presumably by Peirce) of Rolandus' dedicatory letter is given in this article. Burks, *Bibliography;* Fisch, *First Supplement.*

O 00591: (NF)
Scheiner, J.
> *A Treatise on Astronomical Spectroscopy.* A revised and enlarged translation by the author and E.B. Frost of *Die Spectralanalyse der Gestirne,* Boston and London: Ginn & Co., see p. 154, 326, 363-364, 461, 470.

1895

P 00592: F i c h e 107
"Prof. Arthur Cayley."
> *The Evening Post,* New York, vol. 94 (Monday, 28 January), page 7, columns 1-2. See MS 1401 (Robin, *Catalogue*). Fisch, *Third Supplement.*

O 00593: F i c h e 107
Scott, Mary Augusta.
> "Prof. Cayley," *The Evening Post,* New York, vol. 94 (Monday, 4 February), page 7, column 2.

O 00594: (NF)
Royce, Josiah.
> "Natural Law, Ethics, and Evolution," *International Journal of Ethics,* vol. 5, 489-500.

O 00595: (NF)
Schröder, Ernst.
> "Note über die Algebra der binären Relative," *Mathematische Annalen,* vol. 46, 144-158.

1895

P 00596: F i c h e 107
Review of *Logic.* By. Dr. Christoph Sigwart. Second edition
    The Nation, vol. 60 (14 March) 208.

P 00597: F i c h e 107
Review of *Philosophy of Mind: An Essay in the Metaphysics of Psychology.* By George Trumbull Ladd.
    The Nation, vol. 60 (21 March) 226-227. Probably by Peirce.

P 00598: F i c h e 107
Nicolai Ivanovich Lobachevsky. By A. Vasiliev.
    The Nation, vol. 60 (4 April) 265. Probably by Peirce.

P 00599: F i c h e 107
Review of *Comte, Mill and Spencer: An Outline of Philosophy.* By John Watson.
    The Nation, vol. 60 (11 April) 284-285.

P 00600: F i c h e 107
Review of *Herbart and the Herbartarians.* By Charles DeGarmo.
    The Nation, vol. 60 (30 May) 431-432. Probably by Peirce.

P 00601: F i c h e 107
"Some Studies of Reasoning."
    The Nation, vol. 61 (4 July) 14-16.

P 00602: F i c h e 107
Review of *The Source and Mode of Solar Energy throughout the Universe.* By I.W. Heysinger.
    The Nation, vol. 61 (11 July) 34-35.

P 00603: F i c h e 107
Review of *Mental Development in the Child and the Race: Methods and Processes.* By James Mark Baldwin.
    The Nation, vol. 61 (22 August) 139-140. Probably by Peirce.

P 00604: F i c h e 107
Review of *Studies in the Evolutionary Psychology of Feeling.* By Hiram M. Stanley.
    The Nation, vol. 61 (14 November) 353-354.

P 00605: F i c h e 107
Review of *The Psychology of Number, and its Applications to Methods of Teaching Arithmetic.* By James A. McLellan and John Dewey.
    The Nation, vol. 61 (28 November) 395.

O 00606: F i c h e 107
Chemist.
    "Acetylene and Alcohol," *The Nation,* vol. 61 (19 December) 447. Letter.

P 00607: F i c h e 107
Review of *Great Astronomers.* By Sir Robert S. Ball.
    The Nation, vol. 61 (19 December) 453.

P 00608: F i c h e 107
"Acetylene and Alcohol.
    The Nation, vol. 61 (26 December) 464. Signed "S." Probably by Peirce.

1895

O 00609: (NF)
Royce, Josiah.
> "Self-Consciousness, Social Consciousness, and Nature," *Philosophical Review,* vol. 4, 465-485, 577-602, at 592, 602.

O 00610: F i c h e 108
Schröder, Ernst.
> *Vorlesungen über die Algebra der Logik (Exakte Logik),* vol. 3, part 1, Leipzig: B.G. Teubner, at p. 1-75, 114-115.

1896

P 00611: F i c h e 108
Review of *A History of the Warfare of Science with Theology in Christendom.* By Andrew Dickson White.
> *The American Historical Review,* vol. 2 (October), 107-113. Burks, *Bibliography.*

O 00612: F i c h e 108, 109
Peirpont, James.
> "Note on Peirce's Paper on 'A Quincuncial Projection of the Sphere'," *American Journal of Mathematics,* vol. 18 (April), 145-152.

P 00613: F i c h e 109
Translation of "Light and Electricity, According to Maxwell and Hertz," by M. Poincare.
> In *Annual Report of the Board of Regents of the Smithsonian Institution to July 1894,* Washington: Government Printing Office p. 129-139. Fisch, *First Supplement.*

P 00614: F i c h e 109
Translation of "Photographic Photometry," by M.J. Janssen.
> In *Annual Report of the Board of Regents of the Smithsonian Institution to July 1894,* Washington: Government Printing Office, p. 191-196. Fisch, *First Supplement.*

P 00615: F i c h e 109
Translation of "Four Days' Observations at the Summit of Mont Blanc," by M.J. Janssen.
> In *Annual Report of the Board of Regents of the Smithsonian Institution to July 1894,* Washington: Government Printing Office, p. 237-247. Fisch, *First Supplement.*

P 00616: F i c h e 109, 110, 111, 112
Translation of *Genius and Degeneration,* by Dr. William Hirsch. New York: D. Appleton and Co. London: William Heinemann, 1897.
> We have filmed the edition of 1897, published in London by William Heinemann. See drafts in MS 1517 (Robin, *Catalogue*). Burks, *Bibliography.*

O 00617: (NF)
Cajori, Florian.
> *A History of Elementary Mathematics,* New York: Macmillan, at p. 67, 70.

P 00618: F i c h e 113
"Number: A Study of the Methods of Exact Philosophical Thought."
> Lecture before the Mathematical Department, Bryn Mawr College. Cited in *Annual Report of the President of Bryn Mawr College, 1896-1897,* Philadelphia: Alfred J. Ferris, Printer, 1898, p. 35. MS 25 (see Robin, *Catalogue*) is probably for this lecture. Burks, *Bibliography;* Fisch, *First Supplement.*

O 00619: F i c h e 113
Carus, Paul.
> Review of *Algebra und Logik der Relative,* dritter band. By Ernst Schröder. *The Monist,* vol. 6 (January), 312.

1896

P 00620: Fiche 113
"The Regenerated Logic."
The Monist, vol. 7 (October), 19-40. Burks, *Bibliography.*

P 00621: Fiche 113
"Benjamin's History of Electricity."
The Nation, vol. 62 (2 January) 16-18.

O 00622: Fiche 113
Mackintosh, William D.
"Addition and Subtraction," *The Nation,* 62 (9 January) 32-33. Letter.

P 00623: Fiche 113
Review of *Science and Art Drawing.* By J. Humphrey Spanton.
The Nation, vol. 62 (9 January) 42. Probably by Peirce.

P 00624: Fiche 113
Note [on the fourth edition of Halsted's translation of Bolyai's *Absolute Science of Space*].
The Nation, vol. 62 (6 February) 122. Probably by Peirce.

P 00625: Fiche 113
Review of *Molecules and the Molecular Theory of Matter.* By A.D. Risteen.
The Nation, vol. 62 (13 February) 147.

P 00626: Fiche 113
Review of *Mind and Motion,* and *Monism.* By the late George John Romanes.
The Nation, vol. 62 (26 March) 261-262.

P 00627: Fiche 113
Review of *Algebra und Logik der Relative, der Vorlesungen uber die Algebra der Logik.* Von Dr. Ernst Schröder.
The Nation, vol. 62 (23 April) 330-331.

P 00628: Fiche 113
Review of *The Number Concept; Its Origin and Development.* By Levi Leonard Conant.
The Nation, vol. 62 (21 May) 404.

P 00629: Fiche 113
"Külpe's Outlines of Psychology."
The Nation, vol. 63 (23 July) 71-72.

P 00630: Fiche 113
Review of *Elements of the Theory of Functions of a Complex Variable, with especial reference to the Methods of Riemann.* By Dr. H. Durege.
The Nation, vol. 63 (3 September) 181-182.

P 00631: Fiche 113, 114
"On the Logic of Quantity."
Paper read by title (Peirce did not attend) before the National Academy of Sciences, Washington, 21-24 April. Cited in *Report of the National Academy of Sciences for the Year 1896,* Senate Document No. 50, 54th Congress, 2d Session, Washington: Government Printing Office, 1897, p. 9. MSS 14-22 (see Robin, *Catalogue*) may be materials intended for this paper. Burks, *Bibliography;* Fisch, *First Supplement.*

1896

P 00632: Fiche 114
"A Graphical Method of Logic."
>Paper read before the National Academy of Sciences, New York City, 17-18 November. Cited in *Report of the National Academy of Sciences for the Year 1896,* Senate Document No. 50, 54th Congress, 2d Session, Washington: Government Printing Office, 1897, p. 11, filmed at P 00631. MS 480 (see Robin, *Catalogue*) might possibly be a draft of this paper. Burks, *Bibliography.*

P 00633: Fiche 114
"Mathematical Infinity."
>Paper read before the National Academy of Sciences, New York City, 17-18 November. Cited in *Report of the National Academy of Sciences for the Year 1896,* Senate Document No. 50, 54th Congress, 2d Session, Washington: Government Printing Office, 1897, p. 11, filmed at P 00631. Burks, *Bibliography.*

1897

O 00634: Fiche 114
Frischauf, I.
>"Bemerkungen zu Peirce Quincuncial Projection," *American Journal of Mathematics,* vol. 19, 381-382.

P 00635: Fiche 114
"James Joseph Sylvester"
>*The Evening Post,* New York City, vol. 96 (Tuesday, 16 March), page 7, columns 3-4. Burks, *Bibliography.*

O 00636: (NF)
Pritchard, Ada.
>*The Life and Work of Professor Pritchard,* London: Seeley & Co., Ltd, at p. 287.

P 00637: Fiche 114
"The Logic of Relatives."
>*The Monist,* vol. 7 (January), 161-217. Burks, *Bibliography.*

O 00638: Fiche 114
Kempe, A.B.
>"The Theory of Mathematical Form: A Correction and Explanation," *The Monist,* vol. 7 (April), 453-458.

P 00639: Fiche 114
Note [obituary, J.J. Sylvester].
>*The Nation,* vol. 64 (25 March) 227.

P 00640: Fiche 115
Review of *Studies in Psychical Research.* By Frank Podmore.
>*The Nation,* vol. 65 (4 November) 362-363.

P 00641: Fiche 115
Review of *The Principles of Chemistry.* By D. Mendeleef.
>*The Nation,* vol. 65 (25 November) 424.

P 00642: Fiche 115
Note [on Boethius, *The Consolation of Philosophy*].
>*The Nation,* vol. 65 (9 December) 458-459.

1897

O 00643: F i c h e 115
Meldola, Raphael.
    "Proposed Sylvester Memorial," *The Nation,* vol. 65 (30 December) 515.

P 00644: F i c h e 115
Note [on Perry's *Calculus for Engineers*].
    The Nation, vol. 65 (30 December) 518.

P 00645: F i c h e 115
Review of *The Conception of God.* By Josiah Royce, Joseph Le Conte, G.H. Howison, and Sidney Edward Mezes.
    The Nation, vol. 65 (30 December) 524-525.

O 00646: (NF)
Muller, Gustav.
    Die Photometrie der Gestirne, Leipzig: Wilehlm Engelmann, at p. 429, 433, 439, 444-446, 457, 538.

O 00647: F i c h e 115
Halsted, George Bruce.
    "Sylvester," *Science,* new series 5, (Friday 16 April), 597-604.

O 00648: (NF)
Davis, Ellery W.
    "On the Continuity of Chance," *University Studies,* vol. 2, 131-146, at 141-144.

O 00649: (NF)
James, William.
    The Will to Believe and other essays in popuiar philosophy, New York: Longmans, Green, and Co., at dedication and p. 124 (nI), 145 (n2).

1898

P 00650: F i c h e 115
Review of *The "Opus Majus" of Roger Bacon.* Edited, with Introduction and Analytical Table, by John Henry Bridges.
    The American Historical Review, vol. 3 (April), 526-528. Burks, *Bibliography.*

O 00651: (NF)
Muir, Thomas.
    "Reinvestigation of the Problem of the Automorphic Linear Transformation of a Bipartite Quadric," *American Journal of Mathematics,* vol. 20, 215-228, at 225.

P 00652: F i c h e 115
"Reasoning and the Logic of Things."
    Cambridge Conference Lectures.
      1. February 10, Philosophy and the Conduct of Life.
      2. February 14, Types of Reasoning.
      3. February 17, The Logic of Relatives.
      4. February 21, The First Rule of Logic.
      5. February 24, Training in Reasoning.
      6. February 28, Causation and Force.
      7. March 3,   Habit.
      8. March 7,   The Logic of Continuity.

1898

Titles cited in a pamphlet announcing the lecture series. Manuscripts for these lectures survive as follows: 1, MS 437; 2, MS 441; 3, MS 438 or 440 (?); 4, MS 442; 5, MSS 444 and 445; 6, MSS 443 and 446; 7, MS 951; 8, MSS 948-950; also MSS 435, 439, 440, 940, and 941 (see Robin, *Catalogue*). Burks, *Bibliography*.

P 00653: Fiche 115
"The Logic of Mathematics in Relation to Education."
Educational Review, vol. 15 (March), 209-216. The article ends with the phrase, "To be continued," but no continuation has been found. Fisch and Haskell, *Additions to Cohen's Bibliography*; Burks, *Bibliography*.

O 00654: (NF)
Study, E.
"Theorie der Gemeinen and Höheren Complexen Grössen," *Encyklopädie der mathematischen Wissenschaften*, Leipzig: B.G. Teubner, vol. I, p. 147-183, at 169, 170.

O 00655: Fiche 115
Smith, Harriette Knight
The History of the Lowell Institute, Boston: Lamson, Wolff and Company, references to Peirce's Lowell Lectures at p. 63 and 88; see also p. 31.

O 00656: Fiche 115, 116
Schröder, Ernst.
"On Pasigraphy: Its Present State and the Pasigraphic Movement in Italy," *The Monist*, vol. 9, 44-62.

P 00657: Fiche 116
Review of *Some Unrecognized Laws of Nature: An Inquiry into the Causes of Physical Phenomena, with Special Reference to Gravitation*. By Ignatius Singer and Lewis H. Berens.
The Nation, vol. 66 (3 February) 96.

P 00658: Fiche 116
Review of *Social and Ethical Interpretations in Mental Development*. By James Mark Baldwin.
The Nation, vol. 66 (31 March) 250-251.

P 00659: Fiche 116
Review of *Memory and its Cultivation*. By F.W. Edridge-Green.
The Nation, vol. 66 (21 April) 311.

P 00660: Fiche 116
Review of *Astronomy*. By Agnes M. Clerke, A. Fowler, and J. Ellard Gore.
The Nation, vol. 66 (28 April) 330-331. Probably by Peirce.

P 00661: Fiche 116
Review of *Dynamic Idealism: An Elementary Course in the Metaphysics of Psychology*. By Alfred H. Lloyd. *Practical Idealism*. By William De Witt Hyde.
The Nation, vol. 66 (16 June) 467-468. Probably by Peirce.

P 00662: Fiche 116
Note [on Reye's *Geometrie der Lage*].
The Nation, vol. 67 (14 July) 31.

P 00663: Fiche 116
Review of *The New Psychology*. By E.W. Scripture.
The Nation, vol. 67 (14 July) 38-39. Probably by Peirce.

1898

P 00664: F i c h e 116
"The Psychology of Suggestion."
    The Nation, vol. 67 (25 August) 154-155.

P 00665: F i c h e 116
Review of *The Wonderful Century: its Successes and its Failures.* By Alfred Russel Wallace.
    The Nation, vol. 67 (22 September) 228-229.

P 00666: F i c h e 116
Note [on Kerr's *Wireless Telegraphy*].
    The Nation, vol. 67 (29 September) 242.

P 00667: F i c h e 116
"Baldwin's Story of the Mind."
    The Nation, vol. 67 (13 October) 281-282.

P 00668: F i c h e 116
Review of *Logic, Deductive and Inductive.* By Carveth Read.
    The Nation, vol. 67 (20 October) 300-301.

P 00669: F i c h e 116
Note [on Lambert's *Differential and Integral Calculus for Technical Schools and Colleges*].
    The Nation, vol. 67 (24 November) 390.

P 00670: F i c h e 116
Review of *The Story of Marco Polo.* By Noah Brooks.
    The Nation, vol. 67 (24 November) 397.

P 00671: F i c h e 116
Review of *Radiation: An Elementary Treatise on Electromagnetic Radiation and on Röntgen and Cathode Rays.* By H.H. Francis Hyndman.
    The Nation, vol. 67 (1 December) 417-418.

P 00672: F i c h e 116
"Darwin's Tides."
    The Nation, vol. 67 (22 December) 469-470.

O 00673: (NF)
Schröder, Ernst.
    "Uber zwei Definitionen der Endlichkeit und G. Cantor'sche Sätze," *Nova Acta Leopoldina,* vol. 71, 301-362, at 303-315, 361.

P 00674: F i c h e 116
"Note on the Age of Basil Valentine."
    Science, new series 8 (12 August), 169-176. Burks, *Bibliography.*

O 00675: (NF)
Royce, Josiah.
    Studies in Good and Evil, New York: D. Appleton and Co., at 128-9, 237, 248.

O 00676: F i c h e 116, 117
Whitehead, Alfred North.
    A Treatise on Universal Algebra, with Applications, Cambridge University Press, at 3, 10, 37, 42, 115-116, 172.

1898

O 00677: (NF)
James, William.
    "Philosophical Conceptions and Practical Results," *The University Chronicle* (Berkeley, California), vol. 1, 287-310, at 290-291, 307. Reprinted in abridged form in: *Journal of Philosophy,* vol. 1 (1904) 673-687, at 673-674, under the title, "The Pragmatic Method."

O 00678: (NF)
Helmert, Friedrich R.
    "Beitrage zur Theorie des Reversionspendels," *Veröffentlichung des Königl. Preuszischen Geodätischen Instituts und Centralbureau der Internationalen Erdmessung,* at p. 1, 41, 68, 70, 71, 72, 85, 92.

1899

P 00679: F i c h e 117
"Death of Prof. Bunsen."
    The Evening Post, New York City, vol. 98 (Wednesday, 16 August), page 5, columns 4-6. Reprinted in *Progressive Age* (see P 00705). Burks, *Bibliography;* Fisch, *First Supplement.*

O 00680: (NF)
Cajori, Florian.
    A History of Physics in its Elementary Branches, New York: The Macmillan Co., at p. 169-170, 184.

O 00681: (NF)
Carus, Paul.
    Kant and Spencer: A Study of the Fallacies of Agnosticism, Chicago: The Open Court Publishing Co., at p. 51, 77-79.

P 00682: F i c h e 117
Review of *Matter, Energy, Force, and Work.* By Silas W. Holman.
    The Nation, vol. 68 (2 February) 95-96.

P 00683: F i c h e 117
Review of *Leibniz: The Monadology and Other Philosophical Writings.* Translated by Robert Latta.
    The Nation, vol. 68 (16 March) 210.

P 00684: F i c h e 117
Note [on Kepler's *Somnium*].
    The Nation, vol. 68 (20 April) 296.

P 00685: F i c h e 117
Review of *A History of Physics in its Elementary Branches.* By Florian Cajori.
    The Nation, vol. 68 (27 April) 316-317.

P 00686: F i c h e 117
Review of *My Inner Life.* By John Beattie Crozier.
    The Nation, vol. 68 (4 May) 338.

O 00687: F i c h e 117
Cajori, Florian.
    "Galileo's Reasoning," *The Nation,* vol. 68 (18 May) 376.

P 00688: F i c h e 117
"Galileo's Reasoning."
    The Nation, vol. 68 (18 May) 376. Peirce's editorial reply to a letter by Cajori. Filmed at P 00687.

1899

P 00689: Fiche 117
Review of *The Gambling World.* By Rouge et Noir. *The History of Gambling in England.* By John Ashton.
    The Nation, vol. 68 (25 May) 403.

P 00690: Fiche 117
Review of *Outlines of Industrial Chemistry.* By Frank Hall Thorp.
    The Nation, vol. 68 (25 May) 405.

P 00691: Fiche 117
Review of *Stars and Telescopes: A Hand-Book of Popular Astronomy, Founded on the Ninth Edition of Lynn's Celestial Motions.* By David P. Todd.
    The Nation, vol. 68 (22 June) 482-483.

P 00692: Fiche 117
"Marshall's Instinct and Reason."
    The Nation, vol. 68 (29 June) 499-500.

P 00693: Fiche 117
Review of *An Introduction to the Theory of Analytic Functions.* By J. Harkness and F. Morley.
    The Nation, vol. 69 (6 July) 18. Probably by Peirce.

P 00694: Fiche 117
Review of *Old Clocks and Watches and their Makers.* By F.J. Britten.
    The Nation, vol. 69 (27 July) 77-78.

P 00695: Fiche 117
"Leibniz Rewritten."
    The Nation, vol. 69 (3 August) 97-98.

P 00696: Fiche 117
Review of *Through Nature to God.* By John Fiske.
    The Nation, vol. 69 (10 August) 118.

P 00697: Fiche 117
Note [on the fifth edition of Berkeley's works].
    The Nation, vol. 69 (24 August) 154. Probably by Peirce.

P 00698: Fiche 117
Reviews of *From Comte to Benjamin Kidd.* By Robert Mackintosh. *Better-World Philosophy.* By J. Howard Moore.
    The Nation, vol. 69 (7 September) 192-193.

P 00699: Fiche 117
Reviews of *Mathematical Essays and Recreations.* By Hermann Schubert. *The Study and Difficulties of Mathematics.* By Augustus De Morgan.
    The Nation, vol. 69 (21 September) 231.

P 00700: Fiche 117
Review of *Observational Geometry.* By William T. Campbell.
    The Nation, vol. 69 (28 September) 248-249. Probably by Peirce.

P 00701: Fiche 117
Review of *The Boy's Book of Inventions: Stories of the Wonders of Modern Science.* By Ray Stannard Baker.
    The Nation, vol. 69 (19 October) 303-304.

1899

P 00702: Fiche 117
"Ford's Franklin."
> *The Nation*, vol. 69 (9 November) 355-356.

P 00703: Fiche 117
Review of *The Life of James Dwight Dana, Scientific Explorer, Mineralogist, Geologist, Zoologist, Professor in Yale University.* By Daniel C. Gilman.
> *The Nation*, vol. 69 (14 December) 455.

P 00704: Fiche 118
"The Map-coloring Problem."
> Paper read before the National Academy of Sciences, New York City, 14-15 November. Cited in *Report of the National Academy of Sciences for the Year 1899*, Senate Document No. 117, 56th Congress, 1st Session, Washington: Government Printing Office, 1900, p. 13. MSS 153-158 may be related to this presentation (see Robin, *Catalogue*). Burks, *Bibliography*.

P 00705: Fiche 118
"Professor Bunsen."
> *Progressive Age*, vol. 17 (1 September), 393-394. Burks, *Bibliography;* Fisch, *First Supplement*.

O 00706: (NF)
Vailati, Giovanni.
> "La Logique mathématique et sa nouvelle phase de développement dans les écrits de M.J. Peano," *Revue de Métaphysique et de Morale*, vol. 7, 86-102, at 93, 94.

O 00707: (NF)
Royce, Josiah.
> *The World and the Individual*, 2 vols., New York: Macmillan, at I, xiii, 253-255, 510n, 512n, 514n, 562n; II, xvi, 195, 220-221, 234.

O 00708: (NF)
Schumann, R.
> "Uber die Verwendung zweier Pendel auf gemeinsamer Unterlage zur Bestimmung der Mitschwingung," *Zeitschrift für Mathematik und Physik*, vol. 44, 102-138, at 104, 111, 112.

1900

P 00709: Fiche 118
Reviews of *The Spiritual Life*, by George A. Coe; *Introduction to Ethics*, By Frank Thilly.
> *The Bookman*, vol. 11 (July), 491-492. Burks, *Bibliography*.

O 00710: (NF)
Helmert, Friedrich R.
> "Bericht über die relativen Messungen der Schwerkraft mit Pendelapparaten," *Comptes-Rendus des Séances de la treizième conférence générale de L'Association Géodésique Internationale*, vol. 2, 139-385, at 256-258, 276-277, 299, 300, 330-335, 353, 365.

O 00711: (NF)
Kayser, H.
> *Handbuch der Spectroscopie*, Leipzig: S. Hirzee, vol. I: at 122, 403, 447, 705; vol. V (1910): at 47, 50, 56-57; vol. VI (1912): at 8, 54.

O 00712: Fiche 118
Caldwell, W.
> "Pragmatism," *Mind*, new series 9 (October), 433-456.

1900

P 00713: Fiche 118
Note [on Lewis' *Treatise on Crystallography*].
    The Nation, vol. 70 (4 January) 11.

P 00714: Fiche 118
Note [on Pick's *Lectures on Memory Culture*].
    The Nation, vol. 70 (4 January) 12-13.

P 00715: Fiche 118
Review of *A Century of Science, and Other Essays.* By John Fiske.
    The Nation, vol. 70 (4 January) 18.

P 00716: Fiche 118
Review of *A History of Wireless Telegraphy, 1838-1899.* By J.J. Fahie.
    The Nation, vol. 70 (25 January) 78.

P 00717: Fiche 118
Review of *Le Mécanisme de la vie moderne.* Par le Vicomte G. d'Avenel.
    The Nation, vol. 70 (1 February) 97-98.

P 00718: Fiche 118
Note [on Carus' *Kant and Spencer*].
    The Nation, vol. 70 (8 February) 109.

P 00719: Fiche 119
"Lyon Playfair"
    The Nation, vol. 70 (8 February) 114-115.

P 00720: Fiche 119
Note [on Thorp's *Outlines of Industrial Chemistry,* revised edition].
    The Nation, vol. 70 (15 February) 128.

P 00721: Fiche 119
Note [on Ripper's *Steam-Engine Theory and Practice*].
    The Nation, vol. 70 (15 February) 128, filmed at P 00720.

P 00722: Fiche 119
Note [on Atkinson's *Power Transmitted by Electricity*].
    The Nation, vol. 70 (15 February) 128, filmed at P 00720.

P 00723: Fiche 119
Note [on Gay and Yeaman's *An Introduction to the Study of Central Station Electricity Supply*].
    The Nation, vol. 70 (15 February) 128, filmed at P 00720.

P 00724: Fiche 119
Note [on Watson's *A Text-Book of Physics*].
    The Nation, vol. 70 (1 March) 163.

P 00725: Fiche 119
Note [on Pearson's *Grammar of Science,* second edition].
    The Nation, vol. 70 (15 March) 203-204.

P 00726: Fiche 119
Note [on Hertz' *The Principles of Mechanics Presented in a New Form*].
    The Nation, vol. 70 (15 March) 204, filmed at P 00725.

1900

P 00727: F i c h e 119
Review of *The Teaching of Elementary Mathematics.* By David Eugene Smith.
    The Nation, vol. 70 (22 March) 230.

P 00728: F i c h e 119
Review of *The World and the Individual.* By Josiah Royce.
    The Nation, vol. 70 (5 April) 267.

P 00729: F i c h e 119
"Grosseteste."
    The Nation, vol. 70 (19 April) 302-303.

P 00730: F i c h e 119
Review of *Inorganic Evolution as Studied by Spectrum Analysis.* By Sir Norman Lockyer.
    The Nation, vol. 70 (10 May) 366.

P 00731: F i c h e 119
Review of *History of Ancient Philosophy.* By W. Windelband.
    The Nation, vol. 70 (17 May) 384-385.

P 00732: F i c h e 119
Note [on Bottone's *Wireless Telegraphy and Hertzian Waves*].
    The Nation, vol. 70 (31 May) 417.

P 00733: F i c h e 119
Review of *Introduction to Ethics.* By Frank Thilly.
    The Nation, vol. 70 (21 June) 480-481.

P 00734: F i c h e 119
Review of *Illustrations of Logic.* By Paul T. Lafleur.
    The Nation, vol. 70 (28 June) 502-503.

P 00735: F i c h e 119
Review of *A Short History of Free Thought, Ancient and Modern.* By John M. Robertson.
    The Nation, vol. 70 (28 June) 504-505.

P 00736: F i c h e 119
Note [on Sedgefield's edition of Boethius *Consolations*].
    The Nation, vol. 71 (5 July) 14.

P 00737: F i c h e 119
Review of *Theory of Differential Equations.* By Andrew Russell Forsyth.
    The Nation, vol. 71 (19 July) 59.

P 00738: F i c h e 119
Review of *A History of Modern Philosophy: A Sketch of the History of Philosophy from the Close of the Renaissance to Our Own Day.* By Harald Höffding.
    The Nation, vol. 71 (26 July) 78-79.

P 00739: F i c h e 119
Review of *The Kinetic Theory of Gases: Elementary Treatise with Mathematical Appendices.* By Dr. Oskar Emil Meyer.
    The Nation, vol. 71 (26 July) 79, filmed at P 00738.

O 00740: F i c h e 119
Thilly, Frank.
    "Thilly and Wundt," *The Nation,* vol. 71 (16 August) 131.

1900

P 00741: F i c h e 119
Review of *The Theory of Electrolytic Dissociation, and Some of its Applications.* By Harry C. Jones.
    The Nation, vol. 71 (30 August) 178.

P 00742: F i c h e 119
Note [on Perry's mathematical writings].
    The Nation, vol. 71 (6 September) 192-193.

P 00743: F i c h e 119
Review of *Bordeaux and its Wines, Classed by Order of Merit.* By Édouard Feret.
    The Nation, vol. 71 (20 September) 235-236.

P 00744: F i c h e 119
Review of *Acetylene.* By Vivian B. Lewes.
    The Nation, vol. 71 (27 September) 257.

P 00745: F i c h e 119
Review of *Joseph Glanvill.* By Ferris Greenslet.
    The Nation, vol. 71 (11 October) 295-296.

P 00746: F i c h e 119
Review of *A Brief History of Mathematics.* By Dr. Karl Fink.
    The Nation, vol. 71 (18 October) 314-315.

P 00747: F i c h e 119
Review of *The Individual: A Study of Life and Death.* By Nathaniel Southgate Shaler.
    The Nation, vol. 71 (22 November) 410-411.

P 00748: F i c h e 119
Review of *The Progress of Invention in the Nineteenth Century.* By Edward W. Byrn.
    The Nation, vol. 71 (6 December) 449-450.

P 00749: F i c h e 119
Review of *The Story of Nineteenth Century Science.* By Henry Smith Williams.
    The Nation, vol. 71 (27 December) 515-516.

P 00750: F i c h e 119
"Infinitesimals."
    Science, new series 11 (16 March), 430-433. Dated by Peirce as "Milford, Pa., Feb. 18, 1900." *List of Articles;* Burks, *Bibliography.*

P 00751: F i c h e 119
Review of Clark University, 1889-1899. Decennial Celebration. *Worcester, Mass. Published by the University.*
    Science, new series 11 (20 April), 620-622. *List of Articles;* Burks, *Bibliography.*

1901

P 00752: F i c h e S u p. 10
Review of *Thomas Hariot, the Mathematician, the Philosopher, and the Scholar.* By Henry Stevens.
    The American Historical Review, vol. 6 (April), 557-561. Burks, *Bibliography.*

P 00753: F i c h e 120
Translation of "On the Sense of Smell in Birds," by M. Xavier Raspail.
    In *Annual Report of the Board of Regents of the Smithsonian Institution for the Year Ending June 30, 1899,* Washington: Government Printing Office, p. 367-373. Fisch, *First Supplement.*

1901

P 00754: F i c h e 120
Translation of "The Sculptures of Santa Lucia Cozumahualpa, Guatemala, in the Hamburg Ethnological Museum," by Herman Strebel.
> In *Annual Report of the Board of Regents of the Smithsonian Institution for the Year Ending June 30, 1899,* Washington: Government Printing Office, p. 549-561. Fisch, *First Supplement.*

P 00755: F i c h e S u p. 10
Translation of "The Progress of Aeronautics," by M. Janssen.
> In *Annual Report of the Board of Regents of the Smithsonian Institution for the Year Ending June 30, 1900,* Washington: Government Printing Office, p. 187-193. Fisch, *First Supplement.*

P 00756: F i c h e S u p. 10
Translation of "The Growth of Biology in the Nineteenth Century," by Oscar Hertwig.
> In *Annual Report of the Board of Regents of the Smithsonian Institution for the Year Ending June 30, 1900,* Washington: Government Printing Office, p. 461-478. Fisch, *First Supplement.*

P 00757: F i c h e S u p. 10–11
Translation of "Life in the Ocean," by Karl Brandt.
> In *Annual Report of the Board of Regents of the Smithsonian Institution for the Year Ending June 30, 1900,* Washington: Government Printing Office, p. 493-506. Fisch, *First Supplement.*

P 00758: F i c h e S u p. 11
Translation of "The Breeding of the Arctic Fox," by Henry de Varigny.
> In *Annual Report of the Board of Regents of the Smithsonian Institution for the Year Ending June 30, 1900,* Washington: Government Printing Office, p. 527-533. Fisch, *First Supplement.*

P 00759: F i c h e S u p. 11
Translation of "On Ancient Desemers or Steelyards," by Hermann Sŏkeland.
> In *Annual Report of the Board of Regents of the Smithsonian Institution for the Year Ending June 30, 1900,* Washington: Government Printing Office, p. 551-564. Fisch, *First Supplement.*

P 00760: F i c h e S u p. 11
"The Century's Great Men in Science."
> *Annual Report of the Board of Regents of the Smithsonian Institution for the Year Ending June 30, 1900,* Washington: Government Printing Office, p. 693-699. *List of Articles;* Burks, *Bibliography;* Fisch, *First Supplement.*

P 00761: F i c h e 121
"Economy (logical principle of)."
> *Dictionary of Philosophy and Psychology,* ed. J.M. Baldwin, New York: Macmillan, vol. 1, 309. Introductory matter (p. ii-xxiv) for this dictionary is filmed here. Burks, *Bibliography.*

P 00762: F i c h e 121
"Empirical Logic." [with R. Adamson]
> *Dictionary of Philosophy and Psychology,* ed. J.M. Baldwin, New York: Macmillan, vol. 1, 318, see also 318-321. Burks, *Bibliography.*

P 00763: F i c h e 121
"Equipollence or -cy."
> *Dictionary of Philosophy and Psychology,* ed. J.M. Baldwin, New York: Macmillan, vol. 1, 338. Burks, *Bibliography.*

1901

P 00764: Fiche 121
"Genus (in logic)."
>Dictionary of Philosophy and Psychology, ed. J.M. Baldwin, New York: Macmillan, vol. 1, 411. Burks, Bibliography.

P 00765: Fiche 121
"Given."
>Dictionary of Philosophy and Psychology, ed. J.M. Baldwin, New York: Macmillan, vol. 1, 414. Burks, Bibliography.

P 00766: Fiche 121
"Imaging (in logic)." [with H.B. Fine]
>Dictionary of Philosophy and Psychology, ed. J.M. Baldwin, New York: Macmillan, vol. 1, 518-519. Burks, Bibliography.

P 00767: Fiche 121
"Implicit (in logic)."
>Dictionary of Philosophy and Psychology, ed. J.M. Baldwin, New York: Macmillan, vol. 1, 525-526. Burks, Bibliography.

P 00768: Fiche 121
"Inconsistency."
>Dictionary of Philosophy and Psychology, ed. J.M. Baldwin, New York: Macmillan, vol. 1, 529. Burks, Bibliography.

P 00769: Fiche 121
"Independence."
>Dictionary of Philosophy and Psychology, ed. J.M. Baldwin, New York: Macmillan, vol. 1, 530. Burks, Bibliography.

P 00770: Fiche 121
"Index (in exact logic)."
>Dictionary of Philosophy and Psychology, ed. J.M. Baldwin, New York: Macmillan, vol. 1, 531-532. Burks, Bibliography.

P 00771: Fiche 121
"Individual (in logic)."
>Dictionary of Philosophy and Psychology, ed. J.M. Baldwin, New York: Macmillan, vol. 1, 537-538. Burks, Bibliography.

P 00772: Fiche 121
"Inference."
>Dictionary of Philosophy and Psychology, ed. J.M. Baldwin, New York: Macmillan, vol. 1, 542-543. Burks, Bibliography.

P 00773: Fiche 121
"Insolubilia."
>Dictionary of Philosophy and Psychology, ed. J.M. Baldwin, New York: Macmillan, vol. 1, 554. Burks, Bibliography.

P 00774: Fiche 121
"Intention (in logic)."
>Dictionary of Philosophy and Psychology, ed. J.M. Baldwin, New York : Macmillan, vol. 1, 561. Burks, Bibliography.

1901

P 00775: F i c h e 121
"Involution."
> *Dictionary of Philosophy and Psychology,* ed. J.M. Baldwin, New York: Macmillan, vol. 1, 574. Burks, *Bibliography.*

P 00776: F i c h e 121
"Kind."
> *Dictionary of Philosophy and Psychology,* ed. J.M. Baldwin, New York: Macmillan, vol. 1, 600-601. Burks, *Bibliography.*

P 00777: F i c h e 121
"Knowledge (in logic)." [with C. Ladd-Franklin]
> *Dictionary of Philosophy and Psychology,* ed. J.M. Baldwin, New York: Macmillan, vol. 1, 603. Burks, *Bibliography.*

P 00778: F i c h e 121
"Laws of Thought."
> *Dictionary of Philosophy and Psychology,* ed. J.M. Baldwin, New York: Macmillan, vol. 1, 641-643, 644. Part of this article is by C. Ladd-Franklin (643-644). Burks, *Bibliography.*

P 00779: F i c h e 121
"The Century's Great Men in Science."
> *The Evening Post,* New York City, vol. 100 (Saturday, 12 January), section three, page 1, columns 1-3. *List of Articles;* Burks, *Bibliography;* Fisch, *First Supplement.*

O 00780: (NF)
Russell, Bertrand.
> "Recent Work in the Principles of Mathematics," *International Monthly,* vol. 4, 83-101, at 84n.

O 00781: (NF)
Couturat, Louis.
> *La logique de Leibniz d'après des documents inédits,* Paris: Félix Alcan, at p. 303, 387, 408.

P 00782: F i c h e 122
"Wallace's Studies."
> *The Nation,* vol. 72 (10 January) 36-37.

P 00783: F i c h e 122
"William Herschel."
> *The Nation,* vol. 72 (24 January) 72-73.

P 00784: F i c h e 122
Review of *Webster's International Dictionary of the English Language.* W.T. Harris, editor-in-chief.
> *The Nation,* vol. 72 (24 January) 76.

P 00785: F i c h e 122
"Shaftesbury."
> *The Nation,* vol. 72 (31 January) 96-97.

P 00786: F i c h e 122
Note [on Bowley's *Elements of Statistics*].
> *The Nation,* vol. 72 (28 March) 254.

P 00787: F i c h e 122
Review of *By Land and Sea.* By the Rev. John N. Bacon.
> *The Nation,* vol. 72 (28 March) 258-259.

1901

P 00788: Fiche 122
Review of *Essays in Illustration of the Action of Astral Gravitation in Natural Phenomena.* By William Leighton Jordan.
> *The Nation,* vol. 72 (13 June) 479-480.

P 00789: Fiche 122
Review of *Le Vocabulaire Philosophique.* Par Edmond Goblot.
> *The Nation,* vol. 72 (20 June) 497-498.

P 00790: Fiche 122
Note [on Turner's *Knowledge, Belief, and Certitude*].
> *The Nation,* vol. 73 (25 July) 70.

P 00791: Fiche 122
"Berkeley's Works."
> *The Nation,* vol. 73 (1 August) 95-96.

P 00792: Fiche 122
Review of *Bibliotics; or the Study of Documents, Determination of the Individual Character of Handwriting, And Detection of Fraud and Forgery.* By Persifor Frazer.
> *The Nation,* vol. 73 (1 August) 99-100.

P 00793: Fiche 122
Review of *The Philosophy of Religion in England and America.* By Alfred Caldecott.
> *The Nation,* vol. 73 (15 August) 139-140.

P 00794: Fiche 122
"Some Physical Books."
> *The Nation,* vol. 73 (29 August) 172-173.

P 00795: Fiche 122
"Maher's Psychology."
> *The Nation,* vol. 73 (3 October) 267-268.

P 00796: Fiche 122
Review of *Ethics: Descriptive and Explanatory.* By Sidney Edward Mezes.
> *The Nation,* vol. 73 (24 October) 325-326.

P 00797: Fiche 122
"The National Academy at Philadelphia."
> *The Nation,* vol. 73 (21 November) 393-395.

P 00798: Fiche 122
Note [on Wall's *Concise French Grammar*].
> *The Nation,* vol. 73 (28 November) 415.

P 00799: Fiche 122
Review of *Practical X-Ray Work.* By Frank J. Addyman.
> *The Nation,* vol. 73 (12 December) 462.

P 00800: Fiche 122, 123
"On the Logic of Research into Ancient History."
> Paper read before the National Academy of Sciences, Philadelphia, 12-14 November. Cited in *Report of the National Academy of Sciences for the Year 1901*, Senate Document No. 153, 57th Congress, 1st Session, Washington: Government Printing Office, 1902, p. 16. MSS 690-691 and 1344 may be notes used for this lecture (see Robin, *Catalogue*). Burks, *Bibliography*.

1901

P 00801: (NF)
"The Century's Great Men of Science."
    In *The Nineteenth Century,* New York and London: G.P. Putnam's Sons, p. 312-322. Fisch, *First Supplement.*

P 00802: F i c h e 123
"Pearson's Grammar of Science. Annotations on the First Three Chapters."
    The Popular Science Monthly, vol. 58 (January), 296-306. Cohen, *Tentative Bibliography;* Burks, *Bibliography.*

P 00803: F i c h e 123
"Campanus."
    Science, new series 13 (24 May), 809-811. *List of Articles;* Burks, *Bibliography.*

P 00804: F i c h e 123
[References to Peirce's pendulum research]
    Verhandlungen der vom 25 September bis 6 October 1900 in Paris abgehaltenen Dreizehnten Allgemeinen Conferenz der Internationalen Erdmessung, II Theil: Spezialberichte and wissenschaftliche Mittheilungen, Berlin: Verlag von Georg Reimer, Appendix B, I (p. 330-335). Burks, *Bibliography.*

1902

P 00805: F i c h e 123
Translation of "The History of Chronophotography," by Dr. J. Marey.
    In *Annual Report of the Board of Regents of the Smithsonian Institution for the Year Ending June 30, 1901,* Washington: Government Printing Office, p. 317-340. Burks, *Bibliography.*

P 00806: F i c h e 123
"Leading of Proof."
    Dictionary of Philosophy and Psychology, ed. J.M. Baldwin, New York: Macmillan, vol. 2, 1. Introductory matter for vol. 2 (p. iii-xvi) is filmed here. Burks, *Bibliography.*

P 00807: F i c h e 123
"Leading Principle."
    Dictionary of Philosophy and Psychology, ed. J.M. Baldwin, New York: Macmillan, vol. 2, 1-2, filmed at P 00806. Burks, *Bibliography.*

P 00808: F i c h e 123
"Lemma."
    Dictionary of Philosophy and Psychology, ed. J.M. Baldwin, New York: Macmillan, vol. 2, 3. Burks, *Bibliography.*

P 00809: F i c h e 123
"Light of Nature."
    Dictionary of Philosophy and Psychology, ed. J.M. Baldwin, New York: Macmillan, vol. 2, 6. Burks, *Bibliography.*

P 00810: F i c h e 123
"Limitative."
    Dictionary of Philosophy and Psychology, ed. J.M. Baldwin, New York: Macmillan, vol. 2, 6-7, filmed at P 00809. Burks, *Bibliography.*

P 00811: F i c h e 124
"Logic." [with C. Ladd-Franklin]
    Dictionary of Philosophy and Psychology, ed. J.M. Baldwin, New York: Macmillan, vol. 2, 20-23. Burks, *Bibliography.*

1902

P 00812: Fiche 124
"Logic (exact)."
>   *Dictionary of Philosophy and Psychology,* ed. J.M. Baldwin, New York: Macmillan, vol. 2, 23-27, filmed at P 00811. Burks, *Bibliography.*

P 00813: Fiche 124
"Logical."
>   *Dictionary of Philosophy and Psychology,* ed. J.M. Baldwin, New York: Macmillan, vol. 2, 27-28, filmed at P 00811. Burks, *Bibliography.*

P 00814: Fiche 124
"Logical Diagram (or Graph)."
>   *Dictionary of Philosophy and Psychology,* ed. J.M. Baldwin, New York: Macmillan, vol. 2, 28, filmed at P 00811. Burks, *Bibliography.*

P 00815: Fiche 124
"Logomachy."
>   *Dictionary of Philosophy and Psychology,* ed. J.M. Baldwin, New York: Macmillan, vol. 2, 30. Burks, *Bibliography.*

P 00816: Fiche 124
"Major and Minor (extreme, term, premise, *satz,* &c., in logic)."
>   *Dictionary of Philosophy and Psychology,* ed. J.M. Baldwin, New York: Macmillan, vol. 2, 37. Burks, *Bibliography.*

P 00817: Fiche 124
"Mark." [in part, with C. Ladd-Franklin]
>   *Dictionary of Philosophy and Psychology,* ed. J.M. Baldwin, New York: Macmillan, vol. 2, 43. Burks, *Bibliography,*

P 00818: Fiche 124
"Material Fallacy."
>   *Dictionary of Philosophy and Psychology,* ed. J.M. Baldwin, New York: Macmillan, vol. 2, 44. Burks, *Bibliography.*

P 00819: Fiche 124
"Material Logic."
>   *Dictionary of Philosophy and Psychology,* ed. J.M. Baldwin, New York: Macmillan, vol. 2, 44-45, filmed at P 00818. Burks, *Bibliography.*

P 00820: Fiche 124
"Mathematical Logic."
>   *Dictionary of Philosophy and Psychology,* ed. J.M. Baldwin, New York: Macmillan, vol. 2, 47. Burks, *Bibliography.*

P 00821: Fiche 124
"Matter and Form."
>   *Dictionary of Philosophy and Psychology,* ed. J.M. Baldwin, New York: Macmillan, vol. 2, 50-55. Burks, *Bibliography.*

P 00822: Fiche 124
"Maxim (in logic)."
>   *Dictionary of Philosophy and Psychology,* ed. J.M. Baldwin, New York: Macmillan, vol. 2, 55, filmed at P 00821. Burks, *Bibliography.*

1902

P 00823: F i c h e 124
"Method and Methodology, or Methodeutic."
>*Dictionary of Philosophy and Psychology,* ed. J.M. Baldwin, New York: Macmillan, vol. 2, 75. Burks, *Bibliography.*

P 00824: F i c h e 124
"Middle Term (and Middle)." [with C. Ladd-Franklin]
>*Dictionary of Philosophy and Psychology,* ed. J.M. Baldwin, New York: Macmillan, vol. 2, 77. Burks, *Bibliography.*

P 00825: F i c h e 124
"Mixed."
>*Dictionary of Philosophy and Psychology,* ed. J.M. Baldwin, New York: Macmillan, vol. 2, 87. Burks, *Bibliography.*

P 00826: F i c h e 124
"Mnemonic Verses and Words (in logic)."
>*Dictionary of Philosophy and Psychology,* ed. J.M. Baldwin, New York: Macmillan, vol. 2, 87-89, filmed at P 00825. The first few sentences of this article are by J.M. Baldwin. Burks, *Bibliography.*

P 00827: F i c h e 124
"Modality."
>*Dictionary of Philosophy and Psychology,* ed. J.M. Baldwin, New York: Macmillan, vol. 2, 89-93, filmed at P 00825. Burks, *Bibliography.*

P 00828: F i c h e 124
"Modulus."
>*Dictionary of Philosophy and Psychology,* ed. J.M. Baldwin, New York: Macmillan, vol. 2, 94, filmed at P 00825. Burks, *Bibliography.*

P 00829: F i c h e 124
"Modus ponens and Modus tollens."
>*Dictionary of Philosophy and Psychology,* ed. J.M. Baldwin, New York: Macmillan, vol. 2, 94, filmed at P 00825. Burks, *Bibliography.*

P 00830: F i c h e 124
"Monad (Monadism, Monadology)."
>*Dictionary of Philosophy and Psychology,* ed. J.M. Baldwin, New York: Macmillan, vol. 2, 98-99. Only part of this article is by Peirce. Fisch, *Third Supplement.*

P 00831: F i c h e 124
"Multitude (in mathematics)." [with H.B. Fine]
>*Dictionary of Philosophy and Psychology,* ed. J.M. Baldwin, New York: Macmillan, vol. 2, 117-118. Burks, *Bibliography.*

P 00832: F i c h e 124
"Name (in logic)."
>*Dictionary of Philosophy and Psychology,* ed. J.M. Baldwin, New York: Macmillan, vol. 2, 127-128. Burks, *Bibliography.*

P 00833: F i c h e 124
"Necessary (in logic)."
>*Dictionary of Philosophy and Psychology,* ed. J.M. Baldwin, New York: Macmillan, vol. 2, 143. Burks, *Bibliography.*

1902

P 00834: Fiche 124
"Necessity."
>Dictionary of Philosophy and Psychology, ed. J.M. Baldwin, New York: Macmillan, vol. 2, 145-146 filmed at P 00833. Parts of this article are by other authors. Burks, *Bibliography*.

P 00835: Fiche 124
"Negation." [with C. Ladd-Franklin]
>Dictionary of Philosophy and Psychology, ed. J.M. Baldwin, New York: Macmillan, vol. 2, 146-147, filmed at P 00833. The article continues with parts by other authors. Burks, *Bibliography*.

P 00836: Fiche 124
"Negative."
>Dictionary of Philosophy and Psychology, ed. J.M. Baldwin, New York: Macmillan, vol. 2, 148, filmed at P 00833. Another author continues the article. Burks, *Bibliography*.

P 00837: Fiche 124
"Nominal."
>Dictionary of Philosophy and Psychology, ed. J.M. Baldwin, New York: Macmillan, vol. 2, 179. Burks, *Bibliography*.

P 00838: Fiche 124
"Nomology."
>Dictionary of Philosophy and Psychology, ed. J.M. Baldwin, New York: Macmillan, vol. 2, 180. Burks, *Bibliography*.

P 00839: Fiche 124
"Non-A (in logic)."
>Dictionary of Philosophy and Psychology, ed. J.M. Baldwin, New York: Macmillan, vol. 2, 180, filmed at P 00838. Burks, *Bibliography*.

P 00840: Fiche 124
"Non-contradiction."
>Dictionary of Philosophy and Psychology, ed. J.M. Baldwin, New York: Macmillan, vol. 2, 181, filmed at P 00838. Burks, *Bibliography*.

P 00841: Fiche 124
"Nonsequitur."
>Dictionary of Philosophy and Psychology, ed. J.M. Baldwin, New York: Macmillan, vol. 2, 181, filmed at P 00838. Burks, *Bibliography*.

P 00842: Fiche 124
"Norm (and Normality)."
>Dictionary of Philosophy and Psychology, ed. J.M. Baldwin, New York: Macmillan, vol. 2, 182. Part of the article is by another author. Burks, *Bibliography*.

P 00843: Fiche 124
"Nota notae."
>Dictionary of Philosophy and Psychology, ed. J.M. Baldwin, New York: Macmillan, vol. 2, 183, filmed at P 00842. Burks, *Bibliography*.

P 00844: Fiche 124
"Numerical."
>Dictionary of Philosophy and Psychology, ed. J.M. Baldwin, New York: Macmillan, vol. 2, 190. Burks, *Bibliography*.

1902

P 00845: Fiche 124
"Observation." [with J.M. Baldwin]
 Dictionary of Philosophy and Psychology, ed. J.M. Baldwin, New York: Macmillan, vol. 2, 198. Burks, *Bibliography.*

P 00846: Fiche 124
"Obversion."
 Dictionary of Philosophy and Psychology, ed. J.M. Baldwin, New York: Macmillan, vol. 2, 199, filmed at P 00845. Burks, *Bibliography.*

P 00847: Fiche 124
"Opposition (in logic)."
 Dictionary of Philosophy and Psychology, ed. J.M. Baldwin, New York: Macmillan, vol. 2, 206. Part of this article is by J.M. Baldwin. Burks, *Bibliography.*

P 00848: Fiche 124
"Organon."
 Dictionary of Philosophy and Psychology, ed. J.M. Baldwin, New York: Macmillan, vol. 2, 219. Burks, *Bibliography.*

P 00849: Fiche 124
"P (in logic)."
 Dictionary of Philosophy and Psychology, ed. J.M. Baldwin, New York: Macmillan, vol. 2, 253. Burks, *Bibliography.*

P 00850: Fiche 124
"Paradox."
 Dictionary of Philosophy and Psychology, ed. J.M. Baldwin, New York: Macmillan, vol. 2, 258. Burks, *Bibliography.*

P 00851: Fiche 124
"Paralogism."
 Dictionary of Philosophy and Psychology, ed. J.M. Baldwin, New York: Macmillan, vol. 2, 259, filmed at P 00850. Burks, *Bibliography.*

P 00852: Fiche 124
"Parity."
 Dictionary of Philosophy and Psychology, ed. J.M. Baldwin, New York: Macmillan, vol. 2, 263. Burks, *Bibliography.*

P 00853: Fiche 125
"Parsimony (law of)."
 Dictionary of Philosophy and Psychology, ed. J.M. Baldwin, New York: Macmillan, vol. 2, 264. Burks, *Bibliography.*

P 00854: Fiche 125
"Partial."
 Dictionary of Philosophy and Psychology, ed. J.M. Baldwin, New York: Macmillan, vol. 2, 265, filmed at P 00853. Burks, *Bibliography.*

P 00855: Fiche 125
"Particular." [with C. Ladd-Franklin]
 Dictionary of Philosophy and Psychology, ed. J.M. Baldwin, New York: Macmillan, vol. 2, 265-266, filmed at P 00853. Burks, *Bibliography.*

1902

P 00856: Fiche 125
"Particulate."
>Dictionary of Philosophy and Psychology, ed. J.M. Baldwin, New York: Macmillan, vol. 2, 266, filmed at P 00853. Burks, *Bibliography*.

P 00857: Fiche 125
"Parva Logicalia."
>Dictionary of Philosophy and Psychology, ed. J.M. Baldwin, New York: Macmillan, vol. 2, 266, filmed at P 00853. Burks, *Bibliography*.

P 00858: Fiche 125
"Per accidens."
>Dictionary of Philosophy and Psychology, ed. J.M. Baldwin, New York: Macmillan, vol. 2, 276. Burks, *Bibliography*.

P 00859: Fiche 125
"Perseity (1) and (2) Per se."
>Dictionary of Philosophy and Psychology, ed. J.M. Baldwin, New York: Macmillan, vol. 2, 281-282. The first two paragraphs are by John Dewey. Burks, *Bibliography*.

P 00860: Fiche 125
"Perspicuity."
>Dictionary of Philosophy and Psychology, ed. J.M. Baldwin, New York: Macmillan, vol. 2, 286-287. Burks, *Bibliography*.

P 00861: Fiche 125
"Pertinent."
>Dictionary of Philosophy and Psychology, ed. J.M. Baldwin, New York: Macmillan, vol. 2, 287, filmed at P 00860. Burks, *Bibliography*.

P 00862: Fiche 125
"Petitio Principii." [with C. Ladd-Franklin]
>Dictionary of Philosophy and Psychology, ed. J.M. Baldwin, New York: Macmillan, vol. 2, 287-288, filmed at P 00860. Burks, *Bibliography*.

P 00863: Fiche 125
"Philosopheme."
>Dictionary of Philosophy and Psychology, ed. J.M. Baldwin, New York: Macmillan, vol. 2, 290. Burks, *Bibliography*.

P 00864: Fiche 125
"Plurality of Causes."
>Dictionary of Philosophy and Psychology, ed. J.M. Baldwin, New York: Macmillan, vol. 2, 306-307. The last paragraph is by other authors. Burks, *Bibliography*.

P 00865: Fiche 125
"Poly-."
>Dictionary of Philosophy and Psychology, ed. J.M. Baldwin, New York: Macmillan, vol. 2, 309. Part of this article is by J. Jastrow. Burks, *Bibliography*.

P 00866: Fiche 125
"Port Royal Logic."
>Dictionary of Philosophy and Psychology, ed. J.M. Baldwin, New York: Macmillan, vol. 2, 310. Burks, *Bibliography*.

1902

P 00867: F i c h e 125
"Positive."
> *Dictionary of Philosophy and Psychology,* ed. J.M. Baldwin, New York: Macmillan, vol. 2, 311-312, filmed at P 00866. Part of this article is by John Dewey. Burks, *Bibliography.*

P 00868: F i c h e 125
"Possibility, Impossibility, and Possible."
> *Dictionary of Philosophy and Psychology,* ed. J.M. Baldwin, New York: Macmillan, vol. 2, 313-315, filmed at P 00866. Burks (*Bibliography,* p. 292) attributes the entire article to Peirce, probably on the basis of the appearance of Peirce's initials at its end. However, Fisch (*Third Supplement*) states that that part of the article ending with p. 314, col. 1, is by John Dewey.

P 00869: F i c h e 125
"Postpredicament."
> *Dictionary of Philosophy and Psychology,* ed. J.M. Baldwin, New York: Macmillan, vol. 2, 315, filmed at P 00866. Burks, *Bibliography.*

P 00870: F i c h e 125
"Postulate."
> *Dictionary of Philosophy and Psychology,* ed. J.M. Baldwin, New York: Macmillan, vol. 2, 315-316, filmed at P 00866. Burks, *Bibliography.*

P 00871: F i c h e 125
"Pragmatic (1) and (2) Pragmatism."
> *Dictionary of Philosophy and Psychology,* ed. J.M. Baldwin, New York: Macmillan, vol. 2, 321-323. Parts of this article are by other authors. Burks, *Bibliography.*

P 00872: F i c h e 125
"Precise."
> *Dictionary of Philosophy and Psychology,* ed. J.M. Baldwin, New York: Macmillan, vol. 2, 323, filmed at P 00871. Burks, *Bibliography.*

P 00873: F i c h e 125
"Precision."
> *Dictionary of Philosophy and Psychology,* ed. J.M. Baldwin, New York: Macmillan, vol. 2, 323-324, filmed at P 00871. Burks, *Bibliography.*

P 00874: F i c h e 125
"Predesignate."
> *Dictionary of Philosophy and Psychology,* ed. J.M. Baldwin, New York: Macmillan, vol. 2, 324-325, filmed at P 00871. Burks, *Bibliography.*

P 00875: F i c h e 125
"Predicable."
> *Dictionary of Philosophy and Psychology,* ed. J.M. Baldwin, New York: Macmillan, vol. 2, 325, filmed at P 00871. Burks, *Bibliography.*

P 00876: F i c h e 125
"Predicament."
> *Dictionary of Philosophy and Psychology,* ed. J.M. Baldwin, New York: Macmillan, vol. 2, 325, filmed at P 00871. Burks, *Bibliography.*

P 00877: F i c h e 125
"Predicate."
> *Dictionary of Philosophy and Psychology,* ed. J.M. Baldwin, New York: Macmillan, vol. 2, 325-326, filmed at P 00871. Part of this article is by another author. Burks, *Bibliography.*

1902

P 00878: F i c h e 125
"Predication."
>Dictionary of Philosophy and Psychology, ed. J.M. Baldwin, New York: Macmillan, vol. 2, 326-329, filmed at P 00871. Parts of this article are by other authors. Burks, Bibliography.

P 00879: F i c h e 125
"Predicative Proposition."
>Dictionary of Philosophy and Psychology, ed. J.M. Baldwin, New York: Macmillan, vol. 2, 329, filmed at P 00871. Burks, Bibliography.

P 00880: F i c h e 125
"Premise (and Premiss)."
>Dictionary of Philosophy and Psychology, ed. J.M. Baldwin, New York: Macmillan, vol. 2, 330-331. Burks, Bibliography.

P 00881: F i c h e 125
"Presumption."
>Dictionary of Philosophy and Psychology, ed. J.M. Baldwin, New York: Macmillan, vol. 2, 337. Part of this article is by another author. Burks, Bibliography.

P 00882: F i c h e 125
"Presupposition."
>Dictionary of Philosophy and Psychology, ed. J.M. Baldwin, New York: Macmillan, vol. 2, 338. Burks, Bibliography.

P 00883: F i c h e 125
"Prime."
>Dictionary of Philosophy and Psychology, ed. J.M. Baldwin, New York: Macmillan, vol. 2, 341. Burks, Bibliography.

P 00884: F i c h e 125
"Primum cognitum."
>Dictionary of Philosophy and Psychology, ed. J.M. Baldwin, New York: Macmillan, vol. 2, 341, filmed at P 00883. Burks, Bibliography.

P 00885: F i c h e 125
"Principal."
>Dictionary of Philosophy and Psychology, ed. J.M. Baldwin, New York: Macmillan, vol. 2, 341, filmed at P 00883. Burks, Bibliography.

P 00886: F i c h e 125
"Priority (with Prior and Prius)."
>Dictionary of Philosophy and Psychology, ed. J.M. Baldwin, New York: Macmillan, vol. 2, 342-343. Burks, Bibliography.

P 00887: F i c h e 125
"Privation."
>Dictionary of Philosophy and Psychology, ed. J.M. Baldwin, New York: Macmillan, vol. 2, 343, filmed at P 00886. Burks, Bibliography.

P 00888: F i c h e 125
"Probable Inference."
>Dictionary of Philosophy and Psychology, ed. J.M. Baldwin, New York: Macmillan, vol. 2, 353-355. Burks, Bibliography.

1902

P 00889: Fiche 125
"Problem."
>*Dictionary of Philosophy and Psychology,* ed. J.M. Baldwin, New York: Macmillan, vol. 2, 355, filmed at P 00888. Burks, *Bibliography.*

P 00890: Fiche 125
"Problematic."
>*Dictionary of Philosophy and Psychology,* ed. J.M. Baldwin, New York: Macmillan, vol. 2, 355-356, filmed at P 00888. Burks, *Bibliography.*

P 00891: Fiche 125
"Progressive."
>*Dictionary of Philosophy and Psychology,* ed. J.M. Baldwin, New York: Macmillan, vol. 2, 358. Part of this article is by J. Jastrow. Burks, *Bibliography.*

P 00892: Fiche 125
"Proof."
>*Dictionary of Philosophy and Psychology,* ed. J.M. Baldwin, New York: Macmillan, vol. 2, 359, filmed at P 00891. Part of this article is by J.M. Baldwin. Burks, *Bibliography.*

P 00893: Fiche 125
"Proposition." [with J.M. Baldwin]
>*Dictionary of Philosophy and Psychology,* ed. J.M. Baldwin, New York: Macmillan, vol. 2, 361-370. Only part of this article is by Peirce and Baldwin (361-362); the remainder is by other authors. Burks, *Bibliography.*

P 00894: Fiche 125
"Prosyllogism."
>*Dictionary of Philosophy and Psychology,* ed. J.M. Baldwin, New York: Macmillan, vol. 2, 370, filmed at P 00893. Fisch, *Third Supplement.*

P 00895: Fiche 125
"Protasis."
>*Dictionary of Philosophy and Psychology,* ed. J.M. Baldwin, New York: Macmillan, vol. 2, 371, filmed at P 00893. Burks, *Bibliography.*

P 00896: Fiche 125
"Provisional."
>*Dictionary of Philosophy and Psychology,* ed. J.M. Baldwin, New York: Macmillan, vol. 2, 373. Burks, *Bibliography.*

P 00897: Fiche 125
"Proximate."
>*Dictionary of Philosophy and Psychology,* ed. J.M. Baldwin, New York: Macmillan, vol. 2, 373-374, filmed at P 00896. Burks, *Bibliography.*

P 00898: Fiche 125
"Pure (in philosophy)."
>*Dictionary of Philosophy and Psychology,* ed. J.M. Baldwin, New York: Macmillan, vol. 2, 401-402. Part of this article is by J. Dewey. Burks, *Bibliography.*

P 00899: Fiche 125
"Quality (in grammar and logic)."
>*Dictionary of Philosophy and Psychology,* ed. J.M. Baldwin, New York: Macmillan, vol. 2, 408-409. Burks, *Bibliography.*

1902

P 00900: F i c h e 125
"Quantity (in logic and mathematics)."
>*Dictionary of Philosophy and Psychology,* ed. J.M. Baldwin, New York: Macmillan, vol. 2, 410-412. Burks, *Bibliography.*

P 00901: F i c h e 125
"Ratio."
>*Dictionary of Philosophy and Psychology,* ed. J.M. Baldwin, New York: Macmillan, vol. 2, 415. Part of this article is by J.M. Baldwin. Burks, *Bibliography.*

P 00902: F i c h e 125
"Ratiocination."
>*Dictionary of Philosophy and Psychology,* ed. J.M. Baldwin, New York: Macmillan, vol. 2, 415, filmed at P 00901. Burks, *Bibliography.*

P 00903: F i c h e 125
"Rational."
>*Dictionary of Philosophy and Psychology,* ed. J.M. Baldwin, New York: Macmillan, vol. 2, 415, filmed at P 00901. Part of this article is by J.M. Baldwin. Burks, *Bibliography.*

P 00904: F i c h e 126
"Reasoning."
>*Dictionary of Philosophy and Psychology,* ed. J.M. Baldwin, New York: Macmillan, vol. 2, 426-428. Part of this article is by J.M. Baldwin. Burks, *Bibliography.*

P 00905: F i c h e 126
"Reductio ad absurdum."
>*Dictionary of Philosophy and Psychology,* ed. J.M. Baldwin, New York: Macmillan, vol. 2, 434. Burks, *Bibliography.*

P 00906: F i c h e 126
"Reduction."
>*Dictionary of Philosophy and Psychology,* ed. J.M. Baldwin, New York: Macmillan, vol. 2, 434-435, filmed at P 00905. Part of this article is by J. Royce. Burks, *Bibliography.*

P 00907: F i c h e 126
"Regular."
>*Dictionary of Philosophy and Psychology,* ed. J.M. Baldwin, New York: Macmillan, vol. 2, 438-439. Burks, *Bibliography.*

P 00908: F i c h e 126
"Relatives (logic of)."
>*Dictionary of Philosophy and Psychology,* ed. J.M. Baldwin, New York: Macmillan, vol. 2, 447-450. Burks, *Bibliography.*

P 00909: F i c h e 126
"Remote."
>*Dictionary of Philosophy and Psychology,* ed. J.M. Baldwin, New York: Macmillan, vol. 2, 463. Part of this article is by J.M. Baldwin. Burks, *Bibliography.*

P 00910: F i c h e 126
"Represent."
>*Dictionary of Philosophy and Psychology,* ed. J.M. Baldwin, New York: Macmillan, vol. 2, 464. Burks, *Bibliography.*

1902

P 00911: Fiche 126
"Representationism."
    Dictionary of Philosophy and Psychology, ed. J.M. Baldwin, New York: Macmillan, vol. 2, 464-465, filmed at P 00910. Burks, *Bibliography.*

P 00912: Fiche 126
"Repugnance."
    Dictionary of Philosophy and Psychology, ed. J.M. Baldwin, New York: Macmillan, vol. 2, 466. Burks, *Bibliography.*

P 00913: Fiche 126
"Residues (method of)."
    Dictionary of Philosophy and Psychology, ed. J.M. Baldwin, New York: Macmillan, vol. 2, 467-468, filmed at P 00912. Burks, *Bibliography.*

P 00914: Fiche 126
"Rule." [in part, with J.M. Baldwin]
    Dictionary of Philosophy and Psychology, ed. J.M. Baldwin, New York: Macmillan, vol. 2, 481. Burks, *Bibliography.*

P 00915: Fiche 126
"S (in logic)."
    Dictionary of Philosophy and Psychology, ed. J.M. Baldwin, New York: Macmillan, vol. 2, 483. Part of this article is by J.M. Baldwin. Burks, *Bibliography.*

P 00916: Fiche 126
"Saltus."
    Dictionary of Philosophy and Psychology, ed. J.M. Baldwin, New York: Macmillan, vol. 2, 484. Burks, *Bibliography.*

P 00917: Fiche 126
"Scientific Method." [with J.M. Baldwin]
    Dictionary of Philosophy and Psychology, ed. J.M. Baldwin, New York: Macmillan, vol. 2, 500-503. Burks, *Bibliography.*

P 00918: Fiche 126
"Scope (in logic)."
    Dictionary of Philosophy and Psychology, ed. J.M. Baldwin, New York: Macmillan, vol. 2, 503, filmed at P 00917. Burks, *Bibliography.*

P 00919: Fiche 126
"Secundum quid."
    Dictionary of Philosophy and Psychology, ed. J.M. Baldwin, New York: Macmillan, vol. 2, 504. Burks, *Bibliography.*

P 00920: Fiche 126
"Series."
    Dictionary of Philosophy and Psychology, ed. J.M. Baldwin, New York: Macmillan, vol. 2, 521. Part of this article is by J.M. Baldwin. Burks, *Bibliography.*

P 00921: Fiche 126
"Sign."
    Dictionary of Philosophy and Psychology, ed. J.M. Baldwin, New York: Macmillan, vol. 2, 527-528. Part of this article is by J.M. Baldwin. Burks, *Bibliography.*

1902

P 00922: Fiche 126
"Signification (and Application, in logic)." [in part, with C. Ladd-Franklin]
    Dictionary of Philosophy and Psychology, ed. J.M. Baldwin, New York: Macmillan, vol. 2, 528-529, filmed at P 00921. Burks, *Bibliography.*

P 00923: Fiche 126
"Similar (with Similarity, Similitude)."
    Dictionary of Philosophy and Psychology, ed. J.M. Baldwin, New York: Macmillan, vol. 2, 530, filmed at P 00921. Burks, *Bibliography.*

P 00924: Fiche 126
"Simple." [two parts of this article are with J.M. Baldwin]
    Dictionary of Philosophy and Psychology, ed. J.M. Baldwin, New York: Macmillan, vol. 2, 531-532, filmed at P 00921. Burks, *Bibliography.*

P 00925: Fiche 126
"Singular."
    Dictionary of Philosophy and Psychology, ed. J.M. Baldwin, New York: Macmillan, vol. 2, 533, filmed at P 00921. Burks, *Bibliography.*

P 00926: Fiche 126
"Solution."
    Dictionary of Philosophy and Psychology, ed. J.M. Baldwin, New York: Macmillan, vol. 2, 554. Burks, *Bibliography.*

P 00927: Fiche 126
"Some (in logic)." [with C. Ladd-Franklin]
    Dictionary of Philosophy and Psychology, ed. J.M. Baldwin, New York: Macmillan, vol. 2, 555, filmed at P 00926. Parts of this article are by other authors. Burks, *Bibliography.*

P 00928: Fiche 126
"Sophism."
    Dictionary of Philosophy and Psychology, ed. J.M. Baldwin, New York: Macmillan, vol. 2, 556. Part of this article is by J.M. Baldwin. Burks, *Bibliography.*

P 00929: Fiche 126
"Sorites."
    Dictionary of Philosophy and Psychology, ed. J.M. Baldwin, New York: Macmillan, vol. 2, 557, filmed at P 00928. Part of this article is by J.M. Baldwin. Burks, *Bibliography.*

P 00930: Fiche 126
"Species (and Specific Marks, in logic)." [with J.M. Baldwin]
    Dictionary of Philosophy and Psychology, ed. J.M. Baldwin, New York: Macmillan, vol. 2, 567. Part of this article is by J.M. Baldwin. Burks, *Bibliography.*

P 00931: Fiche 126
"Spurious Proposition."
    Dictionary of Philosophy and Psychology, ed. J.M. Baldwin, New York: Macmillan, vol. 2, 588. Burks, *Bibliography.*

P 00932: Fiche 126
"State (and Condition)."
    Dictionary of Philosophy and Psychology, ed. J.M. Baldwin, New York: Macmillan, vol. 2, 593. Part of this article is by J.M. Baldwin. Burks, *Bibliography.*

1902

P 00933: F i c h e 126
"Subalternation."
> *Dictionary of Philosophy and Psychology,* ed. J.M. Baldwin, New York: Macmillan, vol. 2, 606. Burks, *Bibliography.*

P 00934: F i c h e 126
"Subcontrary."
> *Dictionary of Philosophy and Psychology,* ed. J.M. Baldwin, New York: Macmillan, vol. 2, 607, filmed at P 00933. Burks, *Bibliography.*

P 00935: F i c h e 126
"Subject (in logic)."
> *Dictionary of Philosophy and Psychology,* ed. J.M. Baldwin, New York: Macmillan, vol. 2, 608-610. Part of this article is by J.M. Baldwin. Burks, *Bibliography.*

P 00936: F i c h e 126
"Sublation."
> *Dictionary of Philosophy and Psychology,* ed. J.M. Baldwin, New York: Macmillan, vol. 2, 611, filmed at P 00935. Burks, *Bibliography.*

P 00937: F i c h e 126
"Substitution (in logic)."
> *Dictionary of Philosophy and Psychology,* ed. J.M. Baldwin, New York: Macmillan, vol. 2, 614-615. Burks, *Bibliography.*

P 00938: F i c h e 126
"Subsumption."
> *Dictionary of Philosophy and Psychology,* ed. J.M. Baldwin, New York: Macmillan, vol. 2, 615, filmed at P 00937. Part of this article is by K. Groos. Burks, *Bibliography.*

P 00939: F i c h e 126
"Sufficient Reason." [in part, with J.M. Baldwin]
> *Dictionary of Philosophy and Psychology,* ed. J.M. Baldwin, New York: Macmillan, vol. 2, 616-617. Parts of this article are by other authors. Burks, *Bibliography.*

P 00940: F i c h e 126
"Summum Genus."
> *Dictionary of Philosophy and Psychology,* ed. J.M. Baldwin, New York: Macmillan, vol. 2, 621. Burks, *Bibliography.*

P 00941: F i c h e 126
"Supposition."
> *Dictionary of Philosophy and Psychology,* ed. J.M. Baldwin, New York: Macmillan, vol. 2, 624-625. Burks, *Bibliography.*

P 00942: F i c h e 127
"Syllogism." [in part, with J.M. Baldwin]
> *Dictionary of Philosophy and Psychology,* ed. J.M. Baldwin, New York: Macmillan, vol. 2, 628-639. Parts of this article are by other authors. Burks, *Bibliography.*

P 00943: F i c h e 127
"Symbol."
> *Dictionary of Philosophy and Psychology,* ed. J.M. Baldwin, New York: Macmillan, vol. 2, 640. Burks, *Bibliography.*

1902

P 00944: F i c h e 127
"Symbolic Logic or Algebra of Logic." [in part with C. Ladd-Franklin]
> *Dictionary of Philosophy and Psychology,* ed. J.M. Baldwin, New York: Macmillan, vol. 2, 640-651, see P 00887. Parts of this article are by other authors. This entry contains an account of Peirce's system of Existential Graphs. Burks, *Bibliography.* Filmed at P 00943.

P 00945: F i c h e 127
"Symbolical."
> *Dictionary of Philosophy and Psychology,* ed. J.M. Baldwin, New York: Macmillan, vol. 2, 651, filmed at P 00943. Burks, *Bibliography.*

P 00946: F i c h e 127
"Synechism."
> *Dictionary of Philosophy and Psychology,* ed, J.M. Baldwin, New York: Macmillan, vol. 2, 657. Burks, *Bibliography.*

P 00947: F i c h e 127
"Synthetic (-al)."
> *Dictionary of Philosophy and Psychology,* ed. J.M. Baldwin, New York: Macmillan, vol. 2, 658-659. Burks, *Bibliography.*

P 00948: F i c h e 127
"Tautology."
> *Dictionary of Philosophy and Psychology,* ed. J.M. Baldwin, New York: Macmillan, vol. 2, 663. Burks, *Bibliography.*

P 00949: F i c h e 127
"Term."
> *Dictionary of Philosophy and Psychology,* ed. J.M. Baldwin, New York: Macmillan, vol. 2, 675-677. Parts of this article are by other authors. Burks, *Bibliography.*

P 00950: F i c h e 127
"Testimony." [with J.M. Baldwin]
> *Dictionary of Philosophy and Psychology,* ed. J.M. Baldwin, New York: Macmillan, vol. 2, 686. Burks, *Bibliography.*

P 00951: F i c h e 127
"Thema."
> *Dictionary of Philosophy and Psychology,* ed. J.M. Baldwin, New York: Macmillan, vol. 2, 691-692. Burks, *Bibliography.*

P 00952: F i c h e 127
"Theorem."
> *Dictionary of Philosophy and Psychology,* ed. J.M. Baldwin, New York: Macmillan, vol. 2, 693, filmed at P 00951. Burks, *Bibliography.*

P 00953: F i c h e 127
"Theory (in science)." [with C. Ladd-Franklin]
> *Dictionary of Philosophy and Psychology,* ed. J.M. Baldwin, New York: Macmillan, vol. 2, 693-694, filmed at P 00951. Part of this article is by S. Newcomb. Burks, *Bibliography.*

P 00954: F i c h e 127
"Thesis."
> *Dictionary of Philosophy and Psychology,* ed. J.M. Baldwin, New York: Macmillan, vol. 2, 695, filmed at P 00951. Burks, *Bibliography.*

1902

P 00955: F i c h e 127
"Transposition (in logic)." [with C. Ladd-Franklin]
    Dictionary of Philosophy and Psychology, ed. J.M. Baldwin, New York: Macmillan, vol. 2, 713. Burks, *Bibliography;* Fisch, *Third Supplement.*

P 00956: F i c h e 127
"Tree of Porphyry."
    Dictionary of Philosophy and Psychology, ed. J.M. Baldwin, New York: Macmillan, vol. 2, 713-714, filmed at P 00955. Burks, *Bibliography.*

P 00957: F i c h e 127
"Trilemma."
    Dictionary of Philosophy and Psychology, ed. J.M. Baldwin, New York: Macmillan, vol. 2, 715, filmed at P 00955. Burks, *Bibliography.*

P 00958: F i c h e 127
"Trivium."
    Dictionary of Philosophy and Psychology, ed. J.M. Baldwin, New York: Macmillan, vol. 2, 716. Burks, *Bibliography.*

P 00959: F i c h e 127
"Truth and Falsity (1) and (2) Error."
    Dictionary of Philosophy and Psychology, ed. J.M. Baldwin, New York: Macmillan, vol. 2, 716-720, filmed at P 00958. Parts of this article are by other authors. Burks, *Bibliography.*

O 00960: F i c h e 127
Dewey, John
    "Tychism," in *Dictionary of Philosophy and Psychology,* ed. J.M. Baldwin, Macmillan: New York, vol. 2, 721.

P 00961: F i c h e 127
"Ultimate."
    Dictionary of Philosophy and Psychology, ed. J.M. Baldwin, New York: Macmillan, vol. 2, 723-724. Burks, *Bibliography.*

P 00962: F i c h e 127
"Uniformity."
    Dictionary of Philosophy and Psychology, ed. J.M. Baldwin, New York: Macmillan, vol. 2, 726-731. Burks, *Bibliography.*

P 00963: F i c h e 127
"Unity (and Plurality)."
    Dictionary of Philosophy and Psychology, ed. J.M. Baldwin, New York: Macmillan, vol. 2, 734-736. Parts of this article are by J. Dewey. Burks, *Bibliography.*

P 00964: F i c h e 127
"Universal (and Universality)." [in part, with C. Ladd-Franklin]
    Dictionary of Philosophy and Psychology, ed. J.M. Baldwin, New York: Macmillan, vol. 2, 737-741, see P 00906. Part of this article is by J. Dewey. Burks, *Bibliography.* Filmed at P 00963.

P 00965: F i c h e 127
"Universe." [with C. Ladd-Franklin]
    Dictionary of Philosophy and Psychology, ed. J.M. Baldwin, New York: Macmillan, vol. 2, 742. Burks, *Bibliography.*

1902

P 00966: F i c h e 127
"Vague (in logic)."
>Dictionary of Philosophy and Psychology, ed. J.M. Baldwin, New York: Macmillan, vol. 2, 748. Burks, Bibliography.

P 00967: F i c h e 127
"Validity." [with C. Ladd-Franklin]
>Dictionary of Philosophy and Psychology, ed. J.M. Baldwin, New York: Macmillan, vol. 2, 748-749, filmed at P 00966. Burks, Bibliography.

P 00968: F i c h e 127
"Verification."
>Dictionary of Philosophy and Psychology, ed. J.M. Baldwin, New York: Macmillan, vol. 2, 761-762. Burks, Bibliography.

P 00969: F i c h e 127
"Virtual."
>Dictionary of Philosophy and Psychology, ed. J.M. Baldwin, New York: Macmillan, vol. 2, 763-764, filmed at P 00968. Burks, Bibliography.

P 00970: F i c h e 128
"Whole (and Parts)." [in part, with J.M. Baldwin and G.F. Stout]
>Dictionary of Philosophy and Psychology, ed. J.M. Baldwin, New York: Macmillan, vol. 2, 814-815. Burks, Bibliography.

O 00971: F i c h e 128
Jastrow, Joseph.
>"Belief and Credulity," Educational Review, vol. 23 (January), 22-49.

O 00972: F i c h e 128, 129, 130
Burchard, E.L.
>List and Catalogue of the Publications Issued by the U.S. Coast and Geodetic Survey 1816-1902, Washington: Government Printing Office.

P 00973: F i c h e 130
Review of History of Intellectual Development on the Lines of Modern Evolution. By John Beattie Crozier. The Nation, vol. 74 (23 January) 78-79.

P 00974: F i c h e 130
Review of Classification, Theoretical and Practical. I. The Order of the Sciences; II. The Classification of Books. By Ernest Cushing Richardson.
>The Nation, vol. 74 (27 February) 178-179.

P 00975: F i c h e 130
"Pasteur."
>The Nation, vol. 74 (6 March) 192-194.

P 00976: F i c h e 130
"Gidding's Inductive Sociology."
>The Nation, vol. 74 (3 April) 273-274.

P 00977: F i c h e Sup. 11
"The National Academy of Sciences."
>The Nation, vol. 74 (24 April) 322-324.

1902

P 00978: F i c h e 130
Review of *The Story of the Vine.* By Edward R. Emerson.
    The Nation, vol. 74 (29 May) 433-434.

P 00979: F i c h e 130
Note [on Delta's *Charades*].
    The Nation, vol. 75 (10 July) 31.

P 00980: F i c h e 130
Review of *A Study of the Ethics of Spinoza.* By Harold H. Joachim.
    The Nation, vol. 75 (10 July) 36-37.

P 00981: F i c h e 130
Note [on Atkinson's *Electrical and Magnetical Calculations*].
    The Nation, vol. 75 (17 July) 53. Probably by Peirce.

P 00982: F i c h e 130
Note [on Forsyth's *Theory of Differential Equations,* vol. 4].
    The Nation, vol. 75 (24 July) 71. *The Nation* erroneously cites Thorpe as the author of this book.

P 00983: F i c h e 130
Review of *Studies in Physiological Chemistry.* Edited by R.H. Chittenden. *Qualitative Chemical Analysis.* By Albert B. Prescott and Otis C. Johnson. *Victor von Richter's Organic Chemistry.* Edited by Edgar F. Smith. *The Elements of Physical Chemistry.* By Harry C. Jones.
    The Nation, vol. 75 (24 July) 79.

P 00984: F i c h e 130
"Royce's World and the Individual."
    The Nation, vol. 75 (31 July) 94-96.

P 00985: F i c h e 130
Note [on the *Annales* of the Paris International Congress of 1900, section on the History of Science].
    The Nation, vol. 75 (7 August) 115.

P 00986: F i c h e 130
"Thorpe's Essays in Historical Chemistry."
    The Nation, vol. 75 (21 August) 153-154.

P 00987: F i c h e 131
"Paulsen's Kant."
    The Nation, vol. 75 (11 September) 209-211.

P 00988: F i c h e 131
Review of *The Principles of Logic.* By Herbert Austin Aikins.
    The Nation, vol. 75 (18 September) 229-230.

P 00989: F i c h e 131
Review of *The Theory of Optics.* By Paul Drude.
    The Nation, vol. 75 (2 October) 273. A short note on this book is at vol. 75 (24 July 1902) 71. That note could be by Peirce. See P 00982.

P 00990: F i c h e 131
"Aviation."
    The Nation, vol. 75 (23 October) 329-330.

A Comprehensive Bibliography

1902

P 00991: F i c h e 131
Review of *The Origin and Significance of Hegel's Logic: A General Introduction to Hegel's System.* By J.B. Baillie.
    The Nation, vol. 75 (13 November) 390.

P 00992: F i c h e 131
Review of *Theory of Differential Equations. Part III. (Vol. IV.): Ordinary Linear Equations.* By Andrew Russell Forsyth.
    The Nation, vol. 75 (27 November) 430. Compare the earlier note at vol. 75 (24 July 1902) 71, filmed at P 00953.

P 00993: F i c h e 131
"Ellwanger's Pleasures of the Table."
    The Nation, vol. 75 (18 December) 485-486.

P 00994: F i c h e 131
Review of *Sundials and Roses of Yesterday.* By Alice Morse Earl.
    The Nation, vol. 75 (25 December) 506-507.

P 00995: F i c h e Sup. 11
"The Classification of the Sciences."
    Paper read before the National Academy of Sciences, Washington, 15-17 April. Cited in *Report of the National Academy of Sciences for the Year 1902,* Senate Document No. 81, 57th Congress, 2d Session, Washington: Government Printing Office, 1903, p. 13. It is very likely that MS 1339 is the final draft of this paper (Robin, *Catalogue*). Cohen, *Tentative Bibliography;* Burks, *Bibliography.*

P 00996: F i c h e 132
[Majority report, committee on Weights, measures, and coinage, National Academy of Sciences]
    Peirce was a co-signer of the report as a member of this committee of the National Academy of Sciences. The report was presented at the meeting of 15-17 April. Cited in *Report of the National Academy of Sciences for the Year 1902,* Senate Document No. 81, 57th Congress, 2d Session, Washington: Government Printing Office, 1903, p. 13, filmed at P 00995.

P 00997: F i c h e 132
"The Color System."
    Paper read before the National Academy of Sciences, Washington, 15-17 April. Cited in *Report of the National Academy of Sciences for the Year 1902,* Senate Document No. 81, 57th Congress, 2d Session, Washington: Government Printing Office, 1903, p. 13, filmed at P 00995. Cohen, *Tentative Bibliography;* Burks, *Bibliography.*

P 00998: F i c h e 132
"The Postulates of Geometry."
    Paper read before the National Academy of Sciences, Washington, 15-17 April. Cited in *Report of the National Academy of Sciences for the Year 1902,* Senate Document No. 81, 57th Congress, 2d Session, Washington: Government Printing Office, 1903, p. 13, filmed at P 00995. Cohen, *Tentative Bibliography;* Burks, *Bibliography.*

O 00999: (NF)
Rowland, Henry Augustus.
    Physical Papers, Baltimore: The Johns Hopkins Press, at p. 492, 494, 499, 513, 517, 545, 546, 553, 554, 555.

O 01000: (NF)
James, William.
    The Varieties of Religious Experience, London: Longmans, Green, and Co., at p. 444-445.

1903

O 01001: F i c h e 132
Bumstead, Henry A.
> "Josiah Willard Gibbs," *The American Journal of Science,* fourth series 16, whole series 166 (September), 187-202, at 195.

O 01002: F i c h e 132
Davis, Ellery W.
> "Some Groups in Logic," *Bulletin of the American Mathematical Society,* second series 9 (April), 346-348.

O 01003: F i c h e 132
Smith, Percey F.
> "Josiah Willard Gibbs, PH.D., LL.D. A Short Sketch and Appreciation of his Work in Pure Mathematics," *Bulletin of the American Mathematical Society,* second series 10 (October), 34-39, at 36, 38.

P 01004: (NF)
"Pragmatism as a Principle and Method of Right Thinking."
> Harvard University Lectures, delivered from 26 March to 17 May, the first seven sponsored by the Department of Philosophy and the eighth by the Department of Mathematics. See MSS 301-316 (Robin, *Catalogue*). Burks, *Bibliography;* Fisch, *First Supplement.*

P 01005: (NF)
"Some Topics of Logic Bearing on Questions Now Vexed."
> Lectures given at the Lowell Institute, Cambridge, Massachusetts. Lecture I (23 November), What Makes a Reasoning Sound? Lecture II (27 November), A System of Diagrams for Studying Logical Relations. Lecture III (30 November), The Three Universal Categories and Their Utility. Lecture IV (3 December), Exposition of the System of Diagrams. Lecture V (7 December), The Doctrine of Multitude, Infinity and Continuity. Lecture VI (10 December), What is Chance? Lecture VII (14 December), Induction as Doing, Not Mere Cogitation. Lecture VIII (17 December), How to Theorize. MSS for these lectures survive (see Robin, *Catalogue*) as follows: Lecture I, MSS 447-454; Lecture II, MSS 455-456; Lecture III, MSS 457-466; Lecture IV, MS 467; Lecture V, MSS 468-471; Lecture VI, MS 472; Lecture VII, MSS 473-474; Lecture VIII, MSS 475-476. See also MSS 477-478. Burks, *Bibliography.*

P 01006: F i c h e 132
Review of *Euclid: His Life and System.* By Thomas Smith.
> *The Nation,* vol. 76 (29 January) 99-100.

P 01007: F i c h e 132
Note [on *The Physical Papers of Henry Augustus Rowland*].
> *The Nation,* vol. 76 (5 March) 194.

O 01008: F i c h e 132
Ames, J.S. "A Correction." *The Nation,* 76 (19 March) 226. Letter.

P 01009: F i c h e 132
"A Correction."
> *The Nation,* vol. 76 (19 March) 226. Peirce's editorial reply to a letter by J.S. Ames.

P 01010: F i c h e 132
Note [on Fiske's *Cosmic Philosophy*].
> *The Nation,* vol. 76 (2 April) 269.

1903

P 01011: F i c h e 132
"The National Academy Meeting."
>The Nation, vol. 76 (30 April) 349-351.

P 01012: F i c h e 132
Note [on Mellor's *Higher Mathematics for Students of Chemistry and Physics*].
>The Nation, vol. 76 (21 May) 418.

P 01013: F i c h e 132
"Hegel's Logic Interpreted."
>The Nation, vol. 76 (21 May) 419-420, filmed at P 01013.

P 01014: F i c h e 132
Note [on Whittaker's *A Course of Modern Analysis*].
>The Nation, vol. 76 (28 May) 436.

P 01015: F i c h e 132
Review of *Personal Idealism: Philosophical Essays by Eight Members of the University of Oxford.* Edited by Henry Cecil Sturt.
>The Nation, vol. 76 (4 June) 462-463.

P 01016: F i c h e 132
Review of *Dictionary of Philosophy and Psychology.* By James Mark Baldwin.
>The Nation, vol. 76 (11 June) 482.

P 01017: F i c h e 133
Note [on *Kant's Prolegomena to any Future Metaphysics,* edited by Carus].
>The Nation, vol. 76 (18 June) 497-498.

P 01018: F i c h e 133
Review of *Studies in the Cartesian Philosophy.* By Norman Smith.
>The Nation, vol. 77 (16 July) 57-58.

P 01019: F i c h e 133
Review of *Inorganic Chemistry: With the Elements of Physical and Theoretical Chemistry.* By J.I.D. Hinds.
>The Nation, vol. 77 (23 July) 81-82.

P 01020: F i c h e 133
"Clerke's Astrophysics."
>The Nation, vol. 77 (30 July) 98-99.

P 01021: F i c h e 133
Review of *Light Waves and Their Uses.* By A.A. Michelson. *Waves and Ripples in Water, Air, and Ether.* By J.A. Fleming.
>The Nation, vol. 77 (13 August) 141.

P 01022: F i c h e 133
Note [on Cohn's *Tests and Reagents*].
>The Nation, vol. 77 (3 September) 189.

P 01023: F i c h e 133
Note [on Krauch's *The Testing of Chemical Reagents for Purity*].
>The Nation, vol. 77 (10 September) 208.

1903

P 01024: F i c h e 133
Note [on Perrine's *Conductors for Electrical Distribution*].
   The Nation, vol. 77 (10 September) 208, see P 01023.

O 01025: F i c h e S u p. 12
Anonymous.
   Note [on British Science]. *The Nation,* vol. 77 (10 September) 219. Peirce mentions this note at vol. 77 (17 September 1903) 229.

P 01026: F i c h e 133
"British and American Science."
   The Nation, vol. 77 (1 October) 263-264.

O 01027: F i c h e 133
H.T.
   "The Decline of Mathematics in England," *The Nation,* vol. 77 (1 October) 265.

P 01028: F i c h e 133
Reviews of *What is Meaning?* By V. Welby. *The Principles of Mathematics.* By Bertrand Russell.
   The Nation, vol. 77 (15 October) 308-309.

O 01029: F i c h e 133
McMahon, James.
   "Practical Application of the Theory of Functions," *The Nation,* vol. 77 (22 October) 320.

P 01030: F i c h e 133
"Practical Application of the Theory of Functions."
   The Nation, vol. 77 (22 October) 320 see O 00999. Filmed at O 01029.

P 01031: F i c h e 133
"Francis Ellingwood Abbot."
   The Nation, vol. 77 (5 November) 360. Signed letter.

O 01032: F i c h e 133
King, Irving.
   "Pragmatism as a Philosophic Method," *Philosophical Review,* vol. 12, 511-524.

O 01033: (NF)
Russell, Bertrand.
   The Principles of Mathematics, Cambridge: Harvard University Press.

P 01034: F i c h e 133
Translation of "On the Absorption and Emission of Air and Its Ingredients for Light of Wave-Lengths from 250µµ to 100µµ," by Victor Schumann.
   Smithsonian Contributions to Knowledge, vol. 29 (no. 1413), 1-30, Washington: Smithsonian Institution. Fisch and Haskell, *Additions to Cohen's Bibliography;* Burks, *Bibliography.*

P 01035: F i c h e 134
A Syllabus of Certain Topics of Logic.
   Boston: Alfred Mudge & Son, Printers, Dated by Peirce as "Milford, Pa., 1903, Nov. 1."
   List of Articles; Burks, *Bibliography;* Fisch, *First Supplement.*

1904

O 01036: (NF)
Macfarlane, Alexander.
>*Bibliography of Quaternions and Allied Systems of Mathematics,* Dublin, at p. 63.

O 01037: F i c h e 134
Furtwängler, Philip.
>"Die Mechanik der einfachsten physikalischen Apparate und Versuchsanordnungen," in *Encyklopädie der Mathematischen Wissenschaften,* Leipzig: B.G. Teubner, part 2 of vol. 4, p. 1-37.

P 01038: F i c h e 134
"French Academy of Sciences."
>*The Evening Post,* New York City, vol. 103 (Saturday, 5 March), third section, page 1, columns 1-3. Burks, *Bibliography;* Fisch, *First Supplement.*

O 01039: (NF)
James, William.
>"The Pragmatic Method," *Journal of Philosophy,* vol. 1, 673-687.

O 01040: F i c h e 134
Carus, Paul.
>"Pasigraphy — A Suggestion," *The Monist,* vol. 14 (July), 565-582, at 566n.

P 01041: F i c h e 134
Note [on four books on electricity: Walmsley, Foster and Porter, Barnett, and Parr].
>*The Nation,* vol. 78 (11 February) 110. Probably by Peirce.

P 01042: F i c h e 134
"Fahie's Galileo."
>*The Nation,* vol. 78 (11 February) 113-115.

P 01043: F i c h e 134
Note [on Hilton's *Mathematical Crystallography and the Theory of Groups of Movements*].
>*The Nation,* vol. 78 (3 March) 171. Probably by Peirce.

P 01044: F i c h e 134
Note [on Campbell's *Introductory Treatise on Lie's Theory of Finite Continuous Transformation Groups*].
>*The Nation,* vol. 78 (3 March) 171, filmed at P 001043. Probably by Peirce.

P 01045: F i c h e 134
Note [on Woodbridge's *The Philosophy of Hobbes in Extracts and Notes collected from his Writings*].
>*The Nation,* vol. 78 (17 March) 211.

P 01046: F i c h e 134
"The Metric Fallacy."
>*The Nation,* vol. 78 (17 March) 215-216.

P 01047: F i c h e 135
Note [on van't Hoff's *Physical Chemistry in the Service of the Sciences*].
>*The Nation,* vol. 78 (24 March) 231. Probably by Peirce.

P 01048: F i c h e 135
Review of *The Reminiscences of an Astronomer.* By Simon Newcomb.
>*The Nation,* vol. 78 (24 March) 237.

1904

P 01049: Fiche 135
Review of *Lectures on the Logic of Arithmetic.* By M.E. Boole. *Elements of the Theory of Integers.* By Joseph Bowden.
    The Nation, vol. 78 (14 April) 298.

P 01050: Fiche 135
"The National Academy Meeting."
    The Nation, vol. 78 (28 April) 328-330.

P 01051: Fiche 135
"Comte's Philosophy."
    The Nation, vol. 78 (28 April) 335-336.

P 01052: Fiche 135
Note [on Jones's *Notes on Analytical Geometry*].
    The Nation, vol. 78 (19 May) 393.

P 01053: Fiche 135
Note [on Ryder's *Electric Traction*].
    The Nation, vol. 78 (26 May) 411.

P 01054: Fiche 135
Note [on Hawkins and Wallis's *The Dynamo*].
    The Nation, vol. 78 (26 May) 411, see P 01023. Filmed at P 01053.

P 01055: Fiche 135
"Turner's History of Philosophy."
    The Nation, vol. 79 (7 July) 15-16.

P 01056: Fiche 135
Review of *Spinoza's Political and Ethical Philosophy.* By Robert A. Duff.
    The Nation, vol. 79 (21 July) 63.

P 01057: Fiche 135
Review of *Notes on the Composition of Scientific Papers.* By T. Clifford Allbutt.
    The Nation, vol. 79 (28 July) 84-85.

P 01058: Fiche 135
Note [on Buchanan's *Mathematical Theory of Eclipses*].
    The Nation, vol. 79 (25 August) 162.

P 01059: Fiche 135
Review of *The Collected Mathematical Papers of James Joseph Sylvester.*
    The Nation, vol. 79 (8 September) 203-204.

P 01060: Fiche 135
"Logical Lights."
    The Nation, vol. 79 (15 September) 219-220.

P 01061: Fiche 135
Review of *Outlines of Psychology.* By Josiah Royce.
    The Nation, vol. 79 (29 September) 264-265.

P 01062: Fiche 135
Note [on Mendeleef's *An Attempt Toward a Chemical Conception of the Ether*].
    The Nation, vol. 79 (17 November) 396. Probably by Peirce.

1904

P 01063: F i c h e 135
Note [on Murray's *Introduction to Psychology*].
    The Nation, vol. 79 (17 November) 396, filmed at P 01062. Probably by Peirce.

P 01064: F i c h e 135
Note [on Cajori's *Introduction to the Modern Theory of Equations*].
    The Nation, vol. 79 (17 November) 396, filmed at P 01062. Probably by Peirce.

P 01065: F i c h e 135
Review of *Experimental Psychology and its Bearing upon Culture.* By George Malcolm Stratton.
    The Nation, vol. 79 (17 November) 402-403.

P 01066: F i c h e 135
"The National Academy in New York."
    The Nation, vol. 79 (1 December) 432-434.

P 01067: F i c h e 135
Note [on Olsen's *Text-book of Quantative Chemical Analysis*].
    The Nation, vol. 79 (8 December) 460.

P 01068: F i c h e 135
"Note on the Simplest Possible Branch of Mathematics."
    Paper read before the National Academy of Sciences, Washington, 19-21 April. Cited in *Report of the National Academy of Sciences for the Year 1904,* Senate Doc. No. 178, Washington: Government Printing Office, 1905, p. 14. Burks, *Bibliography.*

P 01069: F i c h e 135
"On Topical Geometry."
    Paper read before the National Academy of Sciences, New York City, 15-16 November. Cited in *Report of the National Academy of Sciences for the Year 1904,* Senate Doc. No. 178, Washington: Government Printing Office, 1905, p. 16, filmed at P 01068. Notes for this lecture survive as MS 95 (Robin, *Catalogue).* Burks, *Bibliography.* Fisch, *First Supplement.*

O 01070: (NF)
Royce, Josiah.
    Introduction to *La philosophie en Amérique,* by L. van Becelaere, New York: Eclectic Publishing Co.

P 01071: F i c h e 135
[Letter on a proof of the distributive principle]
    In "Sets of Independent Postulates for the Algebra of Logic," by Edward V. Huntington, *Transactions of the American Mathematical Society,* vol. 5, 288-309, at 300f. Fisch, *Third Supplement.*

O 01072: (NF)
Kayser, H.
    "New Standards of Wave-Length," *Transactions of the International Union for Co-operation in Solar Research,* Transactions of First Conference (St. Louis, 23 September), p. 37.

1905

O 01073: F i c h e 136
Ruger, Henry A.
    What Pragmatism Is. C.S. Peirce. *The Monist,* April, 1905. *The Journal of Philosophy, Psychology, and Scientific Methods,* vol. 2 (7 December), 694-695.

1905

O 01074: (NF)
Prezzolini, Giuseppe.
    "Il Mio Prammatismo," *Leonardo,* vol. 3, at p. 48.

O 01075: (NF)
Vailati, Giovanni.
    "Ch. S. Peirce: What Pragmatism Is," *Leonardo,* vol. 3.

O 01076: F i c h e 136
Schiller, F.C.S.
    "The Definition of 'Pragmatism' and 'Humanism'," *Mind,* new series 14, 235-240.

P 01077: F i c h e 136
Review of *A Treatise on Cosmology.* By Herbert Nichols.
    The Monist, vol. 15 (January), 157-158. Burks, *Bibliography.*

P 01078: F i c h e 136
"What Pragmatism Is."
    The Monist, vol. 15 (April), 161-181. Two internal dates by Peirce are included: main text as "Milford, Pa., September, 1904" and a postscript as "Feb. 9, 1905." Cohen, *Tentative Bibliography;* Burks, *Bibliography.*

P 01079: F i c h e 136
"Substitution in Logic."
    The Monist, vol. 15 (April), 294-295. Signed by Francis C. Russell, though suspected to be by Peirce, based on correspondence in the Harvard MSS. Burks, *Bibliography.*

P 01080: F i c h e 136
"Issues of Pragmaticism."
    The Monist, vol. 15 (October), 481-499. Cohen, *Tentative Bibliography;* Burks, *Bibliography.*

O 01081: F i c h e 136
Peterson, James B.
    "Some Philosophical Terms," *The Monist,* vol. 15 (October), 629-633. This is mentioned by Peirce in "Mr. Peterson's Proposed Discussion," *The Monist,* vol. 16 (January 1906), 147-151.

P 01082: F i c h e 136
Review of *The Preparation of the Child for Science.* By M.E. Boole.
    The Nation, vol. 80 (5 January) 18-19.

P 01083: F i c h e 136
"Royce's Spencer."
    The Nation, vol. 80 (26 January) 71-72.

P 01084: F i c h e 136
Review of *The Becquerel Rays and the Properties of Radium.* By Hon. R.J. Strutt.
    The Nation, vol. 80 (2 February) 100.

P 01085: F i c h e 136
Review of *An Introduction to the Theory of Optics.* By Prof. Arthur Schuster.
    The Nation, vol. 80 (9 March) 198-199.

P 01086: F i c h e 136
Review of *Modern Practical Electricity.* By R. Mullineaux Walmsley.
    The Nation, vol. 80 (16 March) 218-219.

1905

O 01087: Fiche 136
Boole, Mary Everest.
    "The Sorrows of Philosophers," *The Nation,* 80 (23 March) 228.

P 01088: Fiche 136
Note [on Laurent's *Les Grands Écrivains Scientifiques*].
    The Nation, vol. 80 (23 March) 231.

P 01089: Fiche 136
Review of *The Phase Rule and its Applications.* By Alex. Findlay.
    The Nation, vol. 80 (30 March) 255-256.

P 01090: Fiche 137
"The National Academy of Sciences."
    The Nation, vol. 80 (27 April) 327-328.

P 01091: Fiche 137
Review of *Philosophy as Scientia Scientiarum, and a History of the Classification of the Sciences.* By Robert Flint. *A Syllabus of Certain Topics of Logic.* By C.S. Peirce.
    The Nation, vol. 80 (4 May) 360-361.

P 01092: Fiche 137
Note [on Garcin's *N-Rays*].
    The Nation, vol. 80 (11 May) 374.

P 01093: Fiche 137
Note [on Mendeleef's *Principles of Chemistry,* third edition].
    The Nation, vol. 80 (1 June) 438.

P 01094: Fiche 137
Review of *Scientific Fact and Metaphysical Reality.* By Robert Brandon Arnold.
    The Nation, vol. 80 (1 June) 444-445.

P 01095: Fiche 137
Note [on Santayana's *Life of Reason, or the Phases of Human Progress,* volumes I and II].
    The Nation, vol. 80 (8 June) 461.

P 01096: Fiche 137
Note [on Freund's *The Study of Chemical Composition*].
    The Nation, vol. 80 (22 June) 503.

P 01097: Fiche 137
Review of *James Watt.* By Andrew Carnegie.
    The Nation, vol. 80 (29 June) 527-528.

P 01098: Fiche 137
Note [on Bacon's *Balloons, Airships, and Flying Machines*].
    The Nation, vol. 81 (13 July) 33.

P 01099: Fiche 137
Note [on Hampson's *Radium Explained*].
    The Nation, vol. 81 (13 July) 33-34, filmed at P 01098.

P 01100: Fiche 137
Review of *Sociological Papers.* Published by the Sociological Society. *Foundations of Sociology.* By Edward Alsworth Ross.
    The Nation, vol. 81 (13 July) 42-43.

1905

P 01101: F i c h e 137
"Wundt's Principles of Physiological Psychology."
   The Nation, vol. 81 (20 July) 56-57.

P 01102: F i c h e 137
Note [on James's article in the *Archives de Psychologie*].
   The Nation, vol. 81 (3 August) 97.

P 01103: F i c h e 137
Review of *Nos Enfants au Collège.* Par le Dr. Maurice de Fleury.
   The Nation, vol. 81 (7 September) 205.

P 01104: F i c h e 137
Review of *A Treatise on Chemistry.* By Sir H.E. Roscoe and C. Schorlemmer.
   The Nation, vol. 81 (7 September) 205-206, filmed at P 01103.

P 01105: F i c h e 137
Review of *La Nature et la Vie.* Par Henry De Varigny.
   The Nation, vol. 81 (5 October) 286-287.

P 01106: F i c h e 137
Note [on *The Collected Mathematical Works of George William Hill*].
   The Nation, vol. 81 (19 October) 321.

P 01107: F i c h e 137
Note [on Shields's *Philosophia Ultima*].
   The Nation, vol. 81 (26 October) 340.

P 01108: F i c h e 137
Note [on Fine's *College Algebra*].
   The Nation, vol. 81 (26 October) 340-341, filmed at P 01107. Probably by Peirce.

P 01109: F i c h e 137
Note [on de Wiart's *La Cité Ardente*].
   The Nation, vol. 81 (9 November) 382.

P 01110: F i c h e 137
"The National Academy of Sciences at New Haven."
   The Nation, vol. 81 (23 November) 417-419.

P 01111: F i c h e 137
"Gosse's Sir Thomas Browne."
   The Nation, vol. 81 (14 December) 486-488.

P 01112: F i c h e 137, 138
"The Relation of Betweenness and Royce's O-collections."
   Paper read before the National Academy of Sciences, New Haven, 14-15 November. Cited in *Report of the National Academy of Sciences for the Year 1905,* Senate Document No. 144, 59th Congress, 1st Session, Washington: Government Printing Office, 1906, p. 15. Burks, *Bibliography,* p. 5-17, App. p. 21-39.

O 01113: (NF)
Moore, Addison W.
   "Pragmatism and Its Critics," *The Philosophical Review,* vol. 14, 322-343.

1905

O 01114: F i c h e 138
Sabine, George H.
> *What Pragmatism Is.* C.S. Peirce. In *The Philosophical Review,* vol. 14 (September), 628-629.

O 01115: (NF)
Baly, Edward C.C.
> *Spectroscopy.* London, New York and Bombay: Longmans, Green, and Co., at p. 45.

O 01116: (NF)
Maclagan-Wedderburn, J.H.
> "A Theorem on Finite Algebras," *Transactions of the American Mathematical Society,* vol. 6, 349-352, at 349.

O 01117: (NF)
Royce, Josiah.
> "The Relations of the Principles of Logic to the Foundations of Geometry," *Transactions of the American Mathematical Society,* vol. 6, 353-415, at 354, 359, 398n.

O 01118: F i c h e 138
Leith, Charles Kenneth.
> "Rock Cleavage," *United States Geological Survey Bulletin,* No. 239, at 109-110.

1906

O 01119: (NF)
Cattell, J. Mck., and Brimhall, D.R., editors.
> *American Men of Science: A Biographical Dictionary,* Lancaster, Pennsylvania: The Science Press, p. 248.

O 01120: F i c h e 138, 139, 140
Shearman, Arthur Thomas.
> *The Development of Symbolic Logic,* London: Williams and Norgate. (Final chapter and Index are not filmed.)

O 01121: F i c h e 140
Bourgeois, R. and Furtwängler, Ph.
> "Kartographie," in *Encyklopädie der mathematischen Wissenschaften,* part 1 of vol. 6, Leipzig: B.G. Teubner, at p. 17, 248, 287-289.

O 01122: F i c h e Sup. 12
Fullerton, George Stuart.
> *An Introduction to Philosophy,* New York: The Macmillan Co., at p. 219-220.

O 01123: (NF)
James, William.
> "G. Papini and the Pragmatist Movement in Italy," *Journal of Philosophy,* vol. 3, 337-341.

P 01124: F i c h e 140
"Mr. Peterson's Proposed Discussion."
> *The Monist,* vol. 16 (January), 147-151. Cohen, *Tentative Bibliography;* Burks, *Bibliography.*

P 01125: F i c h e 140
"Erratum [to Peirce's article entitled "Mr. Peterson's Proposed Discussion]."
> *The Monist,* vol. 16 (April), 320.

1906

P 01126: F i c h e 140
Review of *Foundations of Sociology.* By Edward Alsworth Ross.
    The Monist, vol. 16 (July), 470-473. Fisch, *Third Supplement.*

O 01127: F i c h e 140, 141
Vailati, Giovanni.
    "Pragmatism and Mathematical Logic (tr. H.D. Austin)," *The Monist,* vol. 16 (October), 481-491.

P 01128: F i c h e 141
"Prolegomena to an Apology for Pragmaticism."
    The Monist, vol. 16 (October), 492-546. Cohen, *Tentative Bibliography;* Burks, *Bibliography.*

P 01129: F i c h e 141
Review of *Radio-Activity.* By E. Rutherford.
    The Nation, vol. 82 (18 January) 61.

P 01130: F i c h e 141
"Alfred Russel Wallace."
    The Nation, vol. 82 (22 February) 160-161.

P 01131: F i c h e 141
"Haldane's Descartes."
    The Nation, vol. 82 (22 March) 242-243.

P 01132: F i c h e 141
"Meeting of the National Academy of Sciences."
    The Nation, vol. 82 (26 April) 341-342.

P 01133: F i c h e 141
Review of *Congress of Arts and Sciences, Universal Exposition, St. Louis, 1904,* Vol. 1. Edited by Howard J. Rogers.
    The Nation, vol. 82 (7 June) 475-476.

P 01134: F i c h e 141
Review of *The Dynamics of Living Matter.* By Jaques Loeb. *Chemistry of the Proteids.* By Gustav Mann.
    The Nation, vol. 83 (5 July) 17-18.

P 01135: F i c h e 141
Review of *The Life and Experiences of Sir Henry Enfield Roscoe.* Written by Himself.
    The Nation, vol. 83 (12 July) 43.

P 01136: F i c h e 141
Note [on Clerke's *System of the Stars*].
    The Nation, vol. 83 (26 July) 78.

P 01137: F i c h e 141
"Aristotle's Ethics."
    The Nation, vol. 83 (13 September) 226-227.

P 01138: F i c h e 142
Review of *An Introduction to Logic.* By Horace William Brindley Joseph.
    The Nation, vol. 83 (25 October) 353-354.

1906

P 01139: F i c h e 142
Review of *Side lights on Astronomy and Kindred Fields of Popular Science: Essays and Addresses.*
By Simon Newcomb.
    The Nation, vol. 83 (20 December) 544-545.

P 01140: F i c h e 142
"Recent Developments of Existential Graphs and their Consequences for Logic."
    Paper read before the National Academy of Sciences, Washington, 16-18 April. Cited in *Report of the National Academy of Sciences for the Year 1906,* Senate Document No. 308, 59th Congress, 2d Session, Washington: Government Printing Office, 1907, p. 15. MS 490 is a set of notes for this presentation (Robin, *Catalogue*). Cohen, *Tentative Bibliography;* Burks, *Bibliography,* pp. 5-20, App. C pp. 33-38.

P 01141: F i c h e 142
"Phaneroscopy, or Natural History of Signs, Relations, Categories, etc.: A method of investigating this subject expounded and illustrated."
    Paper read before the National Academy of Sciences, Boston, 20-22 November. Cited in *Report of the National Academy of Sciences for the Year 1906,* Senate Document No. 308, 59th Congress, 2d Session, Washington: Government Printing Office, 1907, p. 18, filmed at P 01140. MS 299 is probably a draft for this lecture (Robin, *Catalogue*). Cohen, *Tentative Bibliography;* Burks, *Bibliography.*

O 01142: F i c h e 142
Sabine, George H.
    Issues of Pragmaticism. Charles S. Peirce. In *The Philosophical Review,* vol. 15 (September), 565-566.

O 01143: (NF)
Royce, Josiah.
    "The Present State of the Question regarding the First Principles of Theoretical Science," *Proceedings of the American Philosophical Society,* vol. 45, 82-102, at 89, 90, 94.

O 01144: F i c h e 142
Lalande, André.
    "Pragmatisme et Pragmaticisme," *Revue philosophique,* vol. 61, 121-146.

O 01145: (NF)
Keynes, John Neville.
    Studies and Exercises in Formal Logic, 4th ed., London: Macmillan and Co., 336 n2. Sections 268-271 are adapted from Peirce. See also references to *Studies in Logic* at xxiv, 323n, 510n, 517, 518, 519, 520.

P 01146: F i c h e 142
"Men of Science in Session."
    The Sun, New York City, vol. 74 (Wednesday, 28 November), page 6, columns 5-7, page 7, columns 1-4. Fisch, *First Supplement.*

P 01147: F i c h e 142
"Mars as a Place to Inhabit."
    The Sun, New York City, vol. 74 (Sunday, 2 December, first section), page 8, columns 5-6. Fisch, *First Supplement.*

O 01148: (NF)
Kühner, Fr. and Furtwängler, Ph.
    "Bestimmung der Absoluten Grösze der Schwerkraft zu Potsdam mit Reversionspendeln," *Veröffenliehung des Königl. Preuszischen Geodätischen Instituts,* Neue Folge No. 27, Berlin, at p. xii, xiv, 38.

1907

O 01149: (NF)
Enriques, F.
    "Prinzipien der Geometrie," *Encyklopädie der mathematischen Wissenschaften,* Leipzig: B.G. Teubner, 3.1.1.: 1-29, at 12.

P 01150: (NF)
[Lectures on Scientific Method]
    Given before the Harvard University Philosophy Club. The lecture titles as announced were: "Logical Methodeutic: I. Retroduction, or the Framing of Hypothesis; II. Induction, or the Experimental Method." A third lecture on deduction was also given. The lectures were delivered on April 8, 12, 13. A draft of the second lecture survives (see Robin, *Catalogue,* MS 754). Burks, *Bibliography;* Fisch, *First Supplement.*

O 01151: (NF)
Larmor, Joseph, editor.
    Memoir and Scientific Correspondence of the Late Sir George Gabriel Stokes, 2 volumes, Cambridge: Harvard University Press, in vol. 2, at p. 309-313.

O 01152: (NF)
Schiller, F.C.S.
    Review of James' *Pragmatism. Mind,* new series 16, 598-604.

P 01153: F i c h e 142
Review of *The Scientific Papers of J. Willard Gibbs.*
    The Nation, vol. 84 (24 January) 92.

P 01154: F i c h e 142
Review of *A History of Chemistry.* By Ernest von Meyer.
    The Nation, vol. 84 (21 February) 181-182.

P 01155: F i c h e 142
Review of *Thought and Things: A Study of the Development and Meaning of Thought; or Genetic Logic.* By James Mark Baldwin.
    The Nation, vol. 84 (28 February) 203-204.

P 01156: F i c h e 143
Note [on Stickney's *Organized Democracy*].
    The Nation, vol. 85 (12 September) 229.

P 01157: F i c h e 143
Review of *The Collected Mathematical Works of George William Hill.*
    The Nation, vol. 85 (17 October) 355.

O 01158: F i c h e 143
Newcomb, Simon.
    "The Work of George W. Hill."
    The Nation, vol. 85 (31 October), 396.

P 01159: F i c h e 143
"The Work of George W. Hill."
    The Nation, vol. 85 (31 October), 396, filmed at P 00158. Peirce's editorial reply to a letter by Newcomb.

1907

P 01160: F i c h e 143
"Lord Kelvin."
> *The Nation,* vol. 85 (19 December) 570-571. Obituary.

P 01161: F i c h e 143
Note [obituary of Lord Kelvin].
> *The Nation,* vol. 85 (26 December) 579.

O 01162: F i c h e 143
Cunningham, G.W.
> *Prolegomena to an Apology for Pragmaticism.* C.S.S. Peirce. In *The Philosophical Review,* vol. 16 (September), 564-565.

O 01163: (NF)
Vailati, Giovanni.
> "De quelques caractères du mouvement philosophique contemporain en Italie," *La Revue du Mois,* vol. 3, 162-185, at 164, 165, 166.

O 01164: (NF)
Shaw, James Byrnie.
> *Synopsis of Linear Associative Algebra,* Washington, D.C.: Carnegie Institution, at p. 6, 7, 41, 59, 93, 97, 98, 142.

1908

O 01165: F i c h e 143
Stein, Ludwig.
> "Der Pragmatismus," *Archiv für systematische Philosophie,* vol. 14, 1-9, 143-188.

P 01166: F i c h e 143
"A Neglected Argument for the Reality of God."
> *The Hibbert Journal,* vol. 7 (October), 90-112. Burks, *Bibliography.*

O 01167: F i c h e 143, 144
Lovejoy, A.O.
> "The Thirteen Pragmatisms," *The Journal of Philosophy, Psychology and Scientific Methods,* vol. 5, 5-12, 29-39.

O 01168:(NF)
Meyer, Max.
> "The Exact Number of Pragmatisms," *The Journal of Philosophy, Psychology, and Scientific Methods,* vol. 5, 321-326.

O 01169: (NF)
Armstrong, A.C.
> "The Evolution of Pragmatism," *The Journal of Philosophy, Psychology, and Scientific Methods,* vol. 5, 645-650.

O 01170: F i c h e S u p. 12
McTaggart, J. Ellis.
> Review of James' *Pragmatism. Mind,* new series 17, 104-109.

1908

P 01171: F i c h e 144
"Some Amazing Mazes: The First Curiosity."
    The Monist, vol. 18 (April), 227-241. *List of Articles;* Burks, *Bibliography.*

O 01172: F i c h e 144
Boodin, John E.
    "Philosophic Tolerance. A Winter Revery," *The Monist,* vol. 18 (April), 298-306, including the "Editorial Comment" by Carus on page 306.

O 01173: F i c h e 144
Carus, Paul.
    "Pragmatism," *The Monist,* vol. 18 (July), 321-362.

O 01174: F i c h e 144
Russell, Francis C.
    "Hints for the Elucidation of Mr. Peirce's Logical Work," *The Monist,* vol. 18 (July), 406-415.

P 01175: F i c h e 145
"Some Amazing Mazes: Explanation of Curiosity the First."
    The Monist, vol. 18 (July), 416-464. *List of Articles,* Burks, *Bibliography.*

P 01176: F i c h e 145
Review of *Thought and Things: A Study of the Development and Meaning of Thought, or Genetic Logic.* By James Mark Baldwin.
    The Nation, vol. 87 (20 August) 164-165.

P 01177: F i c h e 145
Note [obituary of Oliver Wolcott Gibbs].
    The Nation, vol. 87 (17 December) 609.

P 01178: F i c h e 145
"A Letter from Mr. Peirce."
    The Open Court, vol. 22 (May), 319. The letter refers to an earlier article in the same journal by Paul Carus at vol. 22 (April 1908), 234-246. Fisch, *First Supplement.*

O 01179: (NF)
Gutberlet, Const.
    "Der Pragmatismus," *Philosophisches Jahrbuch* (Görres-Gesellschaft), vol. 21: 4, 437-458.

1909

O 01180: (NF)
Müller, Eugen.
    Abriss der Algebra der Logik. Part I. Leipzig: B.G. Teubner.

O 01181: (NF)
Royce, Josiah.
    "The Problem of Truth in the Light of Recent Discussion," *Bericht uber den III. Internationalen Kongress für Philosophie zu Heidelberg 1. bis 5. Sept. 1908,* Heidelberg: The Elsenhaus, 62-90.

1909

O 01182: (NF)
Carus, Paul.
    [Remarks on pragmatism]. *Bericht uber den III. Internationalen Kongress für Philosophie zu Heidelberg 1. bis 5. September 1908,* Heidelberg: The Elsenhaus, 737.

O 01183: (NF)
Montague, W.P.
    "May a Realist be a Pragmatist? I. The Two Doctrines Defined," *The Journal of Philosophy, Psychology, and Scientific Methods,* vol. 6, 460-463.

O 01184: (NF)
Montague, W.P.
    "May a Realist be a Pragmatist? II. The Implications of Instrumentalism," *The Journal of Philosophy, Psychology, and Scientific Methods,* vol. 6, 485-490.

O 01185: (NF)
Montague, W.P.
    "May a Realist be a Pragmatist? III. The Implications of Psychological Pragmatism," *The Journal of Philosophy, Psychology, and Scientific Methods,* vol. 6, 543-548.

O 01186: (NF)
Montague, W.P.
    "May a Realist be a Pragmatist? IV. The Implications of Humanism and the Pragmatic Criterion," *The Journal of Philosophy, Psychology, and Scientific Methods,* vol. 6, 561-571.

O 01187: (NF)
Lovejoy, A.O.
    "Pragmatism and Realism," *The Journal of Philosophy, Psychology, and Scientific Methods,* vol. 6, 575-580.

O 01188: (NF)
Boodin, J.E.
    "What Pragmatism Is and Is Not," *The Journal of Philosophy, Psychology, and Scientific Methods,* vol. 6, 627-635.

O 01189: (NF)
Kallen, Horace M.
    "The Affiliations of Pragmatism," *The Journal of Philosophy, Psychology, and Scientific Methods,* vol. 6, 655-663.

P 01190: F i c h e 145, 146
"The Fortieth Anniversary of The Nation."
    In *Letters and Memorials of Wendell Philips Garrison, Literary Editor of "The Nation" 1865-1906,* Boston: Houghton Mifflin Company, p. 133-164. Peirce's contributions are at p. 140, 156-157. Fisch and Haskell, *Additions to Cohen's Bibliography.*

O 01191: (NF)
James, William.
    The Meaning of Truth, New York: Longmans, Green, and Co., at 40nl, 51-52.

O 01192: (NF)
Mannoury, Gerrit.
    Methodologisches und Philosophisches zur Elementar-Mathematik, Haarlem, Holland: P. Visser, 75-77.

1909

P 01193: F i c h e 146
"Some Amazing Mazes: A Second Curiosity."
    The Monist, vol. 19 (January), 36-45. *List of Articles;* Burks, *Bibliography.*

O 01194: F i c h e 146
Carus, Paul.
    "A Postscript on Pragmatism," *The Monist,* vol. 19 (January), 85-94.

O 01195: F i c h e 146
Carus, Paul.
    "A German Critic of Pragmatism," *The Monist,* vol. 19 (January), 136-148.

O 01196: F i c h e 146
Carus, Paul.
    "A Letter from Professor James." *The Monist,* 19 (January), 156.

O 01197: F i c h e 146
Anonymous.
    Notice of *Abriss der Algebra der Logik,* part I. By Dr. Eugen Müller. *The Monist,* vol. 19 (July), 475-476.

O 01198: (NF)
Carus, Paul.
    Philosophy as a Science, Chicago: The Open Court Publishing Co., at p. 154, 159.

O 01199: (NF)
James, William.
    A Pluralistic Universe, New York: Longmans, Green, and Co., at p. 398-400.

O 01200: (NF)
Jacoby, Günther.
    Der Pragmatismus: Neue Bahnen in der Wissenschaftslehre des Auslands, Liepzig: Dürr.

P 01201: F i c h e 146
[Research grants to Peirce]
    Summarized in *Report of the National Academy of Sciences for the Year 1908,* Senate Doc. No. 770, Washington: Government Printing Office, 1909, p. 39-41.

O 01202: (NF)
Vailati, Giovanni, and Calderoni, Mario.
    "Le origini e l'idea fondamentale del Pragmatismo," *Rivista di Psicologia Applicata,* 5:1, 10-29.

O 01203: (NF)
Pratt, James B.
    What is Pragmatism? New York: Macmillan Co., at p. 16-19.

1910

O 01204: (NF)
Anonymous.
    "Charles S. Peirce," *American Men of Science,* p. 364.

1910

O 01205: (NF)
McGiffert, A.C.
  "The Pragmatism of Kant," *The Journal of Philosophy, Psychology, and Scientific Methods,* vol. 7, 197-203.

P 01206: F i c h e 146, 147
[Portion of a letter on non-Aristotelian logic]
  In "The Nature of Logical and Mathematical Thought," by Paul Carus, *The Monist,* vol. 20 (January), 33-75, at p. 45.

P 01207: F i c h e 147
[Portion of a letter on non-Aristotelian logic]
  In "Non-Aristotelian Logic," by Paul Carus, *The Monist,* vol. 20 (January), 158-159.

O 01208: F i c h e 147
Boodin, John E.
  "Pragmatic Realism," *The Monist,* vol. 20 (October), 602-614.

O 01209: F i c h e 147
Carus, Paul.
  "Editorial Comment," *The Monist,* vol. 20 (October), 614-615.

O 01210: (NF)
Bawden, H.H.
  The Principles of Pragmatism, Boston.

O 01211: (NF)
Jourdain, Philip E.B.
  "The Development of the Theories of Mathematical Logic and the Principles of Mathematics," *The Quarterly Journal of Pure and Applied Mathematics,* vol. 41, 324-352, at 326, 340; vol. 43, 219-314, at 274.

1911

O 01212: (NF)
Kallen, Horace M.
  "Pragmatism and Its 'Principles'," *The Journal of Philosophy, Psychology, and Scientific Methods,* vol. 8, 617-636.

O 01213: F i c h e 147
Boodin, John Elof.
  "From Protagoras to William James," *The Monist,* vol. 21 (January) 73-91.

P 01214: F i c h e 147
"A method of computation."
  Paper read by title before the National Academy of Sciences, 21-22 November. Cited in *Report of the National Academy of Sciences for the Year 1911,* Senate Doc. No. 343, Washington: Government Printing Office, 1912, p. 24. MSS 212-215 may be relevant to this presentation (Robin, *Catalogue*). Burks, *Bibliography;* Fisch, *Second Supplement.*

P 01215: F i c h e 147
"The reasons of reasoning, or grounds of inferring."
  Paper read by title before the National Academy of Sciences, 21-22 November. Cited in *Report of the National Academy of Sciences for the Year 1911,* Senate Doc. No. 343, Washington: Government Printing Office, 1912, p. 24, filmed at P 01214. Burks, *Bibliography;* Fisch, *Second Supplement.*

1911

O 01216: (NF)
Berthelot, René.
    Un romantisme utilitaire. Etude sur le mouvement pragmatiste, 3 vols., Paris: Alcan, at vol. 1, sec, 2, p. 6-10.

O 01217: (NF)
Vailati, Giovanni.
    Scritti di G. Vailati (1863-1909), Leipzig: Johann Ambrosius Barth; Florence: Successori B. Seeber, at p. 592, 639-640, 753-756, 876-877, 920-932.

O 01218: (NF)
Carus, Paul.
    Truth on Trial, Chicago: The Open Court Publishing Co., at p. 5, 12, 15, 36, 58, 114-116, 118.

O 01219: (NF)
Borrass, E.
    "Der Bericht uber die relativen Messungen der Schwerkraft mit Pendelapparaten in der Zeit von 1808 bis 1909 und uber ihre Darstellung im Potsdamer Schweresystem,"
    Verhandlungen der vom 21 bis 29 September 1909 in London und Cambridge abgehaltenen Sechzehnten Allgemeinen Conferenz der Internationalen Erdmessung, Berlin: Georg Reimer, at p. 241, 242, 247.

1912

O 01220: (NF)
Murray, D.L.
    Pragmatism, New York: Dodge.

O 01221: (NF)
Paget, Violet [under pseudonym of Vernon Lee].
    Vital Lies: Studies of Some Varieties of Recent Obscurantism, London: John Lane, The Bodley Head, see index.

O 01222: (NF)
Royce, Josiah.
    William James and Other Essays on the Philosophy of Life, New York: Macmillan, at 207-208.

1913

O 01223: (NF)
Royce, Josiah.
    "The Principles of Logic," *Encyclopaedia of the Philosophical Sciences,* vol. 1, Logic, London: Macmillan & Co., Ltd., p. 67-135, at 82ff., 86ff., 91, 112n.

O 01224: (NF)
Royce, Josiah.
    "Some Psychological Problems Emphasized by Pragmatism," *Popular Science Monthly,* vol. 83, 394-411, at 402-403, 407, 408.

O 01225: (NF)
Caldwell, William.
    Pragmatism and Idealism, London: Adam and Charles Black.

1913

O 01226: (NF)
Papini, Giovanni.
    Sul Pragmatismo: Saggi e Ricerche, Milano: Libreria editrice Milanese.

O 01227: (NF)
Royce, Josiah.
    The Problem of Christianity. 2 vols., New York: Macmillan, at I, xi; II, 114-117, 138, 139-154, 163, 169-173, 176, 182-186, 196-198, 204, 231, 237, 281-284, 393-396, 406, 413, 422n.

O 01228: (NF)
Royce, Josiah.
    "Some Relations Between Philosophy and Science in the First Half of the Nineteenth Century in Germany," *Science,* new series 38, 567-584, at 580-582.

1914

O 01229: Fiche 147
Peirce, Herbert Henry David.
    "Charles Sanders Peirce" [obituary]," *Boston Evening Transcript* (Saturday 16 May), part 3, page 3, columns 5-6. By C.S. Peirce's brother. Fisch, *Second Supplement.*

O 01230: Fiche Sup. 12
Becker, George F.
    "Charles Santiago Sanders Peirce, '59 [obituary," *Harvard Alumni Bulletin,* vol. 16 (Wednesday 27 May), 549-550.

O 01231: Fiche Sup. 12
Davis, Ellery W.
    "Charles Peirce at Johns Hopkins," *Mid-West Quarterly,* vol. 2, 48-56.

O 01232: Fiche 148
Russell, Francis C.
    "In Memoriam Charles S. Peirce: (Born 1839, died 1914) [obituary]," *The Monist,* vol. 24 (July), 469-472.

O 01233: Fiche 148
Anonymous.
    [obituary of Peirce], *The Nation,* vol. 98 (23 April), 473.

O 01234: Fiche 148
Franklin, Fabian.
    "The Lonely Heights of Science," *The Nation,* vol. 98 (30 April) 489-490.

O 01235: Fiche 148
Jastrow, Joseph.
    "The Passing of a Master Mind," *The Nation,* vol. 98 (14 May) 571. Letter.

O 01236: Fiche Sup. 12
Geyer, Denton Loring.
    The Pragmatic Theory of Truth as Developed by Peirce, James, and Dewey, University of Illinois, Diss.

O 01237: Fiche 149
[Notice of Peirce's death]
    Proceedings of the American Academy of Arts and Sciences, vol. 49 (13 May), p. 659.

1914

O 01238: (NF)
Royce, Josiah.
> "The Mechanical, the Historical and the Statistical," *Science,* new series 39, 551-566, at 562-566.

O 01239: (NF)
Royce, Josiah.
> *War and Insurance,* New York: The Macmillan Co., at iv-v, 50n2.

1915

O 01240: Fiche 149
[Obituary of Peirce]
> *Report of the National Academy of Sciences for the Year 1914,* Senate Doc. No. 989, Washington: Government Printing Office, p. 13, 46.

1916

O 01241: Fiche 149
Royce, Josiah, and Kernan, Fergus.
> "Charles Sanders Peirce," *The Journal of Philosophy, Psychology and Scientific Methods,* vol. 13, 701-709.

O 01242: Fiche 149
Dewey, John.
> "The Pragmatism of Peirce," *The Journal of Philosophy, Psychology, and Scientific Methods,* vol. 13, 709-715, filmed at O 01241.

O 01243: Fiche 149
Ladd-Franklin, Christine.
> "Charles S. Peirce at the Johns Hopkins," *The Journal of Philosophy, Psychology, and Scientific Methods,* vol. 13, 715-722, filmed at O 01241.

O 01244: Fiche 149
Jastrow, Joseph.
> "Charles Sanders Peirce as a Teacher," *The Journal of Philosophy, Psychology, and Scientific Methods,* vol. 13, 723-726, filmed at O 01241.

O 01245: Fiche 149
Cohen, Morris R.
> "Charles S. Peirce and a Tentative Bibliography of his Published Writings," *The Journal of Philosophy, Psychology, and Scientific Methods,* vol. 13, 726-737, filmed at O 01241.

1918

O 01246: Fiche 149
Anonymous.
> "A List of Articles, Mostly Book Reviews, Contributed by Charles Sanders Peirce to 'The Nation'," *The Journal of Philosophy, Psychology, and Scientific Methods,* vol. 15, 578-584.

1918

P 01247: F i c h e 149
"A Philosopher's Political Diagnosis."
    In *New York: A Symphonic Study in Three Parts,* by Melusina Fay Peirce, New York: Neale Publishing Company, p. 100-104. The material by C.S. Peirce printed here was written sometime between 1865 and 1870. Burks, *Bibliography.*

1934

O 01248: F i c h e 149
Jastrow, Joseph.
    "The Widow of Charles Peirce [obituary of Juliette Peirce]," *Science,* new series 80 (Friday 16 November), 440-441.

APPENDIX ONE:
PLACES OF PUBLICATION

American Academy of Arts and Sciences, papers read before the.
    00063, 00087, 00098, 00133

American Association for the Advancement of Science, papers read before the.
    00186

The American Historical Review.
    00611, 00650, 00752

American Journal of Mathematics.
    00111, 00134, 00135, 00167, 00187, 00188, 00296

The American Journal of Psychology.
    00344

The American Journal of Science and Arts.
    00011, 00036, 00100, 00136, 00137.

The American Journal of Science.
    00168, 00218, 00240, 00345, 00346, 00363, 00364.

American Mathematical Society, paper read before the.
    00553

American Metrological Society, paper read before the.
    00270

Annals of the Astronomical Observatory of Harvard College.
    00118, 00219, 00271, 00372

Annual Report of the Board of Regents of the Smithsonian Institution.
    00613, 00614, 00615, 00753, 00754, 00755, 00756, 00757, 00758, 00759, 00760, 00805

Association of Engineers, Cornell University, paper read before the.
    00297

Association geodesique internationale, paper read before the.
    00102

The Atlantic Almanac.
    00023, 00024, 00037, 00038, 00049, 00050, 00051, 00064, 00065, 00071, 00072, 00079, 00080, 00081

The Bookman.
    00709

Boston Daily Evening Traveller.
    00002, 00003, 00004, 00005, 00006, 00007

A Comprehensive Bibliography

"Brief Description of the Algebra of Relatives."
    00220

Cambridge Conference Lectures.
    00652

Cambridge High School Association, oration before the.
    00012

The Century Dictionary and Cyclopedia.
    00373

Chemical News, American Supplement.
    00040

The Christian Register.
    00347

Comptes Rendus des Séances de L'Academie des Sciences.
    00171

Cornell Daily Sun.
    00324

Crónica Cientifica.
    00241

The Democratic Party.
    00089

Dictionary of Philosophy and Psychology.
    00761, 00762, 00763, 00764, 00765, 00766, 00767, 00768, 00769, 00770, 00771, 00772, 00773, 00774, 00775, 00776, 00777, 00778, 00806, 00807, 00808, 00809, 00810, 00811, 00812, 00813, 00814, 00815, 00816, 00817, 00818, 00819, 00820, 00821, 00822, 00823, 00824, 00825, 00826, 00827, 00828, 00829, 00830, 00831, 00832, 00833, 00834, 00835, 00836, 00837, 00838, 00839, 00840, 00841, 00842, 00843, 00844, 00845, 00846, 00847, 00848, 00849, 00850, 00851, 00852, 00853, 00854, 00855, 00856, 00857, 00858, 00859, 00860, 00861, 00862, 00863, 00864, 00865, 00866, 00867, 00868, 00869, 00870, 00871, 00872, 00873, 00874, 00875, 00876, 00877, 00878, 00879, 00880, 00881, 00882, 00883, 00884, 00885, 00886, 00887, 00888, 00889, 00890, 00891, 00892, 00893, 00894, 00895, 00896, 00897, 00898, 00899, 00900, 00901, 00902, 00903, 00904, 00905, 00906, 00907, 00908, 00909, 00910, 00911, 00912, 00913, 00914, 00915, 00916, 00917, 00918, 00919, 00920, 00921, 00922, 00923, 00924, 00925, 00926, 00927, 00928, 00929, 00930, 00931, 00932, 00933, 00934, 00935, 00936, 00937, 00938, 00939, 00940, 00941, 00942, 00943, 00944, 00945, 00946, 00947, 00948, 00949, 00950, 00951, 00952, 00953, 00954, 00955, 00956, 00957, 00958, 00959, 00961, 00962, 00963, 00964, 00965, 00966, 00967, 00968, 00969, 00970

Educational Review.
    00653

The Evening Post.
    00300, 00592, 00635, 00679, 00779, 01038

Genius and Degeneration.
    00616

Graduate Philosophical Society, Harvard University, paper read before the.
    00470

The Harvard Magazine.
    00001

Harvard Philosophical Club, paper given before the.
    00157

Harvard University, lectures given at.
    00039, 00055

Harvard University Lectures.
    00016, 01004

Harvard University Philosophy Club, lectures given before the.
    01150

The Hibbert Journal.
    01166

The Independent.
    00519, 00520

The Johns Hopkins University Circulars.
    00222, 00225, 00242, 00245

The Journal of Speculative Philosophy.
    00025, 00026, 00027, 00028, 00041

Letters and Memorials of Wendell Philips Garrison, Literary Editor of "The Nation" 1865-1906.
    01190

The London, Edinburgh, and Dublin Philosophical Magazine and Journal of Science.
    00105, 00174

Lowell Institute at Cambridge, Mass., lectures given for the.
    00017, 00471, 01005

Mathematical Department, Bryn Mawr College, paper given before the.
    00618

Mathematical Seminary, Cornell University, paper given before the.
    00302

Mathematical Seminary, Johns Hopkins University, papers given before the.
    00175, 00194, 00195, 00226

Mathematical Society, Johns Hopkins University, papers read before the.
    00224, 00273

A Comprehensive Bibliography

Memoirs of the American Academy of Arts and Sciences.
00052

Memoirs of the National Academy of Sciences.
00303

Memoranda Concerning the Aristotelean Syllogism.
00018

Metaphysical Club, Johns Hopkins University, papers read before a meeting of the.
00143, 00176, 00177, 00196, 00197, 00229, 00230, 00232, 00247, 00274, 00275, 00276

Mind.
00099

The Monist.
00439, 00474, 00477, 00480, 00521, 00525, 00620, 00637, 01077, 01078, 01079, 01080, 01124, 01125, 01126, 01128, 01171, 01175, 01193, 01206, 01207

The Nation.
00043, 00044, 00045, 00053, 00056, 00057, 00059, 00066, 00073, 00114, 00148, 00149, 00150, 00198, 00279, 00306, 00307, 00308, 00326, 00376, 00378, 00389, 00390, 00391, 00392, 00393, 00394, 00395, 00396, 00397, 00398, 00441, 00442, 00446, 00447, 00448, 00449, 00450, 00451, 00453, 00454, 00455, 00458, 00460, 00482, 00484, 00485, 00487, 00489, 00491, 00493, 00494, 00495, 00496, 00497, 00498, 00499, 00500, 00501, 00502, 00503, 00504, 00505, 00506, 00507, 00508, 00528, 00529, 00530, 00531, 00532, 00533, 00535, 00536, 00537, 00538, 00539, 00540, 00541, 00542, 00544, 00557, 00558, 00559, 00560, 00561, 00562, 00563, 00564, 00565, 00566, 00567, 00568, 00569, 00570, 00571, 00572, 00573, 00574, 00575, 00576, 00577, 00578, 00579, 00580, 00582, 00583, 00584, 00586, 00587, 00596, 00597, 00598, 00599, 00600, 00601, 00602, 00603, 00604, 00605, 00607, 00608, 00621, 00623, 00624, 00625, 00626, 00627, 00628, 00629, 00630, 00639, 00640, 00641, 00642, 00644, 00645, 00657, 00658, 00659, 00660, 00661, 00662, 00663, 00664, 00665, 00666, 00667, 00668, 00669, 00670, 00671, 00672, 00682, 00683, 00684, 00685, 00686, 00688, 00689, 00690, 00691, 00692, 00693, 00694, 00695, 00696, 00697, 00698, 00699, 00700, 00701, 00703, 00713, 00714, 00715, 00716, 00717, 00718, 00719, 00720, 00721, 00722, 00723, 00724, 00725, 00726, 00727, 00728, 00729, 00730, 00731, 00732, 00733, 00734, 00735, 00736, 00737, 00738, 00739, 00741, 00742, 00743, 00744, 00745, 00746, 00747, 00748, 00749, 00782, 00783, 00784, 00785, 00786, 00787, 00788, 00789, 00790, 00791, 00792, 00793, 00794, 00795, 00796, 00797, 00798, 00799, 00973, 00974, 00975, 00976, 00977, 00978, 00979, 00980, 00981, 00982, 00983, 00984, 00985, 00986, 00987, 00988, 00989, 00990, 00991, 00992, 00993, 00994, 01006, 01007, 01009, 01010, 01011, 01012, 01013, 01014, 01015, 01016, 01017, 01018, 01019, 01020, 01021, 01022, 01023, 01024, 01026, 01028, 01030, 01031, 01041, 01042, 01043, 01044, 01045, 01046, 01047, 01048, 01049, 01050, 01051, 01052, 01053, 01054, 01055, 01056, 01057, 01058, 01059, 01060, 01061, 01062, 01063, 01064, 01065, 01066, 01067, 01082, 01083, 01084, 01085, 01086, 01088, 01089, 01090, 01091, 01092, 01093, 01094, 01095, 01096, 01097, 01098, 01099, 01100, 01101, 01102, 01103, 01104, 01105, 01106, 01107, 01108, 01109, 01110, 01111, 01129, 01130, 01131, 01132, 01133, 01134, 01135, 01136, 01137, 01138, 01139, 01153, 01154, 01155, 01156, 01157, 01159, 01160, 01161, 01176, 01177

National Academy of Sciences, papers read before the.
00115, 00151, 00152, 00153, 00154, 00178, 00199, 00200, 00233, 00234, 00235, 00236, 00281, 00282, 00283, 00327, 00379, 00380, 00461, 00462, 00631, 00632, 00633, 00704, 00800, 00995, 00996, 00997, 00998, 01068, 01069, 01112, 01140, 01141, 01214, 01215

Nature.
     00117, 00155, 00156, 00179, 00204, 00249

New York Daily Tribune.
     00464

New York Mathematical Society, paper presented at a meeting of the.
     00589

New York: A Symphonic Study in Three Parts.
     01247

The New York Times.
     00402, 00416, 00590

The Nineteenth Century.
     00801

The North American Review.
     00013, 00021, 00054, 00060

The Open Court.
     00509, 00510, 00511, 00512, 00513, 00545, 00547, 00548, 01178

Philosophical Society of Washington, papers read before the.
     00061, 00067, 00068, 00075, 00082, 00083

The Popular Science Monthly.
     00107, 00119, 00120, 00121, 00122, 00123, 00802

"The Principles of Philosophy: Or, Logic, Physics and Psychics, Considered as a Unity. In the Light of the Nineteenth Century."
     00552

Proceedings of the American Academy of Arts and Sciences.
     00030, 00031, 00032, 00033, 00034, 00090, 00108, 00125, 00126

Proceedings of the American Society for Psychical Research.
     00352, 00354

Proceedings of the Assay Commission of 1888, Laws of the United States Relating to the Annual Assay, and Rules for the Organization and Government of the Board of Assay Commissioners.
     00368

Progressive Age.
     00705

"Prospectus. The Treatise of Petrus Peregrinus on the Lodestone."
     00551

Report on Gravity at the Smithsonian, Ann Arbor, Madison and Cornell.
     00385

Report of the National Academy of Sciences.
    01201

Report on the Proceedings of the United States Expedition to Lady Franklin Bay, Grinnell Land.
    00369

Report of the Superintendent of the U.S. Coast and Geodetic Survey.
    00008, 00009, 00010, 00015, 00019, 00047, 00048, 00069, 00070, 00076, 00077, 00078, 00085, 00086, 00092, 00093, 00094, 00095, 00096, 00109, 00127, 00128, 00158, 00159, 00160, 00161, 00182, 00183, 00207, 00208, 00237, 00252, 00253, 00254, 00255, 00256, 00257, 00258, 00259, 00260, 00261, 00262, 00263, 00264, 00286, 00287, 00288, 00289, 00290, 00310, 00311, 00312, 00313, 00314, 00315, 00316, 00331, 00332, 00333, 00334, 00335, 00336, 00356, 00357, 00358, 00359, 00360, 00384, 00433, 00465, 00514

Revue Philosophique de la France et de L'Étranger.
    00129, 00162

Science.
    00266, 00292, 00293, 00317, 00674, 00750, 00751, 00803

Science and Immortality; the Christian Register Symposium, Revised and Enlarged.
    00348

The Science of Mechanics.
    00550

Science News.
    00163

Scientific Association, Johns Hopkins University, papers given before the.
    00164, 00210, 00211

Smithsonian Contributions to Knowledge.
    01034

Studies in Logic, By Members of the Johns Hopkins University.
    00268

The Sun.
    01146, 01147

Supreme Court of the United States, in Equity.
    00035

A Syllabus of Certain Topics of Logic.
    01035

Testimony before the Joint Commission.
    00339

Transactions of the American Mathematical Society.
    01071

A Treatise on Projections.
    00238

Verhandlungen [Papers and Proceedings of the International Geodetic Association, title varies from year to year].
      00097, 00110, 00130, 00131, 00165, 00166, 00184, 00215, 00216, 00370, 00804

APPENDIX TWO:
TITLES

"Abbot Against Royce."
    00454

"Dr. F.E. Abbot's Philosophy."
    00326

"Francis Ellingwood Abbot."
    01031

"On the Acceleration of gravity at initial stations."
    00115

"Acetylene and Alcohol."
    00608

Addyman, Frank J. - Peirce's review of his *Practical X-Ray Work.*
    00799

[Administrative Duty].
    00094

[Aide, service as].
    00009

Aikins, Herbert Austin - Peirce's review of his *The Principles of Logic.*
    00988

"Alchemy and Chemistry."
    00576

"Alfred Russel Wallace."
    01130

"On the Algebra of Logic."
    00167

"On the Algebra of Logic."
    00283

'On the Algebra of Logic: A Contribution to the Philosophy of Notation."
    00296

Allbutt, T. Clifford - Peirce's review of his *Notes on the Composition of Scientific Papers.*
    01057

"Some Amazing Mazes: The First Curiosity."
    01171

"Some Amazing Mazes: Explanation of Curiosity the First."
    01175

"Some Amazing Mazes: A Second Curiosity."
01193

Note [on the *Annales* of the Paris International Congress of 1900, section on the History of Science].
00985

"On the Appearance of Encke's Comet as seen at Harvard College Observatory."
00061

"On the Application of Logical Analysis to Multiple Algebra."
00090

"The Architecture of Theories."
00439

"Aristotle's Ethics."
01137

[The Arithmetic of Rollandus, exhibition of].
00589

Arnold, Robert Brandon - Peirce's review of his *Scientific Fact and Metaphysical Reality*.
01094

Ashton, John - Peirce's review of his *The History of Gambling in England*.
00689

"Astronomical."
00064, 00071, 00079.

"Astronomical Explanations."
00023

"Astronomical Information, Etc."
00049

"Astronomical Methods of Determining the Curvature of Space."
00461

[Astronomical Observations].
00219, 00271, 00372.

Note [on Atkinson's *Power Transmitted by Electricity*].
00722

Note [on Atkinson's *Electrical and Magnetical Calculations*].
00981

d'Avenel, Vicomte G. - Peirce's review of his *Le mécanisme de la vie moderne*.
00717

"Aviation."
00990

[Azimuth and magnetic observations].
    00008

Notes [on Babbage and James Mill Peirce].
    00057

Bacon, Rev. John N. - Peirce's review of his *By Land and Sea.*
    00787

Note [on Bacon's Balloons, Airships, and Flying Machines].
    01098

Baillie, J.B. - Peirce's review of his *The Origin and Significance of Hegel's Logic: A General Introduction to Hegel's System.*
    00991

"Bain's Logic."
    00053

Baker, Ray Stannard - Peirce's review of his *The Boy's Book of Inventions: Stories of the Wonders of Modern Science.*
    00701

Baldwin, James Mark - Peirce's review of his *Mental Development in the Child and the Race: Methods and Processes.*
    00603

Baldwin, James Mark - Peirce's review of his *Social and Ethical Interpretations in Mental Development.*
    00658

Baldwin, James Mark - Peirce's review of his *Dictionary of Philosophy and Psychology.*
    01016

Baldwin, James Mark - Peirce's review of his *Thought and Things: A Study of the Development and Meaning of Thought, or Genetic Logic.*
    01155

Baldwin, James Mark - Peirce's review of his *Thought and Things: A Study of the Development and Meaning of Thought, or Genetic Logic.*
    01176

"Baldwin's Story of the Mind."
    00667

Ball, Sir Robert S. - Peirce's review of his *Great Astronomers.*
    00607

Ball, W.W. Rouse - Peirce's review of his *Mathematical Recreations, and Problems of Past and Present Times.*
    00498

Barrès, Maurice - Peirce's review of his *L'Ennemi des Lois.*
    00544

Note [on Beckford's *Vathek*].
    00539

"Benjamin's History of Electricity."
    00621

Note [on the fifth edition of Berkeley's works].
    00697

"Berkeley's Works."
    00791

Note [on Boethius, *The Consolation of Philosophy*].
    00642

Note [on Sedgefield's edition of Boethius' *Consolations*].
    00736

Note [on Bolyai's *Absolute Science of Space*, the fourth edition of Halsted's translation of].
    00624

Boole, M.E. - Peirce's review of her *Lectures on the Logic of Arithmetic*.
    01049

Boole, M.E. - Peirce's review of her *The Preparation of the Child for Science*.
    01082

"The Boston Public Library."
    00506

Note [on Bottone's *Wireless Telegraphy and Hertzian Waves*].
    00732

Note [on Bowley's *Elements of Statistics*].
    00786

Bowden, Joseph - Peirce's review of his *Elements of the Theory of Integers*.
    01049

"Brief Description of the Algebra of Relatives."
    00220

"British and American Science."
    01026

"British Logicians."
    00039

Britten, F.J. - Peirce's review of his *Old Clocks and Watches and their Makers*.
    00694

Brooks, Noah - Peirce's review of his *The Story of Marco Polo*.
    00670

Note [on Buchanan's *Mathematical Theory of Eclipses*].
    01058

Buckley, Arabella B. - Peirce's review of her *Moral Teachings of Science*.
    00499

A Comprehensive Bibliography

Byerly, William Elwood - Peirce's review of his *An Elementary Treatise on Fourier's Series and Spherical and Ellipsoidal Harmonics.*
00569

Byrn, Edward W. - Peirce's review of his *The Progress of Invention in the Nineteenth Century.*
00748

Note [on Cajori's *The Teaching and History of Mathematics in the United States*].
00442

"Cajori's History of Mathematics."
00570

Cajori, Florian - Peirce's review of his *A History of Physics in its Elementary Branches.*
00685

Note [on Cajori's *Introduction to the Modern Theory of Equations*].
01064

Caldecott, Alfred - Peirce's review of *The Philosophy of Religion in England and America.*
00793

"Calendars."
00024, 00037, 00050, 00065, 00072, 00080.

"Campanus."
00803

Campbell, William T. - Peirce's review of his *Observational Geometry.*
00700

Note [on Campbell's *Introductory Treatise on Lie's Theory of Finite Continuous Transformation Groups*].
01044

Carnegie, Andrew - Peirce's review of his *James Watt.*
01097

Carus, Paul - Peirce's review of his *Fundamental Problems: The Method of Philosophy as a Systematic Arrangement of Knowledge.*
00393

Note [on Carus' *Kant and Spencer*].
00718

"Prof. Arthur Cayley."
00592

"The Century Dictionary."
00376

The Century Dictionary, Peirce's definitions in.
00373

"The Century's Great Men of Science."
00760, 00779, 00801.

Chambers, George F. - Peirce's review of his *Pictorial Astronomy for General Readers.*
    00458

"The Chemical Theory of Interpenetration."
    00011

"Chronology, Eclipses, and Tides."
    00038

Clark University, 1889-1899. Decennial Celebration, Peirce's review of.
    00751

"On a Class of Multiple Algebras," Abstract of.
    00224

"The Classification of the Sciences."
    00995

Clerke, Agnes M., A. Fowler, and J. Ellard Gore - Peirce's review of their *Astronomy.*
    00660

"Clerke's Astrophysics."
    01020

Note [on Clerke's *System of the Stars*].
    01136

"The Coast Survey Investigation."
    00300

Note [on the Coast Survey, Peirce and the investigation of].
    00317

Coe, George A. - Peirce's review of his *The Spiritual Life.*
    00709

"Cogito Ergo Sum."
    00547

Note [on Cohn's *Tests and Reagents*].
    01022

"On the Coincidence of Geographical Distribution of Rainfall and of Illiteracy, as shown by the Statistical Maps of the Ninth Census Reports."
    00068

The Collected Mathematical Works of George William Hill, Peirce's review of.
    01157

The Collected Mathematical Papers of James Joseph Sylvester, Peirce's review of.
    01059

Collins, F. Howard - Peirce's review of his *Epitome of the Synthetic Philosophy.*
    00390

"The Color System."
    00997

"On the Colours of the Double Stars."
00179

[Comments on Mitchell's paper].
00195

"A Communication from Mr. Peirce."
00245

"Comparison between the Yard and Metre by Means of the Reversible Pendulum."
00186

"Comparisons of the metre with wave lengths."
00154

[Computations].
00010, 00015, 00019.

"Comte's Philosophy."
01051

"The Comtist Calendar."
00482

Conant, Levi Leonard - Peirce's review of his *The Number Concept; Its Origin and Development.*
00628

Congress of Arts and Sciences, Universal Exposition, St. Louis, 1904, Peirce's review of.
01133

"Connected Pendulums."
00302

"Some Consequences of Four Incapacities."
00027

"Conundrum."
00540

"Was Copernicus a German?"
00535

"A Correction."
01009

[Corrections to an article].
00036

Craik, George L. - Peirce's review of his *The English of Shakespeare.*
00013

"The Critic of Arguments. I. Exact Thinking."
00511

"The Critic of Arguments. II. The Reader is Introduced to Relatives."
00513

"Criticism on 'Phantasms of the Living.' An Examination of an Argument of Messrs. Gurney, Myers, and Podmore."
    00352

Crozier, John Beattie - Peirce's review of his *My Inner Life.*
    00686

Curry, S.S. - Peirce's review of his *The Province of Expression: A search for principles underlying adequate methods of developing Dramatic and Oratoric Delivery.*
    00502

"Darwin's Tides."
    00672

"Death of Prof. Bunsen."
    00679

"On the Deduction of the Ellipticity of the Earth from Pendulum Experiment."
    00254

De Garmo, Charles - Peirce's review of his *Hebart and the Herbartarians.*
    00600

Note [on Delta's *Charades*].
    00979

Note [on De Morgan].
    00056

De Morgan, Augustus - Peirce's review of his *The Study and Difficulties of Mathematics.*
    00699

"Deposition of Charles Saunders [sic] Peirce."
    00035

"Descartes and his Works."
    00587

"Description of an Apparatus for Recording the Mean of the Times of a Set of Observations."
    00128

"Description of a Notation for the Logic of Relatives, Resulting from an Amplification of the Conceptions of Boole's Calculus of Logic."
    00052

"Design and Chance."
    00274

"On the determination of the figure of the earth by the variations of gravity."
    00234

"Determinations of Gravity at Allegheny, Ebensburgh, and York, Pa., in 1879 and 1880."
    00290

"On Determinations of Gravity."
    00380

[Distributive principle, letter on a proof of the].
    01071

"Dmesis."
    00512

"The Doctrine of Necessity Examined."
    00474

Drude, Paul - Peirce's review of his *The Theory of Optics.*
    00989

Duff, Robert A. - Peirce's review of his *Spinoza's Political and Ethical Philosophy.*
    P 01056

Durège, Dr. H. - Peirce's review of his *Elements of the Theory of Functions of a Complex Variable, with especial reference to the Methods of Riemann.*
    00630

Earl, Alice Morse - Peirce's review of her *Sundials and Roses of Yesterday.*
    00994

"Early Magnetical Science. - I."
    00562

"Early Magnetical Science. - II."
    00564

"Economy (logical principle of)."
    00761

Edridge-Green, F.W. - Peirce's review of his *Memory and its Cultivation.*
    00659

"Educational Textbooks. II."
    00066

Note [on Edward's *Elementary Treatise on the Differential Calculus*].
    00497

"On the Effect of Unequal Temperature upon a Reversible Pendulum."
    00336

Note [on four books on Electricity: Walmsley, Foster and Porter, Barnett, and Parr].
    01041

"On the ellipticity of the earth as deduced from pendulum experiments."
    00178

"Ellwanger's Pleasures of the Table."
    00993

Emerson, Edward R. - Peirce's review of his *The Story of the Vine.*
    00978

"Empirical Logic" [with R. Adamson].
    00762

"The English Doctrine of Ideas."
    00045

"Equipollence or -cy."
    00763

"Errata in the Heis Catalogue of Stars."
    00096

"On the errors of pendulum experiments, and on the method of swinging pendulums proposed by Mr. Faye."
    00152

[Eulogy].
    00264

"Evolutionary Love."
    00521

"Experimental Researches on the Force of Gravity."
    00263

Fahie, J.J. - Peirce's review of his *A History of Wireless Telegraphy, 1838-1899.*
    00716

"Fahie's Galileo."
    01042

"A Fallacy of Induction."
    00211

"On a fallacy of induction."
    00233

[Monsieur Faye, letter to].
    00215

Feret, Édouard - Peirce's review of his *Bordeaux and its Wines, Classed by Order of Merit.*
    00743

Ferrero, Annibale - Perice's review of his *Esposizione del Metodo dei Minimi Quadrati.*
    00111

Findlay, Alex - Peirce's review of his *The Phase Rule and its Applications.*
    01089

Note [on Fine's *College Algebra*].
    01108

Fiske, John - Peirce's review of his *Through Nature to God.*
    00696

Fiske, John - Peirce's review of his *A Century of Science, and Other Essays.*
    00715

Note [on Fiske's *Cosmic Philosophy*].
    01010

Fink, Dr. Karl - Peirce's review of his *A Brief History of Mathematics.*
00746

Fleming, J.A. - Peirce's review of his *Waves and Ripples in Water, Air, and AEther.*
01021

Fleury, Dr. Maurice de - Peirce's review of his *Nos Enfants au Collège.*
01103

"On the Flexure of Pendulum Supports."
00253

Flint, Robert - Peirce's review of his *Philosophy as Scientia Scientarium, and a History of the Classification of the Sciences.*
01091

"Floating Magnets."
00117

"Ford's Franklin."
00702

Forsyth, Andrew Russell - Peirce's review of his *Theory of Differential Equations.*
00737

Note [on Forsyth's *Theory of Differential Equations,* vol. 4].
00982

Forsyth, Andrew Russell - Peirce's review of his *Theory of Differential Equations. Part III. (Vol. IV.): Ordinary Linear Equations.*
00992

"The Fortieth Anniversary of The Nation."
01190

[Four-color problem, remarks on the].
00164

"Four Histories of Philosophy.—I."
00578

"Four Histories of Philosophy.—II."
00579

Fraser, Alexander Campbell - Perice's review of his *Locke.*
00396

Frazer, Persifor - Peirce's review of his *Bibliotics; or the Study of Documents, Determination of the Individual Character of Handwriting, and Detection of Fraud and Forgery.*
00792

"French Academy of Sciences."
01038

Note [on Freund's *The Study of Chemical Composition*].
01096

Fullerton, George Stuart - Peirce's review of his *The Philosophy of Spinoza.*
00504

"Funk's Standard Dictionary."
00565

"Galileo's Reasoning."
00688

Note [on Garcin's *N-Rays*].
01092

Note [on Gay and Yeaman's An Introduction to the Study of Central Station Electricity Supply].
00723

"Genus (in logic)."
00764

[Geodetic Association, 1875, participation in the meetings of the Permanent Committee of the].
00097

[Geodetic Conference, Stuttgart, 1877, attendance and remarks at the].
00130

"Ghosts in the diffraction spectra."
00153

"On the Ghosts in Rutherford's Diffraction-Spectra."
00134

"Gidding's Inductive Sociology."
00976

Note [obituary of Oliver Wolcott Gibbs].
01177

[Remarks on Gilman's paper].
00197

Gilman, Daniel C. - Peirce's review of his *The Life of James Dwight Dana, Scientific Explorer, Mineralogist Geologist, Zoologist, Professor in Yale University.*
00703

"Given."
00765

Goblot, Edmond - Peirce's review of his *Le Vocabulaire Philosophique.*
00789

Gore, J. Howard - Peirce's review of his *Geodesy.*
00451

Gorton, David Allyn, *The Monism of Man,* and Hill, David Jayne, *Genetic Philosophy,* Peirce's reviews of.
00568

"Gosse's Sir Thomas Brown."
    01111

Gould, George M. - Peirce's review of his *The Meaning and Method of Life: A Search for Religion in Biology*.
    00530

"A Graphical Method of Logic."
    00632

[Grants, research, to Peirce].
    01201

"Gravimetric Surveys."
    00297

[Gravity, measurement of absolute].
    00258

[Gravity, measurement of absolute, economy of research].
    00259

[Gravity research].
    00260

[Gravity research, reference to].
    00465

"On Gravitation Survey."
    00281

"Nicholas St. John Green."
    00108

Greene, Dascom - Peirce's review of his *An Introduction to Spherical and Practical Astronomy*.
    00460

Greenslet, Ferris - Peirce's review of his *Joseph Glanvill*.
    00745

"Grosseteste."
    00729

"Grounds of Validity of the Laws of Logic: Further Consequence of Four Incapacities."
    00041

"Haldane's Descartes."
    01131

"Hale's New England Boyhood."
    00531

"Hallucinations."
    00583

Hamilton, C.D.P. - Peirce's review of his *Modern Scientific Whist*.
    00586

Note [on Hampson's *Radium Explained*].
    01099

Hanns, Paul H. - Peirce's review of his *Geometry in the Grammar School.*
    00532

Harkness, J., and F. Morley - Peirce's review of their *An Introduction to the Theory of Analytic Functions.*
    00693

Note [on *Annals of the Harvard College Observatory,* vol. XIX, part 2].
    00529

Note [on Hawkins' and Wallis' *The Dynamo*].
    01054

"Hegel's Logic Interpreted."
    01013

"Helmholtz."
    00577

"Herbert Spencer's Philosophy. Is it Unscientific and Unsound?—Its Pretensions Attacked and a Demonstration Called For."
    00402

Note [on Hertz' *The Principles of Mechanics Presented in a New Form*].
    00726

Heysinger, I.W. - Peirce's review of his *The Source and Mode of Solar Energy throughout the Universe.*
    00602

Hill, David Jayne - Peirce's review of his *Genetic Philosophy.*
    00568

Note [on *Hill, The Collected Mathematical Works of George William*].
    01106

Note [on Hilton's *Mathematical Crystallography and the Theory of Groups of Movements*].
    01043

Hinds, J.I.D. - Peirce's review of his *Inorganic Chemistry: With the Elements of Physical and Theoretical Chemistry.*
    01019

History of Intellectual Development on the Lines of Modern Evolution, Peirce's review of.
    00973

"The History of Science."
    00471

Note [on van't Hoff's *Physical Chemistry in the Service of the Sciences*].
    01047

Hoffding, Harald - Peirce's review of his *A History of Modern Philosophy: A Sketch of the History of Philosophy from the Close of the Renaissance to Our Own Day.*
    00738

Holman, Silas W. - Peirce's review of his *Matter, Energy, Force, and Work.*
    00682

Note [a reply to Hoskins in regard to a dispute about the law of *vis viva*].
    00455

Hussey, William J. - Peirce's review of his *Logarithmic and Other Mathematical Tables.*
    00508

"Huxley's Essays."
    00560

Hyde, William De Witt - Peirce's review of his *Practical Idealism.*
    00661

Hyndman, H.H. Francis - Peirce's review of his *Radiation: An Elementary Treatise on Electromagnetic Radiation and on Röntgen and Cathode Rays.*
    00671

"Illustrations of the Logic of Science. First Paper. — The Fixation of Belief."
    00107

"Illustrations of the Logic of Science. Second Paper. — How to make our Ideas Clear."
    00119

"Illustrations of the Logic of Science. Third Paper. — The Doctrine of Chances."
    00120

"Illustrations of the Logic of Science. Fourth Paper. — The Probability of Induction."
    00121

"Illustrations of the Logic of Science. Fifth Paper. — The Order of Nature."
    00122

"Illustrations of the Logic of Science. Sixth Paper. — Deduction, Induction, and Hypothesis."
    00123

"Imaging (in logic)." [with H.B. Fine]
    00766

"Implicit (in logic)."
    00767

"On an Improvement in Boole's Calculus of Logic."
    00030

"Inconsistency."
    00768

"Independence."
    00769

"Index (in exact logic)."
    00770

"Individual (in logic)."
    00771

"Is Induction an Inference?"
    00491

"Inference."
    00772

"Infinitesimals."
    00750

"De l'influence de la flexibilité du trépied sur l'oscillation du pendule à reversion."
    00102

"De l'influence de la flexibilité du trépied sur l'oscillation du pendule à reversion; Note communiquee par Mr. E. Plantamour."
    00131

"On the Influence of Internal Friction upon the Correction of the Length of the Seconds' Pendulum for the Flexibility of the Support."
    00126

"On the Influence of a Noddy on the Period of a Pendulum."
    00335

"Insolubilia."
    00773

"Intention (in logic)."
    00774

"Introductory Lecture on the Sutdy of Logic."
    00225

"Involution."
    00775

"On Irregularities in the Amplitude of Oscillation of Pendulums."
    00218

"Issues of Pragmaticism."
    01080

"James Joseph Sylvester."
    00635

James, Henry - Peirce's review of his *The Secret of Swedenborg: Being an Elucidation of his Doctrine of the Divine Natural Humanity.*
    00054

"James' Psychology. — I."
    00447

"James' Psychology. — II."
    00448

Note [on the abridged edition of James' *Principles of Psychology*].
    00494

Note [on James' article in the *Archives de Psychologie*].
   01102

Jevons, W. Stanley - Peirce's review of his *Studies in Deductive Logic.*
   00198

Jevons, W. Stanley - Peirce's review of his *Pure Logic, and Other Minor Works.*
   00392

Joachim, Harold H. - Peirce's review of his *A Study of the Ethics of Spinoza.*
   00980

Johnson's Universal Cyclopaedia: A New and Enlarged Edition, Peirce's review of.
   00573

Note [on Jones' Notes on *Analytical Geometry*].
   01052

Jones, E.E. Constance - Peirce's review of her *Elements of Logic as a Science of Propositions.*
   00395

Jones, Harry C. - Peirce's review of his *The Elements of Physical Chemistry.*
   00983

Jones, Harry C. - Peirce's review of his *The Theory of Electrolytic Dissociation and Some of its Applications.*
   00741

Jordan, William Leighton - Peirce's review of his *Essays in Illustration of the Action of Astral Gravitation in Natural Phenomena.*
   00788

Joseph, Horace William Brindley - Peirce's review of his *An Introduction to Logic.*
   01138

"On Kant's 'Critic of the Pure Reason' in the light of Modern Logic."
   00177

Note [on Kant's *Prolegomena to any Future Metaphysics,* edited by Carus].
   01017

"Lord Kelvin."
   01160

Note [Lord Kelvin, obituary of].
   01161

Note [on Kepler's *Somnium*].
   00684

Note [on Kerr's *Wireless Telegraphy*].
   00666

Klein, Felix - Peirce's review of his *Lectures on Mathematics.*
00569

"Knowledge (in logic)." [with C. Ladd-Franklin]
00777

Note [on Krauch's *The Testing of Chemical Reagents for Purity*].
01023

"Külpe's Outlines of Psychology."
00629

Lachlan, R. - Peirce's review of his *An Elementary Treatise on Modern Pure Geometry.*
00532

Ladd, George Trumbull - Peirce's review of his *Philosophy of Mind: An Essay in the Metaphysics of Psychology.*
00597

Lafleur, Paul T. - Peirce's review of his *Illustrations of Logic.*
00734

Note [on Lambert's *Differential and Integral Calculus for Technical Schools and Colleges*].
00669

Note [on Langley's *The Internal Work of the Wind*].
00559, 00563.

Note [on Laurent's *Les Grands Écrivains Scientifiques*].
01088

"The Law of Mind."
00477

"The Law of 'Vis Viva'."
00453

"Laws of Thought."
00778

"Lazelle's 'One Law in Nature'."
00073

"Leading of Proof."
00806

"Leading Principle."
00807

Leibniz: The Monadology and Other Philosophical Writings, Peirce's review of.
00683

"Leibniz Rewritten."
00695

"Leland's Memoirs."
    00542

"Lemma."
    00808

"A Letter from Mr. Perice."
    01178

Lewes, Vivian B. - Peirce's review of her *Acetylene.*
    00744

Note [on Lewis' *Treatise on Crystallography*].
    00713

"Light of Nature."
    00809

"Limitative."
    00810

"Linear Associative Algebra."
    00188

"A List of Stars for Observations of Latitude."
    00095

Lloyd, Alfred H. - Peirce's review of his *Dynamic Idealism: An Elementary Course in the Metaphysics of Psychology.*
    00661

Note [on Lobatchevsky's *Non-Euclidean Geometry,* Halstead's translation of].
    00493

"Lockyer's Dawn of Astronomy."
    00567

Lockyer, Sir Norman - Peirce's review of his *Inorganic Evolution as Studied by Spectrum Analysis.*
    00730

Lodge, Oliver - Peirce's review of his *Pioneers of Science.*
    00533

Loeb, Jaques - Peirce's review of his *The Dynamics of Living Matter.*
    01134

"Logic."
    00055

"Logic." [with C. Ladd-Franklin].
    00811

"Logic (exact)."
    00812

"Logical Lights."
    01060

"Upon the Logic of Mathematics."
    00033

"The Logic of Mathematics in Relation to Education."
    00653

"On the Logic of Number."
    00187

"On the logic of number."
    00200

"On the Logic of Number," Abstract of.
    00222

"On the Logic of Quantity."
    00631

"On the logic of relatives."
    00235

"The Logic of Relatives."
    00637

"The Logic of Relation."
    00275

"On the Logic of Research into Ancient History."
    00800

[The logic of science, Harvard University Lectures of 1865 on].
    00016

"The Logic of Science; or, Induction and Hypothesis."
    00017

"Logical."
    00813

"On Logical Algebra."
    00075

"Upon Logical Comprehension and Extension."
    00034

"Logical Contraposition and Conversion."
    00099

"Logical Diagram (or Graph)."
    00814

"Logical Machines."
    00344

"La Logique de la Science. Première Partie. Comment se fixe la croyance."
    00129

"La Logique de la Science. Deuxième Partie. Comment rendre nos idees claires."
    00162

"Logomachy."
    00815

Lombroso, Cesare - Peirce's review of his *The Man of Genius*.
    00487

[Longitude, determination of].
    00289

Love, A.E.H. - Peirce's review of his *A Treatise on the Mathematical Theory of Elasticity*.
    00528

"Lyon Playfair."
    00719

McAulay, A.C. - Peirce's review of his *Utility of Quaternions in Physics*.
    00557

McClelland, William J. - Peirce's review of his *A Treatise on the Geometry of the Circle, and some Extensions to Conic Sections by the Method of Reciprocation*.
    00495

McLellan, James A., and John Dewey - Peirce's review of their *The Psychology of Number, and its Applications to Methods of Teaching Arithmetic*.
    00605

"Mach's Science of Mechanics."
    00536

Mackintosh, Robert - Peirce's review of his *From Comte to Benjamin Kidd*.
    00698

"On 'The Magnet' a fourteenth century manuscript of Petrus Peregrinus."
    00276

"Maher's Psychology."
    00795

"Major and Minor (extreme, term, premise, *satz,* &c., in logic)."
    00816

Mann, Gustav - Peirce's review of his *Chemistry of the Proteids*.
    01134

"Man's Glassy Essence."
    00480

"The Map-coloring Problem."
    00704

"Mark," [in part with C. Ladd-Franklin].
    00817

[Marquand, remarks on a paper by].
   00176

"The Marriage of Religion and Science."
   00545

"Mars as a Place to Inhabit."
   01147

Marsh, George P. - Peirce's review of his *Lectures on the English Language.*
   00013

"Marshall's Instinct and Reason."
   00692

"Material Fallacy."
   00818

"Material Logic."
   00819

"Mathematical Functions."
   00566

"Mathematical Infinity."
   00633

"Mathematical Logic."
   00820

Note [on the *Mathematics, The American Journal of* the current number of].
   00150

"Mathematics Their Theme."
   00590

"Matter and Form."
   00821

"Maxim (in logic)."
   00822

"Measurements of Gravity at Initial Stations in America and Europe."
   00161

[Mechanical units in use in the United States and Great Britain, statement of the].
   00550

"Meeting of the American Association for the Advancement of Science."
   0003, 0004

"Meeting of the National Academy of Sciences."
   01132

Note [on Mellor's *Higher Mathematics for Students of Chemistry and Physics*].
   01012

Memoranda Concerning the Aristotelean Syllogism.
    00018

"Men of Science in Session."
    01146

Mendeleef, D. - Peirce's review of his *The Principles of Chemistry.*
    00641

Note [on Mendeleef's *Principles of Chemistry,* third edition].
    01093

[Metaphysical Club, opening remarks for the].
    00232

"A method of computation."
    01214

"Method and Methodology, or Methodeutic."
    00823

"On a Method of Observing the Coincidence of Vibration of Two Pendulums."
    00255

"On a method of swinging Pendulums for the determination of Gravity, proposed by M. Faye."
    00137

"The Metric Fallacy."
    01046

[Metrology, pendulum research].
    00312, 00313

Meyer, Ernest von - Peirce's review of his *A History of Chemistry.*
    01154

Meyer, Dr. Oskar Emil - Peirce's review of his *The Kinetic Theory of Gases: Elementary Treatise with Mathematical Appendices.*
    00739

Mezes, Sidney Edward - Peirce's review of his *Ethics: Descriptive and Explanatory.*
    00796

Michelson, A.A. - Peirce's review of his *Light Waves and Their Uses.*
    01021

"Middle Term (and Middle)."
    00824

"J.S. Mill's Logic."
    00229

"On Minimum Differences of Sensibility" [with Joseph Jastrow].
    00282

"Mixed."
    00825

"Mnemonic Verses and Words (in logic)."
    00826

"Modality."
    00827

"On the Mode of Representing Negative Quantity in the Logic of Relatives."
    00273

"Modulus."
    00828

"Modus ponens and Modus tollens."
    00829

"Monad (Monadism, Monadology)."
    00830

Note [on the *Monist*, the first number of].
    00397

Moore, J. Howard - Peirce's review of his *Better-World Philosophy.*
    00698

Muir, Thomas - Peirce's review of his *The Theory of Determinants in the Historical Order of its Development. Part I.*
    00394

"Multitude (in mathematics)." [with H.B. Fine]
    00831

Note [on Murray's *Introduction to Psychology*].
    01063

"Mutual Attraction of Spectral Lines."
    00156

"Name (in logic)."
    00832

"Napoleon Intime."
    00519

"Napoleon Intime. Second Article."
    00520

"The National Academy at Philadelphia."
    00797

"The National Academy in New York."
    01066

"The National Academy Meeting."
    01011, 01050.

"The National Academy of Sciences."
00997, 01090.

"The National Academy of Sciences at New Haven."
01110

"On the Natural Classification of Arguments."
00031

"Necessary (in logic)."
00833

"Necessity."
00834

"Negation." [with C. Ladd-Franklin]
00835

"Negative."
00836

"A Neglected Argument for the Reality of God."
01166

Note [on Netto's *Theory of Substitutions*].
00496

"A New Computation of the Compression of the Earth, from Pendulum Experiments."
00210

"On a new edition of Ptolemy's catalogue of stars."
00098

"On a New List of Categories."
00032

"A New Rule for Divison in Arithmetic."
00266

Newcomb, Simon - Peirce's review of his *Popular Astronomy*.
00114

Newcomb, Simon - Peirce's review of his *The Reminiscences of an Astronomer*.
01048

Newcomb, Simon - Peirce's review of his *Sidelights on Astronomy and Kindred Fields of Popular Science: Essays and Addresses*.
01139

Nichols, Herbert - Peirce's review of his *A Treatise on Cosmology*.
01077

Noel, E. - Peirce's review of his *The Science of Metrology; or Natural Weights and Measures. A Challenge to the Metric System*.
00389

Noir, Rouge et - Peirce's review of his *The Gambling World*.
00689

"Nominal."
    00837

"Nominalism versus Realism."
    00025

"Nomology."
    00838

"Non-A (in logic)."
    00839

[Non-Aristotelian logic, portion of a letter on].
    01206, 01207

"Non-contradiction."
    00840

"The Non-Euclidean Geometry."
    00485

"Nonsequitur."
    00841

"Norm (and Normality)."
    00842

"Nota notae."
    00843

"Note on the Age of Basil Valentine."
    00674

"Note on a Device for Abbreviating Time Reductions."
    00334

"Note on the Effect of the Flexure of a Pendulum upon its Period of Oscillation."
    00316

"Note on Grassmann's Calculus of Extension."
    00125

"Note on the Progress of Experiments for comparing a Wave-length with a Meter."
    00136

"Note on the Sensation of Color."
    00100

"Note on the Sensation of Color."
    00105

"Note on the Simplest Possible Branch of Mathematics."
    01068

"Note on the Theory of the Economy of Research."
    00160

"Number: A Study of the Methods of Exact Philosophical Thought."
    00618

"Numerical."
    00844

"The Numerical Measure of the Success of Predictions."
    00292

[Observations]
    00047, 00048, 00069

"Observation." [with J.M. Baldwin]
    00845

"Obversion."
    00846

"The 'Old Stone Mill' at Newport."
    00293

Note [on Olsen's *Text-book of Quantitative Chemical Analysis*].
    01067

"Opinions Concerning the Conduct of Gravitation Work."
    00262

"Opposition (in logic)."
    00847

Peirce's review of The *"Opus Majus" of Roger Bacon*.
    00650

"Organon."
    00848

Ormond, Alexander T. - Peirce's review of his *Basal Concepts in Philosophy*.
    00574

"'Outsider' Wants More Light. He Cometh After his Critics and Searcheth Them - Spencer's Standing in Science - His Theory of Evolution - 'Outsider' is an Inquirer, Not an Assailant."
    00416

"P (in logic)."
    00849

"The Pairing of the Elements."
    00040

"Paradox."
    00850

"Paralogism."
    00851

"Parity."
    00852

"Parsimony (law of)."
    00853

Parsons, Albert Ross - Peirce's review of his *New Light from the Great Pyramid.*
    00572

"Partial."
    00854

"Particular." [with C. Ladd-Franklin]
    00855

"Particulate."
    00856

"Parva Logicalia."
    00857

"Pasteur."
    00975

"Paulsen's Kant."
    00987

Pearson, Karl - Peirce's review of his *The Grammar of Science.*
    00501

Note [on Pearson's *Grammar of Science,* second edition].
    00725

"Pearson's Grammar of Science. Annotations on the First Three Chapters."
    00802

Peirce, C.S. - Perice's review of his own *A Syllabus of Certain Topics of Logic.*
    01091

"C.S. Peirce. — Irregularidades en las oscilaciones del pénduls."
    00241

"Mr. Peirce and the Realists."
    00059

Note [on Peirce's *Principles of Philosophy* and his edition of *On the Lodestone*].
    00558

"Mr. Peirce's Rejoinder."
    00354

[Pendulum Observations]
    00109, 00127, 00158, 00182

"Pendulum Observations."
    00369

[Pendulum Research]
    00093, 00207, 00208, 00257, 00286, 00287, 00314, 00332, 00356, 00357, 00358, 00359, 00384, 00514

[Pendulum researches, references to Peirce's]
    00110, 00165, 00184, 00216, 00370, 00804

[Pendulum researches, report on Peirce's]
    00166

[Pendulum research, metrology]
    00252, 00310, 00311, 00331, 00333

[Pendulum research, metrology, diffraction spectra]
    00237

[Pendulum research at Cornell]
    00324

[Pendulum research, determination of longitude]
    00288

[Pendulum research, records of]
    00360

[Pendulum and metrological research]
    00433

"Per accidens."
    00858

Perrin, Raymond S. - Peirce's review of his *The Religion of Philosophy; or, The Unification of Knowledge.*
    00308

Note [on Perrine's *Conductors for Electrical Distribution*].
    01024

Note [on Perry's *Calculus for Engineers*].
    00644

Note [on Perry's mathematical writings].
    00742

"Perseity (1) and (2) Per se."
    00859

Personal Recollections of Werner von Siemens, Peirce's review of.
    00538

Personal Idealism: Philosophical Essays by Eight Members of the University of Oxford, Peirce's review of.
    01015

"Perspicuity."
    00806

"Pertinent."
    00861

"Mr. Peterson's Proposed Discussion."
    01124

"Erratum [to Peirce's article entitled 'Mr. Peterson's Proposed Discussion']."
    01125

"Petitio Principii." [with C. Ladd-Franklin]
    00862

"Phaneroscopy, or Natural History of Signs, Relations, Categories, etc.: A method of investigating this subject expounded and illustrated."
    01141

"Philosopheme."
    00863

"A Philosopher's Political Diagnosis."
    01247

[On photometric measurement of the stars]
    00063

"Photometric Measurements of the Stars."   "Photometric Researches."
    00087   00118

"Some Physical Books."
    00794

Note [on Pick's *Lectures on Memory Culture*].
    00714

"The Place of Our Age in the History of Civilization."
    00012

"A Plan and an Illustration."
    00089

"Plurality of Causes."
    00864

Podmore, Frank - Peirce's review of his *Studies in Psychical Research*.
    00640

"Poly-."
    00865

"The 'Pons Asinorum' Again. Mr. Peirce sets forth the History of the Phrase from the Times of Duns Scotus's Followers."
    00464

"Port Royal Logic."
    00866

'Positive."
    00867

"Possibility, Impossibility, and Possible."
    00868

"Postpredicament."
    00869

"Postulate."
    00870

"The Postulates of Geometry."
    00998

"Practical Application of the Theory of Functions."
    01030

"Pragmatic (1) and (2) Pragmatism."
    00871

"Pragmatism as a Principle and Method of Right Thinking."
    01004

"Precise."
    00872

"Precision."
    00873

"Predesignate."
    00874

"Predicable."
    00875

"Predicament."
    00876

"Predicate."
    00877

"Predication."
    00878

"Predicative Proposition."
    00879

"Preface to Contributions to Logic by Members of the Johns Hopkins University. C.S. Peirce, Editor. (Little, Brown & Co., Boston, 1882)."
    00242

"Premise (and Premiss)."
    00880

Prescott, Albert B., and Johnson, Otis C. - Peirce's review of their *Qualitative Chemical Analysis.*
    00983

"Presumption."
    00881

"Presupposition."
    00882

"Prime."
  00883

"Primum cognitum."
  00884

"Principal."
  00885

"The Principles of Philosophy: Or, Logic, Physics and Psychics, Considered as a Unity, In the Light of the Nineteenth Century."
  00552

"Priority (with Prior and Prius)."
  00886

"Privation."
  00887

"Probably Inference."
  00888

"Problem."
  00889

"Problematic."
  00890

Proceedings of the Assay Commission of 1888; Also, Laws of the United States Relating to the Annual Assay, and Rules for the Organization and Government of the Board of Assay Commissioners.
  00368

"Professor Bunsen."
  00705

"Professor Porter's 'Human Intellect'."
  00043

"On the progress of pendulum work."
  00199

"Progressive."
  00891

"On the projections of the Sphere which preserve the angles."
  00151

"Prolegomena to an Apology for Pragmaticism."
  01128

"Proof."
  00892

"Proof that there are only Three Linear Associative Algebras in which Division is an Unambiguous Process."
  00194

"Proposition." [with J.M. Baldwin]
>00893

"Prospectus. The Treatise of Petrus Peregrinus on the Lodestone: Latin Text, English Version, and Notes. With an Introductory History of Experimental Science in the Middle Ages. By C.S. Peirce. Printed in two colors on hand-made paper. Bound in full Persion Morocco, hand-tooled. 140 pages."
>00551

"Prosyllogism."
>00894

"Protasis."
>00895

"Provisional."
>00896

"Proximate."
>00897

"The Psychology of Suggestion."
>00664

"On Ptolemy's catalogue of stars."
>00236

"Pure (in Philosophy)."
>00898

"Pythagorics."
>00510

"Quality (in grammar and logic)."
>00899

"Quantity (in logic and mathematics)."
>00900

"On Quaternions, as Developed from the General Theory of the Logic of Relatives."
>00082

"Questions Concerning Certain Faculties Claimed for Man."
>00026

"Questions Concerning certain Faculties, Claimed for Man."
>00143

"A Quincuncial Projection of the Sphere."
>00135, 00183, 00238

"Rainfall."
>00081

"Ratio."
>00901

"Ratiocination."
    00902

"Rational."
    00903

"Read's Theory of Logic."
    00148

Read, Carveth - Peirce's review of his *Logic, Deductive and Inductive*.
    00668

[Reasoning, Art of, announcement, correspondence lessons in the]
    00509

"Reasoning."
    00904

"Reasoning and the Logic of Things."
    00652

"The reasons of reasoning, or grounds of inferring."
    01215

"Recent Developments of Existential Graphs and their Consequences for Logic."
    01140

"The Reciprocity Treaty with Spain."
    00279

"Reductio ad absurdum."
    00905

"Reduction."
    00906

"On the Reference of the Unit of Length to the Wavelengths of Light."
    00133

"The Regenerated Logic."
    00620

"Regular."
    00907

"The Relation of Betweenness and Royce's O-collections."
    01112

"On Relations between Sensations."
    00196

"The Relations of Logic to Philosophy."
    00157

"On the Relative Forms of Quaternions."
    00226

"Relatives (logic of)."
    00908

"Remarks on the above paper [by B.I. Gilman]."
00230

"Remote."
00909

"Reply to Professor Morris on 'Life'."
00247

"Reply to the Necessitarians."
00525

"Report on Gravity at the Smithsonian, Ann Arbor, Madison, and Cornell."
00385

"Represent."
00910

"Representationism."
00911

"Repugnance."
00912

"Residues (method of)."
00913

"Results of Pendulum Experiments."
00168, 00174

"Review of Paper on Color Contrast."
00327

Note [on Reye's *Geometrie der Lage*].
00662

"Ribot's Psychology of Attention."
00391

Richardson, Ernest Cushing - Peirce's review of his *Classification, Theoretical and Practical. I. The Order of the Sciences; II. The Classification of Books.*
00974

Ridgeway, William - Peirce's review of his *The Origin of Metallic Currency and Weight Standards.*
00500

Note [on Ripper's *Steam-Engine Theory and Practice*].
00721

Risteen, A.D. - Peirce's review of his *Molecules and the Molecular Theory of Matter.*
00625

"Ritchie's Darwin and Hegel."
00541

Robertson, John M. - Peirce's review of his *A Short History of Free Thought, Ancient and Modern.*
00735

Romanes, George John - Peirce's review of his *Mind and Motion, and Monism*.
00626

"Rood's Chromatics."
00149

[Rood, O.N., discussion of a paper by]
00462

"Roscoe's Spectrum Analysis."
00044

Roscoe, Sir H.E. and C. Schorlemmer - Peirce's review of their *A Treatise on Chemistry*.
01104

Roscoe, Sir Henry Enfield - Peirce's review of his *The Life and Experiences of Sir Henry Enfield*.
01135

Ross, Edward Alsworth - Peirce's review of his *Foundations of Sociology*.
01126

"Rough notes on geometry. Constitution of real space."
00553

Note [on *The Physical Papers of Henry Augustus Rowland*].
01007

Royce, Josiah, Joseph Le Conte, G.H. Howison, and Sidney Mezes - Peirce's review of their *The Conception of God*.
00645

Royce, Josiah - Peirce's review of his *The World and the Individual*.
00728

"Royce's World and the Individual."
00984

Royce, Josiah - Peirce's review of his *Outlines of Psychology*.
01061

"Royce's Spencer."
01083

"Rule." [in part, with J.M. Baldwin]
00914

Russell, Bertrand - Peirce's review of his *The Principles of Mathematics*.
01028

Russell, John Wellesley - Peirce's review of his *An Elementary Treatise on Pure Geometry*.
00532

Rutherford, E. - Peirce's review of his *Radio-Activity*.
01129

Note [on Ryder's *Electric Traction*].
01053

"S (in logic)."
 00915

"Saltus."
 00916

Note [on Santayana's *Life of Reason, or the Phases of Human Progress,* volumes I and II].
 01095

Schröder, Dr. Ernst - Peirce's review of his *Vorlesungen über die Algebra der Logik.*
 00449

Schröder, Dr. Ernst - Peirce's review of his *Algebra und Logik der Relative, der Vorlesungen über die Algebra der Logik.*
 00627

Schubert, Hermann - Peirce's review of his *Mathematical Essays and Recreations.*
 00699

Schuster, Prof. Arthur - Peirce's review of his *An Introduction to the Theory of Optics.*
 01085

[Science and Immortality, contribution on].
 00347, 00348

"Science in America."
 00484

"Science in America."
 00489

"Scientific Method." [with J.M. Baldwin]
 00917

[Scientific Method, lectures on]
 01150

The Scientific Papers of J. Willard Gibbs, Peirce's review of.
 01153

"Scope (in logic)."
 00918

"Scott's Familiar Letters."
 00561

Scripture, E.W. - Peirce's review of his *The New Psychology.*
 00663

"Secundum quid."
 00919

"On Sensations of Color."
 00379

"Series."
 00920

"Shaftesbury."
00785

Shaler, Nathaniel Southgate - Peirce's review of his *The Individual: A Study of Life and Death*.
00747

Note [on Shea's history of Duns Scotus].
00441

Note [on Shield's *Philosophia Ultima*].
01107

Sidgwick, Alfred - Peirce's review of his *Distinction and the Criticism of Belief*.
00507

"Sign."
00921

"Signification (and Application, in logic)." [in part, with C. Ladd-Franklin]
00922

Sigwart, Dr. Christoph - Peirce's review of his *Logic*. Second edition.
00596

"Similar (with Similarity, Similitude)."
00923

"Simple." [two parts of this article are with J.M. Baldwin]
00924

Singer, Ignatius and Lewis H. Berens - Peirce's review of their *Some Unrecognized Laws of Nature: An Inquiry into the Causes of Physical Phenomena, with Special Reference to Gravitation*.
00657

"Singular."
00925

"Six Reasons for the Prosecution of Pendulum Experiments."
00261

"On Small Differences of Sensation."
00303

Smith, David Eugene - Peirce's review of his *The Teaching of Elementary Mathematics*.
00727

Smith, Norman - Peirce's review of his *Studies in the Cartesian Philosophy*.
01018

Smith, Thomas - Peirce's review of his *Euclid: His Life and System*.
01006

Sociological Papers, Peirce's review of.
01100

[Observations and Research, Solar eclipse of 7 August 1869]
00070

[Observations, Solar Eclipse of 22 December 1870]
    00076, 00078, 00085, 00086

"Solution."
    00926

"Some (in logic)." [with C. Ladd-Franklin]
    00927

"Sophism."
    00928

"Sorites."
    00929

"The Spanish Treaty Once More."
    00306

Spanton, J. Humphrey - Peirce's review of his *Science and Art Drawing.*
    00623

"Species (and Specific Marks, in logic)." [with J.M. Baldwin]
    00930

"The Spectroscope."
    00051

[Spectroscopic studies]
    00155

"Spectroscopic Studies."
    00163

Spencer, Herbert - Peirce's review of his *Essays, Scientific, Political, and Speculative.*
    00450

Spencer, Herbert - Peirce's review of his *Negative Beneficence and Positive Beneficence. Being Parts V. and VI. of the Principles of Ethics.*
    00537

"Spinoza's Ethic."
    00582

"Spurious Proposition."
    00931

Stanley, Hiram M. - Peirce's review of his *Studies in the Evolutionary Psychology of Feeling.*
    00604

Stanton, Edward - Peirce's review of his *Dreams of the Dead.*
    00505

[Star Catalogue, preparation of a]
    00159

"State (and Condition)."
    00932

"On Stellar Photometry."
    00067

Stevens, Henry - Peirce's review of his *Thomas Hariot, the Mathematician, the Philosopher, and the Scholar.*
    00752

Note [on Stickney's *Organized Democracy*].
    01156

Stock, St. George - Peirce's review of his *Deductive Logic.*
    00378

Stratton, George Malcolm - Peirce's review of his *Experimental Psychology and its Bearing upon Culture.*
    01065

[Stringham's paper, comments on]
    00175

Strutt, Hon. R.J. - Peirce's review of his *The Becquerel Rays and the Properties of Radium.*
    01084

Studies in Logic, by Members of the Johns Hopkins University.
    00268

Chittenden, R.H. - Peirce's review of his *Studies in Physiological Chemistry.*
    00983

"Some Studies of Reasoning."
    00601

"Subalternation."
    00933

"Subcontrary."
    00934

"Subject (in logic)."
    00935

"Sublation."
    00936

"Substitution (in logic)."
    00937

"Substitution in Logic."
    01079

"Subsumption."
    00938

"Sufficient Reason." [in part, with J.M. Baldwin]
    00939

"Summum Genus."
    00940

[Supervision of Coast Survey office, responsibility for temporary]
    00092

"Supposition."
    00941

A Syllabus of Certain Topics of Logic.
    01035

"Syllogism." [in part, with J.M. Baldwin]
    00942

Note [obituary, J.J. Sylvester].
    00639

"Symbol."
    00943

"Symbolic Logic or Algebra of Logic." [in part with C. Ladd-Franklin]
    00944

"Symbolical."
    00945

"Synechism."
    00470

"Synechism."
    00946

"Synthetic (-al)."
    00947

"Tautology."
    00948

"The Teaching of Mathematics."
    00446

"Term."
    00949

"Testimony." [with J.M. Baldwin]
    00950

"Thema."
    00951

"Theorem."
    00952

"Theory (in science)." [with C. Ladd-Franklin]
    00953

"On the Theory of Errors of Observations."
    00077

"Thesis."
00954

Thilly, Frank - Peirce's review of his *Introduction to Ethics.*
00733, 00709

"Think Again!"
00001

"The Thirteenth Annual Meeting of the American Association for the Advancement of Science."
00002, 00005, 00006, 00007

Thorp, Frank Hall - Peirce's review of his *Outlines of Industrial Chemistry.*
00690

Thorpe, T.E. - Peirce's review of his *Essays in Historical Chemistry.*
00580

"Thorpe's Essays in Historical Chemistry."
00986

Note [on Thorp's *Outlines of Industrial Chemistry,* revised edition].
00720

Thurston, R.H. - Peirce's review of his *The Animal as a Machine and a Prime Mover, and the Laws of Energetics.*
00575

Todd, David P. - Peirce's review of his *Stars and Telescopes: A Hand-Book of Popular Astronomy, Founded on the Ninth Edition of Lynn's Celestial Motions.*
00691

Todd, Mabel Loomis - Peirce's review of her *Total Eclipses of the Sun.*
00571

"On Topical Geometry."
01069

"Some Topics of Logic Bearing on Questions Now Vexed."
01005

Translation of "On the Absorbtion and Emission of Air and Its Ingredients for Light of Wave-Lengths from $250\mu\mu$ to $100\mu\mu$," by Victor Schumann.
01034

Translation of "On Ancient Desemers or Steelyards," by Hermann Sōkeland."
00759

Translation of "The Breeding of the Arctic Fox," by Henry de Varigny.
00758

Translation of "Four Days' Observations at the Summit of Mont Blanc," by M.J. Janssen.
00615

Translation of *Genius and Degeneration,* by Dr. William Hirsch.
00616

Translation of "The Growth of Biology in the Nineteenth Century," by Oscar Herturg.
00756

Translation of "The History of Chronophotography," by Dr. J. Marey.
00805

Translation of "Life in the Ocean," by Karl Brandt.
00757

Translation of "Light and Electricity, According to Maxwell and Hertz," by M. Poincare.
00613

Translation of "Photographic Photometry," by M.J. Janssen.
00614

Translation of "The Progress of Aeronautics," by M. Janssen.
00755

Translation of "The Sculptures of Santa Lucia Cozumahualpa, Guatemala, in the Hamburg Ethnological Museum," by Herman Strebel.
00754

Translation of "On the Sense of Smell in Birds," by M. Xavier Raspail.
00753

"Transposition (in logic)." [with C. Ladd-Franklin)
00955

"Tree of Porphyry."
00956

"Trilemma."
00957

"Trivium."
00958

"Truth and Falsity (1) and (2) Error."
00959

"Turner's History of Philosophy."
01055

Note [on Turner's *Knowledge, Belief, and Certitude*].
00790

"Ultimate."
00961

"Uniformity."
00962

"Unity (and Plurality)."
00963

"Universal (and Universality)." [in part, with C. Ladd-Franklin]
00964

"Universe." [with C. Ladd-Franklin]
    00965

"On the Use of the Noddy for Measuring the Amplitude of Swaying in a Pendulum Support."
    00315

"Vague (in logic)."
    00966

"Sur la valeur de la pesanteur à Paris."
    00171

"Validity." [with C. Ladd-Franklin]
    00967

"On the Value of Gravity at Paris."
    00256

Varigny, Henry De - Peirce's review of his *La Nature et la Vie*.
    01105

"On Various Hypothesis in Reference to Space."
    00083

Vasiliev, A. - Peirce's review of his *Nicolai Ivanovich Lobachevsky*.
    00598

Venn, John - Peirce's review of his *The Logic of Chance*.
    00021

"Verification."
    00968

Victor von Richter's Organic Chemistry, Peirce's review of.
    00983

"Virtual."
    00969

Wallace, Alfred Russel - Peirce's review of his *The Wonderful Century: its Successes and its Failures*.
    00665

"Wallace's Studies."
    00782

Note [on Wall's *Concise French Grammar*].
    00798

Walmsley, R. Mullineaux - Peirce's review of his *Modern Practical Chemistry*.
    01086

Watson, John - Peirce's review of his *Comte, Mill, and Spencer: An Outline of Philosophy*.
    00599

Note [on Watson's *A Text-Book of Physics*].
    00724

Peirce's review of *Webster's International Dictionary of the English Language*.
00784

"On Weights and Measures."
00270

[Weights, measures, and coinage, National Academy of Science, majority report, committee on]
00996

[Weights and measures, and on the gravimetric survey, Coast Survey, Testimony on the office of
00339

Welby, V. - Peirce's review of her *What is Meaning?*
01028

"What is Christian Faith?"
00548

"What is Meant by 'Determined'."
00028

"What Pragmatism Is."
01078

White, Andrew Dickson - Peirce's review of his *A History of the Warfare of Science with Theology in Christendom*.
00611

White, Richard Grant - Peirce's review of his *The Works of William Shakespeare*.
00013

Note [on Whittaker's *A Course of Modern Analysis*].
01014

"Whole (and Parts)." [in part, with J.M. Baldwin and G.F. Stout]
00970

Note [on Wiart's *La Cité Ardente*].
01109

"William Herschel."
00783

Williams, Henry Smith - Peirce's review of his *The Story of Nineteenth Century Science*.
00749

Williams, R.O. - Peirce's review of his *Our Dictionaries and Other English-Language Topics*.
00398

Windelband, W. - Peirce's review of his *History of Ancient Philosophy*.
00731

Note [on Woodbridge's *The Philosophy of Hobbes in Extracts and Notes Collected from his Writings*].
01045

"The Work of George W. Hill."
01159

The Works of George Berkeley, D.D., formerly Bishop of Cloyne: including many of his Writings hitherto unpublished, Peirce's review of.
     00060

Worthington, A.M. - Peirce's review of his *Dynamies of Rotation: An Elementary Introduction to Rigid Dynamics.*
     00503

Note [on Wundt's *Vorlesungen uber Menschen und Thierseele* (English Translation)].
     00584

Wundt's Principles of Physiological Psychology.
     01101

Note [on U.S. yard no. 57 with British yard no. 1, Peirce's comparison of]
     00249

PART TWO:
BIBLIOGRAPHY
OF
SECONDARY STUDIES

By

Christian J.W. Kloesel
and
Joseph M. Ransdell

INTRODUCTION

This secondary bibliography aims at being comprehensive rather than selective, and it undoubtedly contains a number of items of only marginal interest. We have included all items representing discussions of some substance which are clearly intended to contribute — or which might be construed as contributing — something new towards an understanding of Peirce's life, work, or thought (as distinct from, say, the casual repetition of a stock popular opinion or account, devoid of any interest to the serious student of Peirce). We have not excluded any items because we questioned their truth or reputability. Therefore, if any item of significance is missing from this bibliography, it is due to mechanical error, to poor editorial judgment, or simply to oversight. There are doubtless a number of such oversights, and it is likely that most of these will be items published outside the English-speaking world in journals that are difficult to obtain even in the very best American libraries. Editorial judgment is, of course, equally fallible. The nucleus (actually, a very large part) of this secondary bibliography was provided by Max H. Fisch's three earlier bibliographies; from these we have omitted a few items considered too trivial for inclusion. But many more have been added; so that the present work contains about 2000 items, dealing not only with Peirce's philosophy but with other aspects of his life and work as well.

The items are listed alphabetically by author, and chronologically under authors with multiple entries. Anonymous pieces are entered alphabetically by original title or by supplied title (for example, an originally untitled and anonymous review will be found under "R" for "review"). The bibliographic style represents an editorial compromise that aims chiefly at simplicity and clarity and that tries to avoid unnecessary repetition. We anticipate no difficulties in understanding the principles of our style; but in order to minimize repetition we have resorted to several devices of abbreviation:

1. *"Transactions"* for *"Transactions of the Charles S. Peirce Society."*
2. *"Studies I"* for *"Studies in the Philosophy of Charles Sanders Peirce,* ed. Philip P. Wiener and Frederic H. Young. Cambridge: Harvard University Press, 1952."
3. *"Studies II"* for *"Studies in the Philosophy of Charles Sanders Peirce, Second Series,* ed. Edward C. Moore and Richard S. Robin. Amherst: University of Massachusetts Press, 1964."
4. *"Proceedings 1976"* for *"Proceedings of the C.S. Peirce Bicentennial International Congress, Amsterdam 1976.* Lubbock: Texas Tech Press, forthcoming."
5. *"Collected Papers"* for *"Collected Papers of Charles Sanders Peirce,* 8 vols, ed. Charles Hartshorne, Paul Weiss, and Arthur W. Burks, Cambridge: Harvard University Press, 1931-1958."
6. Secondary studies of Peirce are provided with abbreviated titles whenever such studies are the subject matter of reviews or commentaries. For purposes of cross-referencing such abbreviated titles are always accompanied, in square brackets, by a five-digit number preceded by S; so that the full title, with full bibliographic information, may be easily located in its proper place in this bibliography.

All items in this secondary bibliography have been assigned five-digit numbers preceded by either 'S' or 'O'. Both S numbers and O numbers represent entries for secondary studies. But as explained in the Preface, the O number entries also appear in the primary bibliography (and only there in full form) because they are contemporary with Peirce and because many of them have been filmed in the microfiche collection.

S 00001
Abbagnano, Nicola. Review of *Collected Papers* VII-VIII. *Rivista di Filosofia* 50 (1959), 110.
    (Reviewed by Centioli [S 00249].)

S 0002
Abbagnano, Nicola, and M. Abbagnano, tr. *Caso, amore e logica.* Torino: Taylor, 1956. (Translation of Cohen's *Change, Love, and Logic* [S 00279]). (Reviewed by Bertolini [S 00112], Bosco [S 00142], and Paci [S 01065]).

O 00459
Abbot, Francis E. "Mr. Warner's 'Evidence in Full' Completed." 1891.

S 0003
Abel, Reuben. "Pragmatism and the Outlook of Modern Science." *Philosophy and Phenomenological Research* 27 (1966), 45-54.

S 00004
Achinstein, Peter. "Inference to Scientific Laws."
    Minnesota Studies in the Philosophy of Science 5 (1970), 87-111.

S 00005
Ackermann, Robert. "Sellars and the Scientific Image."
    Noûs 7 (1973), 138-151.

S 00006
Adams, Oscar Sherman. "Elliptic Functions Applied to Conformal World Maps." U.S. Coast and Geodetic Survey Special Publication 112 (Washington, D.C.: Government Printing Office, 1925), 96-103.

S 00007
Aiken, Henry D. "American Pragmatism Reconsidered: I. Charles Sanders Peirce." *Commentary* 34 (1962), 120-130. (See R.W. Hall [S 00602] and Aiken [S 00008]).

S 00008
——— . "Peirce Reconsidered." *Commentary* 35 (1963), 163-164. (Rejoinder to R.W. Hall's reply [S 00602] to Aiken's "American Pragmatism Reconsidered." [S 00007]).

S 00009
——— . Review of Mills' *Sociology* [S 00953]. *New York Review* 4:7 (11 March 1965), 8-10.

S 00010
Aiken, Henry D., and William Barrett, eds. *Philosophy in the Twentieth Century* (New York: Random House, 1962), I:56-63.

S 00011
Alexander, Peter. "On the Logic of Discovery." *Ratio* 7 (1965), 219-232.

S 00012
Ali Jafella, S. "Notas sobre la filosofía y su aplicación a la educación en el tomismo y el pragmatismo." *Revista de Filosofía* 20 (1968), 72-80.

S 00013
Allemand, Edward L. "Peirce's Notion of 'Firstness' and French Phenomenology." *Proceedings 1976*, forthcoming.

S 00014
Almeder, Robert. "The Metaphysical and Logical Realism of Charles Sanders Peirce." Diss. Pennsylvania 1968.

S 00015
———. "Charles Peirce and the Existence of the External World." *Transactions* 4 (1968), 63-79.

S 00016
———. "Peirce's Theory of Perception." *Transactions* 6 (1970), 99-110.

S 00017
———. "The Idealism of Charles S. Peirce." *Journal of the History of Philosophy* 9 (1971), 477-484.

S 00018
———. "Peirce's Pragmatism and Scotistic Realism." *Transactions* 9 (1973), 3-23.

S 00019
———. "Science and Idealism." *Philosophy of Science* 40 (1973), 242-254.

S 00020
———. "Truth and Knowing in Philosophy" (abstract). *International Federation of Philosophical Societies: Abstracts of Communications Presented at the XVth World Congress of Philosophy, Varna* (Sofia: Bulgarian Organizing Committee, 1973), No. 386.

S 00021
———. "Common Sense and the Foundation of Knowledge." *Man and World* 7 (1974), 254-270.

S 00022
———. "The Epistemological Realism of Charles Peirce." *Transactions* 11 (1975), 3-17.

S 00023
———. "Fallibilism and the Ultimate Irreversible Opinion." *American Philosophical Quarterly* 12 (1975), 33-54.

S 00024
Alston, William P. "Pragmatism and the Verifiability Theory of Meaning." *Philosophical Studies* 6 (1955), 65-71.

S 00025
———. "Pragmatism and the Theory of Signs in Peirce." *Philosophy and Phenomenological Research* 17 (1956), 79-88.

S 00026
———. "Sign and Symbol," in Edwards' *Encyclopedia of Philosophy* [S 00386], VII: 437-441.

S 00027
Altshuler, Bruce. "Peirce on Progress and Meaning." *Proceedings 1976*, forthcoming.

O 01008
Ames, J.S. "A Correction." 1903.

S 00028
Ames, Van Meter. *Zen and American Thought* (Honolulu: University of Hawaii Press, 1962), 141-161 ("Peirce and the Use of Signs").

S 00029
Anderson, Alan Ross. Review of Turquette's "Peirce's Icons" [S 01449]. *Journal of Symbolic Logic* 39 (1974), 269.

S 00030
Anderson, Paul Russell, and Max Harold Fisch. *Philosophy in America: From the Puritans to James—With Representative Selections.* New York: Appleton-Century, 1939. (Reviewed by Turner [S 01445]).

S 00031
Angoff, Charles. "Charles Peirce." *American Mercury* 14 (1928), 334-337.

O 00246
Angot, Alfred. Review of Peirce's "On Irregularities in the Amplitude of Oscillation of Pendulums." 1883.

O 00138
Annual Record of Science and Industry for 1878. 1879.

S 00032
Antiseri, D., tr. *Come rendere chiare le nostre idee.* Bergamo: Minerva Italica, 1970. (Translation of "How to Make Our Ideas Clear").

S 00033
Apel, Karl-Otto, ed. *Charles S. Peirce: Schriften I—Zur Entstehung des Pragmatismus* (tr. Gerd Wartenberg) Frankfurt: Suhrkamp, 1967.

S 00034
―――, ed. *Charles S. Peirce: Schriften II — Vom Pragmatismus zum Pragmatizismus* (tr. Gerd Wartenberg Frankfurt: Suhrkamp, 1970.

S 00035
―――. "From Kant to Peirce: The Semiotical Transformation of Transcendental Logic," in *Proceedings of the Third International Kant Congress,* ed. L.W. Beck (Dordrecht-Holland: D. Reidel, 1972), 90-104.

S 00036
―――. "Der semiotische Pragmatismus von Charles S. Peirce und die 'Abstractive Fallacy' in den Grundlagen der Kantschen Erkenntnistheorie und der Carnapschen Wissenschaftslogik" (abstract). *International Federation of Philosophical Societies: Abstracts of Communications Presented at the XVth World Congress of Philosophy, Varna* (Sofia: Bulgarian Organizing Committee, 1973), No. 387.

S 00037
―――. "Programmatische Bermerkungen zur Idee einer 'Transzendentalen Sprach-Pragmatik,'" in *Studia Philosophica in Honorem Sven Krohn* (Annales Universitatis Turkuensis Sarja, Series B Osa, Tom 126, 1973), 11-35.

S 00038
―――. *Transformation der Philosophie.* 2 vols. Frankfurt: Suhrkamp, 1973. (Reviewed by Holmes [S 00684]).

S 00039
―――. "Szientismus oder transzendentale Hermeneutik: Zur Frage nach dem Subjekt der Zeichen-Interpretation in der Semiotik des Pragmatismus," in his *Transformation der Philosophie* [S 00038], II: 178-219.

S 00040
―――. "Von Kant zu Peirce: Die semiotische Transformation der transzendentalen Logik," in his *Transformation der Philosophie* [S 00038], II:157-177.

S 00041
_____ . "The Problem of (Philosophical) Ultimate Justification in the Light of a Transcendental Pragmatic of Language." *Ajatus* 36 (1974), 142-165.

S 00042
_____ . "The Problem of Philosophical Fundamental-Grounding in Light of a Transcendental Pragmatic of Language." *Man and World* 8 (1975), 239-275.

S 00043
_____ . *Der Denkweg von Charles S. Peirce: Eine Einführung in den amerikanischen Pragmatismus.* Frankfurt: Suhrkamp, 1975. (A combination of the Introductions to *Schriften I* and *II* [S 00033] and [S 00034]).

S 00044
Appleby, Peter Clare. "A Critical Study of Peirce's Philosophical Theology." Diss. Texas at Austin 1963.

S 00045
Arata, Carlo. Review of Bosco's *Filosofia pragmatica* [S 00149]. *Giornale di Metafisica* 19 (1964).

S 00046
Archibald, Raymond C. "Benjamin Peirce's Linear Associative Algebra and Charles Sanders Peirce." *American Mathematical Monthly* 34 (1927), 525-527.

S 00047
_____ . *A Semicentennial History of the American Mathematical Society, 1888-1938* (New York: American Mathematical Society, 1938), 6-7. (Contains information concerning Peirce's contributions to various newspapers).

O 01169
Armstrong, A.C. "The Evolution of Pragmatism." 1908.

S 00048
Arnstine, Barbara. "Response to Hullett" [S 00704]. *Philosophy of Education Proceedings* 30 (1974), 432-438.

S 00049
Aronson, Jerrold L. "Connections: A Defense of Peirce's Category of Thirdness." *Transactions* 5 (1969), 158-172.

S 00050
Atkinson, Brooks. "Critic at Large: Dialogue of 2 Writers Finds One Urging a Play About a Man Named Peirce." *New York Times,* 10 September 1963, 40M. (Reprinted as "Journalists Ignore Philosopher: Just Who Was C.S. Peirce?" in *Champaign-Urbana Courier,* 16 September 1963, 20).

S 00051
Aune, Bruce. Review of Ayer's *Origins* [S 00054]. *Transactions* 5 (1969), 255-263.

S 00052
_____ . "Two Theories of Scientific Knowledge." *Critica: Revista Hispano-Americana de Filosofia* 5 (1971), 3-20.

S 00053
_____ . "On an Analytic-Synthetic Distinction." *American Philosophical Quarterly* 9 (1972), 235-242.

S 00054
Ayer, A.J. *The Origins of Pragmatism: Studies in the Philosophy of Charles Sanders Peirce and William James.* San Francisco: Freeman, Cooper, 1968. (Reviewed by Aune [S 00051], Delaney [S 00320], Greenlee [00584], Herbenick [S 00657], Huggett [S 00702], Koehn [S 00774], Mays [S 00914], Rorty [S 01213], Roth, J.K. [S 01243], Roth, R.J. [01248], Stack [S 01372] Tibbetts [S 01424], White, M. [S 01519], and Wood [S 01565]).

S 00055
Ayim, Maryann. "Peirce's View of the Roles of Reason and Instinct in Scientific Inquiry." Diss. Waterloo 1972.

S 00056
———— . "Retroduction: The Rational Instinct." *Transactions* 10 (1974), 34-43.

S 00057
———— . "The Marriage and Divorce of Science and Religion in C.S. Peirce's Philosophy," in *Philosophy in the Life of a Nation* (New York: Bicentennial Symposium of Philosophy, 1976), 217-223.

S 00058
———— . "Theory, Practice, and Peircean Pragmatism." *Proceedings 1976,* forthcoming.

S 00059
Azevedo, M. "Peirce e la semiotica." *Revista de Cultura Vozes* 10 (1970).

S 00060
B., R.   Review of Buchler's *Empiricism* [S 00188]. *Saturday Review of Literature* 21 (3 February 1940), 21.

O 00413
B., W.H.   "A Philosophical Critic." 1890.

O 00424
B., W.H.   "The Evolution of Scientific Religion." 1890.

O 00074
Backhouse, T.W. "Spectrum of Aurora." 1873.

S 00061
Bailey, Solon I. *The History and Work of Harvard Observatory* (New York: McGraw-Hill, 1931), 52, 53, 86, 95, 110, 124, 125, 196, 198-199, 240, 260, 274.

O 01115
Baly, Edward C. C. *Spectroscopy.* 1905.

S 00062
Bambrough, Renford. "Foundations." *Analysis* 30 (1970), 191-197.

S 00063
Barclay, K.C. Review of *Studies* II [S 00968]. *Mind,* NS 75 (1966), 455-456.

S 00064
Barnes, Winston H.F. "Peirce on 'How to Make our Ideas Clear,'" in Studies I [S 01549], 53-60.

S 00065
———. Review of Murphey's *Development* [S 01001]. *Philosophical Quarterly* 13 (1963), 361-366.

S 00066
Barone, Francesco. "Peirce e Schroeder." *Filosofia* 17 (1966), 181-224.

Barrett, William. See Aiken, Henry D., and W. Barrett [S 00010].

S 00067
Barry, Robert M. "Direction of American Philosophy: A Bibliographical View." *American Benedictine Review* 15 (1964), 215-236.

S 00068
Bastian, Ralph J. "The 'Scholastic' Realism of C.S. Peirce." *Philosophy and Phenomenological Research* 14 (1953), 246-249. (Response by Moore [S 00962]).

S 00069
Baum, Maurice. "Pragmatism," in *American Philosophy,* ed. Ralph B. Winn (New York: Philosophical Library, 1955), 162-171.

S 00070
Baumgarten, Edward. *Der Pragmatismus: R.W. Emerson, W. James, J. Dewey.* Frankfurt: Klostermann, 1938.

S 00071
Baumol, William J., and Stephen M. Goldfeld, eds. *Precursors in Mathematical Economics: An Anthology.* Series of Reprints of Scarce Works on Political Economy 19 (London: The London School of Economics and Political Science, 1968), 184-187.

O 01210
Bawden, H.H. *The Principles of Pragmatism.* 1910.

S 00072
Beatty, Richard. "The Logical Foundations of Peirce's Categories, 1867-1885." Diss. Notre Dame 1966.

S 00073
———. "Peirce's Development of Quantifiers and of Predicate Logic." *Notre Dame Journal of Formal Logic* 10 (1969), 64-76.

S 00074
Beauchamp, William T. "Peirce's Conception of the Symbolic Process: An Interpretation for Instructors in College Freshman Composition and Communication." Diss. Columbia 1958.

O 01230
Becker, George F. "Charles Santiago Sanders Peirce, '59." 1914.

S 00075
Beckmann, Peter. "Verbandstheoretische Darstellung der Subzeichen und Zeichenklassen." *Semiosis* 2 (1976), 31-35.

S 00076
Bell, E.T. *The Development of Mathematics* 2nd ed. (New York: McGraw-Hill, 1945), 249-251, 556-557.

O 00310
Bell, Louis. "On the Absolute Wave-Length of Light." 1887.

O 00345
——— . "On the Absolute Wave-Length of Light." 1887.

O 00363
——— . "The Absolute Wave-Length of Light." 1888.

S 00077
Benedict, George Allen. "The Concept of Continuity in Charles Peirce's Synechism." Diss. New York at Buffalo 1973.

S 00078
Beneviste, Emile. "Sémiologie de la langue (I)." *Semiotica* 1 (1969), 1-12.

O 00205
"Benjamin Peirce." 1881.

S 00079
Bense, Max. *Theorie der Texte: Eine Einführung in neuere Auffassungen und Methoden.* Cologne: Kiepenheuer & Witsch, 1962.

S 00080
——— . *Semiotik: Allgemeine Theorie der Zeichen.* Baden-Baden: Agis, 1967.

S 00081
——— . *Einführung in die informationstheoretische Ästhetik.* Reinbek: Rowohlt, 1969.

S 00082
——— . *Zeichen und Design.* Baden-Baden: Agis, 1971.

S 00083
——— . "Semiotik," in *Lexikon der germanistischen Linguistik* (Tübingen: Max Niemeyer, 1973), 13-34.

S 00084
——— *Semiotische Prozesse und Systeme: In Wissenschaftstheorie und Design, Ästhetik und Mathematik.* Baden-Baden: Agis, 1975.

S 00085
——— . "Bemerkungen über die Zeichenbasis." *Semiosis* 2 (1976), 36-40.

S 00086
——— . Semiotische Kategorien und algebraische Kategorien: Zur grundlagentheorie der Mathematik." *Semiosis* 4 (1976), 5-10.

S 00087
——— . Das System der theoretischen Semiotik." *Semiosis* 1 (1976), 24-27.

S 00088
——— . "Zeichenklasse und Realitätsthematik." *Proceedings 1976,* forthcoming.

S 00089
——— . "Das 'Zeichen' als Repräsentationsschema und als Kommunikationsschema." *Semiosis* 5 (1977), 11-18.

——— . See Walther, Elisabeth, and M. Bense [S 01486].

S 00090
Bense, Max, and Elisabeth Walther, eds. *Worterbuch der Semiotik.* Cologne: Kiepenheuer & Witsch, 1973. (Reviewed by Ketner and Kloesel [S 00754]).

S 00091
Bentley, Arthur F. "Truth, Reality, and Behavioral Fact." *Journal of Philosophy* 40 (1943), 169-187.

S 00092
———. "The New 'Semiotic.'" *Philosophy and Phenomenological Research* 8 (1947), 107-132.

S 00093
———. *Inquiry into Inquiries: Essays in Social Theory.* Boston: Beacon Press, 1954.

S 00094
Bently, John E. *An Outline of American Philosophy* (Paterson: Littlefield, Adams, 1963), 144-150.

S 00095
Berger, Wolfgana. "Zur Algebra der Zeichenklassen." *Semiosis* 4 (1976), 20-23.

S 00096
Bergman, Gustav. Discussion of Willis Moore's "The Indexical and the Presentative Function of Signs" [S 00971]. *Philosophy of Science* 9 (1942), 372-374.

S 00097
Berkson, I.B. *The Ideal and the Community: A Philosophy of Education* (New York: Harper, 1958), 63-75.

S 00098
Berleant, A. "E.H. Madden's *Chauncy Wright and the Foundation of Pragmatism* [S 00883]." *Philosophy and Phenomenological Research* 15 (1964), 143-149.

S 00099
Bernadete, José A. Infinity: *An Essay In Metaphysics* (Oxford: Clarendon, 1965), 72-75.

S 00100
Bernstein, Richard J. "Charles Sanders Peirce and the *Nation.*" *Antioch Review* 21 (1961), 15-25.

S 00101
———. Review of Moore's *American Pragmatism* [S 00963]. *Journal of Philosophy* 59 (1962), 272-274.

S 00102
———. "Peirce's Theory of Perception," in *Studies* II [S 00968], 165-189.

S 00103
———. "Action, Conduct, and Self-Control," in his *Perspectives* [S 00105], 66-91.

S 00104
———. Charles Sanders Peirce and *The Nation.*" *Antioch Review* 21:1 (1961), 15-25. (Reprinted in Ketner and Cook [S 00753]).

S 00105
———. *Perspectives on Peirce: Critical Essays on Charles Sanders Peirce.* New Haven: Yale University Press, 1965. (Reviewed by Gill [S 00552], Gustafson [S 00594], and Potter [S 01109]).

S 00106
———. "In Defence of American Philosophy," in Smith's *Contemporary American Philosophy, Second Series* [S 01361], 293-311.

S 00107
———. "Paul Weiss's Recollections of Editing the Peirce Papers" (interview). *Transactions* 6 (1970), 161-188.

S 00108
———. *Praxis and Action: Contemporary Philosophies of Human Activity.* Philadelphia: University of Pennsylvania Press, 1971. (Reviewed by Dearin [S 00316], Hansen [S 00606], and Sharpe [S 01336]).

S 00109
———. "Interpretation and Interpretants." *Proceedings 1976,* forthcoming.

S 00110
Berroth, A. "Schweremessungen." *Handbuch der Physik* (1926), II: 416-486, at 445, 450.

S 00111
Berry, George D. "Peirce's Contributions to the Logic of Statements and Quantifiers," in *Studies* I [S 01549], 153-165. (Reviewed by Wells [S 01502]).

O 01216
Berthelot, René. *Un romantisme utilitaire: Etude sur le mouvement pragmatiste.* 1911-1922.

S 00112
Bertolini, P. Review of Abbagnano's *Caso, amore e logica* [S 00002]. *Rivista Rosminiana di Filosofia e di Cultura* 51 (1957), 311-312.

S 00113
Bierstedt, Robert. Review of Goudge's *Thought* [S 00565]. *Saturday Review of Literature* 34 (16 June 1951), 42.

S 00114
Bikson, Tora Kay Lanto. "Peirce's Logic Treated as Semiotic." Diss. Missouri 1969.

S 00115
Bird, Otto. "Peirce's Theory of Methodology." *Philosophy of Science* 26 (1959), 187-200.

S 00116
———. "What Peirce Means by Leading Principles." *Notre Dame Journal of Formal Logic* 3 (1962), 175-178.

S 00117
Birkhoff, Garrett. *Lattice Theory.* American Mathematical Society Colloquium Publications 25 (New York: American Mathematical Society, 1940), iii, 5n., 16n., 74.

S 00118
Bishop, Donald H. "Peirce on Oriental Philosophy and Religion." *Proceedings 1976,* forthcoming.

S 00119
Blachowicz, James A. "Realism and Idealism in Peirce's Categories." *Transactions* 8 (1972), 199-213.

S 00120
Black, Max. "Vagueness." *Philosophy of Science* 4 (1937), 427-455.

S 00121
———. Review of Feibleman's *Introduction* [S 00451]. *Journal of Symbolic Logic* 12 (1947), 19.

S 00122
———. *Language and Philosophy* (Ithaca: Cornell University Press, 1949), esp. Ch. II.

S 00123
———. Review of *Collected Papers* VII-VIII. *Philosophy of Science* 30 (1963), 299-300.

S 00124
———. *Margins of Precision: Essays in Logic and Language.* Ithaca: Cornell University Press, 1970.

S 00125
Blanshard, Brand. "Unraveling an Idea." (review of Wiener's *Evolution* [S 01533]). *Saturday Review of Literature* 32 (22 October 1949), 15.

S 00126
———. *Reason and Analysis* (La Salle, Ill.: Open Court, 1962), 192-197.

S 00127
Blau, Joseph L. Review of Fisch's *Classic American Philosophers* [S 00469]. *Journal of Philosophy* 48 (1951), 536-537.

S 00128
———. *Men and Movements in American Philosophy* (New York: Prentice-Hall, 1952), 240-252. (Reviewed by Fisch [S 00471]).

S 00129
———. Review of Murphey's *Development* [S 01001]. *American Quarterly* 14 (1962), 511-512.

S 00130
Blomeyer, Gerald R., and Rita M. Helmholtz. "Semiotic in Architecture: A Classifying Analysis of an Architectural Object." *Semiosis* 1 (1976), 42-51.

S 00131
Blum, Manuel. "Properties of a Neuron with Many Inputs," in *Principles of Self-Organization* (Transactions of the University of Illinois Symposium on Self-Organization [ed. Heinz von Foerster and George W. Zoph, Jr.], 1961), 95-119, at 114-119.

S 00132
Bochenski, I.M. *Formale Logik* (Freiburg: Karl Alber, 1956), Part 5. (Translated and edited by Ivo Thomas as *A History of Formal Logic* [South Bend, Ind.: University of Notre Dame Press, 1961]).

O 00486
Bocher, Maxime. "Geometry not Mathematics." 1892.

S 00133
Bochner, Salomon. "Continuity and Discontinuity in Nature and Knowledge," in Wiener's *Dictionary of the History of Ideas* [S 01548], I: 492-504.

S 00134
———. "Mathematical Reflections. Part II: Charles Sanders Peirce." *American Mathematical Monthly* 81 (1974), 838-852. (Criticized by Eisele [S 00409] and Fisch [S 00489]).

S 00135
Boler, John F. "The Structure of Realism in the Philosophy of Charles S. Peirce." Diss. Harvard 1960.

S 00136
——— *Charles Peirce and Scholastic Realism: A Study of Peirce's Relation to John Duns Scotus.* (Reviewed by Bourke [S 00157], Collins [S 00287], Copleston [S 00293], Erpenbeck [S 00416], Llamzon [S 00847], Potter [S 01104] and [S 01109], Potts [S 01114], Rorty [S 01212], and Ross [S 01239]).

S 00137
────── . "Habits of Thought," in *Studies* II [S 00968], 382-400.

O 01172
Boodin, John E. "Philosophic Tolerance. A Winter Revery." 1908.

O 01188
────── . "What Pragmatism Is and Is Not." 1909.

O 01208
────── . "Pragmatic Realism." 1910.

O 01213
────── . "From Protagoras to William James." 1911.

O 01087
Boole, Mary Everest. "The Sorrows of Philosophers." 1905.

S 00138
Boorse, Christopher, "The Origins of the Indeterminacy Thesis." *Journal of Philosophy* 72 (1975), 369-387.

S 00139
Boring, Edwin G. *A History of Experimental Psychology* (New York: Century, 1929), 529, 537, 618, 626.

S 00140
────── . *Sensation and Perception in the History of Experimental Psychology* (New York: Appleton-Century-Crofts, 1942), 40, 51.

O 01219
Borrass, E. "Der Bericht über die relativen Messungen der Schwerkraft mit Pendelapparaten in der Zeit von 1808 bis 1909 und über ihre Darstellung im Potsdamer Schweresystem." 1911.

S 00141
Bosco, Nynfa. "Introduzione allo studio di Peirce." *Filosofia* 7 (1956), 452-469.

S 00142
────── . Review of Abbagnano's *Caso, amore e logica* [S 00002]. *Filosofia* 8 (1957), 351-355.

S 00143
────── . "Charles Sanders Peirce," in *Enciclopedia Filosofica* (Florence: Sansoni, 1957), III: 1250-1251. (2nd ed. 1967, IV: 1447-1452). (Reviewed by Fragata [S 00513]).

S 00144
────── . "Due Pragmatismi: Peirce e James." *Filosofia* 8 (1957), 497-507.

S 00145
────── . "La conoscenza come ricerca in Peirce." *Filosofia* 9 (1958), 568-590.

S 00146
────── . "L'orizzonte storico del pragmaticismo." *Filosofia* 9 (1958), 40-56.

S 00147
────── . "La Conoscenza come significazione in Peirce." *Filosofia* 10 (1959), 90-110.

S 00148
——— . "La metafisica di Charles Sanders Peirce." *Filosofia* 10 (1959), 261-296.

S 00149
——— . *La filosofia pragmatica di C.S. Peirce.* Torino: Edizioni di "Filosofia," 1959. (Reviewed by Arata [S 00045], Gallie [S 00541], Kunz [S 00790], Penati [S 01084], and Schneider [S 01306]).

S 00150
——— . Review of *Collected Papers* VII-VIII. *Filosofia* 10 (1959), 652-655.

S 00151
——— . "Etica ed estetica in Peirce." *Filosofia* 12 (1960), 15-38.

S 00152
——— . "Peirce e la matematica." *Filosofia* 11 (1960), 261-296.

S 00153
——— . "Filosofia della religione e teologia in Peirce." *Filosofia* 12 (1961), 396-402.

S 00154
——— . "La psicologia in Peirce." *Filosofia* 13 (1962), 177-201.

S 00155
——— . "Peirce and Metaphysics," in *Studies* II [S 00968], 345-358.

S 00156
Bouchard, Guy. "Les principales tendances de la sémiologie." *Dialogue* 14 (1975), 649-663.

O 01121
Bourgeois, R., and Ph. Furtwängler. "Kartographie." 1906-1925.

S 00157
Bourke, Vernon J. Review of Boler's *Scholastic Realism* [S 00136]. *Speculum* 39 (1964), 493-494.

S 00158
Bouveresse, Jacques. "Peirce, Popper, l'induction et l'histoire des sciences." *Critique* (Paris), 30 (1974), 736-752.

S 00159
Bowne, G.D. *The Philosophy of Logic 1880-1908.* The Hague: Mouton, 1966.

Boyd, Lyle Gifford. See Jones, Bessie Zaban, and L.G. Boyd [S 00726].

S 00160
Boyer, Carl B. *A History of Mathematics* (New York: John Wiley, 1968), 629, 636f, 644, 661.

S 00161
Braithwaite, R.B. Review of *Collected Papers* I-IV. *Mind,* NS 43 (1934), 487-511.

S 00162
——— . "Peirce on Probability and Induction." *Mind,* NS 43 (1934), 500-511.

S 00163
——— . "Peirce on Signs." *Mind,* NS 43 (1934), 493-500.

S 00164
——— . *Scientific Explanation* (New York: Cambridge University Press, 1953), esp. 187, 264-272, 294.

S 00165
───── . "Moral Principles and Inductive Policies," in *Studies in Philosophy: British Academy Lectures,* ed. J.N. Findlay (New York: Oxford University Press, 1966), 93-114.

S 00166
Brent, Joseph Lancaster, III. "A Study of the Life of Charles Sanders Peirce." Diss. California at Los Angeles 1960.

S 00167
Brinkley, Alan B. "The Phenomenology of Ch. S. Peirce." Diss. Tulane 1960.

S 00168
Britton, Karl. Review of *Collected Papers* VI. *Mind,* NS 46 (1937), 394-399.

S 00169
───── . "Introduction to the Metaphysics and Theology of C.S. Peirce." *Ethics* 49 (1939), 435-465.

S 00170
Brock, Jarrett Ernest. "Charles Sanders Peirce's Logic of Vagueness." Diss. Illinois 1969.

S 00171
───── . "Peirce's Conception of Semiotic." *Semiotica* 14 (1975), 124-141.

S 00172
───── . "Draft of a Critique of Greenlee's *Peirce's Concept of Sign.*" *Transactions* 12 (1976), 111-126. (Criticism of Greenlee [S 00587] ; see also Greenlee's reply [S 00589]).

S 00173
───── . "Peirce and Searle on Assertion." *Proceedings 1976,* forthcoming.

S 00174
Brodbeck, May. "Philosophy in America: 1900-1950," in *American Non-Fiction: 1900-1950,* ed. May Brodbeck *et al.* (Chicago: Henry Regnery, 1952), 3-94, at 17-21.

S 00175
Brodsky, Garry M. "The Pragmatic Movement." *Review of Metaphysics* 25 (1971), 262-291.

S 00176
───── . Critical Comments on Thayer's *Meaning and Action* [S 01402]. *Transactions* 11 (1975), 230-236. (Reply by Thayer [S 01405]).

S 00177
───── . "Peirce on Truth, Reality, and Inquiry." *Monist* 57 (1973), 220-239.

S 00178
Brög, Hans. "Bemerkungen zur semiotischen Bestimmung von Dokumentarfotografie und Portraitmalerei." *Semiosis* 2 (1976), 42-49.

S 00179
Bronstein, Daniel J. "Inquiry and Meaning," in *Studies* I [S 01549], 33-52.

S 00180
Brotherston, Bruce W. "Firstness." *Journal of Philosophy* 36 (1939), 533-543.

S 00181
Brown, D.G. Review of Thompson's *Pragmatic Philosophy* [S 01416]. *Mind,* NS 64 (1955), 561-562.

S 00182
Brown, Warren. "The School Class and the Problem of Fixing Belief." *Proceedings 1976,* forthcoming.

S 00183
Browne, Samuel S.S. *A Pragmatist Theory of Truth and Reality.* Princeton: Princeton University Press, 1930.

S 00184
Browning, Douglas, ed. *Philosophers of Process* (New York: Random House, 1965), 57-109.

S 00185
Broyles, James E. "The Role of Common Sense in the Empiricism of Charles Sanders Peirce." Diss. Washington 1964.

S 00186
_____ . "Charles S. Peirce and the Concept of Indubitable Belief." *Transactions* 1 (1965), 77-89.

S 00187
Buchler, Justus. "The Pragmatism of Charles Sanders Peirce." *Psyche* 17 (1937), 92-131.

S 00188
_____ . *Charles Peirce's Empiricism.* (Reviewed by B., R. [S 00060], Goudge [S 00562], Hartshorne [S 00629], Laird [S 00794], M., W.M. [S 00858], McDonald [S 00872], anonymous [S 01171], Vivas [S 01468], Weiss [S 01495], and Wohlstetter [S 01563]).

S 00189
_____ . "Charles Sanders Peirce, Giant in American Philosophy." *American Scholar* 8 (1939), 400-411.

S 00190
_____ . "Peirce's Theory of Logic." *Journal of Philosophy* 36 (1939), 197-215. (See review by Hempel [S 00653]).

S 00191
_____ . "The Accidents of Peirce's System." *Journal of Philosophy* 37 (1940), 264-269.

S 00192
_____ . "Charles Peirce's Empiricism." Diss. Columbia 1940.

S 00193
_____ , ed. *The Philosophy of Peirce: Selected Writings.* London: Kegan Paul, 1940. (Reprinted as *Philosophical Writings of Peirce.* New York: Dover, 1955). (Noticed by Deledalle [S 00330], Laird [S 00795], Nagel [S 01022], Anonymous [S 01172], and Snyder [S 01366]).

S 00194
_____ . "Reply to Weiss" [S 01496]. *Philosophy and Phenomenological Research* 2 (1941), 261.

S 00195
_____ . Review of Feibleman's *Introduction* [S 00451]. *Journal of Philosophy* 44 (1947), 306-308.

S 00196
_____ . "What Is the Pragmaticist Theory of Meaning?" in *Studies* I [S 01549], 21-32.

S 00197
Buczynska-Garewicz, Hanna. *Peirce.* Warsaw: Wiedza Powszechna, 1965.

S 00198
———. *Wartosc i fact: Rozwazania o pragmatizmie.* Warsaw: Panstwowe Wydawnictwo Naukowe, 1970.

S 00199
———. "Amerykanski kwartalnik poswiecony filozofii Peirce'a." *Studia Filozoficzne* 5 (1972).

S 00200
———. *James.* Warsaw: Wiedza Powszechna, 1973.

S 00201
———. "Actualne badania nad filozofia Peirce'a." *Studia Filozoficzne* 8 (1976), 141-143.

S 00202
———. "Der Interpretant, die Autoreproduktion des Symbols und die pragmatische Maxime." *Semiosis* 2 (1976), 10-16.

S 00203
———. "Miedzynarodowy Kongres Poswiecony Filozofii Peirce'a." *Studia Filozoficzne* 12 (1976), 117-118. (Report of the C.S. Peirce Bicentennial International Congress).

S 00204
———. "Sign and Evidence." *Semiosis* 5 (1977), 5-10.

S 00205
———. "The Idea of Object of Knowledge in Peirce's Theory of Signs." *Proceedings 1976,* forthcoming.

O 01001
Bumstead, Henry A. "Josiah Willard Gibbs." 1903.

S 00206
Bunge, Mario. *Causality: The Place of the Causal Principle in Modern Science.* Cambridge: Harvard University Press, 1959.

S 00207
Bunker, Robert Manson. "The Idea of Failure in Henry Adams, Charles Sanders Peirce, and Mark Twain." Diss. New Mexico 1955.

O 00972
Burchard, E.L. *List and Catalogue of the Publications Issued by the U.S. Coast and Geodetic Survey 1816-1902.* 1902.

S 00208
Burgener, R.J.C. "Peirce's Theory of the Concept." *Review of Metaphysics* 11 (1957), 143-159.

S 00209
Burkamp, Wilhelm. *Wirklichkeit und Sinn* (Berlin: Junker and Dünnhaupt, 1938), esp. II:757-758.

S 00210
Burks, Arthur W. "The Logical Foundations of the Philosophy of Charles Sanders Peirce." Diss. Michigan 1941.

S 00211
———. "Peirce's Conception of Logic as a Normative Science." *Philosophical Review* 52 (1943), 187-193.

S 00212
———. "Peirce's Theory of Abduction." *Philosophy of Science* 13 (1946), 301-306.

S 00213
———. "Icon, Index, and Symbol." *Philosophy and Phenomenological Research* 9 (1949), 673-689.

S 00214
———. "A Theory of Proper Names." *Philosophical Studies* 2 (1951), 35-45.

S 00215
———. "Charles Sanders Peirce," in Fisch's *Classic American Philosophers* [S 00469], 41-53.

S 00216
———, ed. *Collected Papers of Charles Sanders Peirce.* Vols. 7-8. Cambridge: The Belknap Press of Harvard University, 1958.

S 00217
———. "Peirce's Two Theories of Probability," in *Studies* II [S 00968], 141-150.

S 00218
———. "The Pragmatic-Humean Theory of Probability and Lewis' Theory," in *The Philosophy of C.I. Lewis,* ed. P.A. Schilpp (La Salle, Ill.: Open Court, 1968), 415-463.

S 00219
———. "Logic, Computers and Men." *Proceedings and Addresses of the American Philosophical Association* 46 (1972), 39-57.

S 00220
Burks, Arthur W., and Paul Weiss. "Peirce's Sixty-six Signs." *Journal of Philosophy* 42 (1945), 383-388.

S 00221
Burrell, David B. "C.S. Peirce: Pragmatism as a Theory of Judgment." *International Philosophical Quarterly* 5 (1965), 521-540.

S 00222
———. "Knowing as a Passionate and Personal Quest: C.S. Peirce," in *American Philosophy and the Future: Essays for a New Generation,* ed. Michael Novak (New York: Scribner's, 1968), 107-137.

S 00223
Burzlaff, Werner. Review of Walther's *Allgemeine Zeichenlehre* [S 01481]. *Semiosis* 4 (1976), 56.

S 00224
Butler, James Donald. *Four Philosophies and Their Practice in Education and Religion.* 3rd ed. (New York: Harper, 1968), 365-368.

S 00225
Buzzelli, Donald E. "The Argument of Peirce's 'New List of Categories.'" *Transactions* 8 (1972), 63-89.

S 00226
———. "The 'New List of Categories': A Study of the Early Philosophy of Charles Sanders Peirce." Diss. Fordham 1974.

O 00399
C., A.B. "The 'Pons Asinorum.'" 1890.

Cadwallader, Joyce V. See Cadwallader, Thomas C., and J.V. Cadwallader [S 00230].

S 00227
Cadwallader, Thomas C. "Charles S. Peirce (1839-1914): The First American Experimental Psychologist." *Journal of the History of the Behavioral Sciences* 10 (1974), 291-298.

S 00228
───── . "Peirce as an Experimental Psychologist." *Transactions* 11 (1975), 167-186.

S 00229
───── . "Unique Values of Arthival Research." *Journal of the History of the Behavioral Sciences* 11 (1975), 27-33.

S 00230
Cadwallader, Thomas C., and Joyce V. Cadwallader. "America's First Modern Psychologist: William James or Charles S. Peirce?" *Proceedings of the 80th Annual Convention of the American Psychological Association* (1972), 773-774.

S 00231
Cairns, Huntington. *Legal Philosophy from Plato to Hegel* (Baltimore: The Johns Hopkins Press, 1949), 267, 560, 561.

O 00445
Cajori, Florian. "The Teaching of Mathematics." 1891.

O 00617
───── . *A History of Elementary Mathematics.* 1896.

O 00687
───── . "Galileo's Reasoning." 1899.

O 00680
───── . *A History of Physics in its Elementary Branches.* 1899.

S 00232
───── "History of Zeno's Arguments on Motion, VIII." *American Mathematical Monthly* 22 (1915), 215-220.

S 00233
───── . *A History of Mathematics.* 2nd ed. (New York: Macmillan, 1919), 31, 285, 309, 337-339, 407.

S 00234
───── . *A History of Mathematical Notations.* 2 vols. (Chicago: Open Court, 1928-29), paragraphs 449, 681-686, 730.

O 00712
Caldwell, William. "Pragmatism." 1900.

O 01225
───── . *Pragmatism and Idealism.* 1913.

S 00235
Calogero, Guido. "Charles Sanders Peirce," in *Enciclopedia Italiana di Scienze, Lettere ed Arti* (1935), XXVI: 603-604.

S 00236
Capek, Milic. "The Doctrine of Necessity Re-examined." *Review of Metaphysics* 5 (1951), 11-54.

S 00237
———. "James's Early Criticism of the Automaton Theory." *Journal of the History of Ideas* 15 (1954), 260-279.

S 00238
———. "The Theory of Eternal Recurrence in Modern Philosophy of Science, with Special Reference to C.S. Peirce." *Journal of Philosophy* 57 (1960), 289-296. (Response by Van Fraassen [S 01463]).

S 00239
———. *Bergson and Modern Physics* (Dordrecht-Holland: D. Reidel, 1971), 18, 286-287, 290, 299, 310, 350-351, 356.

S 00240
Caponigri, Robert A. *A History of Western Philosophy* (London: Notre Dame University Press, 1971), V:46-48.

S 00241
Cardona, Francisco José. Review of Spirito's *Il pragmatismo* [S 01371] (in Spanish translation). *Philosophy and Phenomenological Research* 8 (1948), 717-720.

S 00242
Carnap, Rudolf. *Logical Foundations of Probability* (Chicago: University of Chicago Press, 1950), 554-555.

S 00243
Carpenter, Frederic I. "Charles Sanders Peirce, Pragmatic Transcendentalist." *New England Quarterly* 14 (1941), 34-48. (Reprinted in *American Literature and the Dream* [New York: Philosophical Library, 1955], 94-104).

S 00244
Carr, William Francis. "Charles Sanders Peirce's Principles of Inquiry." M.A. thesis St. Louis 1953.

S 00245
Cartan, E. "Nombres complexes. Exposé, d'après l'article allemand de E. Study," in *Encyclopédie des sciences mathématiques pures et appliquées* (Paris: Gauthier-Villars, 1915), I:329-468.

O 00431
Carus, Paul. "The Unity of Truth." 1890.

O 00432
———. "The Superscientific and Pure Reason." 1890.

O 00440
———. "The Criterion of Truth." 1891.

O 00475
———. "Mr. Charles S. Peirce on Necessity." 1892.

O 00476
———. "What does Anschauung Mean?" 1892.

O 00478
———. "Mr. Charles S. Peirce's Onslaught on the Doctrine of Necessity." 1892.

O 00481
———. "The Idea of Necessity, Its Basis and Its Scope." 1892.

O 00526
———. "The Founder of Tychism, His Methods, Philosophy and Criticisms: In Reply to Mr. Charles Sanders Peirce." 1893.

O 00546
———. "Religion Inseparable from Science." 1893.

O 00549
———. Note on Peirce's article "What is Christian Faith?" 1893.

O 00619
———. Review of Schröder's *Algebra und Logik der Relative*. 1896.

O 00681
———. *Kant and Spencer: A Study of the Fallacies of Agnosticism*. 1899.

O 01040
———. "Pasigraphy—A Suggestion." 1904.

O 01173
———. "Pragmatism." 1908.

O 01152
———. Remarks on Pragmatism. 1909.

O 01194
———. "A Postscript on Pragmatism." 1909.

O 01195
———. "A German Critic of Pragmatism." 1909.

O 01196
———. "A Letter from Professor James." 1909.

O 01198
———. *Philosophy as a Science*. 1909.

O 01209
———. "Editorial Comment." 1910.

O 01218
———. *Truth on Trial*. 1911.

S 00246
Caspari, C. Ed. "Theorie der Uhren," in *Encyklopädie der mathematischen Wissenschaften* (Leipzig: B.G. Teubner, 1905-1923), 6.2.1.:163-193 (at 178).

O 01119
Cattell, J. McK., and D.R. Brimhall, eds. *American Men of Science: A Biographical Dictionary*. 1906.

S 00247
Caws, Peter. "Three Logics, or the Possibility of the Improbable." *Philosophy and Phenomenological Research* 25 (1965), 516-526.

O 00284
Cayley, Arthur. "On Double Algebra." 1884.

S 00248
Cell, George Croft. "Die Philosophie in Nordamerika," in *Ueberwegs Grundriss der Geschichte der Philosophie,* 13th ed. (Basel: Benno Schwabe, 1953), V:391-392.

S 00249
Centioli, E. Review of Abbagnano's review of Collected Papers VII-VIII [S 00001]. *Humanitas* 13 (1958), 771-773.

O 01204
"Charles S. Peirce." 1910.

S 00250
The Charles S. Peirce Newsletter. Texas Tech University, Institute for Studies in Pragmaticism (biannually since 1973).

O 00517
"Charles Sanders Peirce." 1892.

S 00251
Chatterjee, Margaret. "Progress and Nature." *Dialectics and Humanism* 3 (1976), 67-71.

S 00314
_____ . *Peirce's Epistemology.* The Hague: Martinus Nijhoff, 1972.

O 00606
"Chemist." "Acetylene and Alcohol." 1895.

S 00252
Cheng, Chung-Ying. "Peirce's and Lewis's Theories of Induction." Diss. Harvard 1964.

S 00253
_____ . "Peirce's Probabilistic Theory of Inductive Validity." *Transactions* 2 (1966), 86-112.

S 00254
_____ . "Charles Peirce's Arguments for the Non-Probabilistic Validity of Induction." *Transactions* 3 (1967), 24-39.

S 00255
_____ . "A Note on Charles Peirce's Theory of Induction." *Journal of the History of Philosophy* 5 (1967), 361-364.

S 00256
_____ . "Toward a Theory of Justifying Induction." *Proceedings of the Seventh Inter-American Congress of Philosophy* 2 (1967), 177-185.

S 00257
_____ . "Requirements for the Validity of Induction: An Examination of Charles Peirce's Theory." *Philosophy and Phenomenological Research* 28 (1968), 392-402.

S 00258
_____ . *Peirce's and Lewis's Theories of Induction.* The Hague: Martinus Nijhoff, 1969.

S 00259
Cherry, Colin. *On Human Communication: A Review, a Survey and a Criticism* (New York: John Wiley, 1957), 263-267.

S 00260
Chiaraviglio, Lucio. "Pragmatic Significance." *Monist* 51 (1967), 93-103.

S 00261
Childs, John L. *Education and the Philosophy of Experimentalism* (New York: Century, 1931), 4, 6, 12, 13, 14, 17, 46, 48.

S 00262
_____ . *American Pragmatism and Education: An Interpretation and Criticism* (New York: Holt, Rinehart and Winston, 1956), esp. Part I.

S 00263
Chisholm, Roderick M. "Fallibilism and Belief," in *Studies* I [S 01549], 93-110.

S 00264
Chisholm."Die Lehre Peirces vom Pragmatismus und 'Commonsensismus'." *Unser Weg* 16 (1961), 129-139.

S 00265
Chisholm, Roderick M., et al. *Philosophy* (Englewood Cliffs, N.J.: Prentice-Hall, 1964), 10, 14, 113, 117-122, 139, 228, 256, 328-329, 343, 468, 516.

S 00266
Chomsky, Noam. *Language and Mind* (New York: Harcourt, Brace & World, 1968), 78-79.

S 00267
Church, Alonzo. Review of Keyser's "Charles Sanders Peirce as a Pioneer" [S 00758]. *Journal of Symbolic Logic* 6 (1941), 161-162.

S 00268
_____ . *Introduction to Mathematical Logic, Vol. I*. Princeton: Princeton University Press, 1956.

S 00269
_____ . "Modern Logic," in *Encyclopedia Britannica* (1956), XIV:317-323 (at 320-321).

S 00270
Churgin, Gershon.*Le pragmatisme dans la pensée américaine* (Sura: Ysra'el, 1957-58), 317-357 (in Hebrew).

O 00173
Clarke, A.R. Geodesy. 1880.

S 00271
Clarke, Bowman L. "The Argument from Design: A Piece of Abductive Reasoning." *International Journal for Philosophy of Religion* 5 (1974), 65-78.

S 00272
Clarke, David Sterling, Jr. "An Interpretation of Charles Peirce's Category of Firstness." Diss. Emory 1964.

S 00273
Clendenning, John, ed. *The Letters of Josiah Royce*. Chicago: University of Chicago Press, 1970. (Extracts from Peirce's letters to Royce at 488nn129 and 130, 490n133).

O 00434
Clerke, A.M. *The System of the Stars*. 1890.

O 00321
"The Coast Survey Inquiry." 1885.

O 00320
"The Coast Survey Scandal." 1885.

O 00341
"The Coast Survey Scandal." 1886.

S 00274
Cochrane, Rexmond C. *Measures for Progress: A History of the National Bureau of Standards* (Washington: National Bureau of Standards, 1966), 20-21, 23, 27n, 32, 33, 53n.

S 00275
Cohen, L. Jonathan. Review of M.R. Cohen's *American Thought* [S 00282]. *Philosophy* 31 (1956), 166-167.

S 00276
――――. *The Diversity of Meaning* (London: Methuen, 1962), 4-5, 265-276.

S 00277
――――. Review of Wennerberg's *Pragmatism* [S 01509]. *Philosophical Quarterly* 14 (1964), 271-272.

O 01245
Cohen, Morris R. "Charles S. Peirce and a Tentative Bibliography of his Published Writings." 1916.

S 00279
――――. ed. *Chance, Love and Logic, by Charles Sanders Peirce.* New York: Harcourt, Brace & Co., 1923. (Reprinted New York: George Braziller, 1956). (Translated by Abbagnano [S 00002]). (Reviewed by Dewey [S 00349] and Lewis [S 00834]). Notice of reissue by Gallie [S 00531]).

S 00280
――――. "The Founder of Pragmatism" (review of *Collected Papers* I-II). *Nation* 135 (1932), 368-370. (Reprinted in his *Faith of a Liberal* [New York: Henry Holt, 1946], 391-397).

S 00281
――――. Review of *Collected Papers* I-II. *Ethics* 43 (1933), 220-226.

S 00282
――――. *American Thought: A Critical Sketch,* ed. F.S. Cohen (Glencoe: The Free Press, 1954), 268-275. (Reviewed by L.J. Cohen [S 00275]).

S 00283
Collinge, Francis Brooks. "The Philosophic Method and Temper of Walter Lippmann." Diss. Washington 1964.

S 00284
Collins, James. "Philosophical Discussion in the United States: 1945" *Modern Schoolman* 24 (1947), 61-84.

S 00285
――――. Review of Feibleman's *Introduction* [S 00451]. *Modern Schoolman* 25 (1947), 43-48.

S 00286
────── . "Darwin's Impact on Philosophy." *Thought* 34 (1959), 185-248, esp. 211-219.

S 00287
────── . Notice of Boler's *Scholastic Realism* [S 00136]. *Cross Currents* 14 (1964), 458-459.

S 00288
────── . *Interpreting Modern Philosophy* (Princeton: Princeton University Press, 1972), 21, 56n, 256f, 336-339, 402n, 416, 360-376.

S 00289
Commons, John R. *Institutional Economics* (New York: Macmillan, 1934), 140-157. (Chapter IV: "Hume and Peirce").

S 00290
Conkin, Paul Keith. *Puritans and Pragmatists: Eight Eminent American Thinkers* (New York: Dodd, Mead, 1968), 193-265.

Cook, Guy S. See Heyl, P.R., and G.S. Cook [S 00660].

Cook, James E. See Ketner, Kenneth Laine, and J.E. Cook [S 00753].

S 00291
Cooper, Ted Lincoln. "The Concepts of Knowledge of Peirce and Dewey: The Relation to Education." Diss. Stanford 1970.

Cope, Jackson I. See Fisch, Max H., and J.I. Cope [S 00494].

S 00292
Copi, Irving M. "Matrix Development of the Calculus of Relations." *Journal of Symbolic Logic* 13 (1948), 193-203.

S 00293
Copleston, Frederick. Review of Boler's *Scholastic Realism* [S 00136]. *Heythrop Journal* 5 (1964), 308-310.

S 00294
────── . "The Philosophy of C.S. Peirce," in *A History of Philosophy* (London: Burns and Oates, 1966), VIII:304-329.

S 00295
Cotton, James Harry. *Royce on the Human Self* (Cambridge: Harvard University Press, 1954), 191-237 ("Royce, James, and Peirce"), 295-302 ("Royce-Peirce Correspondence").

O 00781
Couturat, Louis. *La logique de Leibniz d'après des documents inédits*. 1901.

S 00296
Crapo, Henry H., and Don D. Roberts. "Peirce's Algebras and the Distributivity Scandal" (abstract). *Journal of Symbolic Logic* 34 (1969), 153-154.

S 00297
Creary, L.G. "The Pragmatic Justification of Induction: A Critical Examination." Diss. Princeton 1969.

S 00298
Creegan, Robert F. "Radical Empiricism and Radical Historicism: Some Criticisms and a Fundamental Reconstruction." *Journal of Philosophy* 41 (1944), 126-131.

O 00414
"The Critics of Spencer." 1890.

S 00299
Crombie, E. James. "Peirce on our Knowledge of Mind: A Neglected Third Approach," in *Philosophy in the Life of a Nation* (New York: Bicentennial Symposium of Philosophy, 1976), 224-231.

S 00300
Crosser, Paul K. Review of Melvil's *Charles Peirce* [S 00926]. *Philosophy and Phenomenological Research* 32 (1971), 271-272.

O 01162
Cunningham, G.W. Review of Peirce's "Prolegomena to an Apology for Pragmaticism." 1907.

S 00301
Curley, Thomas. "Peirce's Search for a Method." Diss. Fordham 1968.

S 00302
_____ . "The Relation of the Normative Sciences to Peirce's Theory of Inquiry." *Transactions* 5 (1969), 90-106.

S 00303
Curry, Haskell B. *Foundations of Mathematical Logic* (New York: McGraw-Hill, 1963), 160-161.

S 00304
Curtis, Mattoon Monroe. "Die Philosophie in Nordamerika," in *Ueberwegs Grundriss der Geschichte der Philosophie,* 10th ed. (Basel: Benno Schwabe, 1906), IV: 553-554.

S 00305
Cust, Mrs. Henry. *Other Dimensions: A Selection from the Later Correspondence of Victoria Lady Welby* (London: Jonathan Cape, 1931), 144-150, 154-158, 161, 164, 296-314. (Contains some of Lady Welby's side of the Peirce-Welby correspondence. See Lieb [S 00839] and Hardwick [S 00616]).

S 00306
Dauben, Joseph. "Peirce's Critique of Cantorian Set Theory." *Proceedings 1976,* forthcoming.

S 00307
Daugert, Stanley Matthew. *The Philosophy of Thorstein Veblen* (New York: King's Crown Press of Columbia University, 1950), vii-viii, 3, 6, 16-25, 55, 94-96, 113.

S 00308
Davenport, Harbert William. "Peirce's Evolutionary Explanation of Laws of Nature: 1880-1893." Diss. Illinois 1977.

S 00309
_____ . "Peirce's Evolutionism and His Logic: Two Connections." *Proceedings 1976,* forthcoming.

O 00648
Davis, Ellery W. "On the Continuity of Chance." 1897.

O 01002
_____ . "Some Groups in Logic." 1903.

O 01231
_____ . "Charles Peirce at Johns Hopkins." 1914.

S 00310
Davis, H.T. Review of *Collected Papers* I. *Isis* 19 (1933), 217-220.

S 00311
Davis, John W. "The Ethics of Peirce." *Journal of Public Law* 7 (1958), 20-29.

S 00312
Davis, William H. "The Philosophy of C.S. Peirce." Diss. Rice 1965.

S 00313
──── . "Synthetic Knowledge as 'Abduction.'" *Southern Journal of Philosophy* 8 (1970), 37-43.

O 00411
Dawson, Edgar R. "Asking Too Much." 1890.

O 00420
Dawson. "The Spencer Discussion as to Reversed Velocities." 1890.

S 00315
Day, John Patrick. *Inductive Probability* (New York: Humanities Press, 1961), 131-132, 172-175, 205-211, 260, 317.

S 00316
Dearin, Ray D. Review of Bernstein's *Praxis* [S 00108]. *Philosophy and Rhetoric* 6 (1973), 192-193.

S 00317
Deely, John N. "The Two Approaches to Language: Philosophical and Historical Reflections on the Point of Departure of Jean Poinsot's Semiotic." *Thomist* 38 (1974), 856-907 (esp. 876-878).

O 00366
Defforges, Charles. "Sur L'Intensite Absolue de la Pesanteur." 1888.

S 00318
Delacre, Georges. "Peirce y su metodologia." *Dialogos* (Puerto Rico), 6 (1969), 61-77.

S 00319
──── , tr. "C.S. Peirce: 'La doctrina de la necesidad examinada.'" *Dialogos* (Puerto Rico), 9 (1973), 151-166. (Translation of "The Doctrine of Necessity Examined").

S 00320
Delaney, C.F. "Recent Work on American Philosophy." *New Scholasticism* 45 (1971), 457-477. (Reviews Ayer's *Origins* [S 00054] and Potter's *Norms and Ideals* [S 01108]).

S 00321
──── . "Peirce's Justification of Deduction." *Personalist* 53 (1972), 132-140.

S 00322
──── . "Peirce's Critique of Foundationalism." *Monist* 57 (1973), 240-251.

S 00323
──── . "Peirce on Induction and the Uniformity of Nature." *Philosophical Forum* (Boston), 4 (1973), 438-448.

S 00324
──── . "C.S. Peirce on Science and Metaphysics." *Archiv für Geschichte der Philosophie* 56 (1974), 50-70.

S 00325
———. "Foundations of Empirical Knowledge—Again." *New Scholasticism* 50 (1976), 1-19.

S 00326
Deledalle, Gérard. Review of *Studies I* [S 01549]. *Revue de Métaphysique et de Morale* 58 (1953), 212-214.

S 00327
———. *Histoire de la philosophie américaine* (Paris: Presses Universitaires de France, 1954), 92-117.

S 00328
———. "La philosophie américaine classique (1865-1940)." *Critique* (Paris), 10 (1954), 549-559.

S 00329
———. "Les origines du pragmatisme." *L'Ecole,* 1956, 269-271.

S 00330
———. Notice of Buchler's *Philosophical Writings* [S 00193]. *Etudes Philosophiques* 12 (1958), 77-78.

S 00331
———. Notice of Tomas' *Essays* [S 01428]. *Etudes Philosophiques* 13 (1958), 228.

S 00332
———. "Deux lettres de Peirce à Lady Welby sur la phaneroscopie et la sémeiologie." *Revue de Métaphysique et de Morale* 66 (1961), 398-423.

S 00333
———. "Charles S. Peirce et les maîtres à penser de la philosophie européenne d'aujourd'hui." *Etudes Philosophiques* 19 (1964), 283-294.

S 00334
———. *L'idée d'experience dans la philosophie de John Dewey* (Paris: Presses Universitaires de France, 1967), 257-270, 510-513.

S 00335
———. "Charles Sanders Peirce: La nature du pragmatisme." *Revue Philosophique de la France et de l'Etranger* 159 (1969), 31-60. (Translation of "What Pragmatism Is," with brief introduction).

S 00336
———. *Le pragmatisme: Textes choisies.* Paris: Bordas, 1971.

S 00337
———. "Présence du pragmatisme." *Revue Internationale de Philosophie* 26 (1972), 21-41.

S 00338
———. "Qu'est-ce qu'un signe? A propos de *Peirce's Concept of Sign* de Douglas Greenlee [S 00587]." *Semiotica* 10 (1974), 383-397.

S 00339
———. "Peirce ou Saussure." *Semiosis* 1 (1976), 7-13.

S 00340
———. "Peirce et Saussure." *Semiosis* 2 (1976), 18-24.

S 00341
———. "La Joconde: Théorie de l'analyse sémiotique appliquée à un portrait." *Semiosis* 4 (1976), 25-30.

S 00342
———. "For a Semiotic Reading of Peirce," in *Philosophy in the Life of a Nation* (New York: Bicentennial Symposium of Philosophy, 1976), 232-236.

S 00343
Del Valle, Agustin V.F. "Significación y sentido del pragmatismo norteamericano." *Dianoia* 18 (1972), 251-272.

S 00344
DeMarco, Joseph P. "The Nature and Function of the Concept of the Community in the Early and Later Thought of Charles Sanders Peirce." Diss. Pennsylvania State 1969.

S 00345
———. "Peirce's Concept of Community: Its Development and Change." *Transactions* 7 (1971), 24-36.

S 00346
———. "God, Religion, and Community in the Thought of C.S. Peirce." *Modern Schoolman* 49 (1972), 331-347.

S 00347
———. "Peirce's Categories and Normative Inquiry." *Journal of Value Inquiry* 7 (1973), 214-216.

O 00523
Dewey, John. "The Superstition of Necessity." 1893.

O 00960
———. "Tychism." 1902.

O 01242
———. "The Pragmatism of Peirce." 1916.

S 00348
———. "Pragmatic America." *New Republic* 30 (1922), 185-187.

S 00349
———. Review of Cohen's *Chance, Love, and Logic* [S 00279]. *New Republic* 39 (1924), 136-137.

S 00350
———. "The Development of American Pragmatism." *Studies in the History of Ideas* 2 (1925), 353-377. (Reprinted in *Twentieth Century Philosophy,* ed. Runes [New York: Philosophical Library, 1947], 452-468; an earlier French version appeared in *Revue de Metaphysique et de Morale* 29 [1922], 411-430).

S 00351
———. "Charles Sanders Peirce" (review of *Collected Papers* I). *New Republic* 69 (1932), 220-221.

S 00352
———. "The Founder of Pragmatism" (review of *Collected Papers* V). *New Republic* 81 (1935), 338-339.

S 00353
———. "Peirce's Theory of Quality." *Journal of Philosophy* 32 (1935), 701-708.

S 00354
———. "What Are Universals?" *Journal of Philosophy* 33 (1936), 281-288.

S 00355
———. "Charles Sanders Peirce" (review of *Collected Papers* I - VI). *New Republic* 89 (1937), 415-416.

S 00356
———. *Logic: The Theory of Inquiry* (New York: Henry Holt, 1938), 9n, 12, 14, 156, 468, 470.

S 00357
———. "Experience, Knowledge and Value: A Rejoinder," in *The Philosophy of John Dewey*, ed. P.A. Schilpp (Evanston, Ill.: Northwestern University Press, 1939), 517-608 (esp. 572-574).

S 00358
———. "Peirce's Theory of Linguistic Signs, Thought, and Meaning." *Journal of Philosophy* 43 (1946), 85-95. (Letter by Charles Morris, 196; reply by Dewey, 280; rejoinder by Morris, 363-364).

S 00359
Dewey, John, and Arthur F. Bentley. *Knowing and the Known.* Boston: Beacon Press, 1949.

S 00360
———. *A Philosophical Correspondence, 1932-1951,* ed. Sidney Ratner and Jules Altman (New Brunswick, N.J.: Rutgers University Press, 1964).

S 00361
Dilworth, David. "The Platonism-Pragmatism Polarity in Whitehead's Thought." Diss. Fordham 1963.

S 00362
Dipert, Randall R. "Peirce on Mach and Absolute Space." *Transactions* 9 (1973), 79-94.

S 00363
———. "Peirce's Theory of the Dimensionality of Physical Space." *Proceedings 1976,* forthcoming.

S 00364
Dobrosielski, Marian. "The Origins and Genesis of Charles Sanders Peirce's Pragmatism" (in Polish). *Studia Filozoficzne* 2 (1965), 85-114.

S 00365
———. "O Peirce'owskiej koncepcji watpeinia i prezekoania." *Studia Filozoficzne* 2 (1966), 107-137.

S 00366
———. *Filozoficzny pragmatyzn Charles Sanders Peirce'a.* Warsaw: Panstwowe Wydavon, Maukowe, 1967.

S 00367
———. "On C.S. Peirce's Conception of Doubt and Belief." *Studia Filozoficzne* 4 (1970), 5-34.

Doering, Carl R. See Wilson, Edwin B., and C.R. Doering [S 01558].

D 00299
Doolittle, M.H. "The Verification of Predictions." 1885.

S 00368
Dopp, Joseph. Notice of Tomas' *Essays* [S 01428]. *Revue Philosophique de Louvain* 55 (1957), 304.

S 00369
Dougherty, Charles J. "Phenomenological Critiques of Empiricism: A Study in the Philosophies of Husserl and Peirce." Diss. Notre Dame 1975.

S 00370
―――― . "C.S. Peirce's Critique of Psychologism," in *Philosophy in the Life of a Nation* (New York: Bicentennial Symposium of Philosophy, 1976), 237-241.

S 00371
Doyle, Marcian. "The Influence of John Duns Scotus on the Philosophy of Charles Sanders Peirce." M.A. thesis St. Bonaventure 1950.

S 00372
Driscoll, Leo Cornelius. "Methodology of Charles Sanders Peirce." Diss. Fordham 1964.

S 00373
Dubisch, Roy. *The Nature of Number* (New York: Ronald Press, 1952), 117-118.

S 00374
―――― . *Lattices to Logic* (New York: Blaisdell, 1964), 60. (Reviewed by Mullin [S 00997]).

S 00375
Dozoretz, Jerry. "Indubitability and Truth in Peirce's Epistemic Methodology." Diss. California at Santa Barbara 1977.

S 00376
Ducasse, Curt John. Review of *Collected Papers* III. *Saturday Review of Literature* 10 (16 September 1933), 123.

S 00377
―――― . Review of *Collected Papers* IV - V. *Saturday Review of Literature* 11 (22 September 1934), 132.

S 00378
―――― . Letter to Louis J. Lehrman concerning C.S. Peirce. *Social Casework* 36 (1955), 424.

S 00379
Dupuis, Adrian. "The Educational Theory of Charles Sanders Peirce." *Catholic Educational Review* 54 (1956), 179-189.

S 00380
Dürr, Karl. "Lewis and the History of Symbolic Logic," in *The Philosophy of C.I. Lewis,* ed. P.A. Schilpp (La Salle, Ill.: Open Court, 1968), 89-114.

S 00381
Dykeman, King J. "Charles S. Peirce: The Minute Logic" (abstract). *International Federation of Philosophical Societies: Abstracts of Communications Presented at the XVth World Congress of Philosophy, Varna* (Sofia: Bulgarian Organizing Committee, 1973), No. 391.

O 00406
E., R.G. "A Call for Specifications." 1890.

O 00421
―――― . "Force and Life." 1890.

S 00382
Eco, Umberto. *Einführung in die Semiotik.* Munich: Fink, 1972. (German version of *La struttura assente*).

S 00383
———. "Looking for a Logic of Culture." *Times Literary Supplement,* 5 October 1973, 1149-1150.

S 00384
———. *A Theory of Semiotics.* Bloomington: Indiana University Press, 1976. (Reviewed by Walther [S 01483]).

S 00385
———. "Final Interpretant and Dynamical Object." *Proceedings 1976,* forthcoming.

S 00386
Edwards, Paul, ed. *Encyclopedia of Philosophy.* 8 vols. New York: Macmillan and The Free Press, 1967. (Reviewed by Alston [S 00386] and Hesse [S 00659].

S 00387
Eisele, Carolyn. "Charles S. Peirce and the Mathematics of Economics." *Proceedings of the XIII International Congress of the History of Science* (Moscow, 1974), V: 171-175.

S 00388
——— "The *Liber Abaci* through the Eyes of Charles Sanders Peirce." *Scripta Mathematica* 17 (Sept.-Dec. 1951), 236-259.

S 00389
———. "Charles Sanders Peirce and the History of Science." *Year Book of the American Philosophical Society,* 1954, 353-358.

S 00390
———. "Charles Sanders Peirce, American Historian of Science." *Actes du VIIIe Congres International d'Histoire des Sciences* (Florence, 3-9 September 1956), 1196-1200.

S 00391
———. "The Scientist-Philosopher C.S. Peirce at the Smithsonian." *Journal of the History of Ideas* 18 (1957), 537-547.

S 00392
———. "The Charles Sanders Peirce-Simon Newcomb Correspondence." *Proceedings of the American Philosophical Society* 101 (October 1957), 409-433.

S 00393
———. "Some Remarks on the Logic of Science of the Seventeenth Century as Interpreted by Charles Sanders Peirce." *Actes du IIe Symposium International d'Histoire des Sciences* (Pise-Vinci, 16-18 June 1958), 55-64.

S 00394
———. Review of Gardner's *Logic Machines* [S 00543]. *Scripta Mathematica* 24 (1959), 241-242.

S 00395
———. "Charles S. Peirce, Nineteenth Century Man of Science." *Scripta Mathematica* 24 (1959), 305-324.

S 00396
———. "Poincare's Positivism in the Light of Charles Sanders Peirce's Realism." *Actes du IXe Congres International d'Histoire des Sciences* (Barcelona-Madrid, 1959), 461-465.

S 00397
———— . Review of *Collected Papers* VII - VIII. *Scripta Mathematica* 25 (1960), 74-75.

S 00398
———— . "Charles Sanders Peirce and the Problem of Map-Projection." *Proceedings of the American Philosophical Society* 107 (1963), 299-307.

S 00399
———— . "Fermatian Inference and DeMorgan's Syllogism of Transposed Quantity in Peirce's Logic of Science." *Physis: Rivista di Storia della Scienza* 5 (1963), 120-128.

S 00400
———— . "The Influence of Galileo on the Thought of Charles Sanders Peirce." *Atti del Simposio su Galileo Galilei nella Storia e nella Filosofia della Scienza* (Florence-Pisa, 1964), 321-328.

S 00401
———— . "Peirce's Philosophy of Education in his Unpublished Mathematics Textbooks," in *Studies* II [S 00968], 51-75.

S 00402
———— . "The Mathematics of Charles Sanders Peirce." *Actes du XIe Congres International d'Histoire des Sciences* (Warsaw, 1965), 229-234.

S 00403
———— . "The Binary Arithmetic of Charles Sanders Peirce." *International Congress of Mathematicians, Moscow: Abstracts of Brief Scientific Communications* 15 (1966), 5-6.

S 00404
———— . "Charles Sanders Peirce and the Mathematics of the Nineteenth Century" (abstract). *International Congress of Mathematicians, Nice: Les 265 Communications Individuelles* (1970), 285.

S 00405
———— . "Charles Sanders Peirce and the Scientific Philosophy of Ernst Mach." *Actes du XIIIe Congres International d'Histoire des Sciences* (Paris, 1970), II:33-40.

S 00406
———— . "President's Report: Charles S. Peirce Society." *The Charles S. Peirce Newsletter*, November 1973.

S 00407
———— . "Charles Sanders Peirce," in *Dictionary of Scientific Biography,* ed. C.C. Gillispie (New York: Scribner's, 1974), X:482-488.

S 00408
———— . "C.S. Peirce's Search for a Method in Mathematics and the History of Science." *Transactions* 11 (1975), 149-158.

S 00409
———— . "Salomon Bochner on Charles S. Peirce. I." *American Mathematical Monthly* 82 (1975), 477-478. (Criticism of Bochner [S 00134]).

S 00410
———— . "The New Elements of Mathematics by Charles S. Peirce," in *Men and Institutions in American Mathematics,* ed. J.D. Tarwater, J.T. White, and J.D. Miller (Lubbock: Texas Tech Press, 1976), 111-121.

S 00411
—— , ed. *The New Elements of Mathematics, by Charles Sanders Peirce.* 4 vols. (in 5). The Hague: Mouton, 1976.

S 00412
—— . "Modern Mathematical Exactitude in Peirce's 'Doctrine of Exact Philosophy.'" *Proceedings 1976,* forthcoming.

S 00413
Elliott, Richard Lee. "The Hypothesis of Creative Evolution in the Philosophy of Charles Sanders Peirce." Diss. New Mexico 1974.

S 00414
Elton, William. "Peirce's Marginalia in W.T. Harris' *Hegel's Logic."* Journal of the History of Philosophy 2 (1964), 82-84.

O 01149
Enriques, F. "Prinzipien der Geometrie." 1907-1910.

S 00415
Erpenbeck, James. "The Relation of Pragmatism and Realism in the Philosophy of C.S. Peirce." Diss. Notre Dame 1965.

S 00416
—— . Review of Boler's *Scholastic Realism* [S 00136] . *New Scholasticism* 39 (1965), 246-249.

S 00417
Eschbach, Achim, and Wendelin Rader, eds. *Semiotik-Bibliographie I.* Frankfurt: Syndikat, 1976.

S 00418
Esposito, Joseph L. "Synechism, Socialism, and Cybernetics." *Transactions* 9 (1973), 63-78.

S 00419
—— . "Remarks Toward a General Theory of Organization." *International Journal of General Systems* 2 (1975), 133-143.

S 00420
—— . *Schelling's Idealism and Philosophy of Nature* (Lewisburg, Pa.: Bucknell University Press, 1976), Ch. 7.

S 00421
—— . "Peirce and *Naturphilosophie."* *Transactions* 13 (1977), 122-141.

S 00422
—— . "Peirce's Early Speculations on the Categories." *Proceedings 1976,* forthcoming.

S 00423
Evans, D. Luther. Review of Schneider's *History* [S 01303] . *Philosophy and Phenomenological Research* 8 (1948), 463-465.

O 00330
"Executive Proceedings." 1886.

O 00318
"Exorbitant Expenditures." 1885.

O 00426
"Facts about Spencer." 1890.

S 00424
Fain, Haskell. "A Comparison of the Theories of Logic of John Dewey and Charles Sanders Peirce." M.A. thesis Illinois 1949.

O 00415
"A Fair Field and No Favor." 1890.

S 00425
Fairbanks, Matthew J. "C.S. Peirce and Nineteenth Century Positivism." Diss. Notre Dame 1961.

S 00426
―――― . "A Note Concerning Peirce's Debt to Hegel." *New Scholasticism* 36 (1962), 219-224.

S 00427
―――― . "C.S. Peirce and Logical Atomism." *New Scholasticism* 38 (1964), 178-188.

S 00428
―――― . "Charles Sanders Peirce and Positivism." *Modern Schoolman* 41 (1964), 323-337.

S 00429
―――― . "Peirce and the Positivists on Knowledge." *Transactions* 6 (1970), 111-122.

S 00430
―――― . Review of Gallie's *Pragmatism* [S 00534]. *Modern Schoolman* 47 (1970), 357-360.

S 00431
―――― . "Peirce on Man as a Language: A Textual Interpretation." *Transactions* 12 (1976), 18-32.

S 00432
―――― . "Peirce: 'My Language is the Sum Total of Myself'; A Timed Interpretation." *Proceedings 1976,* forthcoming.

S 00433
―――― . "Reality as Language in the Peircean Semiotic." *Proceedings of the First Annual Conference of the Semiotic Society of America* (Atlanta, 1976), forthcoming.

S 00434
Fann, Kuang Tih. "Charles Sanders Peirce's Theory of Abduction." M.A. thesis Illinois 1964.

S 00435
―――― . *Peirce's Theory of Abduction.* The Hague: Mouton, 1970. (Reviewed by Walsh [S 01477]).

S 00436
Farber, Marvin. *The Foundation of Phenomenology* (Cambridge: Harvard University Press, 1943), 85-86.

S 00437
―――― . *Philosophic Thought in France and the United States* (University of Buffalo Publications in Philosophy, 1950), 420-421.

S 00438
―――― . "Le monde-de-la-vie et la tradition de la philosophie américaine." *Etudes Philosophiques* 19 (1964), 209-219.

S 00439
———. *Phenomenology and Existence: Toward a Philosophy within Nature* (New York: Harper and Row, 1967), 15f., 34.

O 00298
Farquhar, Henry. "Empirical Formulae for the Diminution of Amplitude of a Freely-Oscillating Pendulum." 1885.

O 00267
Farrer, T.H. Report of the Board of Trade on their Proceedings and Business under the Weights and Measures Act, 1878. Great Britain, House of Commons. 1883.

S 00440
Faruki, Mohamed Zuhdi Taji. "The Universal Categories of Charles Sanders Peirce." Diss. Indiana 1957.

O 00140
Faye, Hervé. "Théorie mathématique des oscillations d'un pendule double, par M. Peirce." 1879.

O 00172
———. "Rapport sur un Mémoire de M. Peirce concernant la constante de la pesanteur a Paris." 1880.

S 00441
Feibleman, James K. "Une philosophie américaine: La doctrine de Charles Sanders Peirce." *Revue de Métaphysique et de Morale* 46 (1939), 443-459.

S 00442
———. "Peirce's Phanerosocopy." *Philosophy and Phenomenological Research* 1 (1940), 208-216.

S 00443
———. "The Esthetics of Peirce." *Personalist* 22 (1941), 263-273.

S 00444
———. "Systematic Presentation of Peirce's Ethics." *Ethics* 53 (1943), 98-109.

S 00445
———. "Reid and the Origins of Modern Realism." *Journal of the History of Ideas* 5 (1944), 113-120.

S 00446
———. "Individual Psychology and the Ethics of Peirce." *Journal of General Psychology* 31 (1944), 293-295. (Reprinted in his *Revival of Realism* [S 00452], 320-323).

S 00447
———. "The Influence of Peirce on Dewey's Logic." *Education* 66 (1945), 18-24.

S 00448
———. "The Hypothesis of Esthetic Measure," *Philosophy of Science* 12 (1945), 194-217.

S 00449
———. "Peirce's Use of Kant." *Journal of Philosophy* 42 (1945), 365-377.

S 00450
———. "Pragmatism and Inverse Probability." *Philosophy and Phenomenological Research* 5 (1945), 309-319.

S 00451
———. *An Introduction to Peirce's Philosophy Interpreted as a System,* with a foreword by Bertrand Russell. New York: Harper, 1946. (Reprinted Cambridge, Mass.: M.I.T. Press, 1970). (Reviewed by Black [S 00121], Buchler [S 00195], Collins [S 00285], Hartshorne [S 00632], Holmes [S 00683], Morse [S 00987], O'Conner [S 01047], Pollock [S 01102], Anonymous [S 01179], and Schlaretzki [S 01289]).

S 00452
———. *The Revival of Realism: Critical Studies in Contemporary Philosophy* (Chapel Hill: University of North Carolina Press, 1946 [reprinted Port Washington, N.Y.: Kennikat Press, 1972]), esp. 31-45 and 320-323.

S 00453
———. "On the Future of Some of Peirce's Ideas," in *Studies* I [S 01549], 325-334.

S 00454
———. Review of *Collected Papers* VII - VIII. *Philosophy and Phenomenological Research* 20 (1960). 424-425.

S 00455
———. *Foundations of Empiricism*. The Hague: Martinus Nijhoff, 1962.

S 00456
———. *The Two-Story World: Selected Writings,* ed. Huntington Cairns (New York: Holt, Rinehart and Winston, 1966), 483-485.

S 00457
———. "The Leisurely Attitude." *Humanitas* 8 (1972), 279-285.

S 00458
Feldstein, Leonard C. "The Norms of Science: An Evaluation of the Views of Meyerson, Duhem and Peirce." Diss. Columbia 1957.

S 00459
Ferrater Mora, José. "Peirce's Conception of Architectonic and Related Views." *Philosophy and Phenomenological Research* 15 (1955), 351-359.

S 00460
———. "Charles Sanders Peirce," in *Diccionario de filosofía,* 4th ed. (Buenos Aires, 1958), 1036-1037.

S 00461
Ferris, William Henry. "The Distortion of Pragmatism: How Practical-Minded Men, Including Philosophers, Translated an Epistemological Discipline into a Sociological Instrument." Diss. Vanderbilt 1965.

S 00462
Feuer, Lewis S. Review of *Collected Papers* I. *The Campus* (City College of New York), 2 (4 December 1931), 4-6.

S 00463
———. Review of *Collected Papers* VI. *Isis* 26 (1936), 203-208.

S 00464
Findlay, J.N. "Probability Without Nonsense." *Philosophical Quarterly* 2 (1952), 218-239.

S 00465
Fisch, Max H. "Charles Sanders Peirce," in Anderson and Fisch's *Philosophy in America* [S 00030], 447-452.

S 00466
———. "Justice Holmes, the Prediction Theory of Law, and Pragmatism." *Journal of Philosophy* 39 (1942), 85-97.

S 00467
———. "Evolution in American Philosophy." *Philosophical Review* 56 (1947), 357-373.

S 00468
———. Review of Werkmeister's *History* [S 01512] and Weiner's *Evolution* [S 01533]. *American Literature* 22 (1950), 185-189. (Quotes passages from Peirce's unpublished papers concerning the Metaphysical Club at Cambridge).

S 00469
———, ed. *Classic American Philosophers*. New York: Appleton-Century-Crofts, 1951. (Reviewed by Blau [S 00127] and Welsh [S 01508]).

S 00470
———. "General Introduction," in his *Classic American Philosophers* [S 00469], 1-39.

S 00471
———. Review of Blau's *Men and Movements* [S 00128]. *Journal of Philosophy* 49 (1952), 675-677.

S 00472
———. "Alexander Bain and the Genealogy of Pragmatism." *Journal of the History of Ideas* 15 (1954), 413-444.

S 00473
———. Review of Moore's *American Pragmatism* [S 00963]. *American Literature* 34 (1962), 138-140.

S 00474
———. "A Chronicle of Pragmatism, 1865-1879." *Monist* 48 (1964), 441-446.

S 00475
———. "Was There a Metaphysical Club in Cambridge?" in *Studies* II [S 00968], 3-32.

S 00476
———. "A First Supplement to Arthur W. Burks's Bibliography of the Works of Charles Sanders Peirce," in *Studies* II [S 00968], 477-485.

S 00477
———. "Philosophical Clubs in Cambridge and Boston from Peirce's Metaphysical Club to Harris's Hegel Club." *Coranto* 2:1 (1964), 12-23; 2:2 (1965), 12-25; 3:1 (1965), 16-29.

S 00478
———. "Some Correspondents of Charles Sanders Peirce." *Transactions* 1 (1965), 26-31.

S 00479
———. "Peirce's Progress from Nominalism Toward Realism." *Monist* 51 (1967), 159-178. (Criticized by Roberts [S 01200]).

S 00480
———. "Vico and Pragmatism," in *Giambattista Vico: An International Symposium,* ed. Giorgio Tagliacozzo (Baltimore: The Johns Hopkins Press, 1969), 401-424.

S 00481
———. "Dewey's Critical and Historical Studies," in *Guide to the Works of John Dewey,* ed. Jo Ann Boydston (Carbondale: Southern Illinois University Press, 1970), 306-338.

S 00482
———. "Peirce's Arisbe: The Greek Influence in His Later Philosophy." *Transactions* 7 (1971), 187-210.

S 00483
———. "Peirce and Leibniz." *Journal of the History of Ideas* 33 (1972), 485-496.

S 00484
———. "The Peirce Homestead as a National Memorial." *Transactions* 8 (1972), 123-127.

S 00485
———. "Final Report of the Committee on the Peirce Homestead." *Transactions* 9, (1973), 55-59.

S 00486
———. "Supplements to the Peirce Bibliographies." *Transactions* 10 (1974), 94-129.

S 00487
———. "Peirce and the History of Science" (Introduction to a Symposium on Peirce as Scientist, Mathematician, and Historian of Science). *Transactions* 11 (1975), 145-148.

S 00488
———. "Hegel and Peirce," in *Hegel and the History of Philosophy,* ed. J.J. O'Malley, F.G. Weiss, and K.W. Algozin (The Hague: Martinus Nijhoff, 1975), 171-193.

S 00489
———. "Salomon Bochner on Charles S. Peirce.II." *American Mathematical Monthly* 82 (1975), 478-481. (Criticism of Bochner [S 00134]).

S 00490
———. "American Pragmatism Before and After 1898," in *American Philosophy from Edwards to Quine,* ed. Robert W. Shahan and Kenneth R. Merrill (Norman: University of Oklahoma Press, 1977), 77-110.

S 00491
———. "Peirce as Scientist, Mathematician, Logician and Philosopher." *Proceedings 1976,* forthcoming.

S 00492
———. "Peirce's General Theory of Signs," in *Sight, Sound and Sense,* ed. Thomas A. Sebeok (Bloomington: Indiana University Press), forthcoming.

S 00493
———. "The 'Proof' of Pragmatism," in a volume in honor of Thomas A. Goudge (Toronto: University of Toronto Press), forthcoming.

Fisch, Max H. See Anderson, Paul Russell, and M.H. Fisch [S 00030].

S 00494
Fisch, Max H., and Jackson I. Cope. "Peirce at The Johns Hopkins University," in *Studies I* [S 01549], 277-311, 355-360, 363-374. (Reviewed by Wells [S 01503]).

S 00495
Fisch, Max H., and Daniel C. Haskell. "Some Additions to Morris R. Cohen's Bibliography of Peirce's Published Writings," in *Studies* I [S 01549], 375-381.

S 00496
Fisch, Max H., and Atwell Turquette. "Peirce's Triadic Logic." *Transactions* 2 (1966), 71-85. (Noticed by Tucker [S 01440]).

S 00497
Fisch, Max H., Barbara E. Kretzmann, and Victor F. Lenzen. "A Draft of a Bibliography of Writings About Charles Sanders Peirce," in *Studies* II [S 00968], 486-514.

S 00498
Fisch, William Bales. "Charles Peirce's Theory of the Nature of Thought." B.A. thesis Harvard 1957.

S 00499
Fischl, Johann. *Geschichte der Philosophie* (Graz: Altgötting, 1953), IV: 336-338.

S 00500
Fitch, Frederic B. Review of Morris' *Foundations* [S 00981]. *Philosophical Review* 49 (1940), 678-680.

S 00501
_____ . "Peirce's Axioms for Propositional Calculus by A.N. Prior. Critique." *Journal of Symbolic Logic* 25 (1960), 87. (Critique of Prior [S 01122]).

S 00502
Fitzgerald, John J. "Peirce's Theory of Signs as the Foundation of his Pragmatism." Diss. Tulane 1962.

S 00503
_____ . Review of Moore's *American Pragmatism* [S 00963]. *New Scholasticism* 36 (1962), 406-408.

S 00504
_____ . Review of Smith's *Spirit* [S 01357]. *New Scholasticism* 38 (1964), 267-270.

S 00505
_____ . Review of Murphey's *Development* [S 01001]. *Modern Schoolman* 41 (1964), 287-289.

S 00506
_____ . "Peirce's 'How to Make Our Ideas Clear.'" *New Scholasticism* 39 (1965), 53-68.

S 00507
_____ . Review of *Studies* II [S 00968]. *International Philosophical Quarterly* 5 (1965), 677-686.

S 00508
_____ . *Peirce's Theory of Signs as Foundation for Pragmatism.* The Hague: Moutor, 1966. (Reviewed by Potter [S 01109]).

S 00509
_____ . "Peirce's Theory of Inquiry." *Transactions* 4 (1968), 130-143.

S 00510
_____ . "Peirce's Argument for Thirdness." *New Scholasticism* 45 (1971), 409-426.

S 00511
──── . "Ambiguity in Peirce's Theory of Signs." *Transactions* 12 (1976), 127-134. (Criticism of Greenlee [S 00587] ; see also Greenlee's reply [S 00589]).

S 00512
Fraenkel, Abraham A. *Abstract Set Theory* (Amsterdam: North Holland, 1953), 40, 163n, 180n, 272.

S 00513
Fragata, Julio. Review of Bosco's "Charles Sanders Peirce" [S 00143]. *Revista Portuguesa de Filosofia* (Supplemento Bibliografico), 5 (1963), 23.

S 00514
Frank, Jerome. "A Conflict with Oblivion: Some Observations on the Founders of Legal Pragmatism." *Rutgers Law Review* 9 (1954), 424-463.

S 00515
Frank, William A. Notice of Reilly's *Theory of Scientific Method* [S 01162]. *Review of Metaphysics* 26 (1973), 544.

S 00516
Frankel, Charles. *The Golden Age of American Philosophy* (New York: George Braziller, 1960), 47-112.

S 00517
Frankfurt, Harry G. "Peirce's Account of Inquiry." *Journal of Philosophy* 55 (1958), 588-592. (Reply by Murphree [S 01006]).

S 00518
──── . "Peirce's Notion of Abduction." *Journal of Philosophy* 55 (1958), 593-597.

S 00519
──── . "Meaning, Truth and Pragmatism." *Philosophical Quarterly,* 10 (1960), 171-176.

O 01234
Franklin, Fabian. "The Lonely Heights of Science." 1914.

S 00520
Freeman, Eugene. "The Categories of Charles Peirce." Diss. Chicago 1934.

S 00521
──── . *The Categories of Charles Peirce.* La Salle, Ill.: Open Court, 1934. Reviewed by Malik [S 00890], Nagel [S 01017] and Pape [S 01073]).

S 00522
──── . "Objectivity as 'Intersubjective Agreement.'" *Monist* 57 (1973), 168-175.

S 00523
Freeman, Eugene, and Henryk Skolimowski. "The Search for Objectivity in Peirce and Popper," in *The Philosophy of Karl Popper,* ed. P.A. Schilpp (La Salle, Ill.: Open Court, 1974), I:464-519.

S 00524
Fries, Horace. Review of Wiener's *Evolution* [S 01533]. *Philosophy of Science* 17 (1950), 357.

O 00634
Frischauf, I. "Bemerkungen zu Peirces Quincuncial Projection." 1897.

S 00525
Fuller, B.A.G., and Sterling M. McMurrin. *A History of Philosophy.* New York: Holt, Rinehart and Winston, 1955.

O 01122
Fullerton, George Stuart. *An Introduction to Philosophy.* 1906.

S 00526
Furness, Caroline Ellen. *An Introduction to the Study of Variable Stars* (Boston: Houghton Mifflin, 1915), 82, 88-91.

O 01037
Furtwängler, Philip. "Die Mechanik der einfachsten physikalischen Apparate und Versuchsanordnungen." 1904.

Furtwängler, Philip. See Kühner, Fr., and P. Furtwangler [O 01148].

S 00527
G., T. Notice of *Collected Papers* VI. *Nature* 138 (1936), 1037.

S 00528
Gagarin, A.P. *Pragmatizm SSHA.* Moscow: Izdatelstvo Moskovskogo Universiteta, 1963.

S 00529
Gale, Richard M., and Irving Thalberg. "The Generality of Predictions." *Journal of Philosophy* 62 (1965), 195-210.

S 00530
Gallie, W.B. "The Metaphysics of Charles S. Peirce." *Proceedings of the Aristotelian Society* 47 (1946-1947), 27-62.

S 00531
———. Notice of reissue of Cohen's *Chance, Love and Logic* [S 00279]. *Mind,* NS 59 (1950), 282.

S 00532
———. Review of Wiener's Evolution [S 01533]. *Mind,* NS 60 (1951), 433-435.

S 00533
———. "Peirce's Pragmaticism," in *Studies* I [S 01549], 61-74.

S 00534
———. *Peirce and Pragmatism.* Harmondsworth, Middlesex: Penguin, 1952 (rev. ed. New York: Dover, 1966). Reviewed by Fairbanks [S 00430], Goudge [S 00567], Lieb [S 00840], Mayo [S 00911], anonymous [S 01180] and [S 01181], Savan [S 01270], Schalretzki [S 01292], and Wiener [S 01535]).

S 00535
———. Review of von Kempski's *Pragmatismus* [S 00742]. *Philosophical Quarterly* (St. Andrews), 3 (1953), 369.

S 00536
———. Review of Thompson's *Pragmatic Philosophy* [S 01416]. *Philosophical Quarterly* (St. Andrews), 7 (1957), 91-92.

S 00537
———. Review of Wiener's *Values* [S 01538]. *Philosophical Studies* 9 (1959), 200.

S 00538
———. Review of *Collected Papers* VII-VIII. *Philosophy* 35 (1960), 66-68.

S 00539
―――. Review of Murphey's *Development* [S 01001]. *Philosophical Books* (1962), 10-11.

S 00540
―――. Review of Moore's *American Pragmatism* [S 00963]. *Philosophical Books* 3:2 (1962), 16.

S 00541
―――. Review of Bosco's *Filosofia pragmatica* [S 00149]. *Philosophical Quarterly* 14 (1964), 371-372.

S 00542
―――. "The Idea of Practice." *Proceedings of the Aristotelian Society* 68 (1967-68), 63-86.

S 00543
Gardner, Martin. *Logic Machines and Diagrams* New York: McGraw-Hill, 1958. (Reviewed by Eisele [S 00394]).

S 00544
―――. "Mathematical Games: On Map Projections (with special reference to some inspired ones)." *Scientific American* 233:5 (November 1975), 120-125.

S 00545
Geiger, George R. Review of Goudge's *Thought* [S 00565]. *Philosophy of Science* 19 (1952), 182.

S 00546
―――. "Le pragmatisme" (tr. Gerard Deledalle). *Etudes Philosophiques* 19 (1964), 221-232.

S 00547
Geller, P. "Nietzsche, Peirce, et le désaven du sujet." *Annales Publiées Trimestriellement par l'Université de Toulouse: Le Mirail — Philosophie 1,* 8:3 (1972), 95-110.

S 00548
Gentry, George. "Peirce's Early and Later Theory of Cognition and Meaning: Some Critical Comments." *Philosophical Review* 55 (1946), 634-650.

S 00549
―――. "Habit and the Logical Interpretant," in *Studies* I [S 01549], 75-90.

O 00323
"The Geological Survey Next." 1885.

O 01236
Geyer, Denton Loring. *The Pragmatic Theory of Truth as Developed by Peirce, James, and Dewey.* 1914.

O 00329
Gibbs, J. Willard. "Multiple Algebra." 1886.

S 00550
Giere, Ronald Nelson. "Prediction and Confirmation." Diss. Cornell 1968.

S 00551
Gilardoni, G., ed. and tr. *Charles Sanders Peirce: Pragmatismo e pragmaticismo — Saggi scelti.* Padova: Liviana, 1966.

S 00552
Gill, Jerry H. Review of Bernstein's *Perspectives* [S 00105]. *Philosophy and Phenomenological Research* 27 (1967), 458-460.

O 00231
Gilman, B.I. "On Propositions called Spurious." 1882.

S 00553
Gilman, Daniel C., and Jackson I. Cope. "William James' Correspondence with Daniel Coit Gilman, 1877-1881." *Journal of the History of Ideas* 12 (1951), 609-627. (Contains a letter from Peirce to Gilman, dated 13 September 1877, p. 615-616).

S 00554
Glasow, U. "Realität und Wahrheit im Pragmatismus von Charles Sanders Peirce (1839-1914)." *Wissenschaftliche Zeitschrift der Universität Rostock* 21 (1972), 539-544.

Goldfeld, Stephen M. See Baumol, William J., and S.M. Goldfeld [S 00071].

S 00555
Goodman, Leo A., and William H. Kruskal. "Measures of Association for Cross Classifications, II: Further Discussion and References." *Journal of the American Statistical Association* 54 (1959), 123-163, at 127, 129-130, 149, 152.

S 00556
Goodwin, Robert P. "The Metaphysical Pragmatism of Charles Sanders Peirce." Diss. Georgetown 1958.

S 00557
———. "Charles Sanders Peirce: A Modern Scotist?" *New Scholasticism* 35 (1961), 478-509.

S 00558
Goudge, Thomas A. "The Views of Charles Peirce on the Given in Experience." *Journal of Philosophy* 32 (1935), 533-544.

S 00559
———. "Further Reflections on Peirce's Doctrine of the Given." *Journal of Philosophy* 33 (1936), 289-295.

S 00560
———. "The Theory of Knowledge in Charles S. Peirce." Diss. Toronto 1937.

S 00561
———. "Peirce's Treatment of Induction." *Philosophy of Science* 7 (1940), 56-68.

S 00562
———. Review of Buchler's *Empiricism* [S 00188]. *Journal of Philosophy* 37 (1940), 274-276.

S 00563
———. "Charles Peirce, Pioneer in American Thought." *University of Toronto Quarterly* 12 (1942-43), 403-414.

S 00564
———. "The Conflict of Naturalism and Transcendentalism in Peirce." *Journal of Philosophy* 44 (1947), 365-375.

S 00565
───── . *The Thought of C.S. Peirce.* Toronto: University of Toronto Press, 1950. (Peirce's entry in the Harvard class book of 1859, written shortly after his graduation, is reprinted at p. 347-349. The information contained here differs from that of Peirce's biography in the class book, *Harvard College, Records of the Class of 1859,* Cambridge, 1896, p. 49-50 [Cf. p. 9, 74, 76, and 77]). (Reviewed by Bierstedt [S 00113], Geiger [S 00565], Holland [S 00678], Reese [S 01155], anonymous [S 01182], Schlaretzki [S 01291], Smith, J.W. [S 01353], and Thompson [S 01414].

S 00566
───── . "Peirce's Theory of Abstraction," in *Studies* I [S 01549], 121-132.

S 00567
───── . Review of Gallie's *Pragmatism* [S 00534]. *Mind,* NS 63 (1954), 279-281.

S 00568
───── . Review of Wiener's *Values* [S 01538]. *Journal of Philosophy* 55 (1958), 609-610.

S 00569
───── . "Peirce's Evolutionism — After Half a Century," in *Studies* II [S 00968], 323-341.

S 00570
───── . Review of Murphey's *Development* [S 01001] and Wennerberg's *Pragmatism* [S 01509]. *Mind,* NS 73 (1964), 602-603.

S 00571
───── . "Peirce's Index." *Transactions* 1 (1965), 52-70.

S 00572
───── . Review of Thayer's *Meaning and Action* [S 01402]. *Dialogue* 8 (1969), 508-510.

S 00573
───── . "Pragmatism's Contribution to an Evolutionary View of Mind." *Monist* 57 (1973), 133-150.

S 00574
Gouinlock, James. Review of Scheffler's *Four Pragmatists* [S 01281]. *Philosophy and Phenomenological Research* 36 (1976), 436-437.

S 00575
Gould, James A. "R.B. Perry on the Origin of American and European Pragmatism." *Journal of the History of Philosophy* 8 (1970), 431-450.

S 00576
Gowin, D.B. "Teaching, Learning and Thirdness." *Studies in Philosophy and Education* 1 (1961), 87-113.

S 00577
Grathoff, R. "Grenze und Übergang: Bestimmungen einer cartesianischen Sozialwissenschaft." *Soziale Welt* 23 (1972), 383-400.

S 00578
Grattan-Guinness, I. "Wiener on the Logics of Russell and Schröder: An Account of his Doctoral Thesis, and of his Discussion of it with Russell." *Annals of Science* 32 (1975), 103-132 (esp. 117-123).

O 00340
Greely, Adolphus W. *Three Years of Arctic Service.* 1886.

S 00579
Green, Thomas Henry. "The Idea of Novelty in Peirce and Whitehead." Diss. Notre Dame 1968.

S 00580
Greene, John C. *The Death of Adam: Evolution and its Impact on Western Thought* (Ames: Iowa State University Press, 1959), 299-300, 368nn52, 53.

O 00588
Greenhill, A.G. Review of Mach's *Science of Mechanics*. 1894.

S 00581
Greenlee, Douglas A. "The Sign Theory of Charles Sanders Peirce." Diss. Columbia 1964.

S 00582
───── . "Peirce's Hypostatic and Factorial Categories." *Transactions* 4 (1968), 49-58.

S 00583
───── . "The Similarity of Discernibles." *Journal of Philosophy* 65 (1968), 753-763.

S 00584
───── . "On Pragmatism." *Journal of the History of Ideas* 30 (1969), 603-608. (Review of Ayer's *Origins* [S 00054] and Thayer's *Meaning and Action* [S 01402]).

S 00585
───── . "Unrestricted Fallibilism." *Transactions* 7 (1971), 75-92.

S 00586
───── . Review of Reilly's *Theory of Scientific Method* [S 01162]. *Transactions* 8 (1972), 53-55.

S 00587
───── . *Peirce's Concept of Sign*. The Hague: Mouton, 1973. (Criticized by Brock [S 00172], Fitzgerald [S 00511], and Ransdell [S 01146]). (Reviewed by Deledalle [S C0338], Oehler [S 01051], Thayer [S 01407], and Walther and Bense [S 01486]).

S 00588
───── . Critical Comments on Thayer's *Meaning and Action* [S 01402]. *Transactions* 11 (1975), 236-240. (Reply by Thayer [S 01405]).

S 00589
───── . "Peirce's Concept of Sign: Further Reflections." *Transactions* 12 (1976), 135-147. (Reply to Brock [S 00172], Fitzgerald [S 00511], and Ransdell [S 01146]).

S 00590
───── . "Signs as Thirds." *Proceedings 1976*, forthcoming.

S 00591
Grossman, Ross M. "Abduction, Simplicity and Instinct in the Philosophy of Charles Sanders Peirce." M.A. thesis Illinois 1966.

S 00592
Guccione Monroy, Antonio. *Peirce ed il pragmatismo americano*. Palermo: Palumbo, 1959.

S 00593
Gullace, Giovanni. "The Pragmatic Movement in Italy." *Journal of the History of Ideas* 23 (1962), 91-105.

O 00353
Gurney, Edmund. "Remarks on Professor Peirce's Paper." 1887.

O 00381
_____ . "Remarks on Mr. Peirce's Rejoinder." 1889.

S 00594
Gustafson, Donald. Review of Bernstein's *Perspectives* [S 00105]. *Philosophical Review* 76 (1967), 387-389.

O 01179
Gutberlet, Const. "Der Pragmatismus." 1908.

S 00595
Gutmann, James, ed. *Philosophy: A to Z* (New York: Grosset & Dunlap, 1963), 254-258, 301.

S 00596
Haack, R.J. Review of Scheffler's *Four Pragmatists* [S 01281]. *Mind,* NS 85 (1976), 454-456.

S 00597
Haack, Susan. "The Pragmatist Theory of Truth." *British Journal for the Philosophy of Science* 27 (1976), 231-249.

S 00598
Haas, William Paul. *The Conception of Law and the Unity of Peirce's Philosophy.* Studia Friburgensia, 38 (Fribourg: University Press; Notre Dame: The University of Notre Dame Press, 1964). (Reviewed by Potter [S 01109] and Wennerberg [S 01511]). (Noticed by Warner [S 01488]).

S 00599
Habermas, Jürgen. *Erkenntnis und Interesse* (Frankfurt: Suhrkamp, 1968), 116-178.

S 00600
_____ . *Knowledge and Human Interests,* tr. Jeremy J. Shapiro (Boston: Beacon Press, 1971), 90-141. (Reviewed by Ruddick [S 01252]).

S 00601
Hackstaff, L.H. *Systems of Formal Logic* (New York: Gordon and Breach, 1966), 105, 179-181, 204-205.

O 00144
Hall, G. Stanley. "Philosophy in the United States." 1879.

O 00277
Hall, G. Stanley, and E.M. Hartwell. "Bilateral Asymmetry of Function." 1884.

S 00602
Hall, Robert W. "Peirce Reconsidered." *Commentary* 35 (1963), 163-164. (Reply to Aiken's "American Pragmatism Reconsidered" [S 00007], with Aiken's rejoinder [S 00008]).

O 00647
Halsted, George Bruce. "Sylvester." 1897.

S 00603
Hamblin, Frances Murphy. "A Comment on Peirce's 'Tychism'." *Journal of Philosophy* 42 (1945), 378-383.

S 00604
Handbuch der Astrophysik. (Berlin: Julius Springer, 1928-36), I.1:296; II.1:17; II.2:522-554, 711; V.1:226, 246, 260, 261, 275.

S 00605
Handy, Rollo, and E.C. Harwood. *Useful Procedures of Inquiry.* Great Barrington: Behavioral Research Council, 1973.

S 00606
Hansen, James E. Review of Bernstein's *Praxis and Action* [S 00108]. *Philosophy and Phenomenological Research* 34 (1973), 129-130.

S 00607
Hanson, Norwood Russell. "The Logic of Discovery." *Journal of Philosophy* 55 (1958), 1073-1089.

S 00608
_____. *Patterns of Discovery: An Inquiry into the Conceptual Foundations of Science* (New York: Cambridge University Press, 1958), 70-92 (esp. 85-86).

S 00609
_____. "More on 'The Logic of Discovery'." *Journal of Philosophy* 57 (1960), 182-188.

S 00610
_____. "Is There a Logic of Discovery?" in *Current Issues in the Philosophy of Science,* ed. Feigl and Maxwell (New York: Holt, Rinehart and Winston, 1961), 20–35.

S 00611
_____. "Retroductive Inference," in *Philosophy of Science: The Delaware Seminar,* ed. Bernard Baumrin (New York, 1961-63), I:21-37.

S 00612
_____. "The Idea of a Logic of Discovery." *Dialogue* 4 (1965), 48-61.

S 00613
_____. "Notes Towards a Logic of Discovery," in Bernstein's *Perspectives* [S 00105], 42-65.

S 00614
_____. *What I Do Not Believe, and other Essays,* ed. Stephen Toulmin and Harry Woolf (Dordrecht-Holland: D. Reidel, 1971), 288-300.

S 00615
Hardwick, Charles S. "Berkeley and Peirce." *Proceedings 1976,* forthcoming.

S 00616
_____, ed. *Semiotic and Significs: The Correspondence Between Charles S. Peirce and Victoria Lady Welby.* Bloomington: Indiana University Press, 1977.

S 00617
Hare, Peter H. Review of Tursman's *Studies in Philosophy* [S 01455]. *Philosophy and Phenomenological Research* 32 (1971), 284-285.

S 00618
_____. Introduction to a Symposium on H.S. Thayer's *Meaning and Action* [S 01402]. *Transactions* 11 (1975), 229-230.

_____. See Lincourt, John M., and P.H. Hare [S 00846].

O 00062
Harley, Robert. "On Boole's 'Laws of Thought'." 1871.

S 00619
Harris, H.S. *The Social Philosophy of Giovanni Gentile* (Urbana: Illinois University Press, 1960), 258-263.

S 00620
———. "Giovanni Vailati, 1863-1936." *Dialogue* 2 (1963), 328-336.

S 00621
———. "Logical Pragmatism and the Task of Philosophy in Peirce and Vailati." *Revista Critica di Storia della Filosofia* 18 (1963), 311-321.

O 00029
Harris, William Torrey. "Intuition vs. Contemplation." 1868.

S 00622
Harrison, Jonathan. Review of H.K. Wells' *Pragmatism* [S 01501]. *Philosophy* 31 (1956), 167.

S 00623
Harrison, Stanley M. "Man's Glassy Essence: An Attempt to Construct a Theory of Person Based on the Writings of Charles Sanders Peirce." Diss. Fordham 1971.

S 00624
———. "The Unwilling Dead." *Proceedings of the Catholic Philosophical Association* 46 (1972), 199-208.

S 00625
———. "Peirce on Persons." *Proceedings 1976*, forthcoming.

S 00626
Hartshorne, Charles. "Continuity, the Form of Forms, in Charles Peirce." *Monist* 39 (1929), 521-534.

S 00627
———. *The Philosophy and Psychology of Sensation*. Chicago: University of Chicago Press, 1934.

S 00628
———. "Husserl and the Social Structure of Immediacy," in *Philosophical Essays in Memory of Edmund Husserl,* ed. Marvin Farber (Cambridge: Harvard University Press, 1940), 219-230.

S 00629
———. Notice of Buchler's *Empiricism* [S 00188]. *Ethics* 50 (1940), 248.

S 00630
———. "Charles Sanders Peirce's Metaphysics of Evolution." *New England Quarterly* 14 (1941), 49-63.

S 00631
———. "A critique of Peirce's Idea of God." *Philosophical Review* 50 (1941), 516-523.

S 00632
———. Review of Feibleman's *Introduction* [S 00451]. *Philosophy and Phenomenological Research* 9 (1948), 157-159.

S 00633
———. "Chance, Love and Incompatibility." *Philosophical Review* 58 (1949), 429-450.

S 00634
———. "The Relativity of Non-relativity: Some Reflections on Firstness," in *Studies* I [S 01549], 215-224.

S 00635
———. "Charles Peirce, Philosopher-Scientist." *Journal of Public Law* 7 (1958), 2-12.

S 00636
———. "Charles Peirce's 'One Contribution to Philosophy' and His Most Serious Mistake," in *Studies* II [S 00968], 455-474.

S 00637
———. "The Case for Idealism." *Philosophical Forum* 1 (1969), 7-23.

S 00638
———. *Creative Synthesis and Philosophic Method.* London: SCM Press, 1970.

S 00639
———. "The Development of My Philosophy," in Smith's *Contemporary American Philosophy* [S 01361], 211-228.

S 00640
———. *Whitehead's Philosophy: Selected Essays.* University of Nebraska Press, 1972.

S 00641
———. "Charles Peirce and Quantum Mechanics." *Transactions* 9 (1973), 191-201.

S 00642
———. "Synthesis as Polyadic Inclusion: A Reply to Sessions." *Southern Journal of Philosophy* 14 (1976), 245-255. (See Sessions' "Charles Hartshorne and Thirdness" [S 01329]).

S 00643
Hartshorne, Charles, and Paul Weiss. *The Collected Papers of Charles Sanders Peirce,* Vols. I-VI. Cambridge: Harvard University Press, 1931-35.

Harwood, E.C. See Handy, Rollo, and E.C. Harwood [S 00605].

Haskell, Daniel C. See Fisch, Max H., and D.C. Haskell [S 00495].

S 00644
Hausman, Carl R. "Eros and Agape in Creative Evolution: A Peircean Insight." *Process Studies* 4 (1974), 11-25.

S 00645
Hawkins, Benjamin S. "Frege and Peirce on Properties of Sentences in Classical Deductive Systems." Diss. Miami 1971.

S 00646
———. "A Compendium of C.S. Peirce's 1866-1885 Work." *Notre Dame Journal of Formal Logic* 16 (1975), 109-115.

S 00647
———. Review of Roberts' *Existential Graphs* [S 01201]. *Transactions* 11 (1975), 128-139.

S 00648
———. "Peirce and Russell: The History of a Neglected Controversy." *Notre Dame Journal of Formal Logic,* forthcoming.

S 00649
Hawkins, Hugh. *Pioneer: A History of the Johns Hopkins University, 1874-1889* (Ithaca, N.Y.: Cornell University Press, 1960), 191-198.

O 00554
Hearings before the Committee on Naval Affairs, U.S. House of Representatives . . . on the Bill H.R. 6338, to Abolish the Bureau in the Treasury Department Known as the Coast and Geodetic Survey. 1894.

S 00650
Hébert, Marcel. *Le pragmatisme; étude de ses diverses formes: anglo-américaines, francaises, italiennes et de sa valeur religieuse* (Paris: Emile Nourry, 1908 [2nd ed. with response by William James, 1910]), 9-25.

O 00430
Hegeler, Edward C. "Religion and Science." 1890.

S 00651
Heinemann, F.H. Review of Schneider's *History* [S 01303]. Philosophy 23 (1948), 376-378.

S 00652
Held, Virginia. "But Does It Work?" (review of Smith's Spirit [S 01357]). *Reporter* 28 (23 May 1963), 55-57.

O 00678
Helmert, Friedrich R. "Beiträge zur Theorie des Reversionspendels." 1898.

O 00710
―――― . "Bericht über die relativen Messungen der Schwerkraft mit Pendelapparaten." 1900.

Helmholtz, Rita M. See Blomeyer, G.R., and Rita M. Helmholtz [S 00130].

S 00653
Hempel, Carl G. Review of Buchler's "Peirce's Theory of Logic" [S 00190]. *Journal of Symbolic Logic* 4 (1939), 102.

S 00654
Henderson, G.P. "Moral Pragmatism." *Philosophy* 44 (1969), 1-11.

S 00655
Henle, Paul. "Lewis on Meaning and Verification," in *The Philosophy of C.I. Lewis,* ed. Paul A. Schilpp (La Salle, Ill: Open Court, 1968), 60-87.

S 00656
Herbenick, Raymond Michael. "Charles Sanders Peirce and Contemporary Theories of the Systems Concept and Systems Approach to Problem-Solving and Decision-Making: An Introductory Essay on Systems Theory in Philosophical Analysis." Diss. Georgetown 1968.

S 00657
―――― . Review of Ayer's *Origins* [S 00054]. *Personalist* 52 (1971), 121-134.

O 00401
"Herbert Spencer Attacked." 1890.

O 00403
"Herbert Spencer Defended." 1890.

S 00658
Hermes, Hans. *Semiotik: Eine Theorie der Zeichengestalten, als Grundlage für Untersuchungen von formalisierten Sprachen.* Leipzig: Hirzel, 1938 (2nd ed. Hildesheim: Gerstenberg, 1970).

S 00659
Hesse, Mary. Review of Edwards' *Encyclopedia of Philosophy* [S 00386]. *British Journal for the Philosophy of Science* 20 (1969), 263-269.

S 00660
Heyl, Paul R., and Guy S. Cook. "The Value of Gravity at Washington." *Journal of Research of the National Bureau of Standards* 17 (1936), 805-839, at 806, 823.

S 00661
Hicks, G. Dawes. Notice of *Collected Papers* I. *Hibbert Journal* 30 (1932), 522-523.

S 00662
Higgens, David Jeremiah. "Possibility in Peirce and Heidegger: A Propaedeutic for Synthesis." Diss. Missouri 1968.

Hilferty, Margaret M. See Wilson, Edwin B., and M.M. Hilferty [S 01559].

S 00663
Hill, Walker H. "Peirce and Dewey and the Spectator Theory of Knowledge." Diss. Wisconsin 1938.

S 00664
_____. "Peirce and Pragmatism" (abstract). *Journal of Philosophy* 36 (1939), 682-683.

S 00665
_____. "Peirce's 'Pragmatic' Method." *Philosophy of Science* 7 (1940), 168-181.

S 00666
_____. "The Founder of Pragmatism," in *In Commemoration of William James* (New York: Columbia University Press, 1942), 223-234.

S 00667
Hinshaw, Virgil G., Jr. "The Pragmatist Theory of Truth." *Philosophy of Science* 11 (1944), 82-92.

S 00668
Hintikka, Jaakko. "Quine versus Peirce?" *Dialectica* 30 (1976), 7-8.

S 00669
Hobbs, William Gordon. "Abductive Inference: Its Conception and Justification in Transcendental Philosophy." Diss. North Carolina at Chapel Hill 1975.

S 00670
Hocking, W.E. *Types of Philosophy* (New York: Scribner's, 1939), 140, 146, 152ff., 196, 405.

S 00671
_____. "Les moments de la philosophie américaine." *Etudes Philosophiques* 19 (1964), 167-180.

S 00672
Hocutt, Max O. "Peirce's Value Theory." M.A. thesis Tulane 1958.

S 00673
_____. "The Logical Foundations of Peirce's Theory of Values." Diss. Yale 1960.

S 00674
_____. "The Logical Foundations of Peirce's Aesthetics." *Journal of Aesthetics and Art Criticism* 21 (1962), 157-166.

S 00675
Hoensch, Jarmila. "Fragen an die Filmsemiologie." *Semiosis* 3 (1976), 42-52.

S 00676
Hoernle, Reinhold Friedrich. "A Plea for a Phenomenology of Meaning." *Proceedings of the Aristotelian Society* 21 (1921), 71-89.

S 00677
Hoffman, William E. "Vision, Sign and Inference." *Visible Language* 7 (1973), 285-309.

S 00678
Holland, R.F. Review of Goudge's *Thought* [S 00565]. *Mind,* NS 60 (1951), 567-569.

S 00679
Hollinger, Robert. "Aspects of the Theory of Classification." *Philosophy and Phenomenological Research* 36 (1976), 319-338.

S 00680
Holmes, Larry. "Charles S. Peirce and Scientific Metaphysics." Diss. Harvard 1962.

S 00681
_____. "Prolegomena to Peirce's Philosophy of Mind," in *Studies* II [S 00968], 359-381.

S 00682
_____. "Peirce on Self-Control." *Transactions* 2 (1966), 113-130.

S 00683
Holmes, Roger W. Review of Feibleman's *Introduction* [S 00451]. *New York Herald Tribune Weekly Book Review,* 9 March 1947, 23.

S 00684
Holmes, Stephen Taylor. "Karl-Otto Apel's *Transformation der Philosophie"* (review of [S 00038]). *International Philosophical Quarterly* 15 (1975), 215-226.

S 00685
Homblin, Frances Murphy. "A Comment on Peirce's Tychism." *Journal of Philosophy* 42 (1945), 378-383.

S 00686
Hook, Sidney. Review of *Collected Papers* I. *Current History* 36 (1932), iv-v.

S 00687
_____. Review of *Collected Papers* I. *Symposium* 3 (1932), 248-256.

S 00688
_____. "Our Philosophers." *Current History* 41 (March 1935), 698-704.

S 00689
Hookway, C.J. Review of Scheffler's *Four Pragmatists* [S 01281]. *Journal of Philosophy* 73 (1976), 550-554.

S 00690
Horanyi, Ozeb. "Peirce's Term 'Icon'." *Proceedings 1976,* forthcoming.

O 00452
Hoskins, L.M. "The Law of 'Vis Viva'." 1891.

S 00691
Hotopf, W.H.N. *Language, Thought and Comprehension: A Case Study of the Writings of I.A. Richards.* London: Routledge & Kegan Paul, 1965.

O 00319
"How the Money was Spent." 1885.

S 00692
Howard, V.A. "The Pragmatic Maximum" (review of Scheffler's *Four Pragmatists* [S 01281]). *British Journal for the Philosophy of Science* 26 (1975), 343-351.

S 00693
Howard, Wendell T. "A Critical Study of Peirce's Theory of Perceptual Judgment." Diss. Texas at Austin 1955.

S 00694
Hozman, Karel. "Gnoséologie du pragmatisme" (in Czech). *Opera Universitatis Purkynianae Brunensis Facultas Philosophica* (Prague: Tchecosl, 1969), No. 146, p. 109.

S 00695
———. "Über die Stellung des Pragmatismus in der Geschichte der Philosophie." *Sbornik Praci Filosoficke Fakulty Brenske University,* Rada Hudbnevedna: Brno, 1971.

S 00696
Hubig, Christoph. "Can There be a Uniform Conception of the Interpretant? Something about the Relationship Between Semiotics as Philosophy of Science and Semiotics of Art." *Proceedings 1976,* forthcoming.

S 00697
Huff, Toby E. "Discovery and Explanation in Sociology: Durkheim on Suicide." *Philosophy of the Social Sciences* 5 (1975), 241-257.

S 00698
Huggett, William J. "Charles Peirce's Search for a Method." Diss. Toronto 1954.

S 00699
———. Review of Murphey's *Development* [S 01001]. *Dialogue* 1 (1962), 224-227.

S 00700
———. Review of Thompson's *Pragmatic Philosophy* [S 01416]. *Dialogue* 2 (1964), 470-471.

S 00701
———. Review of *Studies* II [S 00968]. *Dialogue* 6 (1967), 419-423.

S 00702
———. Review of Ayer's *Origins* [S 00054]. *Dialogue* 8 (1969), 510-512.

O 00383
Huggins, William. "On the Wave-length of the Principal Line in the Spectrum of the Aurora." 1889.

S 00703
Hull, David L. *Darwin and His Critics: The Reception of Darwin's Theory of Evolution by the Scientific Community.* Cambridge: Harvard University Press, 1973. (Reviewed by Medawar [S 00918]).

S 00704
Hullett, James N. "The Conditions of Inquiry." *Philosophy of Education Proceedings* 30 (1974), 432-438. (Response by Arnstine [S 00048]).

S 00705
Humphries, Barbara. Review of Scheffler's *Four Pragmatists* [S 01281]. *Philosophical Review* 85 (1976), 419-422.

S 00706
Hurst, Martha. "Implication in the Fourth Century B.C." *Mind,* NS 44 (1935), 484-495.

O 00437
Husserl, E.G. Review of Schröder's *Vorlesungen über die Algebra der Logik.* 1891.

O 00467
———. "Der Folgerungscalcül und die Inhaltslogik." 1891.

S 00707
Hutten, E.H. Review of Reingold's *Science in Nineteenth-Century America* [S 01165]. *Nature* 209 (1966), 235.

O 00429
Iles, George. "Seventy Years Old To-Day." 1890.

O 00322
"Intoxicated — Demoralized." 1885.

S 00708
Ivanov, L. "The Idealism of the Sign in the Philosophy and Semiotic of Ch. Peirce and Ch. Morris" (in Bulgarian). *Filosofska Mis'l* (Sofia), 28 (1972), 40-44.

O 01200
Jacoby, Günther. *Der Pragmatismus: Neue Bahnen in der Wissenschaftslehre des Auslands.* 1909.

S 00709
Jaffe, Raymond. *The Pragmatic Conception of Justice.* Berkeley and Los Angeles: University of California Press, 1960.

S 00710
Jager, Ronald. *The Development of Bertrand Russell's Philosophy* (London: Allen and Unwin, 1972), 137-138.

S 00711
Jakobson, Roman. *Selected Writings.* 2 vols. The Hague: Mouton, 1962-1971.

S 00712
———. *Essais de linguistique generale* (tr. Nicolas Ruwet). Paris: Editions de Minuit, 1963.

S 00713
———. "Quest for the Essence of Language." *Bulletin of the American Academy of Arts and Sciences* 18:6 (1965), 3-5.

S 00714
———. "Verbal Communication." *Scientific American,* September 1972, at 73-80.

S 00715
———. *Coup d'oeil sur le developpement de la semiotique* (Bloomington: Indiana University; Lisse: Peter de Ridder Press, 1975), 3, 6-11, 14, 16-17.

S 00716
James, Ralph E. *The Concrete God* (New York: Bobbs-Merrill, 1967), 31-42 ("Peirce: The Continuum").

O 00214
James, William. "Reflex Action and Theism." 1881.

O 00305
———. "On the Function of Cognition." 1885.

O 00456
———. "Abbot Against Royce." 1891.

O 00649
———. *The Will to Believe and Other Essays in Popular Philosophy.* 1897.

O 00677
———. "Philosophical Conceptions and Practical Results." 1898.

O 01000
———. *The Varieties of Religious Experience.* 1902.

O 01039
———. "The Pragmatic Method." 1904.

O 01123
———. "G. Papini and the Pragmatist Movement in Italy." 1906.

S 00717
———. *Pragmatism: A New Name for Some Old Ways of Thinking—Popular Lectures of Philosophy* (London: Longmans-Green, 1907), 46ff. (Reviewed by McTaggart [S 01170] and Schiller [S 01152]).

O 01191
———. *The Meaning of Truth.* 1909.

O 01199
———. *A Pluralistic Universe.* 1909.

S 00718
———. *Collected Essays and Reviews,* ed. R.B. Perry (New York: Russell and Russell, 1920), 20, 406, 410, 448.

O 00428
Janes, Lewis G. "The Grandeur of Spencer's System." 1890.

O 00343
Jastrow, Joseph. "The Psycho-Physic Law and Star Magnitudes." 1887.

O 00362
———. "A Critique of Psycho-Physic Methods." 1888.

O 00971
———— . "Belief and Credulity." 1902.

O 01235
———— . "The Passing of a Master Mind." 1914.

O 01244
———— . "Charles Sanders Peirce as a Teacher." 1916.

O 01248
———— . "The Widow of Charles Peirce." 1934.

S 00719
Jessen, Palle. *Inledning til en almen pragmatologi: med et specielt forsog pa afklaring af den systematiske forbindelse mellem behov og teknik.* Nordisk Sommeruniversitet, Copenhagen 1952.

S 00720
Jessup, John A. "Peirce's Early Account of Induction." *Transactions* 10 (1974), 224-234.

O 00084
Jevons, W. Stanley. *The Principles of Science: A Treatise on Logic and Scientific Method.* 1874.

O 00201
———— . "Recent Mathematico-Logical Memoirs." 1881.

S 00721
Johanson, Arnold E. "Paper Doubt, Feigned Hesitancy, and Inquiry." *Transactions* 8 (1972), 214-230.

S 00722
Johnson, H.A., Jr. "The Speculative Rhetoric of Charles S. Peirce." M.A. thesis Florida 1968.

O 00472
Johnson, William Ernest. "The Logical Calculus." 1892.

S 00723
Johnstone, Henry W., Jr. *Elementary Deductive Logic* (New York: Crowell, 1954), 227-231.

S 00724
———— . "Charles Peirce: Philosopher of Science and Common Sense." *Hermathena* 96 (1962), 3-15.

S 00725
———— . Review of Ross' *Grounds for Grammar* [S 01238] *Transactions* 13 (1977), 153-155.

S 00726
Jones, Bessie Zaban, and Lyle Gifford Boyd. *Harvard College Observatory: The First Four Directorships, 1839-1919* (Cambridge: Harvard University Press, 1971), 149, 165, 168, 172, 174, 176, 184, 185ff., 288, 464n16, 466n11.

S 00727
Jones, Royce Paul. "C.S. Peirce on Intuition and Instinct." Diss. Oklahoma 1972.

S 00728
———— . "Is Peirce's Theory of Instinct Consistently Non-Cartesian?" *Transactions* 12 (1976), 348-366.

S 00729
Jørgensen, Jørgen. *A Treatise of Formal Logic: Its Evolution and Main Branches, with its Relations to Mathematics and Philosophy* (Copenhagen: Levin and Munksgaard, 1931), I: 129-135.

O 01211
Jourdain, Philip E.B. "The Development of the Theories of Mathematical Logic and the Principles of Mathematics." 1910, 1912.

S 00730
Jung, Walter. Review of Thompson's *Pragmatic Philosophy* [S 01416]. *Philosophische Rundschau* 4 (1956), 129-143.

S 00731
———. Review of von Kempski's *Pragmatismus* [S 00742]. *Philosophische Rundschau* 4 (1956), 143-158.

S 00732
———. Review of Wiener's *Values* [S 01538]. *Philosophische Rundschau* 6 (1958), 142-143.

S 00733
Kaden, Lewis B. "Religion in an Evolving Universe." B.A. thesis Harvard 1963.

S 00734
Kagey, Rudolf. Review of *Collected Papers* I. *New York Herald Tribune Books* 81 (13 December 1931), 22.

O 01189
Kallen, Horace M. "The Affiliations of Pragmatism." 1909.

O 01212
———. "Pragmatism and Its 'Principles.'" 1911.

O 00405
"Kappa." "Flaws in 'Outsider's' Reasoning." 1890.

O 00527
"Kappa Kappa." Review of Mach's *The Science of Mechanics*. 1893.

O 00479
"Kappa Rho Sigma." Review of Schröder's *Vorlesungen über die Algebra der Logik (Exakte Logik)* [O 00468]. 1892.

S 00735
Kasher, Asa. "Sentences and Utterances Reconsidered." *Foundations of Language* 8 (1972), 313-345.

S 00736
Katz, Jerrold. "The Role of Doubt in Peirce's Theory of Inquiry." *Dialogue (Journal of Phi Sigma Tau)*, 1 (1956), 1-12.

S 00737
———. *The Problem of Induction and Its Solution* (Chicago: University of Chicago Press, 1962), 17, 45n5.

O 00711
Kayser, H. *Handbuch der Spectroscopie*. 1900.

O 01072
———. "New Standards of Wave-Length." 1904.

S 00738
Kee Soo Shin. "Paul Carus's 'Positive Monism' and Critique of Other Types of Monism (Mach, Haeckel, Peirce)." Diss. Temple 1973.

S 00739
Keeton, Morris T. "Peirce and Montgomery," in *Studies* I [S 01549], 312-324.

O 00355
Kempe, A.B. "Note to a Memoir on the Theory of Mathematical Form." 1887.

O 00638
——— . "The Theory of Mathematical Form: A Correction and Explanation." 1897.

O 00371
Kempf, Paul. Review of Kurlbaum and Bell's "On the Absolute Wave-Length of Light." 1888.

S 00740
von Kempski, Jürgen. "Der Pragmatismus." *Deutsches Adelsblatt* 55 (1937), 1500-1504.

S 00741
——— . "C.S. Peirce und die apagoge des Aristoteles," in *Kontrolliertes Denken: Untersuchungen zum Logikkalkül und zur Logik der Einzelwissenschaften* (Munich: Karl Alber, 1951), 56-64.

S 00742
——— . *Charles Sanders Peirce und der Pragmatismus.* Stuttgart: Kohlhammer, 1952. (Reviewed by Gallie [S 00535], Jung [S 00731], Schlaretzki [S 01293] and Wiener [S 01536]).

S 00743
Kennedy, Gail. "The Pragmatic Naturalism of Chauncey Wright." *Studies in the History of Ideas* 3 (1935), 477-503.

S 00744
——— . "Pragmatism, Pragmaticism, and the Will to Believe: A Reconsideration." *Journal of Philosophy* 55 (1958), 578-588.

S 00745
——— . "Le pragmatisme," in *Les grands courants de la pensée mondiale contemporaine,* ed. M.F. Sciacca (Milan: Marzorati, 1961), II:58-72.

Kennedy, Gail. See Knovitz, Milton Ridvas, and G. Kennedy [S 00781].

S 00746
Kent, Beverley E. "Logic in the Context of Peirce's Classification of the Sciences." Diss. Waterloo 1975.

S 00747
——— . "Peirce's Esthetics: A New Look." *Transactions* 12 (1976), 263-283.

S 00748
——— . "Objective Logic in Peirce's Thought." *Transactions* 13 (1977), 142-146.

S 00749
Kernan, W. Fergus. "The Peirce Manuscripts and Josiah Royce—A Memoir, Harvard 1915-1916." *Transactions* 1 (1965), 90-95.

S 00750
Ketner, Kenneth Laine. "An Essay on the Nature of World Views." Diss. California at Santa Barbara 1972.

S 00751
———. *An Emendation of R.G. Collingwood's Doctrine of Absolute Presuppositions.* Lubbock: Texas Tech Press, 1973.

S 00752
———. "Peirce as an Interesting Failure?" *Proceedings 1976,* forthcoming.

S 00753
Ketner, Kenneth Laine, and James Edward Cook. *Charles Sanders Peirce: Contributions to "The Nation," Part One: 1869-1893.* Lubbock: Texas Tech Press, 1975. (Parts 2 and 3 in press).

S 00754
Ketner, Kenneth Laine, and Christian J.W. Kloesel. "The Semiotic of Charles Sanders Peirce and the First Dictionary of Semiotics." *Semiotica* 13 (1975), 395-414. (Review of Bense and Walther [S 00090]).

S 00755
Keynes, John Maynard. *A Treatise on Probability* (London: Macmillan, 1921), 50n3 (cf. 56-57), 290, 304-306.

O 01145
Keynes, John Neville. *Studies and Exercises in Formal Logic.* 1906.

S 00756
Keyser, Cassius Jackson. "A Glance at Some of the Ideas of Charles Sanders Peirce." *Scripta Mathematica* 3 (1935), 11-37. (Review of *Collected Papers* I - IV, reprinted in Keyser's *Mathematics as a Culture Clue and Other Essays* [New York: Scripta Mathematica, 1947], 155-188).

S 00757
———. *Portraits of Famous Philosophers Who Were Also Mathematicians.* New York: Scripta Mathematica XII (1939).

S 00758
———. "Charles Sanders Peirce as a Pioneer," in *Galois Lectures* (Scripta Mathematica Library, No. 5 [1941]), 87-112. (Reviewed by Church [S 00267]).

O 01032
King, Irving. "Pragmatism as a Philosophic Method." 1903.

S 00759
King, James T. "A Peircean Thread in Our Meta-Ethical Labyrinth." *Journal of Value Inquiry* 3 (1969), 113-125.

S 00760
Kissel, M., and M. Kozlova. Review of Melvil's *Charles Peirce* [S 00926]. *USSR Academy of Sciences* 3 (1968), 203-207.

S 00761
Klaus, Georg. *Semiotik und Erkenntnistheorie.* 2nd ed. Berlin: Deutscher Verlag der Wissenschaften, 1969.

S 00762
———. *Die Macht des Wortes: Ein erkenntnistheoretisches Traktat.* 5th ed. (Berlin: Deutscher Verlag der Wissenschaften, 1969), 57-62.

S 00763
Klausner, Neal W. Review of Werkmeister's *History* [S 01512]. *Philosophy of Science* 19 (1952), 180-181.

S 00764
Kloesel, Christian J.W. "Peirce Edition Project: Eine neue Ausgabe der Schriften von Charles Sanders Peirce." *Semiosis* 4 (1976), 53-54.

S 00765
———. "Speculative Grammar: From Duns Scotus to Charles Peirce." *Proceedings 1976,* forthcoming.

S 00766
———, tr. "The Three Fundamental Structural Categories of Charles S. Peirce" (translation of Krausser's "Strukturkategorien." [S 00783]). *Transactions,* forthcoming.

Kloesel, Christian J.W. See Ketner, Kenneth Laine, and C.J.W. Kloesel [S 00754].

S 00767
Kneale, William. *Probability and Induction* (London: Oxford University Press, 1949), 44n, 150, 166.

S 00768
Kneale, William, and Martha Kneale. *The Development of Logic* (Oxford: Clarendon, 1962), esp. 427-434 ("The Theory of Relations: De Morgan and Peirce").

S 00769
Knight, Thomas S. *Charles Peirce.* New York: Washington Square Press, 1965. (Reviewed by Potter [S 01109]).

O 00106
Knobel, E.B. "The Chronology of Star Catalogues." 1877.

S 00770
Knox, Howard V. Review of Leroux' *Le pragmatisme* [S 00829]. *Mind,* NS 33 (1924), 198-202.

S 00771
Koehn, Donald Robert. "Charles S. Peirce's 'Illustrations of the Logic of Science.'" M.A. thesis Illinois 1966.

S 00772
———. "Peirce's Explanation of the Validity of Synthetic Inference in the 'Illustrations of the Logic of Science.'" Diss. Illinois 1969.

S 00773
———. "The Birth of Pragmatism: Peirce's Attempt to Solve the Problem of Induction," in Tursman's *Studies in Philosophy* [S 01455], 37-51.

S 00774
———. Review of Ayer's *Origins* [S 00054]. *Isis* 61 (1970), 143.

S 00775
———. "Metaphysics and the Problem of Induction." *Southwestern Journal of Philosophy* 2 (1971), 129-138.

S 00776
———. "Charles S. Peirce's 'Illustrations of the Logic of Science' and the Pragmatic Justification of Induction." *Transactions* 9 (1973), 157-174.

S 00777
———. "Logic, Truth, and Action in Peirce's First Public Statement of Pragmatism" (abstract). *International Federation of Philosophical Societies: Abstracts of Communications Presented at the XVth World Congress of Philosophy, Varna* (Sofia: Bulgarian Organizing Committee, 1973), No. 398.

S 00778
Kolakowski, Leszek. *The Alienation of Reason: A History of Positivist Thought,* tr. Norbert Guterman (Garden City, N.Y.: Anchor, 1969), 155-160, 166, 170.

S 00779
Kolenda, Konstantin. "Peirce's Neglected Philosophy of Religion," in *Philosophy in the Life of a Nation* (New York: Bicentennial Symposium of Philosophy, 1976), 242-246.

S 00780
──────. "'Man is a Sign': Peirce and Heidegger." *Proceedings 1976,* forthcoming.

S 00781
Konvitz, Milton Ridvas, and Gail Kennedy, eds. *The American Pragmatists: Selected Writings* (New York: Meridian, 1960), 78-79.

O 00555
Korselt, A. "Bemerkung zur Algebra der Logik." 1894.

Kozlova, M. See Kissel, M., and M. Kozlova [S 00760].

O 00534
Kral, J.J. "Was Copernicus a German?" 1893.

S 00782
Kraus, Elizabeth Muir. "Thought Before It Hardens: A Study in the Evolutionary Philosophy of Charles Sanders Peirce." Diss. Fordham 1970.

S 00783
Krausser, Peter. "Die drei fundamentalen Strukturkategorien bei Charles S. Peirce." *Philosophia Naturalis* 6 (1960), 3-31. (Translated by Kloesel [S 00766]).

S 00784
Kretzmann, Norman. "History of Semantics," in Edwards' *Encyclopedia of Philosophy* [S 00386], VII:395-397 ("Peirce and the Pragmatists").

S 00785
Krikorian, Y.H. Review of Morris' *Pragmatic Movement* [S 00986]. *Philosophy and Phenomenological Research* 32 (1972), 419-421.

S 00786
Krois, John Michael. "Peirce and Cassirer: The Philosophical Importance of a Theory of Signs." *Proceedings 1976,* forthcoming.

S 00787
Krolikowski, Walter P. "The Peircean Vir," in *Studies* II [S 00968], 257-270.

Kruskal, William H. See Goodman, Leo A., and W.H. Kruskal [S 00555].

O 01148
Kühner, Fr., and Ph. Furtwängler. "Bestimmung der absoluten Grösze der Schwerkraft zu Potsdam mit Reversionspendeln." 1906.

S 00788
Kuklick, Bruce. *Josiah Royce: An Intellectual Biography.* New York: Bobbs-Merrill, 1972.

S 00789
Kultgen, J.H. "The 'Future Metaphysics' of Peirce and Whitehead." *Kant-Studien* 51 (1959-1960), 285-293.

O 00365
Kurlbaum, Ferdinand. "Bestimmung der Wellenlänge Fraunhofer'scher Linien." 1888.

S 00790
Kunz, Robert M. Review of Bosco's *Filosofia pragmatica* [S 00149]. *Philosophy and Phenomenological Research* 24 (1964), 604.

S 00791
Kursanov, G.A. *Gnoseologija sovremennogo pragmatizma*. Moscow: Izdatelstvo Sotsialno-Ekonomicheskoi Literature, 1958.

S 00792
Kurtz, Paul. "Charles S. Peirce," in his *American Philosophy in the Twentieth Century: A Sourcebook* (New York: Macmillan, 1966), 45-47.

O 00444
"L., F.H." (F.H. Loud). "The Teaching of Mathematics." 1891.

O 00473
Ladd-Franklin, Christine. Review of Schröder's *Vorlesungen über die Algebra der Logik (Exakte Logik)*. 1892.

O 01243
─────. "Charles S. Peirce at the Johns Hopkins." 1916.

S 00793
Laferrière, Daniel. "What is Semiotics?" *Semiotic Scene* 1:1 (1977), 2-4.

S 00794
Laird, John. Review of Buchler's *Empiricism* [S 00188]. *Philosophy* 15 (1940), 208-209.

S 00795
─────. Review of Buchler's *Philosophy of Peirce* [S 00193]. *Philosophy* 16 (1941), 434.

O 01144
Lalande, André. "Pragmatisme et Pragmaticisme." 1906.

S 00796
Lamanna, Eustachio Paolo. *La filosofia del Novecento* (Florence: Le Monnier, 1962), 155-181.

S 00797
Lancaster, Robert S. "A Note on Peirce, Pragmatism, and Jurisprudence." *Journal of Public Law* 7 (1958), 13-19.

S 00798
Landé, Alfred. *From Dualism to Unity in Quantum Physics* (London: Cambridge University Press, 1960), 13-14, 23.

S 00799
Langford, C.H. Review of Collected Papers III-IV. *Bulletin of the American Mathematical Society* 42 (1936), 795.

Langford, C.H. See Lewis, C.I., and C.H. Langford [S 00837].

O 01151
Larmor, Joseph, ed. Memoir and Scientific Correspondence of the Late Sir George Gabriel Stokes. 1907.

S 00800
Laudan, Laurens. "Peirce and Trivialization of the Self-Correcting Thesis," in *Foundations of Scientific Method: The Nineteenth Century,* ed. R.N. Giere and R.S. Westfall (Bloomington: Indiana University Press, 1973), 275-306.

S 00801
Larrabee, Harold A. Review of Thompson's *Pragmatic Philosophy* [S 01416]. *New England Quarterly* 26 (1953), 426.

S 00802
Lasker, Emanuel. "On the Definition of Logic and Mathematics." *Scripta Mathematica* 3 (1935), 247-249.

S 00803
Lebowitz, Martin. Review of Thayer's *Meaning and Action* [S 01402]. *Yale Review* 59 (1968), 122.

S 00804
Lee, Harold N. "Note to the Editor." *Transactions* 7 (1971), 180-181.

S 00805
────── . *Percepts, Concepts and Theoretic Knowledge: A Study in Epistemology* (Memphis, Tenn.: Memphis State University Press, 1973), vi, 11n, 43n, 76n, 133, 157n, 215n, and 246.

S 00806
────── . "Process and Pragmatism." *Tulane Studies in Philosophy* 23 (1974), 87-97.

S 00807
────── . "Pragmatism and a Behavioral Theory of Meaning." *Journal of the History of Philosophy* 14 (1976), 435-447.

S 00808
Lee, Otis. "Pragmatism and Existence." *Review of Metaphysics* 1:4 (1948), 32-58.

S 00809
Lehde, Norman B. "Arisbe: Project for National Park Service." *Union-Gazette* (Port Jervis, N.Y.), 9 (28 November 1973), 1-4.

S 00810
────── . "Restoration Aspects Pondered for Historical Pike Home." *Union-Gazette* (Port Jervis, N.Y.), 9 (4 December 1973), 1-2.

S 00811
────── . "Arisbe Discusses Furniture for Peirce Home." *Union-Gazette* (Port Jervis, N.Y.) 9 (6 December 1973), 1-3.

S 00812
────── . "Society Ponders Display of Peirce's Work." *Union-Gazette* (Port Jervis, N.Y.) 9 (8 December 1973), 3-5.

S 00813
Lehrman, Louis J. "The Logic of Diagnosis." *Social Casework* 35 (1954), 192-199.

S 00814
────── . "Logic of Diagnosis" (letter to the editor). *Social Casework* 36 (1955), 424.

O 01118
Leith, Charles Kenneth. "Rock Cleavage." 1905.

S 00815
Lenz, John W. "Induction as Self-Corrective," in *Studies* II [S 00968], 151-162.

S 00816
Lenzen, Victor F. "Charles S. Peirce and die europäische Gradmessung." *Actes du Xe Congrès International d'Histoire des Sciences* (Paris, 1964), 781-783.

S 00817
———. "Charles S. Peirce as Astronomer," in *Studies* II [S 00968], 33-50.

S 00818
———. "The Contributions of Charles S. Peirce to Metrology." *Proceedings of the American Philosophical Society* 109 (Philadelphia, 1965), 29-46.

S 00819
———. "Reminiscences of a Mission to Milford, Pennsylvania." *Transactions* 1 (1965), 3-11.

S 00820
———. Review of Murphey's *Development* [S 01001]. *Scripta Mathematica* 27 (1966 for 1964), 361-362.

S 00821
———. "The Role of Science in the Philosophy of C.S. Peirce." Akten des XIV. *Internationalen Kongresses für Philosphie* (Vienna: Herder, 1968), III: 371-376.

S 00822
———. "An Unpublished Scientific Monograph by C.S. Peirce." *Transactions* 5 (1969), 5-24.

S 00823
———. "Charles S. Peirce as Mathematical Geodesist." *Transactions* 8 (1972), 90-105.

S 00824
———. "The Contributions of Charles S. Peirce to Linear Algebra," in *Phenomenology and Natural Existence,* ed. Dale Riepe (State University of New York Press, 1973), 239-254.

S 00825
———. "Peirce, Leibniz, and Infinitesimals" (abstract). *International Federation of Philosophical Societies: Abstracts of Communications Presented at the XVth World Congress of Philosophy, Varna* (Sofia: Bulgarian Organizing Committee, 1973), No. 400.

S 00826
———. "Charles S. Peirce as Mathematical Physicist." *Transactions* 11 (1975), 159-166.

S 00827
Lenzen, Victor F., and Robert P. Multhauf. "Development of the Gravity Pendulum in the 19th Century." *U.S. National Museum Bulletin* 240 (1964), Paper 44, 301-347.

S 00828
Leonard, Henry S. "The Pragmatism and Scientific Metaphysics of C.S. Peirce" (review of *Collected Papers* V-VI). *Philosophy of Science* 4 (1937), 109-121.

S 00829
Leroux, Emmanuel. *Le pragmatisme américain et anglais: Etude historique et critique* (Paris: Félix Alcan, 1923), esp. Pt. II, Chs. 5 and 9. (Reviewed by Knox [S 00770], Schneider [S 01302], and Wright, W.K. [S 01571]).

S 00830
Levi, Albert William. "Peirce and Painting." *Philosophy and Phenomenological Research* 23 (1962), 23-26.

S 00831
Levi, Isaac. "Probability Kinematics." *British Journal for the Philosophy of Science* 18 (1967), 197-209, at 208.

S 00832
Levy, Ronald Brain. "Believing in Action: A study in the Dynamics of Educational Reconstruction." Diss. Columbia 1953.

S 00833
Lewis, C.I. *A Survey of Symbolic Logic.* (Berkeley and Los Angeles: University of California Press, 1918), 79-106.

S 00834
───── . Review of Cohen's *Chance, Love and Logic* [S 00279]. *Journal of Philosophy* 21 (1924), 71-74.

S 00835
───── . "Pragmatism and Current Thought." *Journal of Philosophy* 27 (1930), 238-246.

S 00836
───── . *An Analysis of Knowledge and Valuation.* (LaSalle, Ill.: Open Court, 1946), ix, 72, 308ff.

S 00837
Lewis, C.I., and C.H. Langford. *Symbolic Logic.* New York: Appleton-Century, 1932.

S 00838
Lewis, J. David. "Peirce, Mead, and the Objectivity of Meaning." *Kansas Journal of Sociology* 8 (1972), 111-122.

S 00839
Lieb, Irwin C., ed. *Charles S. Peirce's Letters to Lady Welby.* New Haven, Conn.: Whitlock's, 1953. (Reviewed by Wiener [S 01541]).

S 00840
───── . "New Studies in the Philosophy of Charles S. Peirce." *Review of Metaphysics* 8 (1954), 291-320. (Reviews of Gallie's *Pragmatism* [S 00534], Thompson's *Pragmatic Philosophy* [S 01416], and *Studies* I [S 01549]).

S 00841
───── . Review of *Collected Papers* VII-VIII. *Review of Metaphysics* 12 (1959), 602-611.

S 00842
───── . Review of *Studies* II [S 00968]. *British Journal for the Philosophy of Science* 18 (1967), 241-250.

S 00843
───── . "Charles Hartshorne's Recollections of Editing the Peirce Papers: An Interview." *Transactions* 6 (1970), 149-159.

O 00425
"Light for 'Outsider.'" 1890.

S 00844
Limper, Peter Frederick. "Value and the Individual in the Philosophies of Whitehead and Peirce." Diss. Yale 1975.

S 00845
Lincourt, John M. "Charles S. Peirce and Psychiatry." *Transactions* 12 (1976), 33-45.

S 00846
Lincourt, John M., and Peter H. Hare. "Neglected American Philosophers in the History of Symbolic Interactionism." *Journal of the History of the Behavioral Sciences* 9 (1973), 333-338.

O 01246
"A List of Articles, Mostly Book Reviews, Contributed by Charles Sanders Peirce to *The Nation*." 1918.

O 00101
"List of Latitude Stars Employed in the Coast Survey." 1877.

S 00847
Llamzon, Benjamin S. Review of Boler's *Scholastic Realism* [S 00136]. *Modern Schoolman* 42 (1964), 111-114.

O 00367
Lockyer, J. Norman. "Notes on the Spectrum of the Aurora." 1888.

O 00382
———. "Appendix to the Bakerian Lecture, Session 1887-1888." 1889.

S 00848
Lohkamp, Richard J. "The Meaning and Significance of Charles S. Peirce's 'On a New List of Categories.'" Diss. Notre Dame 1971.

S 00849
Long, Wilbur. Review of *Collected Papers* VII-VIII. *Philosophy* 41 (1960), 85-86.

Loud, F.H. See L., F.H. [S 00444].

O 01167
Lovejoy, Arthur "The Thirteen Pragmatisms." 1908.

O 01187
———. "Pragmatism and Realism." 1909.

S 00850
———. "A Note on Peirce's Evolutionism." *Journal of the History of Ideas* 7 (1946), 351-354. (Reprinted in Wiener's *Evolution* [S 01533], 227-230).

S 00851
———. "What is the Pragmaticist Theory of Meaning? The First Phase," in *Studies* I [S 01549], 3-20.

S 00852
———. *The Thirteen Pragmatisms, and Other Essays*. Baltimore: The Johns Hopkins Press, 1963.

S 00853
Lowe, Victor. "Peirce and Whitehead as Metaphysicians," in *Studies* II [S 00968], 430-454.

S 00854
Luchins, Abraham S., and Edith H. Luchins. *Logical Foundations of Mathematics of Behavioral Scientists* (New York: Holt, Rinehart and Winston, 1965), 109, 112-113, 170, 247-248, 256, 273, 298, 319.

S 00855
Lukasiewicz, Jan. *Aristotle's Syllogistic* (Oxford: Clarendon, 1951), 83.

S 00856
―――― . *Elements of Mathematical Logic* (Oxford: Pergamon, 1963), 4, 92.

S 00857
Lunine, Myron J. "An Examination of Charles Peirce's Metaphysical Generalization of Charles Darwin's Scientific Theory of Evolution." M.A. thesis Illinois 1963.

O 00543
M., F.E. Note on Peirce's review of Leland's *Memoirs.* 1893.

S 00858
M., W.M. (William Marias Malisoff). Review of Buchler's *Empiricism* [S 00188]. *Philosophy of Science* 7 (1940), 134.

S 00859
McCabe, Russell Tyler. "The Origin and Role of the Categories in Experience and Inquiry: A Comparison of the Theories of Kant and Peirce." Diss. North Carolina at Chapel Hill 1973.

S 00860
McCarthy, Jeremiah E. "Peirce's Critical Commonsensism and Metaphysics," in *Philosophy in the Life of a Nation* (New York: Bicentennial Symposium of Philosophy, 1976), 247-251.

S 00861
McCarthy, Thomas A. "Responses to 'Theory and Practice.'" *Cultural Hermeneutics* 2 (1975), 355-356.

S 00862
Maccia, George S. "The Epistemology of Charles Sanders Peirce and Its Implications for a Philosophy of Education." Diss. Southern California 1953.

S 00863
―――― . "The Educational Aims of Charles Peirce." *Educational Theory* 4 (1954), 206-212.

S 00864
―――― . "A Comparison of the Educational Aims of Charles Peirce and John Dewey." *Educational Theory* 4 (1954), 289-296.

S 00865
―――― . "The Peircean School." *Educational Theory* 5 (1955), 29-33.

O 00202
McColl, Hugh. "Symbolical Logic." 1881.

O 00203
―――― . "Symbolical Logic." 1881.

O 00206
―――― . "A Note on Prof. Peirce's Probability Notation of 1867." 1881.

O 00524
McCrie, G.M. "The Issues of 'Synechism'." 1893.

S 00866
McCulloch, Warren S. *Embodiments of Mind* (Cambridge, Mass.: M.I.T. Press, 1965), 8, 143, 160-161, 221, 389-391.

S 00867
McDermott, John J. Review of Moore's *American Pragmatism* [S 00963]. *International Philosophical Quarterly* 1 (1961), 725.

S 00868
MacDonald, Audrey. "Peirce's Philosophy of Mind." Diss. Texas at Austin 1963.

S 00869
———— . "Peirce's Logic: An Objective Study of Reasoning." *Monist* 48 (1964), 332-345.

S 00870
MacDonald, Margaret. "Charles Sanders Peirce on Language." *Psyche* 15 (1935), 108-128.

S 00871
———— . "Language and Reference." *Analysis* 4 (1936), 33-41.

S 00872
———— . Review of Buchler's *Empiricism* [S 00188]. *Mind,* NS 50 (1941), 81-83.

O 01036
Macfarlane, Alexander. *Bibliography of Quaternions and Allied Systems of Mathematics.* 1904.

O 01205
McGiffert, A.C. "The Pragmatism of Kant." 1910.

S 00873
Machan, Tibor. "Peirce, Kuhn, and Absolute Truth." *Proceedings 1976,* forthcoming.

S 00874
Mackay, Donald S. "Pragmatism," in *A History of Philosophical Systems,* ed. Vergius Ferm (New York: Philosophical Library, 1950), 387-404.

S 00875
McKeon, Charles K. "Peirce's Scotistic Realism," in *Studies* I [S 01549], 238-250.

S 00876
MacKinnon, Barbara A. Review of Moore's *Essential Writings* [S 00966]. *Review of Metaphysics* 27 (1973), 408-409.

O 00622
Mackintosh, William D. "Addition and Subtraction." 1896.

O 01116
Maclagan-Wedderburn, J.H. "A Theorem on Finite Algebras." 1905.

O 01029
McMahon, James. "Practical Application of the Theory of Functions." 1903.

S 00877
McMurray, Gudelia Abacar. "The Pragmatic Theory of Meaning as a Potential Resource for Educational Theory." Diss. Illinois 1969.

S 00878
McPeck, John Edward. "A Logic of Discovery: Lessons from History and Current Prospects." Diss. Western Ontario 1973.

O 01170
McTaggart, J. Ellis. Review of James' *Pragmatism* [S 00717]. 1908.

S 00879
Madden, Edward H. "Chance and Counterfacts in Wright and Peirce." *Review of Metaphysics* 9 (1956), 420-432.

S 00880
——— . "Charles Peirce e la ricerca di un metodo." *Rivista di Filosofia* 49 (1958), 1-20.

S 00881
——— . "Inducción y probabilidad en la filosofía de Charles Sanders Peirce." *Philosophia* 22 (1959), 36-43.

S 00882
——— . "Charles Sanders Peirce's Search for a Method," in *Theories of Scientific Method,* by Ralph M. Blake, Curt J. Ducasse, and Edward H. Madden, (Seattle: University of Washington Press, 1960), 248-262.

S 00883
——— . *Chauncey Wright and the Foundations of Pragmatism* (Seattle: University of Washington Press, 1963), 79-91, 104-107. (Reviewed by Berleant [S 00098] and Rorty [S 01211]).

S 00884
——— . "Peirce on Probability," in *Studies* II [S 00968], 122-140.

S 00885
——— . "Peirce and Current Issues in the Philosophy of Science," in *Contemporary Philosophy: A Survey,* ed. Raymond Klibansky (Florence: La Nuova Italia, 1968), 31-44.

S 00886
——— . Review of White's *Pragmatism* [S 01521]. *Journal of the History of Philosophy* 11 (1973), 277-280.

S 00887
Mahowald, Mary B. *An Idealistic Pragmatism: The Development of the Pragmatic Element in the Philosophy of Josiah Royce.* The Hague: Martinus Nijhoff, 1972.

S 00888
——— . "Peirce's Concept of Community: Another Interpretation." *Transactions* 9 (1973), 175-186.

S 00889
——— . "Peirce's Concepts of God and Religion." *Transactions* 12 (1976), 367-377.

S 00890
Malik, Charles. Review of Freeman's *Categories* [S 00521]. *Isis* 23 (1935), 296-297.

S 00891
——— . Review of *Collected Papers* V. *Isis* 23 (1935), 477-483.

Malisoff, W.M. See M., W.M. [S 00858].

S 00892
Manning, Thomas G. "Peirce, the Coast Survey, and the Politics of Cleveland Democracy." *Transactions* 11 (1975), 187-194.

O 01192
Mannoury, Gerrit. *Methodologisches und Philosophisches zur Elementar-Mathematik.* 1909.

S 00893
Marcuse, Ludwig. "Amerikanischer und deutscher Pragmatismus." *Zeitschrift für philosophische Forschung* 9 (1955), 257-262.

S 00894
───── . *Amerikanisches Philosophieren* (Hamburg: Rowohlt, 1959), Ch. 2.

S 00895
───── . *La philosophie américaine,* tr. Danielle Bohler (Paris: Gallimard, 1967), Ch. 2.

S 00896
Marks, Robert W., ed. *Great Ideas in Modern Science* (New York: Bantam Books, 1967), 3-22.

S 00897
Markus, R.A. "St. Augustine on Signs." *Phronesis* 2 (1957), 60-83, at 82-83.

S 00898
Maron, Stanley. "The Origin of Pragmatism." *Philosophical Quarterly* (Amalner, India), 26 (1953), 139-151.

O 00328
Marquand, Allan. "A New Logical Machine." 1886.

S 00899
Martens, Ekkehard, ed. *Texte der Philosophie des Pragmatismus: Ch. S. Peirce, W. James, F.C.S. Schiller, J. Dewey* (Stuttgart: Reclam, 1975), 3-127.

S 00900
───── . "C.S. Peirce on Speech Acts." *Proceedings 1976,* forthcoming.

S 00901
Martin, Edwin, Jr. "On the Nature and Relevance of Indeterminacy." *Foundations of Language* 12 (1974), 49-71.

S 00902
Martin, Richard M. "On Acting on a Belief," in *Studies* II [S 00968], 212-225.

S 00903
───── . "On Peirce's Icons of Second Intention." *Transactions* 1 (1965), 71-76.

S 00904
───── . "On the Peirce Representation Relation." *Transactions* 5 (1969), 143-157.

S 00905
───── . *Logic, Language and Metaphysics* (New York: New York University Press, 1971), 37-50, 63, 78.

S 00906
———. "Some Comments on De Morgan, Peirce, and the Logic of Relations." *Transactions* 12 (1976), 223-230.

S 00907
———. "On Individuality and Quantification in Peirce's Published Logic Papers, 1867-1885." *Transactions* 12 (1976), 231-245.

S 00908
Marty, Robert "Topologie du champ théorique en sémiologie et en sémiotique." *Semiosis* 2 (1976), 25-29.

S 00909
Maurer, Armand A. "Pragmatism: Charles Sanders Peirce," in *Recent Philosophy: Hegel to the Present*, ed. E. Gilson, T. Lanzan, and A.A. Maurer (New York: Random House, 1962), 624-634.

S 00910
Mayberry, Thomas C. "God and Moral Authority." *Monist* 54 (1970), 106-123.

O 00116
Mayer, A.M. "Floating Magnets." 1878.

S 00911
Mayo, Bernard. Review of Gallie's *Pragmatism* [S 00534]. *Philosophy* 29 (1954), 89-90.

S 00912
———. "The Open Future." *Mind,* NS 71 (1962), 1-14.

S 00913
Mays, Wolfe. Review of Smith's *Spirit* [S 01357]. *Philosophical Books* 5:2 (1964), 26-27.

S 00914
———. Review of Ayer's *Origins* [S 00054] and Thayer's *Meaning and Action* [S 01402]. *Philosophical Books* 10:2 (1969), 1-4.

S 00915
———. Review of Scheffler's *Four Pragmatists* [S 01281]. *Philosophical Books* 16:2 (1975), 25-27.

S 00916
Medawar, Peter Brian. *The Art of the Soluble.* London: Methuen, 1967.

S 00917
———. *Induction and Intuition in Scientific Thought* (London: Methuen, 1969), Preface.

S 00918
———. Review of Hull's *Darwin and His Critics* [S 00703]. *New York Review of Books,* 15 November 1973, 12.

S 00919
Megill, Kenneth A. "Peirce and Marx." *Transactions* 3 (1967), 55-65.

O 00643
Meldola, Raphael. "Proposed Sylvester Memorial." 1897.

S 00920
Mellor, David Hugh. *The Matter of Chance* (Ithaca, N.Y.: Cornell University Press, 1972), 66, 73.

S 00921
Melvil, Yuri K. "One More Attempt to Uphold Pragmatism" (review of Moore's *American Pragmatism* [S 00963]). *Voprosy Filosofii,* September 1961, 154-158 (in Russian).

S 00922
―――― . "The Semiotic of Charles Peirce" (in Russian). *Filosofia Nauki* 3 (1965), 80-89.

S 00923
―――― . "The Conflict Between Science and Religion in the Philosophy of Charles Peirce" (in Russian). *Voprosy Filozofii* 18:9 (1965), 88-98.

S 00924
―――― . "The Conflict of Science and Religion in Charles Peirce's Philosophy." *Transactions* 2 (1966), 33-50.

S 00925
―――― . "The Pragmatist 'Reconstruction' in Philosophy and Its True Meaning" (in Russian). *Voprosy Filozofii* 20:10 (1966), 61-69.

S 00926
―――― . *Charles Peirce i pragmatizm: U istokov amerik, burshchuaznoi filosofii XX v.* Moscow: Moscow State University Press, 1968. (Reviewed by Crosser [S 00300] and Kissel and Kozlova [S 00760]).

O 00515
Mendenhall, Thomas Corwin. Note on Peirce's resignation from the Coast Survey. 1892.

S 00927
Menne, A. "Extension und Comprehension bei Peirce und Bolzano." *Proceedings 1976,* forthcoming.

S 00928
Merrill, G.H. "Peirce on Probability and Induction." *Transactions* 11 (1975), 90-109.

O 00407
Messenger, H.J., Jr. "Two Points Fairly Met." 1890.

S 00929
Mester, Richard Arnold. "The Concrete Embodiment of Thirdness in the Philosophy of Charles S. Peirce." Diss. Pennsylvania State 1971.

S 00930
Metz, Rudolf. Review of *Collected Papers* I-II. *Kant-Studien* 38 (1933), 188-189.

O 01168
Meyer, Max. "The Exact Number of Pragmatisms." 1908.

S 00931
Meyers, Robert G. "Belief and Truth in Charles Peirce." Diss. State University of New York at Buffalo 1966.

S 00932
―――― . "Peirce on Cartesian Doubt." *Transactions* 3 (1967), 13-22.

S 00933
―――― . "Truth and Ultimate Belief in Peirce." *International Philosophical Quarterly* 11 (1971), 87-103.

S 00934
———. "Ayer on Pragmatism." *Metaphilosophy* 6 (1975), 44-53.

S 00935
Michael, Emily. "The Early Logic of C.S. Peirce." Diss. Pennsylvania 1973.

S 00936
———. "Peirce's Early Study of the Logic of Relations, 1865-1867." *Transactions* 10 (1974), 63-75.

S 00937
———. "Peirce's Paradoxical Solution to the Liar's Paradox." *Notre Dame Journal of Formal Logic* 16 (1975), 369-374.

S 00938
———. "Peirce's Earliest Contact with Scholastic Logic." *Transactions* 12 (1976), 46-55.

S 00939
———. "Peirce on Individuals." *Transactions* 12 (1976), 321-329.

O 00221
Michaelis, C.T. "C.S. Peirce. On the Algebra of Logic." 1882.

O 00272
———. "C.S. Peirce. Remarks." 1884.

O 00351
Michelson, Albert A., and Edward W. Morley. "On a Method of making the Wave-length of Sodium Light the actual and practical Standard of Length." 1887.

S 00940
Midonick, Henrietta O., ed. *The Treasury of Mathematics* (New York: Philosophical Library, 1965), xi, 626-642.

S 00941
Miller, James Wilkinson. Review of Wiener's *Evolution* [S 01533]. *Philosophy and Phenomenological Research* 11 (1950), 276-277.

S 00942
Miller, Richard Warner. "C.S. Peirce's First Series of Papers in Logic." M.A. thesis Illinois 1966.

S 00943
———. "Peirce's First Series of Papers in Logic," in Tursman's *Studies in Philosophy* [S 01455], 72-86.

S 00944
———. "Charles S. Peirce's Theory of Probability." Diss. Illinois 1970.

S 00945
———. "Propensity: Popper or Peirce?" *British Journal for the Philosophy of Science* 26 (1975), 123-132.

S 00946
———. "Peirce on Probability." *Proceedings 1976,* forthcoming.

S 00947
Miller, Willard M. "The Synechistic Philosophy of Charles Sanders Peirce: A Hypothetical Cosmology in Accord with the Logic of Science." B.A. honors thesis Illinois 1966.

S 00948
──── . "History of Science in the Philosophy of Charles Sanders Peirce." M.A. thesis Illinois 1968.

S 00949
──── . "C.S. Peirce on the Philosophy of History." Diss. Illinois 1970.

S 00950
──── . "Peirce on the Use of History." *Transactions* 7 (1971), 105-126.

S 00951
──── . "Further Thoughts on Peirce's Use of History." *Transactions* 8 (1972), 115-122.

S 00952
Mills, C. Wright. "A Sociological Account of Some Aspects of Pragmatism." Diss. Wisconsin 1942, 89-176.

S 00953
──── . *Sociology and Pragmatism: The Higher Learning in America,* ed. Irving Louis Horowitz (New York: Paine-Whitman, 1964), 123-212. (Reviewed by Aiken [S 00009]).

S 00954
Min, Yung Wha Kim. "Pragmatism and Realism in Peirce's Philosophy." M.A. thesis Illinois 1963.

O 00342
"Mr. Thorn Heard From." 1886.

S 00955
Moloff, Paul Gregory. "Duns Scotus in the Systematic Philosophy of Charles Sanders Peirce." Diss. New York 1969.

S 00956
Montague, Richard. "Pragmatics and Intensional Logic." *Synthese* 22 (1970), 68-94.

O 01183
Montague, W.P. "May a Realist be a Pragmatist? I. The Two Doctrines Defined." 1909.

O 01184
──── . "May a Realist be a Pragmatist? II. The Implications of Instrumentalism." 1909.

O 01185
──── . "May a Realist be a Pragmatist? III. The Implications of Psychological Pragmatism." 1909.

O 01186
──── . "May a Realist be a Pragmatist? IV. The Implications of Humanism and the Pragmatic Criterion." 1909.

S 00957
──── . *The Ways of Knowing or the Methods of Philosophy* (New York: Macmillan, 1925), 131-133.

S 00958
──── . "The Story of American Realism." *Philosophy* 12 (1937), 140-161.

O 01113
Moore, Addison W. "Pragmatism and Its Critics." 1905.

S 00959
Moore, Asher. "The Promised Land." *Monist* 57 (1973), 176-190.

S 00960
Moore, Edward C. "Metaphysics and Pragmatism in the Philosophy of C.S. Peirce." Diss. Michigan 1950.

S 00961
———. "The Scholastic Realism of C.S. Peirce." *Philosophy and Phenomenological Research* 12 (1952), 406-417.

S 00962
———. "Professor Bastian's Comments on Peirce's Scholasticism." *Philosophy and Phenomenological Research* 14 (1953), 250-251. (See Bastian [S 00068]).

S 00963
———. *American Pragmatism: Peirce, James and Dewey.* New York: Columbia University Press, 1961. (Reviewed by Bernstein [S 00101], Fisch [S 00473], Fitzgerald [S 00503], Gallie [S 00540], McDermott [S 00867], Melvin [S 00921], Naus [S 01026] and Sibley [S 01342]).

S 00964
———. "The Influence of Duns Scotus on Peirce," in *Studies* II [S 00968], 401-413.

S 00965
———. "On the World as General." *Transactions* 4 (1968), 90-100.

S 00966
———, ed. *Charles S. Peirce: The Essential Writings.* New York: Harper & Row, 1972. (Reviewed by MacKinnon [S 00876]).

S 00967
———. "On an Alleged Incompatibility between Peirce's Metaphysics and his Pragmaticism." *Proceedings 1976,* forthcoming.

S 00968
Moore, Edward C., and Richard S. Robin. *Studies in the Philosophy of Charles Sanders Peirce, Second Series.* Amherst: University of Massachusetts Press, 1964. (Reviewed by Barclay [S 00063], Lieb [S 00842], Potter [S 01109], Ransdell [S01142], Schlaretzki [S 01296], and Schneider [S 01307]).

S 00969
Moore, Harold. "Ayer and the Pragmatic Maxim." *Transactions* 7 (1971), 168-175.

S 00970
Moore, Jared Sparks. "Charles Sanders Peirce." *Harvard Alumni Bulletin* 45 (1942), 37.

S 00971
Moore, Willis. "The Indexical and the Presentative Functions of Signs." *Philosophy of Science* 9 (1942), 367-371. (Discussed by Bergman [S 00096]).

S 00972
Morgan, Charles G. "Peirce—Semantics for Modal Logics." *Proceedings 1976,* forthcoming.

S 00973
Morgan, Douglas N. "Icon, Index, and Symbol in the Visual Arts." *Philosophical Studies* 6 (1955), 49-54.

S 00974
Morier, Claude. *Charles Sanders Peirce et la sémiotique.* Travaux du Centre de Recherches Sémiologiques 9 (Neuchâtel, 1971).

S 00975
―――. "La sémiotique de Charles Sanders Peirce." Diss. Lausanne, forthcoming.

S 00976
Morris, Charles. "Philosophy of Science and Science of Philosophy." *Philosophy of Science* 2 (1935). (Reprinted in his *Logical Positivism* [S 00979], 7-21).

S 00977
―――. "The Relation of the Formal and Empirical Sciences within Scientific Empiricism." *Erkenntnis* 5 (1935). (Reprinted in his *Logical Positivism* [S 00979], 46-55).

S 00978
―――. "Semiotic and Scientific Empiricism." *Proceedings of the First International Congress for the Unity of Science* (Paris: Hermann, 1936). (Reprinted in his *Logical Positivism* [S 00979], 56-71).

S 00979
―――. *Logical Positivism, Pragmatism and Scientific Empiricism.* Paris: Hermann, 1937.

S 00980
―――. "Peirce, Mead, and Pragmatism." *Philosophical Review* 47 (1938), 109-127.

S 00981
―――. *Foundations of the Theory of Signs.* Chicago: University of Chicago Press, 1938. (Published as Number 2 of Volume 1 of the *International Encyclopedia of Unified Science*). (Reviewed by Fitch [S 00500] and Nagel [S 01020]).

S 00982
―――. *Signs, Language and Behavior.* New York: Prentice-Hall, 1946.

S 00983
―――. "Signs about Signs about Signs." *Philosophy and Phenomenological Research* 9 (1948), 115-133.

S 00984
―――. "Pragmatism and Logical Empiricism," in *The Philosophy of Rudolf Carnap,* ed. P.A. Schilpp (La Salle, Ill.: Open Court, 1963), 87-98.

S 00985
―――. *Signification and Significance.* Cambridge, Mass.: M.I.T. Press, 1964. (Reviewed by Tibbetts [S 01426]).

S 00986
―――. *The Pragmatic Movement in American Philosophy.* New York: Braziller, 1970. (Reviewed by Krikarian [S 00785]).

S 00987
Morse, J. Mitchell. Review of Feibleman's *Introduction* [S 00451]. *New York Times Book Review* 51 (22 December 1946), 8.

S 00988
Mosier, Richard D. "The Peircean Critique of American Universities." *Harvard Educational Review* 16 (1946), 282-285.

S 00989
Mosteller, Frederick. "Nonsampling Errors." *International Encyclopedia of the Social Sciences* (1968), V:113-132, at 123-124.

O 00651
Muir, Thomas. "Reinvestigation of the Problem of the Automorphic Linear Transformation of a Bipartite Quadric." 1898.

S 00990
Muirhead, John Henry. "Peirce's Place in American Philosophy." *Philosophical Review* 37 (1928), 460-481. (Reprinted in his *The Platonic Tradition in Anglo-Saxon Philosophy* [New York: Macmillan, 1931]).

S 00991
———. Review of *Collected Papers* I. *Philosophy* 7 (1932), 245-246.

O 01180
Müller, Eugen. *Abriss der Algebra der Logik.* 1909. Reviewed by Anonymous [O 01197].

O 00251
Müller, Gustav. "Photometrische Untersuchungen." 1883.

O 00646
———. *Die Photometrie der Gestirne.* 1897.

S 00992
Müller, Gustav. "Charles Peirce." *Archiv für Geschichte der Philosophie* 40 (1931), 227-238.

S 00993
———. *Amerikanische Philosophie.* 2nd ed. (Stuttgart: Frommann, 1950), 135-149.

S 00994
Mullin, Albert A. *Philosophical Comments on the Philosophies of Charles Sanders Peirce and Ludwig Wittgenstein.* Urbana: Electrical Engineering Research Laboratory, Engineering Experiment Station, University of Illinois, 1961.

S 00995
———. Review of *Collected Papers* I-VI. *Mathematical Reviews* 22 (1961), 261.

S 00996
———. Review of Murphey's *Development* [S 01001]. *Mathematical Reviews* 23A (1962), 691-692.

S 00997
———. Review of Dubisch's *Lattices to Logic* [S 00374]. *American Journal of Physics* 33 (1965), 354-355.

S 00998
———. "C.S.S. Peirce and E.G.A. Husserl on the Nature of Logic." *Notre Dame Journal of Formal Logic* 7 (1966), 301-304.

S 00999
———. "On Reconciling the Logical Systems of Charles Sanders Peirce and Moses Maimonides: Preliminary Report" (abstract). *Journal of Symbolic Logic* 36 (1971), 698.

Multhauf, Robert P. See Lenzen, Victor F., and R.P. Multhauf [S 00827].

S 01000
Murphey, Murray G. "The Synechism of Charles Sanders Peirce." Diss. Yale 1954.

S 01001
―――. *The Development of Peirce's Philosophy.* Cambridge: Harvard University Press, 1961. (Reviewed by Barnes [S 00065], Blau [S 00129], Fitzgerald [S 00505], Gallie [S 00539], Goudge [S 00570], Huggett [S 00699], Mullin [S 00996], Potter [S 01109], Thompson [S 01417], and Wiener [S 01540]).

S 01002
―――. "On Peirce's Metaphysics." *Transactions* 1 (1965), 12-25.

S 01003
―――. "Charles Sanders Peirce," in Edwards' *Encyclopedia* [S 00386], VI:70-78.

S 01004
―――. "Toward an Understanding of C.S. Peirce" (review of *Studies* II [S 00968]). *Massachusetts Review* 8 (1967), 213-218.

S 01005
―――. "Kant's Children, the Cambridge Pragmatists." *Transactions* 4 (1968), 3-33.

S 01006
Murphree, Idus. "Peirce's Theory of Inquiry" (reply to Frankfurt [S 00517]). *Journal of Philosophy* 56 (1959), 667-678.

S 01007
―――. "The Theme of Positivism in Peirce's Pragmatism," in *Studies* II [S 00968], 226-241.

S 01008
―――. Review of Wennerberg's *Pragmatism* [S 01509]. *Philosophy of Science* 33 (1966), 189-190.

S 01009
Murphy, Frances H. "The Place of Moral Responsibility in the Philosophies of Whitehead and Peirce." Diss. Brown 1941.

O 01220
Murray, D.L. *Pragmatism.* 1912.

S 01010
Muses, C.A. "Centrality in the Ethics of Peirce." *Personalist* 31 (1950), 289-303.

O 00217
N., H.A. Review of Benjamin Peirce's *Linear Associative Algebra.* 1882.

O 00417
N., W.S. "Mathematical Weakness of Spencer's Philosophy." 1890.

S 01011
Nadin, Mihai. "The Repertory of Signs." *Semiosis* 1 (1976), 29-33.

S 01012
―――. "Sign and Fuzzy Automata." *Semiosis* 5 (1977), 19-26.

S 01013
Nagel, Ernest. Review of *Collected Papers* I. *Saturday Review of Literature* 8 (1932), 592.

S 01014
———. "Charles Peirce's Guesses at the Riddle" (review of *Collected Papers* I-II). *Journal of Philosophy* 30 (1933), 365-386. (Reply by Paul Weiss: 31 (1934), 251; Nagel's reply to Weiss: 31 (1934), 252).

S 01015
———. "Master of Logic" (review of *Collected Papers* III-IV). *New Republic* 80 (1934), 315-316.

S 01016
———. Review of *Collected Papers* III-IV. *Journal of Philosophy* 31 (1934), 188-190.

S 01017
———. Review of Freeman's *Categories* [S 00521]. *Journal of Philosophy* 31 (1934), 277-278.

S 01018
———. Review of *Collected Papers* V. *Journal of Philosophy* 31 (1934), 582-583.

S 01019
———. Review of *Collected Papers* VI. *Journal of Philosophy* 33 (1936), 107-109.

S 01020
———. Review of Morris' *Foundations* [S 00981]. *Journal of Philosophy* 35 (1938), 689-693.

S 01021
———. "Charles S. Peirce, Pioneer of Modern Empiricism." *Philosophy of Science* 7 (1940), 69-80.

S 01022
———. Review of Buchler's *Philosophy of Peirce* [S 00193]. *Journal of Philosophy* 38 (1941), 189-190.

S 01023
———. *Sovereign Reason* (Glencoe, Ill.: The Free Press, 1954), 58-100.

S 01024
———. "Charles Sanders Peirce, a Prodigious but Little-Known American Philosopher" (review of *Collected Papers* VII-VIII). *Scientific American* 200 (1959), 185-192.

O 00387
Nagy, Albino. "Fondamenti del calcolo logico." 1890.

S 01025
Natanson, Maurice. "The Concept of the Given in Peirce and Mead." *Modern Schoolman* 32 (1955), 143-157.

S 01026
Naus, J.E. Review of Moore's *American Pragmatism* [S 00963]. *Modern Schoolman* 40 (1963), 406-409.

S 01027
Nauta, Doede, Jr. "Peirce's Three Categories Regained." *Proceedings 1976,* forthcoming.

S 01028
Nedeljkovic, Dusan. *Pragmatizam i djalektika.* Belgrade: Kultura, 1960.

S 01029
Nelson, Raymond J. "Peirce's Theory of Knowledge." Diss. Chicago 1950.

S 01030
Nesher, Dan. "Peirce on Realism and Existence." *Proceedings 1976,* forthcoming.

S 01031
Nethery, Wallace. "C.S. Peirce to W.T. Harris." *Personalist* 43 (1962), 35-45.

O 00375
Newcomb, Simon. "The Century Dictionary." 1889.

O 00377
———— . "The Century Dictionary." 1889.

O 01158
———— . "The Work of George W. Hill." 1907.

S 01032
Newman, James R., ed. *The World of Mathematics: A Small Library of the Literature of Mathematics from A'h-mose the Scribe to Albert Einstein* (New York: Simon and Schuster, 1956), II:1334-1354; III:1767-1783.

S 01033
Newman, Jay. "The Faith of Pragmatists." *Sophia* (Melbourne), 13 (1974), 1-15.

S 01034
Nidditch, Peter H. *Elementary Logic of Science and Mathematics* (New York: The Free Press, 1960), 17, 67, 287-288, 309-326, 339-345.

S 01035
———— . *The Development of Mathematical Logic* (New York: The Free Press, 1962), 44, 48-57, 73, 81.

S 01036
Nissen, Lowell. *John Dewey's Theory of Inquiry and Truth* (The Hague: Mouton, 1966), 87-100.

S 01037
Northrop, F.S.C. "The Relation Between Naturalistic Scientific Knowledge and Humanistic Intrinsic Values in Western Culture," in Smith's *Contemporary American Philosophy* [S 01361], 107-151 (esp. 122-125, 148, 151).

S 01038
Norton, John Clyde. "The Politics of Pragmatism." Diss. Illinois 1965.

O 01025
Note on British Science. 1903.

O 00337
Note on investigation of Coast Survey. 1886.

O 00280
Note on Peirce's "'Old Stone Mill' at Newport." 1884.

O 00516
Note on Peirce's *Open Court* articles. 1892.

O 00585
Note on Peirce's review of Spinoza's *Ethic.* 1894.

O 00581
Note on the Proceedings of the Psychical Research Society. 1894.

S 01039
Nöth, Winfried. *Semiotik: Eine Einführung mit Beispielen für Reklameanalysen* (Tübingen: Max Niemeyer, 1975), 9-25.

O 00112
Notice of Peirce's *Photometric Researches*. 1878.

O 00124
Notice of Peirce's *Photometric Researches*. 1878.

O 00250
Notice of *Studies in Logic*. 1883.

S 01040
Nott, Kathleen. *Philosophy and Human Nature* (New York: New York University Press, 1971), 73-74, 78-79, 81-87, 92-99, 101-102, 191, 223, 228-229.

S 01041
Novak, Michael, ed. *American Philosophy and the Future: Essays for a New Generation* (New York: Scribner's, 1968), 107-137, 277-298.

O 01233
Obituary of Peirce. 1914.

S 01042
"An Ocean Ship from the Ohio River" (launching of hydrographic research ship, the *Peirce*). *Business Week* 10 (November 1962), 159-160.

S 01043
O'Connell, James O. "Charles Sanders Peirce and the Problem of Knowledge." *Philosophica I Studies* (Maynooth), 7 (1957), 3-42.

S 01044
———. "Charles Sanders Peirce's Conception of Philosophy." *Downside Review* 77 (1959), 277-295.

S 01045
———. "Charles Sanders Peirce," in *The Concise Encyclopedia of Western Philosophy and Philosophers,* ed. J.O. Urmson (London: Hutchinson, 1960), 287-290.

S 01046
O'Connor, Daniel D. "Peirce's Debt to F.E. Abbot." *Journal of the History of Ideas* 25 (1964), 534-564.

S 01047
O'Connor, Daniel J. Review of Feibleman's *Introduction* [S 00451]. *Ethics* 57 (1947), 233.

S 01048
O'Donnell, Sister Patricia A. "The Concepts of Explanation, Cause, Law and Reality in the Philosophy of Charles Sanders Peirce." Diss. Notre Dame 1976.

S 01049
Oehler, Klaus. *Charles S. Peirce, Über die Klarheit unserer Gedanken.* Frankfurt: Vittorio Klostermann, 1968. (Translation of "How to Make Our Ideas Clear," with introduction and commentary).

S 01050
———. "Peirce Research in West Germany." *The Charles S. Peirce Newsletter,* December 1973.

S 01051
———. Review of Greenlee's *Concept of Sign* [S 00587]. *Transactions* 10 (1974), 185-189.

S 01052
———. "Zur Logik einer Universalpragmatik." *Semiosis* 1 (1976), 14-22.

S 01053
———. "Peirce contra Aristotle: Two Forms of the Theory of Categories." *Proceedings 1976,* forthcoming.

S 01054
Ogden, C.K. Editorial. *Psyche* 15 (1935), 5-18.

S 01055
———. "Word Magic." *Psyche* 18 (1938), 19-126 (at 119-121).

S 01056
Ogden, C.K., and I.A. Richards. *The Meaning of Meaning* (London: Routledge and Kegan Paul, 1923), esp. 279-290. (Reprinted New York: Harcourt, Brace, 1930).

S 01057
O'Leary, Paul Thomas. "Peirce's Conception of Belief." Diss. Toronto 1973.

S 01058
———. "Peirce's First Property of Belief." *Transactions* 12 (1976), 284-290.

S 01059
Oliver, W. Donald. Review of *Studies* I [S 01549]. *Journal of Philosophy* 50 (1953), 528-535.

S 01060
———. "Peirce on 'The Ethics of Terminology.'" *Philosophical Quarterly*, 13 (1963), 238-245.

S 01061
———. "The Final Cause and Agapasm in Peirce's Philosophy," in *Studies* II [S 00968], 289-303.

S 01062
Olshewsky, Thomas M. "Realism and Semiosis." *Proceedings 1976,* forthcoming.

O 00412
Opperg, Carl. "Experience and Intuition." 1890.

O 00213
von Oppolzer, Theodor. *Syzygien-tafeln für den Mond.* 1881.

O 00295
———. "Ueber die Bestimmung der Schwere mit Hilfe verschiedener Apparate." 1884.

O 00239
von Orff, Carl. "Bestimmung der Länge des einfachen Secundenpendels auf der Sternwarte zu Bogenhausen." 1883.

S 01063
Ormiston, Gayle L. "Pragmaticism of Imagination in Wittgenstein's *Philosophical Investigations.*" M.A. thesis Kent State 1973.

S 01064
_____. "Categories in Peirce's Semiotic." *Proceedings of the First Annual Conference of the Semiotic Society of America* (Atlanta, 1976), forthcoming.

O 00410
Osborn, Henry Fairfield. "The Spencerian Biology." 1890.

O 00418
P., H.L. "Specialists and Generalizers." 1890.

S 01065
Paci, Enzo. Review of Abbagnano's *Caso, amore e logica* [S 00002]. *Aut Aut* 39 (1957), 310-311.

O 01221
Paget, Violet (under pseudonym Vernon Lee). *Vital Lies: Studies of Some Varieties of Recent Obscurantism.* 1912.

S 01066
Palmer, Humphrey. "Are Recurring Questions Serious?" *Proceedings 1976*, forthcoming.

S 01067
Pannekoek, Antonie. "Researches on the Structure of the Universe." *Publications of the Astronomical Institute of the University of Amsterdam* 1 (1924), 28.

S 01068
Pape, Helmut. "On a Connection Between Peirce's Theory of Perception and His Theory of Indexical Identification." *Proceedings 1976*, forthcoming.

S 01069
Pape, Leslie M. Review of *Collected Papers* I. *Annals of the American Academy of Political and Social Science* 162 (1932), 291.

S 01070
_____. Review of *Collected Papers* II. *Annals of the American Academy of Political and Social Science* 164 (1932), 271.

S 01071
_____. Review of *Collected Papers* III. *Annals of the American Academy of Political and Social Science* 169 (1933), 211-212.

S 01072
_____. Review of *Collected Papers* IV. *Annals of the American Academy of Political and Social Science* 174 (1934), 216.

S 01073
_____. Review of Freeman's *Categories* [S 00521]. *Annals of the American Academy of Political and Social Science* 174 (1934), 216.

S 01074
———. Review of *Collected Papers* V. *Annals of the American Academy of Political and Social Science* 177 (1935), 291.

S 01075
———. Review of *Collected Papers* VI. *Annals of the American Academy of Political and Social Science* 185 (1936), 253.

O 01226
Papini, Giovanni. *Sul Pragmatismo: Saggi e Ricerche.* 1913.

S 01076
Parente, Alfredo. "Il 'Primato del fare' e il prammatismo: Attivita in genere e attivita pratica." *Rivista di Studi Crociani* 8 (1971), 121-137.

S 01077
Parisi, D. Notice of Tomas' *Essays* [S 01428]. *Rassegna di Filosofia* 6 (1957), 193.

S 01078
Parks, R.Z. "The Mystery of Phi and Psi." *Transactions* 7 (1971), 176-177.

S 01079
Pasquinelli, Alberto. "Filosofia e scienza in Vailati e Peirce." *Rivista Critica di Storia della Filosofia* 18 (1963), 322-331.

S 01080
Passmore, John. *A Hundred Years of Philosophy* (London: Duckworth, 1957), 103-105, 111-112, 139-146.

S 01081
Patin, Henry A. "Pragmatism, Intuitionism, and Formalism." *Philosophy of Science* 24 (1957), 243-252.

O 01237
Peirce (notice of his death). *Proceedings of the American Academy of Arts and Sciences.* 1914.

O 01240
Peirce (obituary). *Report of the National Academy of Sciences for the Year 1914.* 1915.

O 00294
Peirce (references to his pendulum researches). *Verhandlungen der vom 15. bis zum 24. Oktober 1883 in Rom abgehaltenen siebenten Allgemeinen Conferenz der europäischen Gradmessung.* 1884.

O 00014
Peirce, Benjamin. Astronomical Works. 1864.

O 00046
———. "Computing Division." 1869.

O 00091
———. "On the Uses and Transformations of Linear Algebra." 1875.

O 00104
———. "Qualitative Algebra." 1877.

O 00193
———. *Ideality in the Physical Sciences.* 1881.

O 00223
———. Abstract of *Linear Associative Algebra.* 1882.

O 00240
Peirce, Benjamin Osgood, Jr. "On the Sensitiveness of the Eye to Slight Differences of Color." 1883.

S 01082
"Peirce, Charles Sanders Santiago," in *National Cyclopedia of American Biography* (New York: James T. White, 1924), VIII:409-410.

O 00180
Peirce, Frederick C. *Peirce Genealogy.* 1880.

O 01229
Peirce, Herbert Henry David. "Charles Sanders Peirce." 1914.

O 00612
Peirpont, James. "Note on Peirce's Paper on 'A Quincuncial Projection of the Sphere.'" 1896.

S 01083
Peixoto, D.S. "Algunos estudios sobre Charles S. Peirce." *Revista Portuguesa de Filosofia* 24 (1968), 454-456.

S 01084
Penati, Giancarlo. Review of Bosco's *Filosofia pragmatica* [S 00149]. *Rivista di Filosofia Neoscolastica* 54 (1962), 510-511.

S 01085
Percy, Walker. "Toward a Triadic Theory of Meaning." *Psychiatry* 35 (1972), 1-19.

S 01086
Perrier, Joseph Louis. "The Permanent Contributions of the Pragmatists." *Journal of Philosophy* 13 (1916), 267-273.

S 01087
Perry, Ralph Barton. *The Thought and Character of William James* (Boston: Little, Brown, 1935), I:533-542; II: 104-108, 406-440.

S 01088
Perry, Reginald C. "Some Observations Concerning the Philosophy of Charles S. Peirce." *Philosophical Quarterly* (St. Andrews), 9 (1959), 131-141.

S 01089
Peterfreund, Sheldon P. *An Introduction to American Philosophy* (New York: Odyssey, 1959), 7-59.

O 01081
Peterson, James B. "Some Philosophical Terms." 1905.

S 01090
Peterson, Sven R. "Benjamin Peirce: Mathematician and Philosopher." *Journal of the History of Ideas* 16 (1955), 89-112.

S 01091
Petrick, Joseph Anthony. "Peirce on Hegel." Diss. Pennsylvania State 1972.

S 01092
Pfeifer, David Elmer. "The Summum Bonum in the Philosophy of C. S. Peirce." Diss. Illinois 1971.

S 01093
──── . "Charles Peirce's Contribution to Religious Thought." *Proceedings 1976,* forthcoming.

S 01094
Pfeiffer, Raymond Smith. "Pragmatism and the Epistemology of Willard Van Orman Quine." Diss. Washington 1974 (esp. Ch. 1).

S 01095
Pfunter, Carl Herman. "An Examination of the Extent of Philosophical Dependence, Methodological and Metaphysical, of John Dewey on Charles Peirce." Diss. Georgetown 1966.

O 00118
Photometric Researches, Made in the Years 1872-1875. 1878.

O 00189
Pickering, Edward C. "Schreiben des Herrn Professor Edward C. Pickering an den Herausgeber." 1881.

S 01096
Pignatari, Decio. *Semiotica e literatura* (Sao Paulo: Perspectiva S.A., 1974), esp. 9-66.

S 01097
Pinkham, Gordon N. "Some Comments on Cheng, Peirce and Inductive Validity." *Transactions* 3 (1967), 96-107.

S 01098
Platt, David. "Transcendence of Subjectivity in Peirce and Whitehead." *Personalist* 49 (1968), 238-255.

S 01099
──── . "God: From Experience to Inference—A Phenomenological Study." *International Philosophical Quarterly* 10 (1970), 598-610.

S 01100
Pochmann, Henry A. *German Culture in America: Philosophical and Literary Influences, 1600-1900.* Madison: University of Wisconsin Press, 1957.

S 01101
Pollak, Gustav. *Fifty Years of American Idealism: The New York "Nation," 1865-1915* (New York: Houghton Mifflin, 1915), 50.

S 01102
Pollock, Robert C. Review of Feibleman's *Introduction* [S 00451]. *Thought* 23 (1948), 352-355.

S 01103
Pospesel, Howard Andrew. "The Existence of Propositions." Diss. North Carolina at Chapel Hill 1967.

S 01104
Potter, Vincent G. Review of Boler's *Scholastic Realism* [S 00136]. *International Philosophical Quarterly* 4 (1964), 317-320.

S 01105
───── . "Peirce's Ontological Pragmatism." Diss. Yale 1965.

S 01106
───── . "Peirce's Analysis of Normative Science." *Transactions* 2 (1966), 5-32.

S 01107
───── . "Normative Science and the Pragmatic Maxim." *Journal of the History of Philosophy* 5 (1967), 41-53.

S 01108
───── . *Charles S. Peirce on Norms and Ideals.* Amherst: University of Massachusetts Press, 1967. (Reviewed by Delaney [S 00320], Savan [S 01275], Schneider [S 01308], Stearns [S 01376], and Thompson [S 01421]).

S 01109
───── . "A Survey of Recent Peirce Literature." *International Philosophical Quarterly* 8 (1968), 593-618. (Reviews Bernstein [S 00105], Boler [S 00136], Fitzgerald [S 00508], Haas [S 00598], Knight [S 00769], Murphey [S 01001], *Studies* II [S 00968], and Wennerberg [S 01509]).

S 01110
───── . "'Vaguely like a Man': The Theism of Charles S. Peirce," in *God Knowable and Unknowable*, ed. Robert J. Roth (New York: Fordham University Press, 1973), 241-254.

S 01111
───── . "Peirce's Pragmatic Maxim." *Tijdschrift voor Filosofie* 35 (1973), 507-517.

S 01112
Potter, Vincent G., and Paul B. Shields. "Peirce's Definitions of Continuity." *Transactions* 13 (1977), 20-34.

S 01113
───── . "Peirce on Continuity." *Proceedings 1976,* forthcoming.

S 01114
Potts, Timothy C. Review of Boler's *Scholastic Realism* [S 00136]. *Philosophical Quarterly* 15 (1965), 361-362.

S 01115
Powell, Sumner C. "Charles S. Peirce, Semiosis, and the 'Mind.'" *ETC.: A Review of General Semantics* 10 (1953), 201-208.

S 01116
Power, William L. "Informative Discourse and Theology." *Religious Studies* 12 (1976), 21-36.

O 01203
Pratt, James B. *What Is Pragmatism?* 1909.

O 00338
"The Present Condition of the Coast Survey." 1886.

O 00466
Preston, E.D. "Determinations of Gravity and the Magnetic Elements in Connection with the U.S. Scientific Expedition to the West Coast of Africa, 1889-1890." 1891.

O 01074
Prezzolini, Giuseppe. "Il Mio Prammatismo." 1905.

S 01117
Prior, Arthur N. "On Some Consequentiae in Walter Burleigh." *New Scholasticism* 27 (1953), 433-446 (at 443-444).

S 01118
———. *Formal Logic* (New York: Oxford University Press, 1955), 48-51.

S 01119
———. Comment on Ueyama's "Development of Peirce's Theory of Logic" [S 01457]. *Journal of Symbolic Logic* 20 (1955), 170.

S 01120
———. "The Logic Game." *Listener* 57 (1957), esp. 675, 718-719.

S 01121
———. *Time and Modality* (New York: Oxford University Press, 1957), 111-116.

S 01122
———. "Peirce's Axioms for Propositional Calculus." *Journal of Symbolic Logic* 23 (1958), 135-136. (Critiqued by Fitch [S 00501]).

S 01123
———. "The Formalities of Omniscience." *Philosophy* 37 (1962), 114-129.

S 01124
———. "The Theory of Implication." *Zeitschrift für mathematische Logik und Grundlagen der Mathematik* 9 (1963), 1-6.

S 01125
———. "The Algebra of the Copula," in *Studies* II [S 00968], 79-94.

S 01126
———. "Postulates for Tense-Logic." *American Philosophical Quarterly* 3 (1966), 153-161.

S 01127
———. "Stratified Metric Tense-Logic." *Theoria* 33 (1967), 28-38.

S 01128
———. "Peirce" (in "History of Logic"), in Edwards' *Encyclopedia of Philosophy* [S 00386], IV:546-549.

S 01129
———. *Past, Present and Future* (Oxford: Clarendon, 1967), 128-136, 172.

S 01130
———. "Egocentric Logic." *Noûs* 2 (1968), 191-207 (at 203-207).

S 01131
———. *Papers on Time and Tense* (Oxford: Clarendon, 1968), 44, 72, 96-97.

S 01132
———. *Objects of Thought* (Oxford: Clarendon, 1971), 105, 145-149, 153.

O 00636
Pritchard, Ada. *The Life and Work of Professor Pritchard.* 1897.

O 00228
Pritchard, C. "Photometric Determination of the Relative Brightness of the Brighter Stars North of the Equator." 1882.

S 01133
Pritchard, Ilona Kemp. "A Critical Examination of the Role of Continuity in Peirce's Thought." Diss. State University of New York at Stony Brook 1976.

S 01134
Pulsifer, Susan Nichols. *Witch's Breed: The Peirce-Nichols Family of Salem* (Cambridge, Mass.: Dresser, Chapman and Grimes, 1967), 223-232 ("Charles Sanders Peirce and Continuance").

S 01135
Quine, Willard Van Orman. Review of *Collected Papers* II. *Isis* 19 (1933), 220-229.

S 01136
―――. Review of *Collected Papers* III. *Isis* 22 (1934), 285-297.

S 01137
―――. Review of *Collected Papers* IV. *Isis* 22 (1934), 551-553.

S 01138
―――. *Ontological Relativity and Other Essays* (New York: Columbia University Press, 1969), 78-80.

O 00419
R., S.D. "Where Spencer Fails."

S 01139
Rademacher, Hans. "Zum Problem der transzendentalen Apperzeption bei Kant." *Zeitschrift für philosophische Forschung* 24 (1970), 28-49.

S 01140
Ramakrishna, Rao I. *Gandhi and Pragmatism: An Intercultural Study.* Calcutta: Oxford and IBH Pub. Co., 1968.

S 01141
Ramsey, Frank Plumpton. *The Foundations of Mathematics and Other Logical Essays* (London: Kegan Paul, 1931), 156, 185, 186, 194-198, 201-203.

S 01142
Ransdell, Joseph. Review of *Studies* II [S 00968]. *Philosophy and Phenomenological Research* 26 (1965), 295-297.

S 01143
―――. "Charles Peirce: The Idea of Representation." Diss. Columbia 1966.

S 01144
―――. "Book Notes" (Comments on Scheffler's *Four Pragmatists* [S 01281], Morris's *Pragmatic Movement* [S 00986], and Roberts' *Existential Graphs* [S 01201]). *The Charles S. Peirce Newsletter,* April 1975.

S 01145
―――. "Book Notes" (review of Rosensohn's *Phenomenology* [S 01220]). *The Charles S. Peirce Newsletter,* April 1976.

S 01146
———. "Another Interpretation of Peirce's Semiotic." *Transactions* 12 (1976), 97-110. (Criticism of Greenlee [S 00587] ; see also Greenlee's reply [S 00589]).

S 01147
———. *The Pursuit of Wisdom: A History of Philosophy* (Santa Barbara, Calif.: Intelman Books, 1976), Ch. 12 ("Communication and Community: Wittgenstein and Peirce").

S 01148
———. "A Misunderstanding of Peirce's Phenomenology" (criticism of Tibbetts [S 01427]). *Philosophy and Phenomenological Research,* forthcoming.

S 01149
———. "On the Aim and Application of Peirce's Semiotic." *Proceedings of the First Annual Conference of the Semiotic Society of America* (Atlanta, 1976), forthcoming. (Revised version forthcoming in *Semiotica* as "Some Leading Ideas of Peirce's Semiotic.")

S 01150
———. "Semiotic Causation: A Partial Explication." *Proceedings 1976,* forthcoming.

O 00141
Ranyard, A.C. "Observations Made During Total Solar Eclipses." 1879.

S 01151
Rawlins, F.I.G. Review of Collected Papers VII-VIII. *Nature* 183 (1959), 276-277.

S 01152
Ray, Binayendranath. "Pragmatism," in *History of Philosophy Eastern and Western,* ed. Saprepalli Radhakrishnan (London: Allen and Unwin, 1957), II: 336ff.

S 01153
Rayleigh, Baron John William Strutt. *Scientific Papers,* Vol. III (London: Cambridge University Press, 1902), 111.

S 01154
Reck, Andrew J. Review of Thayer's *Meaning and Action* [S 01402] and Pragmatism: The Classic Writings [S 01403]. *Man and World* 4 (1971), 331-341.

S 01155
Reese, William. Review of Goudge's *Thought* [S 00565]. *Philosophy and Phenomenological Research* 11 (1951), 600-601.

S 01156
———. "Philosophic Realism: A Study in the Modality of Being in Peirce and Whitehead," in *Studies* I [S 01549], 225-237.

S 01157
———. Review of Thompson's *Pragmatic Philosophy* [S 01416]. *Philosophy and Phenomenological Research* 15 (1954), 133-135.

S 01158
———. "Peirce on Abstraction." *Review of Metaphysics* 14 (1961), 704-713.

S 01159
Reichenbach, Hans. "Dewey's Theory of Science," in *The Philosophy of John Dewey,* ed. P.A. Schilpp (Evanston, Ill.: Northwestern University Press, 1939), 159-192, esp. 187-190.

S 01160
──── . *The Theory of Probability: An Inquiry into the Logical and Mathematical Foundations of the Calculus of Probability.* 2nd ed. (Berkeley and Los Angeles: University of California Press, 1949), 446n.

S 01161
Reilly, Francis Eagan. "The Method of the Sciences According to Charles Sanders Peirce." Diss. St. Louis 1959.

S 01162
──── . *Charles Peirce's Theory of Scientific Method.* New York: Fordham University Press, 1970. (Noticed by Frank [S 00515]). (Reviewed by Greenlee [S 00586]).

S 01163
Reinert, Harry F., Jr. "Evolutionary Ethics." *Ethics* 62 (1951), 48-54.

S 01164
Reinfrank, Arno. "In Memoriam Charles Sanders Peirce (1839-1914)" (poem). *Dimension: Contemporary German Arts and Letters* 6:3 (1973), 560-561.

S 01165
Reingold, Nathan. *Science in Nineteenth-Century America: A Documentary History* (New York: Hill and Wang, 1964), 226-235. (Reviewed by Hutten [S 00707]).

S 01166
Rescher, Nicholas. *Many-Valued Logic* (New York: McGraw-Hill, 1969), 3-5, 20.

S 01167
──── . "Peirce and the Economy of Research." *Philosophy of Science* 43 (1976), 71-98.

S 01168
──── . "Peirce on Scientific Progress." *Proceedings 1976,* forthcoming.

S 01169
Rescher, Nicholas, and Thomas C. Vinci. "The Truth-Relevancy of the Pragmatic Utility of Beliefs." *Review of Metaphysics* 28 (1975), 443-452.

S 01170
Réthoré, Joëlle. "Sémiotique de la syntaxe et de la phonologie." *Semiosis* 3 (1976), 5-18.

S 01171
Review of Buchler's *Empiricism* [S 00188]. *Times Literary Supplement* 39 (1940), 68.

S 01172
Review of Buchler's *Philosophy of Peirce* [S 00193]. *Times Literary Supplement* 39 (1940), 640.

S 01173
Review of *Collected Papers* I. *Revue de Métaphysique et de Morale* 40 (Supplément Avril-Juin, 1933), 10-11.

S 01174
Review of *Collected Papers* I. *Harvard Alumni Bulletin* 34 (1931), 316-317.

S 01175
Review of *Collected Papers* II. *Times Literary Supplement* 31 (1932), 656.

S 01176
Review of *Collected Papers* III-V. *Nature* 135 (1935), 131.

S 01177
Review of *Collected Papers* III-VI. *Times Literary Supplement* 35 (1936), 272.

S 01178
Review of *Collected Papers* VII-VIII. *Times Literary Supplement* 58 (1959), 181.

O 01197
Review of Eugen Müller's *Abriss der Algebra der Logik,* I [O 01180]. 1909.

S 01179
Review of Feibleman's *Introduction* [S 00451]. *Times Literary Supplement* 60 (1961), 568.

S 01180
Review of Gallie's *Pragmatism* [S 00534]. *Listener* 48 (1952), 733-735.

S 01181
Review of Gallie's *Pragmatism* [S 00534]. *Times Literary Supplement* 51 (1952), 521.

S 01182
Review of Goudge's *Thought* [S 00565]. *Times Literary Supplement* 51 (1952), Religion and Philosophy Section, iv.

O 00325
Review of Peirce and Jastrow's *On Small Differences of Sensation.* 1886.

O 00146
Review of Peirce's *Photometric Researches.* 1879.

S 01183
Review of *Studies* I [S 01549]. *Revue de Métaphysique et de Morale* 58 (1953). 212.

S 01184
"La Revue trimestrielle américaine consacrée à la philosophie de Peirce." *Studia Filosoficzne* 16 (1972), 197-200.

S 01185
Rey, Alain. "On Peirce's Definition of the Semiotic Process: Some Implications." *Proceedings 1976,* forthcoming.

O 00436
Reyes y Prósper, Ventura. "Cristina Ladd Franklin: Matemática Americana y su influencia en la logica simbolica." 1891.

O 00469
———— . "Charles Santiago Peirce y Oscar Honward Mitchell." 1892.

S 01186
Reznikow, Lasar O. "The Antiscientific Nature of the Pragmatic Concepts of Sign, Meaning and Thing" (in Russian). *Filosofskie Nauki* 1 (1963), 74-82.

S 01187
"Rho". Review of *Encyclopedia of the Philosophical Sciences,* Vol. I, by Arnold Ruge et al. *Monist* 25 (1915), 160.

Richards, I.A. See Ogden, C.K., and I.A. Richards [S 01056].

S 01188
Riley, Gresham. "The Self, Self-Knowledge and Pragmaticism." Diss. Yale 1965.

S 01189
——— . "Existence, Reality and Objects of Knowledge: A Defense of C.S. Peirce as a Realist." *Transactions* 4 (1968), 34-38.

S 01190
——— . Review of Thayer's *Meaning and Action* [S 01402]. *Metaphilosophy* 2 (1971), 171-184.

S 01191
——— . "Peirce's Theory of Individuals." *Transactions* 10 (1974), 135-165.

S 01192
——— . Critical Comments on Thayer's *Meaning and Action* [S 01402]. Transactions 11 (1975), 249-257. (Reply by Thayer [S 01405]).

S 01193
Riley, Isaac W. *American Thought from Puritanism to Pragmatism and Beyond.* New York: Holt, Rinehart, 1923.

S 01194
Ring, John Walter. "Peirce's Contribution to a Logic of Discovery." Diss. Minnesota 1970.

S 01195
Ringer, Virginia Hartt. Notice of Tomas' *Essays* [S 01428]. *Philosophy* 39 (1958), 178.

S 01196
Riverso, Emmanuele. *Metafisica e scientismo: Con un' appendice sulla logica di C.S. Peirce* (Napoli: Istituto Editoriale del Mezzogiorno, 1957), 126-146.

S 01197
Rivetti Barbò, Francesca. *L'antinomia del mentitore nel pensiero contemporaneo de Peirce a Tarski: Studi-testi-bibliografia* (Milan: Società editrice "Vita e pensiero", 1961), xxxi, 1-37, 334-345.

S 01198
Roberts, Don Davis. "The Existential Graphs of Charles S. Peirce." Diss. Illinois 1963.

S 01199
——— . "The Existential Graphs and Natural Deduction," in *Studies* II [S 00968], 109-121. (Reviewed by Zeman [S 01585]).

S 01200
——— . "On Peirce's Realism." *Transactions* 6 (1970), 67-83. (Criticism of Fisch [S 00479]).

S 01201
——— . *The Existential Graphs of Charles S. Peirce.* The Hague: Mouton, 1973. (Reviewed by Hawkins [S 01201] and Zeman [S 01587]).

S 01202
——— . "Peirce's Proof of Pragmaticism and his Existential Graphs." *Proceedings 1976,* forthcoming.

Roberts, Don Davis. See Crapo, Henry H., and D.D. Roberts [S 00296].

S 01203
Robin, Richard S. "Critical Common-Sensism: A Critical Study in the Philosophy of C.S. Peirce." Diss. Harvard 1958.

S 01204
———. "Peirce's Doctrine of the Normative Sciences," in *Studies* II [S 00968], 271-288.

S 01205
———. *Annotated Catalogue of the Papers of Charles S. Peirce.* Amherst: University of Massachusetts Press, 1967.

S 01206
———. "The Peirce Papers: A Supplementary Catalogue." *Transactions* 7 (1971), 37-57.

S 01207
———. "Peirce and the Foundations of Knowledge." *Proceedings 1976,* forthcoming.

Robin, Richard S. See Moore, Edward C., and R.S. Robin [S 00968].

O 00361
Rogers, William A. "Report of Professor William A. Rogers." 1887.

S 01208
Rollins, C.D. Review of *Studies* I [S 01549]. *Australasian Journal of Philosophy* 3 (1958), 222-231.

O 00145
Rood, Ogden N. *Modern Chromatics, With Applications to Art and Industry.* 1879.

S 01209
Rorty, Amelie, ed. *Pragmatic Philosophy: An Anthology* (Garden City, N.Y.: Anchor Books, 1966), 3-118.

S 01210
Rorty, Richard. "Pragmatism, Categories, and Language." *Philosophical Review* 70 (1961), 197-223.

S 01211
———. Review of Madden's *Chauncey Wright* [S 00883]. *Philosophical Review* 73 (1964), 287-289.

S 01212
———. Review of Boler's *Scholastic Realism* [S 00136]. *Philosophical Review* 75 (1966), 116-119.

S 01213
———. Review of Ayer's *Origins* [S 00054]. *Philosophical Review* 80 (1971), 96-100.

S 01214
Rosenberg, Jay F. "What's Happening in Philosophy of Language Today: A Metaphysician's-Eye View." *American Philosophical Quarterly* 9 (1972), 101-106.

S 01215
———. "Transcendental Arguments Revisited." *Journal of Philosophy* 72 (1975), 611-624.

S 01216
Rosenblatt, David. "On the Graphs and Asymptotic Forms of Finite Boolean Relation Matrices and Stochastic Matrices." *Naval Research Logistics Quarterly* 4 (1957), 151-167.

S 01217
———. "On Some Aspects of Models of Complex Behavioral Systems," in Information and Decision Processes, ed. R.E. Machol (New York: McGraw-Hill, 1960), 62-86.

S 01218
—— . "On the Graphs of Finite Idempotent Boolean Relation Matrices." *Journal of Research of the National Bureau of Standards—Mathematics and Mathematical Physics* 67B (1963), 249-256.

S 01219
Rosensohn, William L. "The Phenomenology of Charles S. Peirce." Diss. State University of New York at Buffalo 1972.

S 01220
—— . *The Phenomenology of Charles S. Peirce: From the Doctrine of Categories to Phaneroscopy.* Amsterdam: B.R. Grüner, 1974. (Reviewed by Ransdell [S 01145]).

S 01221
Rosenthal, Aaron. "Epistemology and Public Understanding: A Methodological Orientation," in *Philosophy in the Life of a Nation* (New York: Bicentennial Symposium of Philosophy, 1976), 252-258.

S 01222
Rosenthal, Sandra B. "A Pragmatic Concept of 'The Given'." *Transactions* 3 (1967), 74-95.

S 01223
—— . "A Systematic Expansion of C.I. Lewis' Conceptual Pragmatism with Reference to the Philosophies of Peirce and Mead." Diss. Tulane 1968.

S 01224
—— . "A Comment on Some Comments." *Dialectica* 22 (1968), 318-320.

S 01225
—— . "The Would-be Present of C.S. Peirce." *Transactions* 4 (1968), 155-163.

S 01226
—— . "Peirce, Mead and the Logic of Concepts." *Transactions* 5 (1969), 173-187.

S 01227
—— . "Peirce's Theory of the Perceptual Judgment: An Ambiguity." *Journal of the History of Philosophy* 7 (1969), 303-314.

S 01228
—— . "Charles Peirce and the Category of Firstness." *Tulane Studies in Philosophy* 21 (1972), 39-50.

S 01229
—— . "Pragmatism, Process, and Potentiality." *Southern Journal of Philosophy* 10 (1972), 307-312.

S 01230
—— . "Pragmatism and the Methodology of Metaphysics." *Monist* 57 (1973), 252-264.

S 01231
—— . "On the Metaphysical Significance of What Peirce is Not." *Southern Journal of Philosophy* 12 (1974), 455-467.

S 01232
—— . "Recent Perspectives on American Pragmatism (Part One)." *Transactions* 10 (1974), 76-93; (Part Two), 166-184. (See Wilshire, B.W. [S 01555] and Rosenthal [S 01234]).

S 01233
——— . "On the Epistemological Significance of What Peirce Is Not," in *Philosophy in the Life of a Nation* (New York: Bicentennial Symposium of Philosophy, 1976), 259-266.

S 01234
——— . "Pragmatism and Phenomenology: The Significance of Wilshire's Reply." *Transactions* 13 (1977), 56-66. (See Wilshire, B.W. [S 01555] and Rosenthal [S 01232]).

S 01235
——— . "C.S. Peirce: Pragmatism, Semiotic Structure, and Lived Perceptual Experience." *Proceedings 1976*, forthcoming.

S 01236
Ross, Dorothy. *G. Stanley Hall: The Psychologist as Prophet* (Chicago: University of Chicago Press, 1972), 135-138.

S 01237
Ross, Gregory A. "Peirce, Strawson and the Quest for Categories." Diss. State University of New York at Buffalo 1969.

S 01238
——— . *Grounds for Grammar*. Washington, D.C.: University Press of America, 1976. (Reviewed by Johnstone [S 00725]).

S 01239
Ross, James F. Review of Boler's *Scholastic Realism* [S 00136]. *Journal of Philosophy* 62 (1965), 80-83.

S 01240
Ross, Stephen D. "Truth in Science: Unrestricted Validity." *Transactions* 6 (1970), 46-57.

S 01241
Rossi, Mario M. Review of *Collected Papers* V. *Logos* 19 (1936), 152-157.

S 01242
Roth, Friederike, tr. *Charles Sanders Peirce; Graphen und Zeichen—Prolegomena Zu einer Apologie des Pragmatizismus*. rot 44 (Stuttgart: edition rot, 1971).

S 01243
Roth, John K. Review of Ayer's *Origins* [S 00054]. *Journal of the History of Philosophy* 10 (1972), 375-376.

S 01244
Roth, Robert J. Review of Smith's *Spirit of American Philosophy* [S 01357]. *International Philosophical Quarterly* 3 (1963), 629-630.

S 01245
——— . "Charles Sanders Peirce, 1839-1914: A Philosopher Whose Religious Writings Foreshadowed Ideas being Expressed Today." *America* 111 (1964), 108-110.

S 01246
——— . "Is Peirce's Pragmatism Anti-Jamesian?" *International Philosophical Quarterly* 5 (1965), 541-563.

S 01247
——— . "American Philosophy and the Future of Man." *Proceedings of the American Catholic Philosophical Association* 42 (1968), 209-216.

S 01248
—— . Review of Ayer's Origins [S 00054] and Thayer's *Meaning and Action* [S 01402]. *International Philosophical Quarterly* 9 (1969), 297-299.

S 01249
Rothe, Hermann. "Systeme Geometrischer Analyse," in *Encyklopädie der mathematischen Wissenschaften* (Leipzig: B.G. Teubner, 1914-31), III.1.2: 1307, 1381, 1420.

O 00181
Rowland, Henry Augustus. "Remarks on Charles Sanders Peirce's Paper on the Ghosts in Rutherford's Grating." 1880.

O 00269
—— . "Remarks in accepting the Rumford Medal." 1884.

O 00346
—— . "On the Relative Wave-Length of the Lines of the Solar Spectrum." 1887.

O 00349
—— . "On the Relative Wavelengths of the Lines of the Solar Spectrum." 1887.

O 00999
—— . *Physical Papers.* 1902.

O 00594
Royce, Josiah. "Natural Law, Ethics, and Evolution." 1895.

O 00609
—— . "Self-Consciousness, Social Consciousness, and Nature." 1895.

O 00675
—— . *Studies in Good and Evil.* 1898.

O 00707
—— . *The World and the Individual.* 1899.

O 01070
—— . Introduction to *La philosophie en Amérique,* by L. van Becelaere. 1904.

O 01117
—— . "The Relations of the Principles of Logic to the Foundations of Geometry." 1905.

O 01143
—— . "The Present State of the Question Regarding the First Principles of Theoretical Science." 1906.

O 01181
—— . "The Problem of Truth in the Light of Recent Discussion." 1909.

O 01222
—— . *William James and Other Essays on the Philosophy of Life.* 1912.

O 01223
—— . "The Principles of Logic." 1913.

O 01224
—— . "Some Psychological Problems Emphasized by Pragmatism." 1913.

O 01227
——— . *The Problem of Christianity.* 1913.

O 01228
——— . "Some Relations Between Philosophy and Science in the First Half of the Nineteenth Century in German." 1913.

O 01238
——— . "The Mechanical, the Historical and the Statistical." 1914.

O 01239
——— . *War and Insurance.* 1914.

S 01250
——— . "Mind," in *Encyclopedia of Religion and Ethics* (1915), VIII: 649-657. (Reprinted in Royce's *Logical Essays* [S 01251], 146-178).

S 01251
——— . *Logical Essays,* ed. D.S. Robinson. Dubuque: Wm. C. Brown, 1951.

O 01241
Royce, Josiah, and Fergus Kernan. "Charles Sanders Peirce." 1916.

S 01252
Ruddick, Sara. Critical Notice of Habermas' *Knowledge and Human Interest* [S 00600]. *Canadian Journal of Philosophy* 2 (1973), 545-569.

O 01073
Ruger, Henry A. Review of Peirce's *What Pragmatism Is.* 1905.

S 01253
Rugg, Harold. *Foundations for American Education* (Yonkers-on-Hudson: World Book Co., 1947), 73-87.

S 01254
Rukeyser, Muriel. *Willard Gibbs* (New York: Doubleday, Doran & Co., 1942), 217, 250, 280, 378.

O 00780
Russell, Bertrand. "Recent Work in the Principles of Mathematics." 1901.

O 01033
——— . *The Principles of Mathematics.* 1903.

S 01255
——— . "Dewey's New *Logic*," in *The Philosophy of John Dewey,* ed. P.A. Schilpp (Evanston, Ill.: Northwestern University Press, 1939), 137-156, at 144-146.

S 01256
——— . *A History of Western Philosophy* (New York: Simon & Schuster, 1945), 816, 824.

S 01257
——— . Foreword to Feibleman's *Introduction* [S 00451].

S 01258
——— . *Wisdom of the West,* ed. Paul Faulkes (New York: Doubleday, 1959), 276-278, 279, 296.

S 01259
——— . Unpublished notes on Peirce's "On the Algebra of Logic" (1880) and "On the Algebra of Logic: A Contribution to the Philosophy of Notation" (1885), preserved in the Russell Archives at McMaster University.

O 00522
Russell, Francis C. "Logic as Relation-Lore." 1893.

O 00556
——— . "Logic as Relation-Lore: Rejoinder to M. Mouret by Mr. Russell." 1894.

O 01174
——— . "Hints for the Elucidation of Mr. Peirce's Logical Work." 1908.

O 01232
——— . "In Memoriam Charles S. Peirce: (Born 1839, died 1914)." 1914.

O 00490
S., J. McL. "Is Induction an Inference?" 1892.

O 00422
S., W.E. "Space and Form." 1890.

O 00400
S., W.L. "The 'Pons Asinorum'." 1890.

O 01114
Sabine, George H. Review of Peirce's *What Pragmatism Is*. 1905.

O 01142
——— . Review of Peirce's *Issues of Pragmaticism*. 1906.

S 01260
Sabra, Nancy Sutton. Review of Tomas' *Essays* [S 01428] and Wiener's *Values* [S 01538]. *British Journal for the Philosophy of Science* 12 (1961), 72-73.

S 01261
Saint-Maurice, Beraud. "The Contemporary Significance of Duns Scotus' Philosophy," in *Studies in Philosophy and the History of Philosophy,* ed. J.K. Ryan and B.M. Bonansea (Washington, D.C.: The Catholic University of America Press, 1965), III:345-367.

S 01262
Salanitro, Niccolò. *Peirce e i problemi dell' interpretazione.* Genoa: Silva, 1969.

S 01263
Sanders, Gary. "Peirce's Sixty-six Signs." *Transactions* 6 (1970), 3-16.

S 01264
Santayana, George. Letter to Justus Buchler. *Journal of Philosophy* 51 (1954), 54.

S 01265
Santucci, Antonio. *Il pragmatismo in Italia*. Bologna: Mulino, 1963.

S 01266
——— . "Vailati e il pragmatismo americano." *Rivista Critica di Storia della Filosofia* 18 (1963), 322-331.

S 01267
──── . "Peirce e la critica del senso comune." *Rivista di Filosofia* 60 (1969), 401-432.

S 01268
──── . "Peirce, Hegel e la dottrina delle categoria," in *Incidenza di Hegel,* ed. F. Tessitore (Naples: Morano, 1970), 965-984.

S 01269
Savan, David. "On the Origins of Peirce's Phenomenology," in *Studies* I [S 01549], 185-194.

S 01270
──── . "Peirce and Pragmatism" (review of Gallie's *Pragmatism* [S 00534]). *University of Toronto Quarterly* 22 (1952), 90-93.

S 01271
──── . Review of Thompson's *Pragmatic Philosophy* [S 01416]. *Philosophical Review* 64 (1955), 329-330.

S 01272
──── . "Peirce as Man and Philosopher" (review of *Collected Papers* VII-VIII). *Canadian Forum* 39 (1959), 87-88.

S 01273
──── . "Peirce's Infallibilism," in *Studies* II [S 00968], 190-211.

S 01274
──── . "Decision and Knowledge in Peirce." *Transactions* 1 (1965), 35-51.

S 01275
──── . Review of Potter's *Norms and Ideals* [S 01108]. *Transactions* 4 (1969), 163-168.

S 01276
──── . "Peirce's Semiotic Theory of Emotion." *Proceedings 1976,* forthcoming.

S 01277
──── . "Some Questions Concerning Certain Trichotomies Claimed for Signs." *Proceedings of the First Annual Conference of the Semiotic Society of America* (Atlanta, 1976), forthcoming (also forthcoming in *Semiotica).*

S 01278
Savery, William." Chance and Cosmogony." *Philosophical Review* 41 (1932), 147-179.

S 01279
──── . "Concatenism." *Journal of Philosophy* 34 (1937), 337-354.

S 01280
──── . "The Significance of Dewey's Philosophy," in *The Philosophy of John Dewey,* ed. P.A. Schilpp (Evanston, Ill.: Northwestern University Press, 1939), 481-513.

O 00132
Sawitsch, M.A. "E. Plantamour's recherches expérimentales sur le mouvement simultané d'un pendule et de ses supports." 1878.

O 00142
──── . "Les longueurs du pendule à secondes à Poulkova, à St.-Petersbourg, et aux différents points de la Russie occidentale, corrigées de l'influence produite par la flexion des supports du pendule construits par M. Repsold." 1879.

O 00438
Scheffers, Georg. "Zuruckfuhrung complexer Zahlensysteme auf typische Formen." 1891.

S 01281
Scheffler, Israel. *Four Pragmatists: A Critical Introduction to Peirce, James, Mead, and Dewey.* London: Routledge & Kegan Paul, 1974. (Reviewed by Gouinlock [S 00574], Haack [S 00596], Hookway [S 00689], Howard [S 00692], Humphries [S 00705], Mays [S 00915], Ransdell [S 01144], and Thompson [S 01423].

O 00591
Scheiner, J. *A Treatise on Astronomical Spectroscopy.* 1894.

S 01282
Scheler, Max. *Die Wissensformen und die Gesellschaft* (Leipzig: Der Neue Geist, 1926), 259-323.

O 01076
Schiller, F.C.S. "The Definition of 'Pragmatism' and 'Humanism'." 1905.

O 01152
——— . Review of James' *Pragmatism* [S 00717] 1907.

S 01283
——— . Review of *Collected Papers* I. *Personalist* 13 (1932), 142-143.

S 01284
——— . Review of *Collected Papers* II. *Personalist* 14 (1933), 140-141.

S 01285
——— . Review of Collected Papers III. *Personalist* 15 (1934), 174-177.

S 01286
——— . Review of *Collected Papers* IV. *Personalist* 16 (1935), 78-80.

S 01287
——— . Review of *Collected Papers* V. *Personalist* 16 (1935), 169-173.

S 01288
——— . Review of *Collected Papers* VI. *Personalist* 17 (1936), 196-201.

S 01289
Schlaretzki, Walter Ernest. Review of Fiebleman's *Introduction* [S 00451]. *Philosophical Review* 56 (1947), 695-702.

S 01290
——— . Review of Wiener's *Evolution* [S 01533]. *Philosophical Review* 60 (1951), 131-133.

S 01291
——— . Review of Goudge's *Thought* [S 00565]. *Philosophical Review* 60 (1951), 249-252.

S 01292
——— . Review of *Studies* I [S 01549] and Gallie's *Pragmatism* [S 00534]. *Philosophical Review* 62 (1953), 631-636.

S 01293
——— . Review of von Kempski's *Pragmatismus* [S 00742]. *Philosophical Review* 63 (1954), 444-445.

S 01294
───── . "The Idea of Community in Royce, Peirce and Mead." Diss. Cornell 1958.

S 01295
───── . "Scientific Reasoning and the Summum Bonum." *Philosophy of Science* 27 (1960), 48-57.

S 01296
───── . Review of *Studies* II [S 00968]. *Philosophical Review* 76 (1967), 241-244.

O 00301
Schlegel. "C.S. Peirce. On the relative forms of quaternions." 1885.

S 01297
Schmalriede, Manfred. "Bemerkungen zu den Interpretanten bei Ch. S. Peirce." *Semiosis* 3 (1976), 26-30.

S 01298
Schmehl, H. "Schwerkraftmessungen." *Handbuch der Experimentalphysik* 25 (1931), 192-242, at 204, 206, 209, 210.

S 01299
Schmidt, H. Arnold. *Mathematische Gesetze der Logik, I* (Berlin: Springer-Verlag, 1960), 109, 212, 214, 362.

S 01300
Schneider, Erna F. "Recent Discussions of Subjunctive Conditionals." *Review of Metaphysics* 6 (1953), 623-649.

S 01301
Schneider, Hans J. "Towards a Pragmatic Foundation of Linguistic Categories." *Proceedings 1976*, forthcoming.

S 01302
Schneider, Herbert W. Review of Leroux' *Pragmatisme américain* [S 00829]. *Journal of Philosophy* 21 (1924), 184-191.

S 01303
───── . *A History of American Philosophy* (New York: Columbia University Press, 1946), 334-337, 516-523, 546-550. (Reviewed by Evans [S 00423] and Heinemann [S 00651]).

S 01304
───── . Review of Wiener's *Evolution* [S 01533]. *Journal of the History of Ideas* 11 (1950), 241-245.

S 01305
───── . "Fourthness," in *Studies* I [S 01549], 209-214.

S 01306
───── . Review of Bosco's *Filosofia pragmatica* [S 00149]. *Journal of the History of Philosophy* 1 (1963), 110-112.

S 01307
───── . Review of *Studies* II [S 00968]. *Journal of the History of Philosophy* 3 (1965), 281-283.

S 01308
───── . Notice of Potter's *Norms and Ideals* [S 01108]. *Journal of the History of Philosophy* 6 (1968), 420.

S 01309
Scholz, Heinrich. Review of *Collected Papers* I-II. *Deutsche Literaturzeitung* 55:9 (4 March 1934), 392-395.

S 01310
―――. Review of *Collected Papers* III-V. *Deutsche Literaturzeitung* 57:4 (26 January 1936), 137-144.

O 00285
Schröder, Ernst. "Exposition of a Logical Principle, as disclosed by the Algebra of Logic, but overlooked by the Ancient Logicians." 1884.

O 00435
―――. *Vorlesungen über die Algebra der Logik (Exakte Logik)*. 1890.

O 00468
―――. *Vorlesungen über die Algebra der Logik (Exakte Logik)*. 1891. (Reviewed by "Kappa Rho Sigma" [O 00479]).

O 00595
―――. "Note über die Algebra der binären Relative." 1895.

O 00610
―――. *Vorlesungen über die Algebra der Logik (Exakte Logik)*. 1895.

O 00656
―――. "On Pasigraphy: Its Present State and the Pasigraphic Movement in Italy." 1898.

O 00673
―――. "Über zwei Definitionen der Endlichkeit und G. Cantor'sche Sätze." 1898.

O 00304
Schubert, Johannes. Review of Peirce's "The Numerical Measure of the Success of Predictions." 1885.

S 01311
Schulz, Theodore Albert. "Panorama der Ästhetik von Charles Sanders Peirce." Diss. Stuttgart 1961.

O 00708
Schumann, R. "Über die Verwendung zweier Pendel auf gemeinsamer Unterlage zur Bestimmung der Mitschwingung." 1899.

S 01312
Scott, Frederick J. Down. "Peirce and Schiller and Their Correspondence." *Journal of the History of Philosophy* 11 (1973), 363-386.

S 01313
―――. "A Note on James's Aid of Peirce." *Transactions* 12 (1976), 71-76.

O 00593
Scott, Mary Augusta. "Prof. Cayley." 1895.

O 00103
Searle, Arthur. "Historical Account of the Astronomical Observatory of Harvard College, from October, 1855, to October, 1876." 1877.

S 01314
Searles, Herbert L. "Pragmatism Today." *Philosophy* 32 (1951), 137-152.

S 01315
Sebeok, Thomas A. "Between Animal and Animal." *Times Literary Supplement,* 5 October 1973, 1187-1189.

S 01316
——— . "Six espèces de signes: Propositions et critiques." *Degrés: Revue de Synthèse à Orientation Sémiologique* 6 (1974), b1-b42.

S 01317
——— . "Six Species of Signs: Some Propositions and Strictures." *Semiotica* 13 (1975), 233-260. (Reprinted in his *Contributions* [S 01318], 117-142).

S 01318
——— . *Contributions to the Doctrine of Signs.* Bloomington: Indiana University; Lisse: Peter de Ridder Press, 1976.

S 01319
——— . "Semiotics: A Survey of the State of the Art," in his *Contributions* [S 01318], 1-45.

S 01320
——— . "'Semiotics' and Its Congeners," in his *Contributions* [S 01318], 47-58.

S 01321
——— . "The Semiotic Web: A Chronicle of Prejudices," in his *Contributions* [S 01317], 149-188. (An earlier version in *Bulletin of Literary Semiotics* 2 [1975], 1-63).

S 01322
——— . "Iconicity." *Modern Language Notes* 91 (1976), 1427-1456.

S 01323
——— . "The French Swiss Connection." *Semiotic Scene* 1:1 (1977), 27-32.

S 01324
——— . "The Pertinence of Peirce to Linguistics" (Presidential Address delivered to the Linguistic Society of America, San Francisco, 30 December 1975). *Language* 53 (1977).

S 01325
Seger, Jon. "Peirce and the Public." *The Charles S. Peirce Newsletter,* December 1973.

S 01326
Seidensticker, William David. "Peirce's Theory of Esthetics and Normative Science." Diss. Fordham 1968.

S 01327
Sellars, Roy Wood. "Panpsychism or Evolutionary Materialism."*Philosophy of Science* 27 (1960), 329-350.

S 01328
Semerena, Wade Kinsey. "Pragmaticism and Realism in the Philosophy of C.S. Peirce." Diss. Miami 1973.

S 01329
Sessions, William Lad. "Charles Hartshorne and Thirdness." *Southern Journal of Philosophy* 12 (1974), 239-252. (See Hartshorne's "Synthesis as Polyadic Inclusion." [S 00642]).

S 01330
Settle, Tom. "Propensity Theories of Probability Unscathed: A Reply to White" [S 01515]. *British Journal for the Philosophy of Science* 23 (1972), 331-335.

S 01331
Shapiro, Gary. "Peirce's Theory of Habit." Diss. Columbia 1970.

S 01332
_____ . "Habit and Meaning in Peirce's Pragmatism." *Transactions* 9 (1973), 24-40.

S 01333
_____ . "Peirce and Hegel on Absolute Meaning." *Proceedings 1976,* forthcoming.

S 01334
Shapiro, Michael. "Peirce's Interpretant from the Perspective of Linguistic Theory." *Proceedings 1976,* forthcoming.

S 01335
Shapiro, Michael, and Marianne Shapiro. *Hierarchy and the Structure of Tropes.* Bloomington: Indiana University; Lisse: Peter de Ridder Press, 1976.

S 01336
Sharpe, R.A. Review of Bernstein's *Praxis and Action* [S 00108]. *Inquiry* 17 (1974), 249-256.

S 01337
Sharpe, Robert. "Induction, Abduction and the Evolution of Science." *Transactions* 6 (1970), 17-33.

O 01164
Shaw, James Byrnie. *Synopsis of Linear Associative Algebra.* 1907.

S 01338
Shea, William R. Review of Tursman's *Studies in Philosophy* [S 01455]. *Dialogue* 10 (1971), 182.

O 01120
Shearman, Arthur Thomas. *The Development of Symbolic Logic.* 1906.

S 01339
Shenker, Israel. "A Thinker's Thinker is Honored Belatedly." *New York Times,* 12 October 1976, 39.

S 01340
Sheridan, James F. "Paul Carus: A Study of the Thought and Work of the Editor of The Open Court Publishing Company." Diss. Illinois 1957, 133-139.

Shields, Paul. See Potter, Vincent J., and P. Shields [S 01112] and [S 01113].

S 01341
Short, Thomas Lloyd. "Objectivity Without a Cognitive Given: Peirce's Philosophy of Science." Diss. Texas at Austin 1974.

S 01342
Sibley, William M. Review of Moore's *American Pragmatism* [S 00963]. *Dialogue* 1 (1962), 223-224.

S 01343
Sidgwick, Alfred. Review of *Collected Papers* V. *Mind,* NS 44 (1935), 223-230.

S 01344
Simons, Leo. "The Doctrine of Fallibilism." Diss. Columbia 1951.

S 01345
Singer, Beth J. Critical Comments on Thayer's *Meaning and Action* [S 01402]. *Transactions* 11 (1975), 240-249. (Reply by Thayer [S 01405]).

S 01346
Skidmore, Arthur. "Studies in Peirce's Theories of Logic." Diss. Texas at Austin 1968.

S 01347
———. "Peirce and Triads." *Transactions* 7 (1971), 3-23.

Skolimowski, Henryk. See Freeman, Eugene, and H. Skolimowski [S 00523].

S 01348
Sleeper, R.W. "Pragmatism, Religion, and 'Experienceable Difference'," in *American Philosophy and the Future: Essays for a New Generation,* ed. Michael Novak (New York: Scribner's, 1968), 277-298.

S 01349
Smith, C.M. "The Aesthetics of Charles S. Peirce." *Journal of Aesthetics and Art Criticism* 31 (1972), 21-29.

S 01350
Smith, D.G. "Pragmatism and the Group Theory of Politics." *American Political Science Review* 58 (1964), 600-610.

S 01351
Smith, Grover, ed. *Josiah Royce's Seminar, 1913-1914, as Recorded in the Notebooks of Harry T. Costello.* New Brunswick, N.J.: Rutgers University Press, 1963.

O 00655
Smith, Harriette Knight. *The History of the Lowell Institute.* 1898.

S 00278
[Smith, Irving C.]. "A List of Articles, Mostly Book Reviews, Contributed by Charles S. Peirce to 'The Nation' to which is appended Some Additions to the Bibliography of his Published Writings in this Journal, Dec. 21, 1916." *The Journal of Philosophy, Psychology, and Scientific Methods,* 15 (1918), 578-584.

S 01352
Smith, James Ward. "Pragmatism, Realism and Positivism in the United States." *Mind,* NS 61 (1952), 190-208.

S 01353
———. Review of Goudge's *Thought* [S 00565]. *Philosophical Quarterly* (St. Andrews), 2 (1952), 271-273.

S 01354
Smith, John E. *Royce's Social Infinite: An Analysis of the Theory of Interpretation and Community* (New York: Liberal Arts Press, 1950), 19-31, 69-74.

S 01355
———. "Religion and Theology in Peirce," in *Studies* I [S 01549], 251-267.

S 01356
———. "Purpose in American Philosophy: I." *Intermational Philosophical Quarterly* 1 (1961), 390-406.

S 01357
———. *The Spirit of American Philosophy* (New York: Oxford University Press, 1963), 3-37 ("Charles S. Peirce: Meaning, Belief and Love in an Evolving Universe"). (Reviewed by Fitzgerald [S 00504], Held [S 00652], Mays [S 00913], and Roth [S 01244]).

S 01358
———. "Community and Reality," in Bernstein's *Perspectives* [S 00105], 92-119.

S 01359
───── . "The Reflexive Turn, the Linguistic Turn, and the Pragmatic Outcome." *Monist* 53 (1969), 588-605.

S 01360
───── . *Themes in American Philosophy: Purpose, Experience and Community* (New York: Harper & Row, 1970), 20-23, 80-108.

S 01361
───── , ed. *Contemporary American Philosophy, Second Series.* New York: Humanities Press, 1970.

S 01362
───── . "Signs, Selves and Interpretation," in his *Contemporary American Philosophy, Second Series* [S 01361], 312-328.

S 01363
Smith, Michael D. "Peirce and Piaget: Pragmatic Functions Underlying the Acquisition of Word Meaning and Syntax." *Proceedings of the First Annual Conference of the Semiotic Society of America* (Atlanta, 1976), forthcoming.

O 01003
Smith, Percey F. "Josiah Willard Gibbs, PH.D., LL.D. A Short Sketch and Appreciation of his Work in Pure Mathematics." 1903.

O 00488
Smith, William Benjamin. "Science in America." 1892.

S 01364
Smullyan, Arthur F. "Some Implications of Critical Commonsensism," in *Studies* I [S 01549], 111-120.

S 01365
Smyth, Richard. "The Pragmatic Maxim in 1878." *Transactions* 13 (1977), 93-111.

S 01366
Snyder, William S. Review of Buchler's *Philosophical Writings* [S 00193]. *Philosophy* 38 (1957), 81.

S 01367
───── . Review of Wiener's *Values* [S 01538]. *Philosophy* 40 (1959), 181.

S 01368
Sorel, Georges. *De l'utilité du pragmatisme* (Paris: Marcel Rivière, 1921), 4-6.

O 00404
"Spencer Ably Defended." 1890.

O 00409
"Spencer's Philosophy." 1890.

S 01369
Spiegelberg, Herbert. "Husserl's and Peirce's Phenomenologies: Coincidence or Interaction." *Philosophy and Phenomenological Research* 17 (1956), 164-185.

S 01370
───── . *The Phenomenological Movement* (The Hague: Martinus Nijhoff, 1960), I:17-19.

S 01371
Spirito, Ugo. *Il pragmatismo nella filosofia contemporanea.* Florence: Vallecchi, 1921. (Translated by Leon Ostrov: *El pragmatismo en la filosofía contemporanea.* Buenos Aires: Editorial Losada, 1945). (Reviewed by Cardona [S 00241]).

S 01372
Stack, George J. Review of Ayer's *Origins* [S 00054]. *Modern Schoolman* 47 (1970), 351-354.

S 01373
Stanley, Albert A. "A Quincuncial Projection of the World." *Surveying and Mapping* 61 (1946), 19.

S 01374
Stearns, Isabel. "Firstness, Secondness, and Thirdness," in *Studies* I [S 01549], 195-208.

S 01375
——— . "The Apparent Amphiboly of Peirce's Reality." *Transactions* 4 (1968), 80-89.

S 01376
——— . Review of Potter's *Norms and Ideals* [S 01108]. *Man and World* 3 (1970), 136-138.

O 00388
Stearns, J.W. "Philosophy in American Colleges and Universities: University of Wisconsin." 1890.

S 01377
Stebbing, L.S. "Sounds, Shapes and Words." *Proceedings of the Aristotelian Society, Supplementary Volume* 14 (1935), 1-21.

S 01378
——— . Review of *Collected Papers* IV-V. *Philosophy* 11 (1936), 116-118.

S 01379
——— . Review of *Collected Papers* VI. *Philosophy* 12 (1937), 230-232.

O 01165
Stein, Ludwig. "Der Pragmatismus." 1908.

S 01380
Stiebing, Hans Michael. "Dreistelligkeit der Relationenlogik: Kommentierende Bemerkungen zu Peirce's 'The Logic of Relatives'." *Semiosis* 3 (1976), 20-24.

S 01381
Stiker, Henri-Jacques. "Le langage intégre la sémantique chez Roman Jakobson." *Archives de Philosophie* 37 (1974), 601-616.

O 00483
Stille, Werner A. "Science in America." 1892.

O 00492
——— . "Experimental Psychology." 1892.

O 00518
Strobel, Fr. "Namenregister zum 1-15 Bande (1877-1891), von Fr. Strobel." *Beiblätter zu den Annalen der Physik und Chemie.* 1893.

S 01382
Stroh, Guy W. "Professor Feiblemen's Philosophy in Relation to Currents of Twentieth-Century Realism, Empiricism and Naturalism, Especially Peirce and Santayana." *Studium Generale* 24 (1971), 718-735.

S 01383
Struhl, Paula Rothenberg. "Peirce's Defense of the Scientific Method." *Journal of the History of Philosophy* 13 (1975), 481-490.

O 00265
"Studies in Logic." 1883.

O 00654
Study, E. "Theorie der Gemeinen und Höheren Complexen Grössen." 1898.

S 01384
Stumpf, Samuel E. *Socrates to Sartre: A History of Philosophy* (New York: McGraw, Hill, 1966), 404-407.

S 01385
Styazhkin, N.I. *History of Mathematical Logic from Leibniz to Peano* (Cambridge, Mass.: M.I.T. Press, 1969), 253-263. (Translated from the Russian).

S 01386
Suhr, Martin. "On the Relation of Peirce's 'Universal Categories' and Hegel's 'Stages of Thought'." *Proceedings 1976,* forthcoming.

S 01387
Sullivan, Denis F. "C.S. Peirce: On the Foundations of Human Knowledge." Diss. Fordham 1975.

S 01388
———. "Peirce's Notion of Pre-perceptual Cognition: A Reinterpretation." *Transactions* 12 (1976), 182-198.

S 01389
———. "Peirce and the Possibility of Metaphysics." *New Scholasticism* 51:1 (1977).

S 01390
Sweet, Albert. "The Pragmatics of First Order Languages. I." *Notre Dame Journal of Formal Logic* 13 (1972), 145-160.

O 00227
Sylvester, J.J. Remarks on C. Peirce's Logic of Relatives, given before the Mathematical Seminary, Johns Hopkins University, April. 1882.

O 00243
———. "Erratum." 1883.

O 00244
———. "A Note from Professor Sylvester." 1883.

S 01391
Szasz, Gabor. *Introduction to Lattice Theory* (New York: Academic Press, 1963), 15, 42, 123, 221.

O 01027
T., H. "The Decline of Mathematics in England." 1903.

O 00386
Taber, Henry. "On the Theory of Matrices." 1890.

O 00209
Tannery, Paul. "C.S. Peirce—On the Algebra of Logic." 1881.

S 01392
Tarr, Elvira R. "The Epistemology of Charles Sanders Peirce and Its Relation to Education." Diss. New York 1968.

S 01393
──── . "Roots and Ramifications: The Social Thought of Charles S. Peirce." *Proceedings 1976*, forthcoming.

S 01394
Tarski, Alfred. "On the Calculus of Relations." *Journal of Symbolic Logic* 6 (1941), 73-89 (at 73-74).

S 01395
──── . *Introduction to Logic* (New York: Oxford University Press, 1941), 14, 38, 88, 105.

S 01396
──── . *Logic, Semantics, Mathematics* (Oxford: Clarendon, 1956), 40, 54.

S 01397
Thagard, Paul R. "The Unity of Peirce's Theory of Hypothesis." *Transactions* 13 (1977), 112-121.

S 01398
──── . "Explanation and Scientific Inference." Diss. Toronto 1977.

S 01399
──── . "Peirce on Hypothesis and Abduction." *Proceedings 1976*, forthcoming.

Thalberg, Irving. See Gale, Richard M., and I. Thalberg [S 00529].

S 01400
Thayer, Horace S. "Pragmatism," in *A Critical History of Western Philosophy*, ed. D.J. O'Connor (New York: The Free Press, 1964), 437-462.

S 01401
──── . "Pragmatism," in Edwards' *Encyclopedia of Philosophy* [S 00386], VI:430-436.

S 01402
──── . *Meaning and Action: A Critical History of Pragmatism* (Indianapolis: Bobbs-Merrill, 1968), esp. 79-132. (Criticized by Brodsky [S 00176], Greenlee [S 00588], Riley [S 01192], and Singer [S 01345]). (Reviewed by Goudge [S 00572], Greenlee [S 00584], Lebowitz [S 00803], Mays [S 00914], Reck [S 01154], Riley [S 01190], Roth [S 01248], and Tibbetts [S 01425]).

S 01403
──── , ed. *Pragmatism: The Classic Writings*. New York: New American Library, 1970. (Reviewed by Reck [S 01154]).

S 01404
──── . *Meaning and Action: A Study of American Pragmatism*. Indianapolis: Bobbs-Merrill, 1973. (A shortened, revised version of the original 1968 hardback).

S 01405
—— . "Reply to Criticisms." *Transactions* 11 (1975), 258-288. (Reply to Brodsky [S 00176], Greenlee [S 00588], Riley [S 01192], and Singer [S 01345]).

S 01406
—— . "Peirce on Truth," in *Philosophy in the Life of a Nation* (New York: Bicentennial Symposium of Philosophy, 1976), 267-277.

S 01407
—— . Review of Greenlee's *Concept of Sign* [S 00587]. *Journal of the History of Philosophy* 14 (1976), 115-117.

O 00088
"The Theory of Errors of Observation." 1875.

S 01408
Thibaud, Pierre. "La logique de Charles Sanders Peirce: De l'algebre aux graphes." Diss. University of Provence, forthcoming.

O 00740
Thilly, Frank. "Thilly and Wundt." 1900.

S 01409
Thomas, Ivo. "The Rule of Peirce." *Notre Dame Journal of Formal Logic* 9 (1968), 34.

S 01410
—— . "Axiom Sets Equivalent to Syllogism and Peirce." *Notre Dame Journal of Formal Logic* 17 (1976), 248.

S 01411
Thompson, Bruce. "The Pragmaticist Theory of Meaning." M.A. thesis Denver 1977.

S 01412
Thompson, Manley. "The Pragmatic Philosophy of C.S. Peirce." Diss. Chicago 1942.

S 01413
—— . "The Logical Paradoxes and Peirce's Semiotic." *Journal of Philosophy* 46 (1949), 513-536. (Reviewed by Turquette [S 01447]).

S 01414
—— . Review of Goudge's *Thought* [S 00565]. *Ethics* 61 (1951), 159-161.

S 01415
—— . "The Paradox of Peirce's Realism," in *Studies* I [S 01549], 133-142.

S 01416
—— . *The Pragmatic Philosophy of C.S. Peirce.* Chicago: University of Chicago Press, 1953. (Reprinted 1963 as a Phoenix Books paperback, with a new Foreword). (Reviewed by Brown [S 00181], Gallie [S 00536], Huggett [S 00700], Jung [S 00730], Larrabee [S 00801], Lieb [S 00840], Reese [S 01157], and Savan [S 01271].

S 01417
—— . Review of Murphey's *Development* [S 01001] *Philosophical Review* 72 (1963), 117-119.

S 01418
—— . Review of Wennerberg's *Pragmatism* [S 01509] *Philosophical Review* 73 (1964), 415-417.

S 01419
_____ . "Peirce's Experimental Proof of Scholastic Realism," in *Studies* II [S 00968], 414-429.

S 01420
_____ . "Abstract Entities and Universals." *Mind,* NS 74 (1965), 365-381.

S 01421
_____ . Review of Potter's *Norms and Ideals* [S 01108]. *Ethics* 79 (1969), 244-246.

S 01422
_____ . "Quine and the Inscrutablity of Reference." *Revue Internationale de Philosophie* 26 (1972), 42-62.

S 01423
_____ . Review of Scheffler's *Four Pragmatists* [S 01281]. *Transactions* 12 (1976), 88-93.

S 01424
Tibbetts, Paul. "A.J. Ayer's *The Origins of Pragmatism*" [S 00054]. *Personalist* 52 (1971), 121-134.

S 01425
_____ . Review of Thayer's *Meaning and Action* [S 01402]. *New Scholasticism* 46 (1972), 248-258.

S 01426
_____ . Review of Morris' *Signification and Significance* [S 00985]. *Personalist* 53 (1972), 448-453.

S 01427
_____ . "Peirce and Mead on Perceptual Immediacy and Human Action." *Philosophy and Phenomenological Research* 36 (1975), 222-232. (Criticized by Ransdell [S 01148]).

S 01428
Tomas, Vincent, ed. *Charles S. Peirce: Essays in the Philosophy of Science.* New York: Liberal Arts Press, 1957. (Reviewed by Sabra [S 01260]). (Noticed by Deledalle [S 00331], Dopp [S 00368], Parisi [S 01077], Ringer [S 01195], and Wiener [S 01539]).

S 01429
Townsend, H.G. "The Pragmatism of Peirce and Hegel." *Philosophical Review* 37 (1928), 297-303.

S 01430
_____ . Review of *Collected Papers* I. *Philosophical Review* 41 (1932), 621-623.

S 01431
_____ . *Philosophical Ideas in the United States* (New York: American Book Co., 1934), 196-224 ("Logical Realism: Chance").

S 01432
_____ . Review of *Collected Papers* II. *Philosophical Review* 43 (1934), 209-212.

S 01433
_____ . "Some Sources and Early Meanings of American Pragmatism as Reflected in Volume V of The Collected Papers of Charles Sanders Peirce." *Journal of Philosophy* 32 (1935), 181-187.

S 01434
_____ . Review of *Collected Papers* III-IV. *Philosophical Review* 44 (1935), 85-87.

S 01435
_____ . Review of *Collected Papers* V-VI. *Philosophical Review* 45 (1936), 418-420.

S 01436
Trammell, Richard Louis. "Charles S. Peirce's Understanding of Religion." Diss. Columbia 1971.

S 01437
―――. "Religion, Instinct and Reason in the Thought of Charles S. Peirce." *Transactions* 8 (1972), 3-25.

S 01438
―――. "Charles Sanders Peirce and Henry James the Elder." *Transactions* 9 (1973), 202-220.

S 01439
―――. "Charles Peirce's 'Final Opinion'" (abstract). *International Federation of Philosphical Societies: Abstracts of Communications Presented at the XVth World Congress of Philosophy, Varna* (Sofia: Bulgarian Organizing Committee, 1973), No. 407.

O 00364
Trowbridge, John. "Wave-lengths of standard lines." 1888.

S 01440
Tucker, J. Notice of Fisch and Turquette's "Peirce's Triadic Logic" [S 00496]. *Mathematical Reviews* 35 (1968), 5.

S 01441
Turley, Peter T. "Peirce on the Laws of Nature." Diss. Fordham 1967.

S 01442
―――. "Peirce on Chance." *Transactions* 5 (1969), 243-254.

S 01443
―――. "A Problem in Peirce: The Law of Nature and Its Occurrence." *Modern Schoolman* 46 (1969), 140-142.

S 01444
―――. "Peirce's Cosmic 'Sheriff.'" *Journal of the History of Ideas* 36 (1975), 717-720.

S 01445
Turner, J.E. Review of Anderson and Fisch's *Philosophy in America* [S 00030]. *Philosophy* 15 (1940), 215-216.

S 01446
Turner, Karon Jack. "Mind as a Principle of Order in the Philosophy of C.S. Peirce." Diss. Missouri 1972.

S 01447
Turquette, Atwell R. Review of Thompson's "Logical Paradoxes" [S 01413]. *Journal of Symbolic Logic* 16 (1951), 214-215.

S 01448
―――. "Modality, Minimality, and Many-Valuedness." *Acta Philosophica Fennica* 16 (1963), 261-276.

S 01449
―――. "Peirce's Icons for Deductive Logic," in *Studies* II [S 00968], 95-108. (Reviewed by Anderson [S 00029]).

S 01450
———— . "Peirce's Phi and Psi Operators for Triadic Logic." *Transactions* 3 (1967), 66-73.

S 01451
———— . "Peirce's Complete System of Triadic Logic." *Transactions* 5 (1969), 199-210.

S 01452
———— . "Dualism and Trimorphism in Peirce's Triadic Logic." *Transactions* 8 (1972), 131-140.

S 01453
———— . "Implications for Peirce's Triadic Logic" (abstract). *International Federation of Philosophical Societies: Abstracts of Communications Presented at the XVth World Congress of Philosophy, Varna* (Sofia: Bulgarian Organizing Committee, 1973), No. 408.

S 01454
———— . "Minimal Axioms for Peirce's Triadic Logic" (abstract). *Abstracts of Communications: International Congress of Mathematicians* (Vancouver, 1974).

Turquette, Atwell R. See Fisch, Max H., and A.R. Turquette [S 00496].

S 01455
Tursman, Richard Allen, ed. *Studies in Philosophy and in the History of Science: Essays in Honor of Max Fisch* (Lawrence, Kansas: Coronado Press, 1970), 37-51, 72-86, 159-167, 168-181. (Reviewed by Hare [S 00617] and Shea [S 01338]).

S 01456
———— . "Will's Criticisms of Peirce's Frequency Theory of Probability," in his *Studies in Philosophy* [S 01455], 159-167.

S 01457
Ueyama, Shumpei. "Development of Peirce's Theory of Logic." *Science of Thought* (Tokyo), 1 (1954), 25-32. (Commented upon by Prior [S 01119]).

S 01458
———— . "Mathematical and Dialectical Logic in Peirce's Logical Theory" (in Japanese). *Toho Gakuho* (Kyoto), 25 (1954), 495-512.

S 01459
Ullian, Joseph S. "Peirce, Gamblin, and Insurance." *Philosophy of Science* 29 (1962), 79-80.

S 01460
"USC&GS Ship Peirce Is Launched." *Personnel Panorama* 11:8 (1962), 1, 6.

O 00309
United States Coast and Geodetic Survey. *Determination of Gravity at Stations in Pennsylvania, 1879-1880. Appendix No. 19, Report for 1883.* 1885.

O 00147
"Uranometry." 1879.

O 00706
Vailati, Giovanni, "La logique mathematique et sa nouvelle phase de developpement dans les ecrits de M. J. Peano." 1899.

O 01075
———. "Ch. S. Peirce: What Pragmatism Is." 1905.

O 01127
———. "Pragmatism and Mathematical Logic" (tr. H. D. Austin), 1906.

O 01163
———. "De quelques caractères du mouvement philosophique contemporain en Italie." 1907.

O 01217
———. *Scritti di G. Vailati (1863-1909)*. 1911.

O 01202
Vailati, Giovanni, and Mario Calderoni. "Le origini e l'idea del pragmatismo." 1909.

S 01461
Vandamme, F. "On Axioms and Semantics of Natural Language." *Proceedings 1976,* forthcoming.

S 01462
Van Der Borgert, Frans. "On Some Pragmatic Conditions of Reasonable Induction." Diss. Cornell 1973.

S 01463
Van Fraassen, Bas C. "Capek on Eternal Recurrence." *Journal of Philosophy* 59 (1962), 371-375. (Response to Capek [S 00238]).

S 01464
Van Marter, Leslie Edward. "Categories as Non-Arbitrary, Finite System of Mutually Irreducible Simple Unities: A Study Based on Comparative Analysis of Aristotle, Kant, and Charles Sanders Peirce." Diss. Chicago 1964.

S 01465
Van Wesep, Henry B. *Seven Sages: The Story of American Philosophy* (New York: Longmans, Green, 1960), 317-391)"Charles Sanders Peirce: Trail-Blazing Logician").

O 00212
Venn, John. *Symbolic Logic.* 1881.

O 00248
———. *Studies in Logic.* 1883.

S 01466
Vetter, Patricia Louise. "The Theory of Community in Charles S. Peirce." Diss. St. Louis 1968.

S 01467
Veysey, Laurence Russ. "The Emergence of the American University, 1865-1910: A Study in the Relations Between Ideals and Institutions." Diss. California 1961 (esp. 387, 420, 650, 660-661, 853, 1136-1139).

S 01468
Vivas, Eliseo. "The Philosophy of Peirce" (review of Buchler's *Empiricism* [S 00188]). *Nation* 151 (1940), 483-484.

S 01469
Voigt, Vilmos. "Peircean Semiotics in Hungary." *Proceedings 1976,* forthcoming.

O 00463
W. "Not 'Pons,' But 'Pontes Asinorum,' Perhaps." 1891.

O 00185
W., Th. "Peirce, C.S., Photometric researches. Made in the years 1872-1875." 1880.

S 01470
Waibel, Edwin. "Studien zum Pragmatismus." *Archiv für systematische Philosophie* 21 (1915), 1-43.

S 01471
─── . "Die pragmatische Wahrheitslehre." *Archiv für systematische Philosophie* 21 (1915), 113-126.

S 01472
─── . "Metaphysische Grundlagen des Pragmatismus und dessen Erkenntnistheorie." *Archiv für systematische Philosophie* 22 (1916), 1-30.

S 01473
Wallis, Mieczyslaw. "On Iconic Signs," in *Recherches sur les systemes signifiants: Symposium de Varsovie 1968,* ed. Josette Rey-Debove (The Hague: Mouton, 1973), 481-498.

S 01474
Walraven, Pieter Louis. "On the Bezold-Brücke Phenomenon." *Journal of the Optical Society of America* 51 (1961), 1113-1116.

S 01475
─── . *On the Mechanisms of Colour Vision* (Utrecht: Kemink en Zoon, 1962), 27, 30, 32-33, 36, 88, 93.

S 01476
Walsh, Dorothy. "Literature and the Categories." *Journal of Philosophy* 55 (1958), 846-855.

S 01477
Walsh, F. Michael. Review of Fann's *Theory of Abduction* [S 00435]. *Philosophy* 47 (1972), 377-379.

S 01478
Walther, Elisabeth. "Die Begründung der Zeichentheorie bei Ch. S. Peirce." *Grundlagenstudien aus Kybernetik und Geisteswissenschaft* 3 (1962), 33-44.

S 01479
─── , ed. *Die Festigung der Überzeugung und andere Schriften.* Baden-Baden: Agis, 1967.

S 01480
─── , ed. *Lectures on Pragmatism—Vorlesungen über Pragmatismus.* Hamburg: Felix Meiner, 1973.

S 01481
─── . *Allgemeine Zeichenlehre: Einführung in die Grundlagen der Semiotik.* Stuttgart: Deutsche Verlags-Anstalt, 1974. (Reviewed by Berzlaff [S 00223]).

S 01482
─── . "Die Haupteinteilungen der Zeichen von C. S. Peirce." *Semiosis* 3 (1976), 32-41.

S 01483
─── . Review of Eco's *Theory of Semiotics* [S 00384]. *Semiosis* 1 (1976), 54-55.

S 01484
———. "Erste Überlegungen zur Semiotik von C.S. Peirce in den Jahren 1860-1866." *Semiosis* 1 (1976), 35-41.

S 01485
———. "Ein als Zeichen verwendetes Natur-Objekt." *Semiosis* 5 (1977), 54-60.

Walther, Elisabeth. See Bense, Max, and E. Walther [S 00090].

S 01486
Walther, Elisabeth, and Max Bense. Review of Greenlee's *Concept of Sign* [S 00587]. *Semiosis* 1 (1976), 52-54.

S 01487
Wand, B. Review of *Studies* I [S 01549]. *University of Toronto Quarterly* 22 (1953), 207-208.

S 01488
Warner, Clifford. Notice of Haas' *Conception of Law* [S 00598]. *Review of Metaphysics* 19 (1965), 374.

O 00457
Warner, Joseph B. "The Suppression of Dr. Abbot's Reply." 1891.

S 01489
Wartenberg, Gerd. *Logischer Sozialismus: Die Transformation der Kantschen Transzendental-philosophie durch Ch. S. Peirce.* Frankfurt: Suhrkamp, 1971.

———. Translation of Apel's *Schriften* [S 00033] and [S 00034].

O 00042
Wasson, David A. "Being and Nothing—In What Sense They Are Identical." 1869.

S 01490
Weaver, Harold F. "The Development of Astronomical Photometry." *Popular Astronomy* 54 (1946), 211-230.

S 01491
Wedderburn, J.H.M. *Lectures on Matrices.* American Mathematical Society Colloquium Publications XVII (1934), 173.

S 01492
Weiss, Paul. "Charles Sanders Peirce," in *Dictionary of American Biography* (1934), XIV:398-403. (Reprinted in Bernstein's *Perspectives* [S 00105], 1-12).

S 01493
———. Letter to the Editors. *Journal of Philosophy* 31 (1934), 251.

S 01494
———. "The Essence of Peirce's System." *Journal of Philosophy* 37 (1940), 253-264.

S 01495
———. Review of Buchler's *Empiricism* [S 00188]. *Philosophical Review* 49 (1940), 595.

S 01496
———. Review of Buchler's *Philosophy of Peirce* [S 00194]. *Philosophy and Phenomenological Research* 2 (1941), 259-261. (Buchler's reply to Weiss, 261; Weiss' reply to Buchler, 261-262).

S 01497
———. "Charles Sanders Peirce." *Sewanee Review* 50 (1942), 184-192.

S 01498
———. "The Logic of the Creative Process," in *Studies* I [S 01549], 166-182.

S 01499
———. "Charles S. Peirce, Philosopher," in Bernstein's *Perspectives* [S 00105], 120-140.

Weiss, Paul. See Bernstein [S 00107].

———. See Hartshorne, Charles, and P. Weiss [S 00643].

S 01500
Weiss, Paul, and Arthur W. Burks. "Peirce's Sixty-six Signs." *Journal of Philosophy* 42 (1945), 383-388.

S 01501
Wells, Harry K. *Pragmatism: Philosophy of Imperialism* (New York: International Publishers, 1954), 26-40. (Reviewed by Harrison [S 00622]).

S 01502
Wells, Rulon. Review of Berry's "Peirce's Contributions" [S 00111]. *Journal of Symbolic Logic* 24 (1959), 209-211.

S 01503
———. Review of Fisch and Cope's "Peirce at the Johns Hopkins" [S 00494]. *Journal of Symbolic Logic* 24 (1959), 211.

S 01504
———. "The True Nature of Peirce's Evolutionism," in *Studies* II [S 00968], 304-322.

S 01505
———. "Charles S. Peirce as an American," in Bernstein's *Perspectives* [S 00105], 13-41.

S 01506
———. "Distinctively Human Semiotic." *Social Science Information* 66 (1967), 103-124.

S 01507
———. "Peirce's Notion of the Symbol." *Proceedings of the First Annual Conference of the Semiotic Society of America* (Atlanta, 1976), forthcoming (also forthcoming in *Semiotica*).

S 01508
Welsh, Paul. Review of Fisch's *Classic American Philosophers* [S 00469]. *Philosophical Review* 61 (1952), 133.

S 01509
Wennerberg, Hjalmar. *The Pragmatism of C.S. Peirce: An Analytical Study.* Lund: C.W.K. Gleerup, 1962. (Reviewed by Cohen, L.J. [S 00277], Goudge [S 00570], Murphree [S 01008], Potter [S 01109], and Thompson [S 01418]).

S 01510
———. "Peirce's Theory of Meaning," in *Filosofiska studier tillägnade Konrad MarcWogau den 4 April 1962,* ed. Ann-Mari Henschen-Dahlquist (Uppsala: Filosofiska Föreningen i Uppsala, 1962), 35-44.

S 01511
———. Review of Haas' *Conception of Law* [S 00598]. *Philosophical Quarterly* 16 (1966), 284.

S 01512
Werkmeister, W.H. *A History of Philosophical Ideas in America* (New York: Ronald Press, 1949), 171-203. (Reviewed by Fisch [S 00468] and Klausner [S 00763]).

S 01513
———. "The Universalistic Evolutionism of Charles Sanders Peirce." *Southern Journal of Philosophy* 9 (1971), 327-333.

O 00423
West, George E. "Evolution and Gravitation." 1890.

O 00408
"Where are the Foes of Spencer?". 1890.

S 01514
White, Alan R. *Truth* (New York: Macmillan, 1970), 90, 122-126.

S 01515
———. "The Propensity Theory of Probability." *British Journal for the Philosophy of Science* 23 (1972), 35-43. (Reply by Settle [S 01330]).

S 01516
White, John J. "The Argument for a Semiotic Approach to Shaped Writing: The Case of Italian Futurist Typographs." *Visible Language* 10 (1976), 53-86.

S 01517
White, Morton. *The Age of Analysis.* Boston: Houghton Mifflin, 1955.

S 01518
———. "Pragmatism and the Scope of Science," in *Paths of American Thought,* ed. Arthur M. Schlesinger, Jr. and Morton White (Boston: Houghton Mifflin, 1963), 190-202.

S 01519
———. Review of Ayer's *Origins* [S 00054]. *New York Review of Books,* 30 January 1969, 24-27.

S 01520
———. *Science and Sentiment in America: Philosophical Thought from Jonathan Edwards to John Dewey* (New York: Oxford University Press, 1972), 144-169 ("C.S. Peirce: Pragmatist and Metaphysician").

S 01521
———. *Pragmatism and the American Mind: Essays and Reviews in Philosophy and Intellectual History* (New York: Oxford University Press, 1973), 96-107. 110-114. (Reviewed by Madden [S 00886]).

S 01522
White, Richard B. "A Cut-Elimination Theorem for a Peircean Logic." *Transactions* 12 (1976), 253-262.

O 00676
Whitehead, Alfred North. *A Treatise on Universal Algebra, with Applications.* 1898.

S 01523
Whiting, Douglas. "The Meaning of Love in Education: Charles Peirce's Conception in Educational Perspective." Diss. Pittsburgh 1967.

S 01524
Whittaker, E.T. "Chance, Free Will and Necessity in the Scientific Conception of the Universe." *Proceedings of the Physical Society of London* 55 (1943), 459-471 (at 465).

S 01525
Whittemore, Robert Clifton. *Makers of the American Mind* (New York: William Morrow, 1964), 357-363 ("The Pragmatic Creed: Charles Sanders Peirce").

S 01526
Whittier, Duane H. "Language and the Self," in Tursman's *Studies in Philosophy* [S 01455], 168-181.

S 01527
Wichelhaus, Barbara. "C.S. Peirce Bicentennial International Congress." *Semiosis* 3 (1976), 73-75.

S 01528
Wick, Warner Arms. *Metaphysics and the New Logic.* Chicago: University of Chicago Press, 1942.

O 00204
"Width of Mr. Rutherford's Rulings." 1881.

S 01529
Wiebe, D. "The Religious Experience Argument." *Sophia* (Melbourne), 14 (1975), 19-28.

O 00139
Wiedemann, E. German abstract of "Fortschritt von Versuchen, die Wellenlänge mit einem Meter zu vergleichen." 1879.

O 00169
———. German abstract of "Ueber eine Methode mit schwingenden Pendeln die Schwere zu bestimmen." 1880.

O 00170
———. German abstract of "Gegenseitige Anziehung von Spectrallinien." 1880.

O 00190
———. German abstract of "Resultate von Pendelversuchen." 1881.

O 00191
———. German abstract of "Ueber Gespenster (ghosts) in den Rutherford'schen Beugungsspectren." 1881.

O 00192
———. German abstract of "Ueber die Weite der Gitterabstände in Rutherford's Gittern." 1881.

O 00113
Wiedemann, G. German abstract of "Schwimmende Magnete." 1878.

S 01530
Wiener, Philip P. "Peirce's Metaphysical Club and the Genesis of Pragmatism." *Journal of the History of Ideas* 7 (1946), 218-233. (Incorporated in Ch. 2 of his *Evolution* [S 01533]).

S 01531
———. "The Evolutionism and Pragmaticism of Peirce." *Journal of the History of Ideas* 7 (1946), 321-350. (Incorporated in Ch. 4 of his *Evolution* [S 01533]).

S 01532
———. "The Peirce-Langley Correspondence and Peirce's Manuscript on Hume and the Laws of Nature." *Proceedings of the American Philosophical Society* 91 (1947), 201-228.

S 01533
———. *Evolution and the Founders of Pragmatism.* Cambridge: Harvard University Press, 1949. (Reviewed by Blanshard [S 00125], Fries [S 00524], Gallie [S 00532], Lovejoy [S 00850], Miller [S 00941], Schlaretzki [S 01290], and Schneider [S 01304]).

S 01534
———. "Peirce's Evolutionary Interpretations of the History of Science," in *Studies* I [S 01549], 143-152.

S 01535
———. Review of Gallie's *Pragmatism* [S 00534]. *Philosophy and Phenomenological Research* 13 (1953), 575-576.

S 01536
———. Review of von Kempski's *Pragmatismus* [S 00742]. *Journal of Philosophy* 50 (1953), 535-538.

S 01537
———. "Peirce's Experimentalism and Practicalism." *Philosophical Studies* 7 (1956), 65-68.

S 01538
———. ed. *Values in a Universe of Chance: Selected Writings of Charles Sanders Peirce.* New York: Doubleday Anchor, 1958 (reprinted 1966; see [S 01542]). (Reviewed by Gallie [S 00537], Goudge [S 00568], Jung [S 00732], Sabre [S 01260], and Snyder [S 01367]).

S 01539
———. Review of Tomas' *Essays* [S 01428]. *Philosophy of Science* 27 (1960), 312-313.

S 01540
———. Review of Murphey's *Development* [S 01001]. *Journal of Philosophy* 59 (1962), 265-269.

S 01541
———. Review of Lieb's *Letters* [S 00839]. *Journal of Philosophy* 59 (1962), 270-272.

S 01542
———, ed. *Charles S. Peirce: Selected Writings.* New York: Dover, 1966. (Reprint of his *Values* [S 01538]).

S 01543
———. "A Soviet Philosopher's View of Peirce's Pragmatism." *Transactions* 3 (1967), 3-12. (Reprinted in *Philosophy, Science, and Method: Essays in Honor of Ernest Nagel,* ed. S. Morgenbesser *et al.* [New York: St. Martin's, 1969]).

S 01544
———. "Charles Sanders Peirce," in *International Encyclopedia of the Social Sciences,* ed. David L. Sills (New York: Macmillan, 1968), XI:511-513.

S 01545
———. "W.M. Miller on Peirce's Interpretation of the History of Science." *Transactions* 7 (1971), 233-236.

S 01546
———. "More Thoughts About Miller's 'Further Thoughts on Peirce's Use of History.'" *Transactions* 8 (1972), 187-195.

S 01547
———. "Pragmatism," in his *Dictionary of the History of Ideas* [S 01548], III:551-570.

S 01548
———. ed. *Dictionary of the History of Ideas*. 5 vols. New York: Scribner's, 1973-1974.

S 01549
Wiener, Philip P., and Frederic H. Young, eds. *Studies in the Philosophy of Charles Sanders Peirce*. Cambridge: Harvard University Press, 1952. (Reviewed by Lieb [S 00840], anonymous [S 01183], Rollins [S 01208], Schlaretzki [S 01292], and Wand [S 01487]).

S 01550
Wigner, E.P. "The Unreasonable Effectiveness of Mathematics in the Natural Sciences." *Communications on Pure and Applied Mathematics* 13 (1960), 1-14.

S 01551
Will, Frederick L. "The Preferability of Probable Beliefs." *Journal of Philosophy* 62 (1965), 57-67.

S 01552
Willer, David. *Scientific Sociology*. Englewood Cliffs, N.J.: Prentice-Hall, 1967.

S 01553
Williams, Donald. "Tokens, Types, Words and Terms." *Journal of Philosophy* 33 (1936), 701-707.

S 01554
———. *The Ground of Induction* (Cambridge: Harvard University Press, 1947), 196-201.

S 01555
Wilshire, Bruce W. "William James, Phenomenology and Pragmatism: A Reply to Rosenthal." *Transactions* 13 (1977), 45-55. (See Rosenthal [S 01232] and [S 01234]).

S 01556
Wilson, Curtis. "Newton and Some Philosophers on Kepler's 'Laws.'" *Journal of the History of Ideas* 35 (1974), 231-258.

S 01557
Wilson, Edwin B. "The Contributions of Gibbs to Vector Analysis and Multiple Algebra," in *A Commentary on the Scientific Writings of J.Willard Gibbs,* ed. Arthur Haas (New Haven: Yale University Press, 1936), II:127-160 (at 141).

S 01558
Wilson, Edwin B., and Carl R. Doering. "The Elder Peirce's." *Proceedings of the National Academy of Sciences* 12 (1926), 424-432.

S 01559
Wilson, Edwin B., and Margaret M. Hilferty. "Note on C.S. Peirce's Experimental Discussion of the Law of Errors." *Proceedings of the National Academy of Sciences* 15 (1929), 120-125.

O 00022
Winlock, Joseph. "Observations of Asteroids Made With the Fifteen Inch Equatoreal of the Observatory of Harvard College, Cambridge, U.S." 1868.

S 01560
Winn, Ralph B., ed. *American Philosophy*. New York: Philosophical Library, 1955.

S 01561
———. "Charles Sanders Peirce," in his *American Philosophy* [S 01560], 268-270.

S 01562
Wisdom, John. Review of *Collected Papers* III. *Philosophy* 9 (1934), 379-380.

S 01563
Wohlstetter, Albert. Review of Buchler's *Empiricism* [S 00188]. *Isis* 32 (1949), 399-403.

O 00374
Wolf, C. "Collection de Memoires relatifs a la Physique." 1889.

S 01564
Wolff, Theodor. Review of Peirce's *Photometric Researches. Vierteljahrsschrift der astronomischen Gesellschaft* 15 (1880), 193-208.

S 01565
Wood, Michael. Review of Ayer's *Origins* [S 00054]. *New Statesman* 76 (1968), 541.

S 01566
Woodburne, A.S. Review of *Collected Papers* I. *Crozer Quarterly* 9 (1932), 242.

S 01567
_____ . Review of *Collected Papers* II. *Crozer Quarterly* 9 (1932), 370.

S 01568
Workman, Rollin. "Pragmatism and Realism," in *Studies* II [S 00968], 242-253.

O 00020
Wright, Chauncey. "Mathematics in Court." 1867.

O 00058
_____ . Note on Peirce's review of the works of Berkeley in the *North American Review*. 1871.

S 01569
von Wright, Georg Henrik. *The Logical Problem of Induction* (Helsinki: Acta Philosophica Fennica, 1941), III:177-181.

S 01570
_____ . *A Treatise on Induction and Probability* (New York: Harcourt, Brace, 1951), 165, 293-294.

S 01571
Wright, William Kelley. Review of Leroux' *Pragmatisme* [S 00829]. *Philosophical Review* 33 (1924), 607-612.

S 01572
Wu, Joseph S. "The Problem of Existential Import." *Notre Dame Journal of Formal Logic* 10 (1969), 415-424.

S 01573
Wykoff, William. "Semiosis and Infinite Regressus." *Semiotica* 2 (1970), 59-67.

O 00443
X. "A Caricature" 1891.

O 00427
Youmans, W.J. "Mr. Spencer's Rank as a Philosopher." 1890.

S 01574
Young, Frederic H. "Charles Sanders Peirce, America's Greatest Logician and Most Original Philosopher" (paper delivered 15 October 1945, at Milford, Pennsylvania, before the Pike County Historical Society). Privately printed 1946.

S 01575
―――. "Charles Sanders Peirce: 1839-1914," in *Studies* I [S 01549], 271-276.

Young, Frederic H. See Wiener, Philip P., and F.H. Young [S 01549].

S 01576
Young, William. "Did Peirce Exorcise the Spirit of Cartesianism?" *International Federation of Philosophic Societies: Abstracts of Communications Presented at the XVth World Congress of Philosophy, Varna* (Sofia: Bulgarian Organizing Committee, 1973), No. 410.

S 01577
―――. "C.S. Peirce on Type and Token." *Proceedings 1976,* forthcoming.

S 01578
Zanoni, Candido P. "Logical Pragmatism: The Philosophy of G. Vailati." Diss. Minnesota 1968.

S 01579
Zarnecka-Bialy, Ewa. "Negation in Charles S. Peirce's Propositional Calculus." *Reports on Mathematical Logic* 1 (1973), 99-101.

S 01580
Zeeck, Beatrice. "Philosopher Gains Wide Recognition as Time Goes By." *Lubbock Today* 44 (1974), 12.

S 01581
Zemach, E.M. "The Pragmatic Paradox in Aesthetics." *British Journal of Aesthetics* 7 (1967), 215-224.

S 01582
Zeman, J. Jay. "The Graphical Logic of C.S. Peirce." Diss. Chicago 1965.

S 01583
―――. "A System of Implicit Quantification." *Journal of Symbolic Logic* 32 (1967), 484-504.

S 01584
―――. "Peirce's Graphs—the Continuity Interpretation." *Transactions* 4 (1968), 144-154.

S 01585
―――. Review of Roberts' "Existential Graphs and Natural Deduction" [S 01199]. *Journal of Symbolic Logic* 35 (1970), 320-321.

S 01586
―――. *Modal Logic: The Lewis-Modal Systems* (Oxford: Clarendon, 1973), v, 14, 129-131, 295.

S 01587
―――. "Peirce's Logical Graphs" (review article of Roberts' *Existential Graphs* [S 01201]). *Semiotica* 12 (1974), 239-256.

S 01588
───── . "Modality and the Peircean Concept of Belief." *Semiotica* 10 (1974), 205-220.

S 01589
Zeni, Silvio. *Il pragmatismo americano: Peirce, James, Dewey.* Asti: P. Monticone, 1957.

S 01590
Zivotić, Miladin. *Pragmatizam i savermena filozofiza.* Belgrade: "Nolit," 1966.

S 01591
van Zoest, A.J.A. "De bruikbaarheid van Peirce's begrip 'icon' bij het benoemen van bepaalde verschijnselen in Franse peozie." *Handelingen van bet 32e Nederlands Filologencongres* (Amsterdam, 1974), 187-193.

DATE DUE

DEMCO, INC. 38-2931